BELOW THE LINE

Michele & Rachhael, sp!
thanks for the hospitality!

BELOW THE LINE

MEREDITH JORDAN

Meredith Jordan
6·26·20

Above the Line: The writer, director, actors and producers. **Below the Line:** Everyone else.

Contents

PART THREE: WRAP

PREFACE
How Did a Reporter Get In Here?

By the time *Last Vegas* finished wrap I was behind in nearly everything in my life. Making a major motion picture is intense and time consuming and very little else got done in the five months I had been watching them do it. In that, I was just like the crew. The nature of being embedded, whether with the military or on a dusty movie set, is that the observer lives the experience. It's empathy building, to say the least, and I was exhausted.

There was never any doubt I was different. The crew knew I was there to write a book about behind-the-scenes movie-making because I told them, but they could also see it. My name was on the phone list but not on the crew list. I had a badge but no IMDb page, which is how crew reviews credits to size up who they're working with. I was blessed because the vast majority of crew welcomed me, to varying degrees. Many were extraordinarily patient, sitting for multiple interviews. Even the roughly 10 percent who weren't interested were polite, with one exception.

When I introduced myself and said I was a journalist, I almost always added, "I'm friendly." I didn't realize until a few months in that my nuanced meaning could be lost. What I meant was that I was a friendly *journalist*. I don't do hack jobs. What some apparently heard was, 'She's telling us she's friendly, like a puppy.' Not everyone likes puppies or journalists.

The exception, and the worst of it, was a confrontation with a short-term department head. Through a misstep on my part I had gotten on her bad side about a week into location work in Las Vegas. Attempts to pivot into safe territory failed so I had tried to steer clear. About three days before the company was to move to Atlanta I found myself face to face with her.

"I understand you're *friendly*," she said, angrily quoting me from three weeks earlier. "I don't want to say you don't belong here, but you don't belong here!" Her eyes were bloodshot from exhaustion, and I imagine mine were as well. I don't know what I said to prompt that, or even recall what I said in response. But I was definitely friendly as I backed out of the room.

A couple of days later something else happened to push me closer to beam's edge. That was Day 13 of principal photography, the last day in Las

Vegas. They were shooting scenes at McCarran International Airport. The video assist operator routinely set up several mobile work-stations around any set they worked on. Each had monitors that reflected what each camera saw. Jon Turteltaub, with his immediate team, had the largest workstation, aptly termed director's village. Directors chairs were set up in front of the monitors. It was miked so crew at a smaller group of monitors could hear when he wanted something.

I was with the monitors on the receiving end, which were perhaps 100 feet away from Directors Village that day. They were between setups so I wasn't paying attention. I saw an assistant hurry up but didn't think anything of it until I heard my name on the speaker. The assistant warned Turteltaub of my presence, telling him I could hear everything. The director thanked him.

As I watched him scurry away my heart skipped a beat. What just happened? Jon knows what I'm doing. Doesn't he? My brain flipped through pages of memory. I'd asked the director occasional questions in prep, gone with him on a scout. I'd interviewed the first and second assistant directors at length, typing frantically into my laptop. I spun that through: No experienced assistant directors, as they both were, kept things like that from a director.

I was unnerved and sat as long as I could, perhaps five minutes. Then I walked casually inside the airport and out of sight. Once I rounded a bend I called an editor friend, who of course didn't answer. Then I saw a department supervisor coming out of an office. She had been candid with me on several occasions and I decided to see what she thought. She listened patiently, first with a look of surprise and then slight amusement. "Jon Turteltaub knows exactly who you are," she said. "This is Jon's movie. If he didn't want you here, you'd *already* be gone." That rang as true to me as anything I'd heard thus far. I got back to work.

I've thought a lot about that, particularly why I'd reacted that way. Being embedded is a strange thing. You're not living in your own space and that creates a level of vulnerability. It's someone else's world. Even if they're only going to inhabit it a short time, it's theirs. You're the interloper. If I felt insecure when the worst-case scenario was losing my dream-reporting gig, imagine what a journalist in a war zone feels when confronted with an angry, red-eyed sergeant.

It also illustrates just how bizarre it was, to them, that I was there at all. Crew told me that repeatedly, particularly once they got to know me. Many said they'd never even seen a journalist on set or perhaps once. Others said if they were there at all, it was for a brief period and with a publicist or producer. That leads to the next logical question: How did a journalist get on set with free rein? What follows next is a reporter's journey, so okay for you movie people to skip to the chase, which is two pages before this preface ends.

As an East Coast journalist, my only experience with Hollywood-style reporting came in 1997 when I was in Los Angeles to cover a banking conference. The public relations department of a major credit card issuer invited a group of journalists to attend a special event marking the 25th anniversary of Rodeo Drive. Dubbed "A Tribute to Style," it included a fashion show and a $1,000-a-plate dinner, which required special permission from my employer because of its value. The charity event was attended by dozens of actors, from Sylvester Stallone and Warren Beatty to Jennifer Tilly and Michael Richards.

Like most Americans, I grew up with the television set on, so I recognized many other celebrities. When I found the red carpet, I moved to the back to watch. The famous faces were surreal but it was something else that pushed my jaw open. The entertainment media was squashed together behind a chest-high barrier, shouting questions at the celebrities who posed for the cameras. It went on at least 30 minutes, maybe more, a parade of people safely protected from the media animals. My favorite memory is of Mary Hart of "Entertainment Tonight" who first walked the carpet as a celebrity interviewee and then scooted behind the fence as an interviewer.

I was still young but had grown up the child of journalists near Washington, D.C. Reporting was a respected and valued endeavor. I didn't understand that the entertainment media worked differently than mainstream media. I assumed they were a lot better paid than I was! I also remember being grateful that I wasn't covering the event. Getting behind the barricade would have been emotionally tantamount to having my eyebrows shaved off. That was enough Hollywood journalism for me. I worked in the news business in Washington for a long time and eventually relocated to Atlanta for a job.

Instead, my vantage point to the movie and television industry came through friends who worked in it. I would visit one on set every year or two. At first, it was like a day at a rare and exotic museum. But with each visit my fascination grew.

On the set of *Rendition* (2007) I watched crew hoist a huge black tarp stretched like a trampoline vertically along one side of the area. It was a tool for lighting but in this case, it was to protect the actors by blocking the lenses of paparazzi high up in other buildings. They had successfully hunted them the day before. "All in a day's work," said one of the men who had put it place, to laughter. It turned out they were grips. The joke was that sometimes they installed equipment to shoot the movie, sometimes to protect stars.

That's when the movie business got its lure into my fleshy cheek. It wasn't the actors, Reese Witherspoon, Jake Gyllenhaal and Peter Sarsgaard, although they were great. Through the osmosis of celebrity culture I already knew about them, at least as much as I needed to know.

What was interesting and ultimately became riveting was what I didn't know. I had been a lifelong consumer of Hollywood products but had no idea how they were made or the magic happened. Who were the people behind the scenes? Why were there so many and what did they do? And finally, why was it that I had no idea?

I looked for a book that could fill in the blanks and found "The Devil's Candy: The Anatomy of a Hollywood Fiasco." In it, Julie Salamon chronicles the making of Brian De Palma's *Bonfire of the Vanities* (1990). I also found "Picture," which dated back to 1951. Lillian Ross followed John Huston for the making of *Red Badge of Courage*. Those books were closest to what I wanted because they were journalism, done by outsiders.

The most recent example, at least that I'm aware of, is "The Man Who Heard Voices: Or, How M. Night Shyamalan Risked His Career on a Fairy Tale," which came out in 2006. That book was written by Michael Bamberger, who shadowed Shyamalan for the making of *Lady in the Water* (2006).

There were wonderful legacy books done about iconic movies. There were great insider books, like "Final Cut: Dreams and Disasters in the Making of Heaven's Gate" (1985), which was written by Steven Bach, a United Artists senior vice president. It is a remarkable account of the 1980 movie, which remains one of the best-known failures in Hollywood film history. There were thousands of general books about Hollywood and people above the line, an accounting term that refers to writers, actors, producers and directors.

'The making of' is a whole category on its own where the story of a popular movie is generously told, often through the work of the still photographer on crew. All of those, with rare exception, are controlled by the studio.

But I couldn't find where anyone had followed a production in a way that would explain how it all tied together, including all the players. I decided I wanted to do that. I wanted to keep tabs on all departments, from art to costumes to production. I wanted to see how they worked together, and how it operated as a business. My initial goal was to write a magazine story and then continue on with my normal work as a contracted writer and researcher, which actually made money.

For years I pitched anyone I met in a position of power in the industry to let me follow crew along for one production cycle. I had an East Coast ignorance of how things worked in Hollywood, which turned out to be a blessing. I didn't know what I didn't know, which was that not letting journalists hang around was so entrenched as policy that it might have been legislated.

One of the people I pitched over those years was Billy Badalato who had spent his life around the movie business. In 2010 he was in Atlanta working as unit production manager, along with executive producer Jeremiah Samuels, on *Big Momma's House: Like Father, Like Son.* The movie they were making was number three in Martin Lawrence's lucrative franchise about a cross-dressing FBI agent.

Badalato gave me an interview and about two hours at the studio. I made as strong a pitch as I could to write a longer piece on production, perhaps even a book. He saw genuine need for something holistic that would explain how movies are made. Even people with degrees from film schools needed a practical understanding of how and why things were done a certain way. He said he had seen many of them come to set without that, to their detriment.

Badalato didn't say much to the pitch, and certainly not "yes." But there was a consolation prize. He invited me to return to the set of *Big Momma's House* toward the end of production when they filmed the big dance scene. I watched from the side of the stages and from the monitors as the choreographer worked with the dancers. Before the day ended I again made the case to Badalato. He didn't say "no" but there wasn't much encouragement either. *Big Momma's House* wrapped shortly thereafter and he was gone.

I widened the scope to include television shows and zeroed in on showrunners, whose jobs are what the title suggests. A television show about zombies was being shot in Atlanta and I had an inroad there. I also honed in on Kurt Sutter, the creator and showrunner of "Sons of Anarchy."

Sutter was a likely candidate in my mind. I was an unexpected fan of his show and had done a freelance story for The Washington Post about being an extra on it. He was a rule-breaker and occasional reprobate, brilliant and committed to doing things his way to great success. "Sons of Anarchy," a story about an outlaw motorcycle club, was well on its way to garnering 10 million weekly viewers, according to FX Networks. If anyone would break the rule of letting a reporter in for an entire episode, surely it would be him.

I had part of that right because I got an interview with Sutter. We talked for more than an hour in his offices on the show's soundstages in North Hollywood. By the end of the meeting, he said I could do the story. The show was in hiatus between seasons and I would return. I was so elated I might have floated back to Atlanta without a plane. Finally!

I pulled out the stops, reaching out to contacts at the larger mainstream news organizations to get the story placed. I did research. I interviewed Jon Landgraf, CEO at FX Networks, professors of popular culture who follow television, ratings people, crew on the show. Neighborhood friends who held weekly dinners asked me how much money I had in the story before I left. I estimated it would be $2,500 by the time it was done, all for a piece that would net less than $1,000.

Once I returned to L.A. for the story I reached out to Sutter to set it up. The reply didn't come from him this time. Instead an FX network public relations person swooped in. The new season was starting and Sutter was extremely busy. Who was I and what did I want? We went back and forth. No, the flack finally said, I would not be spending two weeks or even one week on set to write about the show. Perhaps I could just write up that interview with Landgraf and the earlier conversation with Sutter?

My closest friend in the industry had told me from the outset that no one would let me do the story, and he said it again. "It's like there is a 'veil of secrecy,'" I said. "It's more of a Teflon curtain painted a red-velvet hue," he replied. But I was too subdued to joke. "So, you tell me, how does it serve the industry to not write about the other people who work in it?"

"It's not their job to serve the industry. It's their job to make money," he said. Then he softened. "There's not enough upside for them. And way too much can go wrong." I must have muttered something about pressing on because he said, "Good luck" with a tone that registered the opposite. But I'd be lying if I said something hadn't changed. He'd gotten through to me, or maybe it was the FX flack.

Past momentum carried me a little farther. I talked to the showrunner of "The Walking Dead" when I did another story for The Washington Post, that one about a makeup artist. Separately, I mentioned the idea to Andrew Lincoln, an acquaintance and the actor who played Rick on the show. Lincoln thought it was a great idea. "Crew deserves a lot more of the glory than they get," he said. He even agreed to put a word in for me with the showrunner, but the idea ultimately fizzled.

Then, out of the blue, I got an email from Badalato, a primary character in the pages of "Below the Line." I'd kept up with him and his wife a little bit in the three years since they'd been in Atlanta on *Big Momma's House*. Living thousands of miles apart, the interactions had amounted to a single brunch when I was in L.A. and a handful of emails.

Was I still interested in writing about production? Badalato was coming back to Atlanta, this time on *Last Vegas*. We agreed that I would collaborate on a manual for him called "The Cost of Words." He was an educator at heart and had wanted to do a manual for a decade or more. He was also newly inspired by an experience at the University of Texas at Arlington. A professor in the department of Radio-Television-Film had invited Badalato to speak to a film studies class, and he ended up returning several times. He wasn't paid but it reaffirmed his commitment.

He would pay me a stipend of $6,000 over the five-month run of production to work on "The Cost of Words" and I could write whatever else I wanted on my own. I would have a desk in the bullpen. Most importantly, no one had to talk to me. That was up to me.

I received no pay from Four Fellas Production LLC, the business entity that made the movie. My focus was on what was happening around me and the people and process that happened on the ground level. Aside from Samuels and Badalato, I wasn't sure what other producers and executives knew about the project. Anyone who was on location or on the soundstages saw me. Well after the movie wrapped I contacted the key producer, the one most responsible for getting the movie made, for an interview. The request was denied, via a publicist. The producer was unaware of the book and granting an interview could be misconstrued as approval. I was disappointed but I understood. There was no non-disclosure agreement in place or anything to limit the scope of the narrative.

The story wasn't about people above the line so I didn't seek them out. The exception was the director, who was at the center of the action. It was clear to me that Turteltaub understood I was a journalist and taking notes. I did a follow-up interview with him in his offices at Disney Studios well after box office results for *Last Vegas* were determined. "I had *nothing* to do with it," he said, shortly into the meeting. I laughed but it was true. At the core, that is what makes "Below the Line" different than the other books mentioned. The authors of those books were there to follow the directors.

Turteltaub deserves credit for not making it about him, and he might have. He gets even more credit for not kicking me out.

The independence of this book is good news for readers who want an inside look at process. I would assert it's also good news for people above the line on *Last Vegas* because this is a positive book. It's just as true, however, that if it had been a debacle this book would be about a debacle -- no matter how much I liked them. That's what journalists do. Even Brian De Palma admitted *Bonfire of the Vanities* was a mess, noting it was all there, in Julie Salamon's book.

My goal was to understand how a quality major motion picture was made and to try to explain it to others. It wasn't until day 36 of the 38 days of photography, while I watched them shoot the culminating scene, that I realized I had the story, or enough. It came with a bolt of clarity that movies were a collaborative art form. The crew wasn't just help, they were an integral part of the process. Some of them were as talented as the best actor in front of any camera. I hadn't understood that in two hours, the time period typically afforded journalists. Nor was it true at three weeks. It had taken me every minute of the past months to get to that point. It's taken every bit of the years since, and every minute of research, to get to this one. It's a complicated business, but it's brilliant.

Thank you to Billy Badalato and to everyone above the line, especially Turteltaub and the producer most responsible for getting the movie made. But most of all, thank you to the crew.

Meredith Jordan, Rancho Mirage, CA, February, 2019

INTRODUCTION

The story of *Last Vegas* begins nearly four years before the start of production in Atlanta in August 2012. That's when the idea of the movie first made it into a news story. There was no short story forming a basis for it, no spec script. But the "untitled boomers-in-Vegas comedy" pitch was strong enough to lead to a bidding contest and a $1 million payday for writer Dan Fogelman, according to Variety.

Hollywood describes a pitch as an idea for a movie and a really good idea a "high concept." Generally, it's attached to someone with a track record or someone's personal story. In the case of *Last Vegas*, even the logline was vague at that point, since the screenplay was unwritten: "Four semi-retired guys embarking on a getaway to SinCity." It moved through the pipelines as an "unnamed project by Dan Fogelman."

Fogelman's career, animated by luck, took hold in the mid-2000s. He was an unpublished writer of 25 or so when he landed an interview with John Lasseter at Pixar. That turned into a job writing *Cars* in 2006 and then *Fred Claus* in 2007. Meanwhile, he had other screenplays in development, including *Crazy, Stupid, Love.*

IMDb, the Internet movie database, lists the pitch for *Last Vegas* coming in March 2008, with the script delivered in August 2009 and revised by April 2010. News reports that Jon Turteltaub would direct started a year before production, in summer 2011.

Amy Baer, then president and CEO of CBS Films, pulled the trigger on the pitch. If the reported $1 million she promised for the script that became *Last Vegas* rolled any eyes at the time, it would seem prescient after *Crazy, Stupid, Love* cemented Fogelman as a major scriptwriter. The movie made an estimated $143 million after it was released in 2011. It also was nominated for more than a dozen awards. It featured Steve Carell as a drab, middle-aged guy whose wife asks for a divorce, leaving him to reclaim his manhood with the help of a newfound friend played by Ryan Gosling.

To fans of classic television, Baer may be more known for her father, actor Tom Bosley, who played Howard Cunningham, the dad for 255 episodes of "Happy Days." Born in 1966, she grew up in Hollywood. For her, take-your-kid-to-work day included two appearances on the show, which ran from 1974 to 1984. Instead of becoming an actress, she became an executive. She spent 17 years as a senior production executive at Sony before taking the lead role at CBS Films in 2007. When she left in late 2011 it was with plans to produce, *Last Vegas* her first project in that capacity.

Hollywood icon Laurence "Larry" Mark had a career on par with any other living producer. His credits spanned decades but more than that, the pictures he's worked on were memorable. He produced *Dreamgirls*, which won two Academy Awards and three Golden Globe Awards, including one for Best Picture. He received an Academy Award nomination for producing Best Picture nominee *Jerry Maguire*. He executive-produced *As Good As It Gets* and *Working Girl*, both of which were nominated for Best Picture.

There are different kinds of producers. Baer and Mark were creative producers, although that isn't a formal title. The job includes things like delivering talent to a project or assisting in casting, weighing in on creative hires like the production and costume designers, and handling high-level issues as they arise.

Other producers have more day-to-day managerial roles, like Jeremiah Samuels. He would have an executive producer credit on *Last Vegas*. He was on site day-to-day, managing expenditures and overseeing all aspects of production. A good line producer, and Samuels also had a long list of credits, put out small fires so effectively that a Baer or Mark never even smelled smoke.

There's only one director. For *Last Vegas*, it needed to be someone comfortable with telling actors like Robert De Niro, Michael Douglas, and Morgan Freeman to do another take. Jon Turteltaub was experienced and he understood Hollywood. A graduate of Beverly Hills High School, he had grown up around television shows. His father, Saul Turteltaub, was a television industry mainstay, producing TV programs like "That Girl," "Sanford and Son," and "What's Happening." His father and Baer's had even worked on some of the same projects, starting in 1964 when the elder Turteltaub was a writer and throughout the '70s, after he become a producer.

Turteltaub started making movies in his late 20s. The first two are best remembered for getting him his third job, *3 Ninjas*, which came out in 1992. It was a martial arts comedy with kids at the center that cost about $6.5 million to make. Critics didn't rave but kids liked it, dragging their parents along in high enough numbers to gross $40 million.

That got the attention of Jeffrey Katzenberg, then chairman of Disney Studios. He put the young director at the helm of *Cool Runnings* but there was a catch. Turteltaub had to agree to give Disney exclusive rights to his next two movies. And he had to agree to be paid scale for *Cool Runnings*.

That 1993 movie, about the Jamaican bobsled team's attempt to make it to the Olympics, cost $15 million and touched the number 1 slot, if briefly. It was quirky and charming. Joel Siegel at Good Morning America announced it "goes for the gold and gets it." Roger Ebert called it "surprisingly entertaining with a nice sweetness." It grossed $155 million.

But it was 1995's *While You Were Sleeping*, starring Sandra Bullock, that really put Turteltaub on the map. Bullock, coming off the success of *Speed* the year earlier, won the hearts of moviegoers as Lucy, who pretends to be the girlfriend of a man in a coma. It cost $17 million to make and brought in $182 million worldwide. Turteltaub, then 32, had arrived. *Phenomenon* was next. The $32 million budget ultimately resulted in $142 million worldwide. The Los Angeles Times called him "hot as a pistol."

Hot directors get movies with bigger budgets, and sometimes more room to fail. His next movie was *Instinct*, starring Anthony Hopkins as a primatologist lost in the jungle for two years. He becomes like his charges and commits two murders, which land him in a prison with the criminally insane. *Instinct* (1999) cost $80 million to make and returned a paltry $34 million.

Turteltaub bounced back with Disney's *The Kid*. It wasn't a grand slam, but it made money. It starred Bruce Willis as a mean guy who changes his ways when his eight-year-old self appears out of nowhere to visit him. The film made $110 million to its $65 million cost. It was a competent return for Turteltaub, particularly given it had to stand next to Willis' other recent effort, *The Sixth Sense*. That movie hit the stratosphere. It was nominated for six Oscars and earned $662 million worldwide.

Turteltaub had proved himself to the powers that be. He was the rare contemporary director who stuck with the same studio, and he had turned in far more successes than failures. The *National Treasure* movies starring Nicolas Cage, in 2003 and 2007, were both big budget movies that yielded respectable returns. The first one cost about $100 million to make and netted $173 million. The sequel, *National Treasure: Book of Secrets* cost $130 million and returned $220 million. Then came *The Sorcerer's Apprentice*, with a $150 million budget. It earned an underwhelming $63 million in the U.S. but ultimately made it up oversees with a final gross estimated at $251 million.

Last Vegas would succeed, Turteltaub would see to that. So what if the budget was 20 percent that of *The Sorcerer's Apprentice*?

PART ONE: PRE-PRODUCTION
Weeks 1-10

CHAPTER ONE
10 Weeks Out
Aug. 13-17

Billy BADALATO GLANCED at a piece of paper in his hand as he led nine people through Mailing Avenue Stageworks in Atlanta, Ga. It was still cool inside at 8:30 a.m. relative to the 80 degrees outside. At 85,000 square feet, the mixed-use warehouse space was much larger than a football field. They would make *Last Vegas* here, a comedy starring some of the longest reigning stars in Hollywood. Before they could hire costumers, build soundstages or bring in high-end trailers for the actors, there were significant structural changes to be made. The creased paper in Badalato's hand, an architectural layout of the facility covered with penciled notes, held its promise. Otherwise the place, which had never been a movie studio, was echoingly empty, dusty and smelly.

Badalato, the unit production manager, seemed undaunted. "We're the Movie Marines," he told them. "We're the first to parachute in and the last to leave." The "we" might have referred to the people in front of him, a combination of building owners, contractors, two production assistants and an interloping journalist. It more readily meant his boss, Jeremiah Samuels, the executive producer of the movie. Badalato and Samuels would be the business-side team that would manage the details of its production. They had worked together for seven years, twice in Georgia. The first time was on Robert Redford's *The Conspirator*, shot in Savannah, and the second on *Big Momma's House: Like Father Like Son* in Atlanta.

Samuels was in a van on that Atlanta-hot August day scouting locations with Jon Turteltaub, who would direct *Last Vegas*. There had been discussion about why he would be taking a relatively small budget movie, given his biggest financial successes had been the *National Treasure* movies starring Nicholas Cage. *The Sorcerer's Apprentice* was his most recent project.

Samuels' role was line producer, a term close to his actual job description, which meant follow the budget lines, keep a grip on the wallet. Everyone else was on the creative side of the equation. As the production designer, David Bomba was in charge of the overall "look" of the movie based on Turteltaub's direction. The location manager was there to show them places they could shoot in Atlanta, while a member of the film commission weighed in. There was a lot of ground to cover. The working script had 118 scenes, which correlated to 45 sets.

Last Vegas, a comedy about four guys in their late sixties who throw a bachelor party for the last one of them to get married, had a stellar cast in Robert De Niro, Michael Douglas, Morgan Freeman, and Kevin Kline. Mary Steenburgen would play the enchantress, although the ink wasn't dry on her deal yet. With seven Academy Awards among these stars, the studios were betting their collective stature and popularity ensured a hit. The actors would arrive in Las Vegas in ten weeks for the start of principal photography. That's how long they had to prep the movie, which would be shot in the two cities, and include 50 people in the cast, 4,000 extras and a crew of 360.

To understand why it was happening in Georgia, and how the producers laid the framework for location work in Las Vegas, is to take a quantum leap into the business of Hollywood in the new millennium. Aside from a handful of mega-pictures, the days of free-flowing capital were gone. This movie, with its $36 million budget, was business. It was a creative venture but they would pay close attention to the bottom line, which was much more typical of how films happen in the new millennium.

Georgia offered compelling savings to movie and television productions through generous tax credits. It was so significant in the deciding where to make *Last Vegas* that the budget itself reflected the discount. The total budget was $36 million, but they factored in 20 percent savings, which made it a $30 million movie on paper.

Runaway production, a term once used to describe a project shot abroad for distribution in the United States, was now used to describe projects lured away from Hollywood to other parts of the country. It was a seismic shift that had challenged California's lead as a production state, something it was working to change behind the scenes.

Only a few states provided deep incentives like Georgia, and Nevada was not one of them. One way to cut costs in Las Vegas was through embedded marketing, or the inclusion of a branded product into a story. It's better known as product placement. Most consumers considered it to be Tom Cruise wearing Ran-Ban's Wayfarer sunglasses in *Risky Business* (1983) or James Bond drinking a Heineken instead of his trademark martini in *Skyfall* (2012). Its practice dates back to the early days of Hollywood, starting with a short film called *The Garage* (1920), which featured Crown Gasoline. Better known is the Hershey's Chocolate Bar that appeared in a scene in *Wings* (1927), which received a lot more notice. *Wings* was the first movie to win an Oscar for Best Picture, then known as Best Production.

The product placement business was estimated at $4.7 billion in 2012 and expected to touch $11.5 billion in 2019, according to Statista. The numbers surprised most people. While consumers had grown increasingly weary of traditional advertising they didn't necessarily notice it in the fabric of their entertainment, a least not to the extent it was there. Studios that had once shunned the idea now had executives in charge of 'product integration' or 'strategic partnerships' or some variation of that because product placement provided corporate benefit.

An impressive deal had been done before *Last Vegas* got to prep. The original script envisioned the story taking place at Planet Hollywood Hotel and Casino. Now it was set at Aria Resort and Casino, a huge casino-resort jewel in the MGM crown. That wasn't happenstance. In exchange for the actors saying its name on screen, among other things, Aria would provide 3,000 room nights. It was invaluable marketing for the resort and greatly reduced costs of shooting in Las Vegas for the movie production.

The business of making the movie fell under the umbrella of Four Fellas Productions LLC, the business entity that would spend millions of dollars putting the movie together, leasing everything from studio space to camera equipment and furniture. It would buy insurance, food, office supplies and copy machines, rent clothing racks and mirror stations and pay the crew. Then it would cease operations and shift resources to post production. Eventually the LLC would cease to operate except to pay residuals, assuming it was successful and made money.

What made an LLC a desirable business structure was that investors, whether studios or otherwise, were only on the hook for what they put in. They could lose it all, but it wasn't a partnership where they could be pursued for more money. More than $10 million in spending would be managed by the production accountant in the next five months. He would work closely with Badalato and Samuels, which meant there were two sides keeping track. The accountant was already working, just operating from his hotel room until the office space was ready.

The group followed Badalato through the executive offices and into the general office space, coming to a stop in a giant room. A huge pile of construction debris anchored the center of the room, electrical outlets from its previous configuration still dangling in wait for an electrician. Six offices a

3

week earlier, they had been gutted to create the bullpen, which would be the center of the movie production. No one was sure how it came to be called the bullpen. But it centered on the production department, which was the working hub of the movie. All the other departments were spokes, as Badalato explained it.

There was a loud grinding noise in the distance and a wafting smell of wet limestone as workers transformed the gritty concrete halls into a smooth surface. The mood was light, everyone happy to be there and chatting away as they went the short distance to the large corner office across the hallway from the bullpen. This would be Badalato's office. He took the cap off a Sharpie and walked toward one of the walls.

"I think I've cut in windows or doors on every show I've worked on," he said as he drew four neat arrows and then brackets for the planned corners of the window on the wall. The window would go between his office and one next door, which would house the production manager, his second in command. "It encourages communication," he said.

This prompted a laugh but they had laughed at all of Badalato's jokes. He was the man with control of the gate and the checkbook. To varying degrees, every one of them needed his approval. They wanted to like him, too. Though he seemed likable, it wasn't clear yet if he was.

Badalato looked like a movie executive. In his mid-40s, he had broad shoulders and a balding, horseshoe-pattern haircut. His striking, bright blue eyes were topped with healthy eyebrows and balanced with gleaming white Hollywood teeth. The clothes he wore were casual, a black short-sleeve polo shirt and jeans, but they looked expensive. He wore a thick watch and two rings. Most importantly, he spoke with authority, like a producer who expected to be heard more than he listened.

A temporary production assistant, a young man who wouldn't be long on the show, checked the swing of the door between the two offices. He noted gingerly that with a new window, the door between the two offices would open the wrong way. It was a good point and it was duly noted with the Sharpie that the door had to be reversed and rehung. Badalato went to another wall and marked the corners for a second window, this one on the side of the office that faced a long hallway of offices.

"This way I can see traffic as it approaches," he said, as he wrote four more neat sideways Ls on the wall precisely where he wanted the window.

The paper in Badalato's hand might have been time coded. The executive suites—particularly Turteltaub's and Samuels' offices—had been easy. They were functional if given a little paint, although neither man was likely to spend a lot of time there. What part of the building would be occupied in what order? Production, Accounting and Art needed to move into permanent offices right away. Transportation, the mill shop, Hair and Makeup, Grip and Electric, could wait.

The office on the other side of Badalato's was for the first assistant director, the lead manager on the director's team. There was a large mirror on one wall of the room and someone remarked that it should be a producer's office. It was one of those jokes that made people nervous until Badalato laughed. The accounting offices were next, then the locations department, cinematographer's office and payroll. The costume department occupied a series of offices at the end of the hall. Eventually that department would need a lot of space for storage, cages and dressing rooms, all of it in proximity to the stages. There was time for that.

Bristie Stephens, the second production assistant, or PA, had shoulder-length dark hair and sharp, dancing eyes. She wore comfortable clothes, a brown shirt with thick dark stripes, baggy pants, and a maroon hoodie that read "Teen Wolf." She had worked as a production assistant on the MTV series. She was pretty and shorter than the others, the only African American, and aside from a visitor, the only woman in the group.

Everyone took notes, electronically or the old-fashioned way, but it was Stephens who wrote most ferociously. Her to-do list not only grew quickly but she also kept track of everyone else's. Stephens wanted a bump up to production secretary, the next rung in the production office hierarchy, and she meant to prove her worthiness. She wrote everything down, big projects and smaller ones, details about furniture and signs for the office, changes to HVAC. Taking down the walls and rebuilding them was just the start. They had to be trimmed and painted, and rooms carpeted. Stops grew less frequent as they made their way through the warehouse spaces, past a spray booth and the mill shop and offices built within the spaces.

They stopped at the far end of the building, about 100 steps into the 38,000-square-foot warehouse where most of the stages would be built. Workers had poured concrete to repair the floor after they'd removed 30-foot steel columns that had held up the roof. The columns now lay on the ground, temporary braces in place until the two 80-foot steel trusses were installed to support the roof. It was all done to create unencumbered space. The penthouse set, where the most scenes would be shot for *Last Vegas*, would be perhaps 9,000 square feet. It couldn't have steel columns in the middle. It was a major renovation but beneficial to the facility in general, since it planned to cater to movie productions when this one finished.

The building's owners also planned to remove fencing and then re-grade the space behind the warehouse to make it more hospitable to trucks, trailers, equipment and trailers for the actors. Something also would have to be done about the top of the roof to quiet any potential rain. The existing roof was fine for a regular warehouse but not one where they would record sound. The sound of a significant rain pelting the existing roof could ruin an entire shooting day.

The group was showing signs of wear as they went back up the other side of Mailing Avenue. The last stop was the area that would house the art department. That space was U-shaped with offices around a storage room in the middle. One side had three offices and windows facing the parking lot. Badalato wanted to take down one wall between two smaller offices on the far side to create a bigger room with space for three artist workstations. All the rooms around the U would have windows cut between them for better communication.

The tour was about to come to an end when Badalato said something that left them dumbfounded: He wanted it all done by Friday, which was days away. That would tee up the offices for the influx of crew starting next week. The art department space needed to be ready.

"This Friday?" The lead contractor asked the question with a light enough tone to prompt more nervous laughter. It wasn't just taking the walls down and cutting in windows. It was trim work, paint and features like fiberboard. That provided a place to tack calendars and photos, renderings and paperwork, and anything else without damaging walls. It wasn't just going in the art department but in many of the offices.

Badalato hadn't laughed. "Are we good?"

"Sure," the contractor said. "No problem."

"Great. Thanks, guys," said Badalato, as he and the two PAs disappeared from the room.

The men who remained looked at each other. Most people can't renovate a kitchen in a week and the Hollywood guy wanted 18,000 square feet of office space finished now. The building owner huddled with the contractor while the others checked studs in the walls that would soon come down.

Badalato and the production assistants moved into the pea-soup green room, the first room off the foyer in the executive suites. It had been empty with a vague smell of mold but the building owner had alerted them to furniture dumped by a previous tenant in office space near the back warehouse.

The temporary PA, a young man who was both a screenwriter and a teacher, had proved adept with the hand truck. Three banquet-style tables were set up in front of the walls with chairs behind them, so everyone faced the center of the room. A fourth table leaned against the last wall. All of the tables were wobbly except one, but not so bad they couldn't hold laptops. By 11 a.m. they were all seated and working, complete with new phone lines installed.

The phones had started to ring almost immediately with Samuels, the studios, and then Michael Douglas' hair and makeup people in rapid succession. De Niro, Douglas and Freeman were allotted the same number of people in their entourage. The actors said whom they wanted hired and if they didn't, the production would find crew. In all cases it was up to Badalato or a designee to negotiate their deals. Above the line people had a contract. Below the line people had a deal memo. Above the line, an accounting term, referred to the writer, director, actors and producers. Everyone else was below the line.

Badalato reached in his pocket and handed the PA petty cash to go to the store. They needed virtually everything at that point.

"Here's ninety bucks," Badalato said. "Save all your receipts." Then, almost as an afterthought, he reminded him to count the money. The PA flipped through the thin pile of money.

"It's a hundred," the young man said quickly. "Not ninety."

"Is it?" Badalato grinned like he might have known that. "Okay, thanks for telling me."

The young man soon returned with a coffee pot and accoutrements. This was makeshift "craft service," which provided food and beverages to the crew. It would be its own department when the movie started shooting, providing meaningful snacks, even mini-meals. It was separate from catering, which would provide full meals for cast and crew.

Today it provided coffee mixers, other nonalcoholic beverages, crackers and cookies and fruit. The comfort was appreciated but also assumed as part of life on a movie production. It also ensured the focus remained on work. Even in "prep," the term given the next ten weeks used to prepare for principal photography, they would work a minimum of ten hours each day.

The PA also picked up general supplies, like cleaning equipment, soap, paper towels and toilet paper. He was responsible for wiping the built-in cabinets on the back wall and otherwise cleaning up the place and keeping the coffee pot gurgling. The coffee aroma did the most to eradicate the lingering moldy smell.

It was Stephens who turned the place into an office, aided by her kit. A "kit" in movie set parlance consisted of different tools or supplies crew needed to do their respective jobs. They were freelancers who brought it with them, whether hammers or lists of vendors, manuals or clothing racks. The temporary PA had one too, in a sense, in that he wore a belt with tools of his trade. It was a little like a construction belt, but smaller, with tape measure and a tool knife, notepad and sundry items. The side benefit to having a kit at the ready -- how quickly people could get to work -- was in evidence.

In Stephens' case, the kit amounted to a moveable office, compact enough to fit in the trunk of her pristine 1998 Mercedes 320. These weren't light supplies. She provided the fourth folding table in the office, the only one that wasn't vulnerable to collapse, and brought the best chair. She even had a giant physio-ball for ergonomic sitting and a compressor in her black shiny car just outside to pump it up if needed. She had a newer laptop, a quality printer and enough paper, scissors, tape, pencils and pens for anyone who needed them. She had a miscellaneous box with objects like office-grade hole punchers and notebooks and magic markers, the larger items with her name taped to them.

Stephens had a long to-do list but one immediate priority. She had created a list of furniture needed in each room, nearly 100 pieces, featuring desks, chairs, bookcases and couches. Badalato had talked about pricing them with different companies. Was it cheaper to rent or purchase? Leaving intrinsic value out of it, what had the least impact to the bottom line of the production company? Stephens used a spreadsheet to organize it and huddled over it at her desk.

"Price tables, too," Badalato said at one point, in a room that had gone quiet aside from occasional outside phone calls. It was funny in one sense, coming out of context, but it had quickly become the norm. "They're cheaper and not everybody needs a desk."

It was clear by now to everyone he meant to save money. This wasn't a big-budget movie -- $30 million was nothing to the likes of De Niro, Douglas and Freeman -- and Badalato figured the more people understood that the better. Stephens quickly narrowed it down to two companies. Once she had all prices side by side, she returned to the bidders to negotiate better rates. Then she gave Badalato her report, which he immediately signed off on. They got the order in fast because they wanted the furniture delivered fast.

Mailing Avenue was dusty but it was a nice facility. It had been quality construction to begin with and the new ownership group wanted to make it better. That wasn't true of all places leased to make movies, even with higher-end budgets. At full capacity, the 18,000 square feet of total office space, which included the executive wing, was 20 percent roomier than others Badalato had negotiated for similar projects. Better still, he and Samuels had brought it in under budget, and it was a larger space.

"I'm saving money on my movie so there's more money for my movie," said Badalato.

By midweek when they were pricing high-end copying machines it was clear Badalato would spend money. The production would need at least two of them to begin with and both had to be state-of-the-art. The one for the art department had to be color. The other one would be the size of a Smart Car that among many talents could collate and print 100 scripts in half an hour. Leased machines broke too easily, Badalato said. He'd had it happen. The thought of a copier going down on a shooting day, leaving cast and crew on the clock standing around waiting for updated script pages, was more than he could stand. The potential risk justified the expense. Besides, they would sell the machines later and recoup at least half of the money. The combination of those things more than justified the expense.

Badalato and Samuels had a rhythm, one in-house, one out, and were in regular phone communication. Much of the conversation was about hires. It was focused on the immediate, but nothing was ignored either. *Last Vegas* still needed several department heads. Generally the director could pick whom he wanted in conjunction with producers, who played a huge role in those decisions.

A likely costume designer had been identified in L.A., a pick of the screenwriter Dan Fogelman, although the decision wasn't final. The search for a director of photography (DP) continued. Also known as the cinematographer, it was the highest paid position below the line and hugely important to the success of the movie. It was the DP who hired the Camera crew, oversaw the Grip and Electric departments and delivered the physical product. Turteltaub's first choice had a scheduling conflict. Both creative department heads were needed soon.

Other department hires weren't as pressing but still very important. Who would handle transportation when principal photography began? Setting up base camps, moving trucks and trailers, transporting cast and crew, and managing the Teamsters who did the work under union rules was a big job. Shooting in two different locations like Las Vegas and Atlanta made it all that much more challenging.

The scouting van with the director pulled in to Mailing Avenue for the first time midweek. Badalato had been acutely aware of the planned visit. When Samuels called to tell him they were pulling up he hurried out to meet them. The hive of men -- Turteltaub in the center -- entered the building and moved as a swarm toward the interior. The building owner, ever present, was cued in to the visit and he blended right in with the group.

The PAs kept working as though they didn't know the director was in the building. But they knew. Everyone from the highest level to the lowest had done homework on him long before now. There had been full discussions about his work in the temporary bullpen. One of them loved *Phenomenon,* his 1996 movie starring John Travolta as a simple country mechanic who gets thumped with a bright light and becomes a brain trust. Someone else liked the *National Treasure* franchise and thought they should make a third movie. Not one of them had seen *The Sorcerer's Apprentice.* They wanted to meet the director but it was also nervous-making.

After about fifteen minutes the scouting group exited the far door near where the art department would be, the sound of their voices wafting from the parking lot. There was a sense of unspoken relief. Then the voices were back, louder, this time at the main door. Suddenly Turteltaub burst through it, down the hall and into the temporary office where they all sat wide-eyed. Badalato and Samuels were in close pursuit, introducing the director over his shoulder.

Turteltaub was a big man, maybe 6'2", with shaggy graying hair. He was laughing out loud. "Are you people working?" he boomed. There was silence as they stared back, stunned and smiling, afraid to speak. Then he said it again, the room fully under command. He noted the air conditioning -- good air conditioning. That was something he had in short supply as he toured around outside in summertime Atlanta. Now they were all laughing. The director made the rounds, stopping at every desk to shake hands and chat briefly. Then he was gone, creating a vacuum that pulled Samuels and Badalato out behind him.

"Wow!" said the PA.

"WOW," echoed Stephens.

They were wide-eyed and grinning, shaking their heads.

It was a good sign, no doubt about that. When Badalato returned he was grinning, too. Mailing Avenue had been well received, its spaciousness noticed. "It's a plus for production," he said. "We did the right thing in choosing the space." It wasn't always the case that everyone had plenty of room to work.

"Sure, it's all puppies and flowers in prep," joked Stephens. "Then shooting starts."

Badalato assured everyone it was going to be a great show. It comes from the top, he told them, and an easygoing director made all the difference. The director shaped the movie, all aspects of it, even the production department, which would spend little time on set. He or she could make the experience miserable or happy.

Turteltaub was the creative boss of the movie and it was the expressed goal to keep him happy -- assuming it was possible. Some directors want what they want without thought to cost. If he were that kind of director he would need to be reined in, which would fall to Samuels as line producer or Badalato as his henchman. The two sides, creative and business, were an industry dynamic. It generally worked, which didn't mean it ended up a love fest, just that it spared the need for studio intervention.

Later the group in the provisional office processed Turteltaub's visit. He had been a surprise. "Jon looks great," Badalato said. Then he paused a few seconds. "I sure hope I get to work with him on a big-budget movie sometime."

As Friday neared and the smell of paint grew thicker, it appeared Badalato would succeed in finishing his Rome-building-in-a-day to-do list. All kinds of construction work, large and small, had coalesced. The warehouse had new steel beams, the art department offices trimmed out. The hallways gleamed, trendy and gorgeous, while new carpet went into the offices where paint had dried.

Then a problem emerged. The winning furniture company insisted it be paid upon delivery. Badalato and the accountant, who was in Atlanta but working from his hotel room, couldn't make it happen. The studio insisted on signing off and they couldn't cut the check that quickly. The soonest it could be delivered was Monday. Stephens tried to get company rep to change his mind to no avail.

CHAPTER TWO
9 Weeks Out
Aug. 20 24

D AMIANA KAMISHIN HADN'T BEEN THERE five minutes before she and Badalato disappeared into the hinterlands of Mailing Avenue. As de facto production manager she would have been working on *Last Vegas* from day one except she'd needed time to wrap her last show. She had spent the last few months in Boston on *Labor Day* starring Kate Winslet and Josh Brolin. There was a lot to catch her up on, even just one week into prep.

In a perfect world a movie crew would have a few weeks or even months off between shows to recuperate. A movie is a condensed work cycle that leaves little time for anything else. There were consistently long hours, union defined and compensated, and details like when people would be fed, where they stayed on site. That left no time for personal errands during the workweek, which otherwise amounted to prime resting time. By the end of any show, most crew was well behind in things they needed to do for themselves and their families.

At the same time, there could be big gaps between projects. The inclination of most crew was to take the next job when they got it, because who knew when the next one would line up. That's why scheduling was an issue for managers who wanted to re-hire people they'd used before. For Kamishin, by all accounts very good at her job, that happened a lot. She worked so much she hadn't spent a lot of time at home. While she had been based in Los Angeles for four years the amount of time she actually lived there was closer to one year.

Kamishin worked with Samuels and Badalato on *Big Momma's House,* so they knew what they were getting. The office next to Badalato's with the freshly cut window would be hers. Her presence immediately lightened the load for both Badalato and Stephens bringing a sense of relief.

But she was tired and said as much. "Back-to-backs," as Kamishin termed this, were exhausting.

She and Badalato had barely taken their seats from the studio tour when the office landline rang, Samuels on the other end. After a quick greeting, Badalato waved for her to come to the phone. She hurriedly dug into her bag for a notebook.

"It's just a welcoming call," he whispered. "You don't need your notebook."

Kamishin laughed. She was about 5'6," slender with shoulder-length hair and wore jeans and sandals and a frilly tank top. "Yeah. I know how he rolls," she said with a smile. "This could take a while." She went over to the wobbly desk and put the phone to her ear, placing the notebook and pen in front of her. Then she lowered herself to a crouch and leaned over the desk, poised to write on the pad. Within a minute she was jotting away.

Afterward she handed the phone back to Badalato for his and Samuels' morning call. Samuels had gone to L.A. for the weekend and had stayed Monday. He had a full office there and wasn't set up yet in Atlanta, in part due to the delay in furniture delivery. The head accountant for *Last Vegas*, who was working from his Atlanta hotel room since he didn't have an office with furniture, had convinced the executive to overnight it to Mailing Avenue. Badalato confirmed the check had arrived.

That handled, Badalato and Samuels moved on. Badalato's eyes following silently down the list of items he had prepared for the conversation, checking things off one by one, as bits of disconnected conversation funneled into the room.

"Sounds bombastic. He's going to have to get over it."

"She's in her summer home. She can stay in her own house here, but I have to fly her in for the interview," he said. "But I can't imagine it's a bigger deal than that."

"It's his schedule on "Newsroom," said Badalato, referring to the HBO series. "He thinks he can make the Vegas portion work." This had to do with transportation for the movie. The discussion turned to someone else they had worked with before and liked for the job. Maybe they could split up transportation and have someone else handle it in Atlanta.

Badalato had a bad back and while surgery helped, sitting could aggravate it. He often stood for longer calls, as he was now. Suddenly his tenor changed and he took a seat somewhat quickly.

"Wow. That's heavy."

Everyone in the office was focused on work but the shift in his tone was hard to ignore. Everyone tuned in, heads on their work.

14

"Very sorry to hear that," he said. "He was a really creative force in the business."

The news was bad. Producer-director Tony Scott had died overnight. He'd jumped to his death from the Vincent Thomas Bridge in San Pedro, Calif. Samuels, on West Coast time, had seen coverage of it. Badalato had come to the office early and gone right to work without looking at news. The talk turned to Scott's artistic brilliance, the suffering that must have preceded an apparent suicide, and concern for the family and production company staff, and his brother, Ridley Scott, another widely respected director. Badalato wondered out loud if Bill, his father, knew.

Bill Badalato had been executive producer of *Top Gun* in 1986, the film directed by Scott that launched both him and Tom Cruise to stardom. Billy, then nineteen, had grown up on movie sets with his father but *Top Gun* was his first paid job. That's what sealed his fate with the movie business. He had earlier talked about those days, hanging out with the crew and becoming a part of the magic of it. Cruise, an unknown at that point, had often joined them.

Scott had had a stellar career since, compiling a list of movies that included a lot of big-budget action films, generally directing one every three to five years. His most recent offering, 2010's *Unstoppable* with Denzel Washington, was a critical success. It had been praised for covering new terrain, an action movie with a full range of tension and intrigue without featuring guns. Ridley Scott was now a powerhouse in Hollywood. Bill Badalato senior had likewise had a successful career as a producer.

Someone asked Badalato if he had any memories of Tony Scott. He said there were many but one in particular stood out. It was a conflict between his father and Scott when they were shooting *Top Gun*. The production was on location out in the ocean to do scenes on the aircraft carrier. It was late afternoon and Scott was looking into the distance, watching the sun go down, his two hands squared to block out the shot. It was the money shot, a gorgeous sunset. Then the sun started to shift in his view as the aircraft carrier began to bend away with a new heading. Scott turned and looked up at the bridge. "Wait. What are you doing?" he said. "Turn it back!"

They quickly radioed the bridge with the director's wishes but were told the captain had been instructed to return to shore. Scott called out to Badalato, who was at the same moment headed over to talk to him. The line producer coolly explained that if they didn't turn back now it would cost another $10,000. The time allocated for the aircraft carrier was up.

Scott was having none of that.

"I need this shot!" he said.

"Sorry, Tony. No."

"Turn it back! Now."

"No!"

Scott was flustered but he wasn't about to give up. He found his checkbook and wrote a personal check to the production for $10,000 and threw it at the senior Badalato. The ship turned back and the director got his shot. The sunset scene is in the movie. Scott's check was eventually returned and the men ended up laughing about it. They'd stayed in contact for a number of years after the movie struck gold.

Top Gun, which cost $15 million to make, went on to a worldwide gross of $345 million, according to estimates. Physical producers like Badalato don't control budgets on the basis of potential, or at least not ones the studios rehire. The movie's creators had known it would be good but no one had anticipated it would become iconic.

At one point telling the story, Badalato looked like a kid, awe on his face and small in his chair. His inner child vanished as soon as the story ended. He looked at Stephens. "Where are we with the furniture?"

Stephens had handled the furniture and she had been the one to pass on the news they would not deliver on credit, after being told they would. And she had kept in contact with the company rep like close family. She told him the furniture was arriving in three trucks.

By the end of the day the first truck deposited 29 rolling desk chairs in the foyer. The other two trucks loaded with desks and couches and tables and bookcases arrived early Tuesday morning, and by noon everyone had moved to the bullpen or other permanent offices

Stephens, 24, was new to the movie business and she meant to succeed. Her most recent job had been on a pilot for MTV called "Cassandra French's Finishing School for Boys" and *Last Vegas* was her first feature film. She was essentially acting as a production coordinator, since the woman with that job title was wrapping another movie and wouldn't arrive until next week. They consulted on the phone and by email but the brunt of responsibility had fallen to Stephens.

Badalato made it clear he wanted precise cost details, and everything, no matter how small, was priced from then on. It could be something simple like the microwave and refrigerator for the kitchen, which he wanted as soon as possible, or something more expensive. Stephens didn't need to be told anything twice. She wrote everything down and followed up, which helped catch things early if they started to go awry, as had happened with the furniture.

It helped that the other PA was solid. Stephens had met him on another production, liked his work, and recommended him for the PA job on *Last Vegas* although he was temporary. A phone list was in the works. They started a short list of candidates for Samuels' assistant. Badalato would mention cleaning services and a shredding company and she and the other PA would make eye contact that determined who was going to handle it.

The best PAs do what they are asked while trying to anticipate what will be needed but she also had a degree of charm. She was smart but it was actually more simple than that. Stephens knew when to listen and she was pleasant to everyone, whether studio personnel or crew seeking work. The latter had increased dramatically as the landline became known to the outside world.

Soon Stephens was soon rewarded for her effort. Badalato announced she would be production secretary. She had been hired as a temporary PA. The new role meant she would manage the other office PAs and get a bump in pay.

That coincided with the move to the permanent bullpen. It smelled new, a mix of the fresh paint and the chemicals that accompany new carpet, but it also felt palatial after the original makeshift office. There were five work-stations in the rectangular space, three desks and two banquet tables around the perimeter of the room and facing inward. A couch was set up on the far end, a waiting area for crew coming in for interviews that would start in a few hours. It was a big enough space that it had gobbled up the furniture, leaving the middle of the room very empty.

"It feels bigger than it did without furniture," said Stephens. "There would be an echo in here if it wasn't for the carpet!" The carpet squares had a modish look like something out of a movie theater. It had been bulk sale to the building owners, discounted if they took all of it, and Badalato hadn't cared what the carpet looked like.

The art department had undergone the same renovation as the other rooms, including a conference room space across the hall without windows. It was a little behind but not much. Fiberboard, in this case used like giant bulletin boards, was installed on all of its walls, as it would be in many offices.

The art director was on board, which served to make it happen that much faster. As the second in the department, his job was to manage the department and the artists who worked there while advancing Bomba's plans. He had immediately hired a coordinator, someone Bomba knew and liked. She soon made the rounds to meet everyone.

Stephens and the PA made a phone list and systematically checked the 30 phone lines, going to every station in the bullpen and in every office, listened for a dial tone, and matched the corresponding extensions. The last line was for the fax machine. Another table was set up for the fax, incoming and outgoing mail, and receiving. Someone had brought in an older fax machine and Stephens tested it and it worked. Why buy a new one? They steadily downloaded resumes from the email address created for that purpose.

The phones started to ring immediately as if callers sensed there were more of them to be rung. Word spread quickly that there was a movie looking for crew. A production newsletter had listed it and then a local reporter covered a town event where a location manager said they were looking for places to shoot. That got the information online.

A game started between Stephens and the PA and anyone else in the bullpen. The main phone line could be picked up at any of the desks in the bullpen. The challenge was to see who could answer the phone first. They would race to the nearest phone from wherever they were, sometimes from across the room, and grab for the cradle.

"Production office. Can I help you?" The only rule was that the caller not recognize their haste.

This was the beauty of Stephens. She was going to make it fun. Sure it was a tough, pressure-packed job, but they were making a movie! She approached it like that and her infectious laugh roped others in. At the same time she was sharp as the container of brads she had pulled out of her kit. Her container was labeled "Brad Pitt," a pit for brads, which are used to bind scripts together.

Organizing the bullpen came with a long list of other details. Stephens and the PA changed the placement of the three bookcases in the room. One went behind Stephens' desk, the other where her boss, the assistant production office coordinator (APOC) would sit, the largest on the far end for crew paperwork. Production manager Kamishin came out of her office to look at the bullpen now that it was laid out. She liked it with one change.

Kamishin wanted to switch the location of Stephens' desk with that of the APOC. It was the same reasoning that had Badalato cut a hole in the wall. She needed to be able to communicate easily with the person in that role and nothing was more efficient than proximity.

It also revealed something more elemental to the movie industry. It was all about hierarchy. In most businesses there are top managers, middle managers and worker bees. This too was a lineage, top to bottom, and existed in every department, defined by the concept of a "second." The titles varied by department, many of them containing word "assistant." But a second wasn't a role of subservience. That person had a lot of power and distinct responsibilities within their department.

The hierarchy was first visible in production, because they had to lay the framework for every other department. Samuels had Badalato as a second, Badalato had Kamishin, Kamishin would have the APOC, and she would have Stephens, who would manage PAs. The same was true on the creative side, but in all cases the vision belonged to the first person while the second carried it out.

Badalato and Kamishin's first choice for APOC was a woman they worked with on *Big Momma's House*, but she had another commitment. It was Stephens' assignment to come up with a list of candidates. As the keeper of the email address created to collect resumes submitted to the movie, she had a growing list of candidates. She also had connections.

Hiring crew was a top priority across the board. From the outset Badalato and Kamishin had culled through their phone books for Atlanta-based crew. There was pressure to hire locally as part of the tax reduction agreement with Georgia. At the same time, they wanted to hire known quantities. Too much happened too fast for positions of responsibility to involve on-the-job training or worse, difficult personalities. The movie industry made room for difficult personality types in a way few others did. There was leeway for craziness from people above the line -- particularly actors -- but it also extended to department heads and certain others. There were good reasons for it.

In a condensed work cycle it was generally easier to live with a challenging personality than replace one. Even firing someone lower in the ranks could be problematic given the brief lifespan of the project. Further, they might have come in as a referral or become well-liked by an actor, say, who would inquire where they went. As a general practice it was best to live with the choices made. That boosted the importance of hiring people who came recommended.

Paper signs with the person's name and their jobs or the names of departments were affixed near each office door or by individual desks and through the hallways leading to the production offices. A few went up before to help people acclimate but these were more permanent. Some were more creative than others. Badalato's sign read "Chief of Staff." The chief accountant's office proclaimed him "Chancellor of the Exchequer," the Brits' name for their minister of finance.

The production accountant and his second, a husband and wife team, had moved in on the tail of the furniture delivery. He was in a private office while she set anchor in the accounting bullpen. In time another four people would be hired in the department. The payroll accountant would start shortly, although her office was at the other end of the hall closer to where costume would be. These were serious people: No names, please.

The duo wouldn't have been cast as accountants. Burly with graying hair and a little bit of a gut, he might have played high school or even college football. She looked bookish the first time she came in, a central casting stereotype, but later emerged stylishly well-dressed. Someone commented that the transformation was like Susan Sarandon's character in the first *The Witches of Eastwick*, the proper cellist character letting her hair down as she moves from bookish to coquettish.

The accountant and Badalato were an internal checks-and-balances system, the structure of the relationship long preceding them. Their responsibilities overlapped enough to help ensure nothing hinky happened to the money, since both were paying close attention. But it was a big job to manage the money and the accountant, who had numerous movie and television credits, had been at it for years.

It was all about the budget. There was a lot of back and forth between Badalato and the accountant. Even at this early juncture they were talking about potential cost overruns. Both of them said it repeatedly: It was about planning. Changes could be made, funds designated for one part of the budget could go to another if needed. But you had to be paying attention to the day and looking ahead at the same time.

Petty cash alone would require significant management. In a movie the size of *Last Vegas*, once it was crewed up, $40,000 a week in petty cash, "PC" as the crew referred to it, wouldn't be unusual. That would rise to roughly

$80,000 when principal photography began, given the per diem, the living expenses provided to crews based on their deals on the show. PC had to be meticulously monitored and documented differently from other expenditures. The accounting department paid close attention, even to postage stamps it distributed.

Most companies with large operating budgets call the top accountant the "chief financial officer," often with a flurry of letters after their names. They oversee annual budgets based on existing infrastructure, fixed costs, predictable variables and perhaps a capital expenditure list where big-ticket items are amortized over time. Movie production bean counters aren't CPAs or even necessarily people with accounting degrees. Production accounting is so highly specialized that it takes on-the-job training, experience more highly valued than letters after a name. It may change with time, but in 2012 it was still a fact of life that the average chief accountant came up through the ranks or was apprenticed in some way to learn the ropes.

The production accountant had the same type of responsibility as anyone overseeing a big budget but it happened in a condensed fashion. This part of the movie production would happen in the course of five months. That made it an entirely different beast. Every bit of infrastructure, every employee, all goods and services, from dolly tracks to clothing racks, from catering to auto rentals, had to not only be acquired but disposed of for accounting purposes. If that wasn't complicated enough, they had an abacus of rules to follow that varied by state, by union, by contract, by person.

Most people on the movie never dreamed of seeing the budget. It was off-limits, certainly to the people below the line but most people above the line wouldn't see it either. The actors and writers wouldn't ask for it because it wasn't appropriate. They were hired to do a job. Turteltaub had access to it but he understood well enough what limitations he faced.

The budget for *Last Vegas* showed a grand total of nearly $36 million. It appeared to be almost an even split: $18.7 million staying above the line and $17.4 below it. But the business strategy imagined it in three parts. A third would go above the line, a third for physical production, and a third for marketing and distribution.

The budget had total cast expenses at a little over $11 million. De Niro, Douglas and Freeman would each be paid $2.5 million and get a $100,000 per package to cover on-set requirements. Kline would earn $500,000 and Mary Steenburgen, $250,000. All four men would work somewhere between 37 and 40 days to shoot the movie; Steenburgen's role required about 20 days on set.

That essentially valued the five leads on two levels, De Niro, Douglas and Freeman on one and Kline and Steenburgen on another. That was an assumption based on the amount of work required of each actor. Kline was working twice the number of days as Steenburgen, making their pay roughly equal. Yet Kline would work about the same number of days as De Niro, Douglas and Freeman.

It was bizarre to think of the actors as commodities. De Niro, Douglas and Freeman had bigger fan bases and would draw more people to the movie. De Niro, in particular, had international draw. Kline and Steenburgen had name recognition and good followings, but not at the same level. All of them were highly respected.

Pay equity had long been a topic in the industry. What the head of a studio might say -- off the record lest they end up with unwanted media attention -- was that this was a business and its rules clearly defined. Union contracts determined the lowest allowable pay, something known as "scale."

Actors at this level were paid way above scale. How much above scale was a matter of negotiation. Yes, there should be pay equity, but don't beat them up for getting the best price they could. That was the American way regardless of industry. At least Hollywood's workers and talent had unions and agents.

In order to use union labor, Four Fellas was a signatory of the respective union contracts, which meant it abided by union rules. Unless otherwise negotiated, *Last Vegas* was to pay scale, which was predetermined by the Writers Guild of America (WGA), the Directors Guild of America (DGA), the Screen Actors Guild (SAG), and the International Alliance of Theatrical Stage Employees (IATSE), with its myriad locals. The unions were listed on the top half of the fold of the budget document.

The budget identified pay for the "executive producer" at $2 million, while "producers" would divide $1.5 million. Another $250,000 went to producer overhead. That didn't include things like transportation costs or hotel/lodging. It set aside money to have Samuels on site for 143 days, Mark for 32 nights and Baer, 31. Mark and Baer, with producer credits, and

Samuels with an executive producer credit, would have the most influence on the final product -- aside from Turteltaub. Samuels was one of four people with an executive producer credit, the others connected to the studios.

It was the director's appearance in the budget that provided the real surprise. It showed a salary of $181,700. This was Jon Turteltaub, who earned a reported $5 million for *The Kid* with Bruce Willis in 2000. Even a bad guess was that his pay for *The Sorcerer's Apprentice* was at least that much. But the salary figure wasn't necessarily the full picture. It was possible that Turteltaub would have his payday later.

Hollywood does a better job of keeping its numbers shrouded than perhaps any other legal business in the United States. The distribution of proceeds was not part of the operating budget, which revealed only the front end of a movie. The real money, assuming a success and that it actually got through, often came on the backend for people above the line. How proceeds would be distributed was based on "points," with one percent being one point.

Points are divided as a movie is planned. Lawyers who design the legal structures say a typical breakdown is a split, where the businesses behind a movie -- studios or investors or financiers -- get 50 percent of the points. The producers who bring it all together, control the distribution of the other 50 percent. Writers typically get 3 percent, directors from 5 to 7 percent. Lead actors, particularly at the level of De Niro, Douglas and Freeman, can command as much as five points, with most falling somewhere between 1 to 5 percent. Producers can end up with 5 to 20 percent, depending on what remains after handed out points under their control. That was a generic overview. All of it was negotiable and varied by picture.

Turteltaub could have agreed to be paid in popcorn for directing *Last Vegas* for all it mattered to the cast or crew. The director is the CEO of the movie. It's their vision, their direction, theirs to make or break. It was "Jon's movie," as both Samuels and Badalato, and various crew, said at different junctures. The job of the UPM -- they split the credit -- was to keep Turteltaub on budget or just under it. Samuels had a reputation for getting that job done, for not going back to the studios to ask for more money. At the same time, they couldn't come in too much under budget. If a movie failed for any reason and they hadn't used money available it looked bad for them for skimping on necessary ingredients. But it was the director who would take most of the blame.

Many directors handpick the heads of all creative departments -- if it's possible. Scheduling conflicts weren't helping here, as some of the people Turteltaub wanted to hire were committed elsewhere. But he had lined up the most important role. The first assistant director for the movie would be Gary Rake, who he had worked with on a television show. The 1st AD was the director's next in charge and often key to the success of a movie. That person builds the shooting schedule, which means they plan the movie. When principal photography begins, the 1st AD manages the set. A good "first" enables a director to keep their highest focus on the creative.

Badalato considered the position of 1st AD on par with his as unit production manager. Both were the top jobs below the line, Badalato on the business side and the 1st AD on the creative, even with the giant caveat that the UPM controlled the money.

Rake wasn't technically on the clock but he might as well have been. He was working from his home in Los Angeles and in regular contact with Turteltaub and to a lesser extent, the production office. His main focus was "breaking down" the script, which was still in draft form.

Virtually everyone in a leadership position analyzes the script for production elements that relate to their jobs, so they all break it down differently. The unit production manager read it for dollar signs. The production designer saw the "look" of the movie and each scene in sets. The set decorator would see each set furnished. The costume supervisor looked at it for what the actors would wear, keeping script days in mind. The props department would see objects the actors touched. Locations saw it in scenes to be shot outside the studio. Grips would read it for rigging, electric for cable and power distribution, and camera for lenses, all of them at the direction of the cinematographer. But in the end, they would work from Rake's breakdown, which created the schedule. He would run the show with Turteltaub, who had read the script with a vision that steadily evolved.

The schedule was just the start of responsibilities. The 1st AD would shadow Turteltaub every step of the way, joining in location scouts, hiring decisions and problem-solving as they prepped for shooting. Once photography began, he would remain the proverbial number two running the movie, managing the AD department and interacting with other department heads, all within confines of union and OSHA regulations. Among other duties, the 1st AD was in charge of safety. Rake would have a team of people in his department to help him with all these responsibilities. They were actively looking for a second assistant director and there would be another manager from there, a "second-second." That was the language at play: "Who's the First?" or "Do we have a Second yet?"

There had been some challenges in lining up a 2nd AD. Rake's first candidate had accepted the job weeks earlier. When the man called the studio for more details, eager to get started, he was routed to the mid-level executive involved with *Last Vegas*, who reacted with great umbrage. Who was calling him? How come no one told him they had a second lined up? Insulted, the man accepted a different offer, this one involving several projects, a rare opportunity in the industry, and begged off of *Last Vegas*.

The next candidate was a woman, well known and respected. Badalato had worked hard to get her. He knew Rake wanted her but he was also motivated by the calendar. Time was passing and they needed the person to start soon. Badalato followed up with her on the phone several times, each time more of the salesman, coaxing and cajoling her to take the assignment. In the end she declined, saying something else had come up.

To an outsider, *Last Vegas* might look like a great job for an AD. But not everybody was bowled away by the opportunity. Movie stars are a normal part of the equation, but the issue for *Last Vegas* was that it paid scale. An ancillary issue for experienced crew was that pay could establish their rates going forward. When they came to negotiate the next project, they'd be asked what they were paid for their last show. The search for a 2nd AD would continue.

It wasn't unusual to hear veteran crew joke that they got paid their rate whether a movie made money or not. But they all wanted to be on a good movie. High-profile actors help increase the chances of a success, which meant more people willing to work for scale. At the same time, Badalato and Samuels could improve the individual packages of crew in other ways, through kit rentals, duration of the work contract, or improved travel perks.

There were other side benefits to being on *Last Vegas* with its name cast. Actors of their stature had deals that limited their workdays to 12 hours. Crew hours would be much longer than the actors, but the 12-hour perimeter still limited the overall hours per day during principal photography and made for an easier show.

The hours weren't that long in prep, certainly not like some shows. But they weren't short either. The bullpen was a steady stream of assignments:

Find reinforced paper for De Niro's scripts; get movie posters on this list for the hallway art; create a dozen oversized laminated production calendars that synchronized work dates for each department; find 34 good quality lamps at the best price.

They all seemed like straightforward requests but each required a fair amount of effort. Underlying it was constant focus on the budget. From staying with the old fax machine, which by now had befuddled anyone who tried to use it, to finding office supplies, they had internalized Badalato's frugality. More to the point, he and Kamishin were paying attention. Had they shopped whatever it was thoroughly?

The paper De Niro wanted -- strengthened on the hole-punch side -- wasn't readily available. They easily found vendors who carried white paper reinforced for use in binders but the crew needed differently colored paper as well, since scripts will go through changes identified by color as they are updated.

The movie posters on the list were specific, some of them older, and not easy to find. Each one was a project someone involved in *Last Vegas* had worked on, generally someone above the line, but not all.

The calendars had to be professional grade. They would be adorned with sticky notes that distinguished the production periods -- prep, principal photography and wrap -- as well as locations, scout dates, travel dates and holidays, with plenty of room for departments to write in specifics to them. It was an organizational tool used at movie and television productions all over.

All of this needed to be finished by Friday.

The lamps should have been easy to find, but were proving a conundrum. They didn't come in bulk as a rule and when they did, they were pricier. The young man shopped online and went out to local retailers. He looked at breaking up the order with different kinds of lamps. The costs seemed too high for what he was getting, so he kept searching.

The Art department felt like it had been feng shuied, given the sense of flow that came with the finished renovations. The elimination of walls and addition of four windows between the offices in the U-shaped department, done in the name of improving communication, gave it an open feel. But that wasn't what brought it to life. That credit belonged to Chloe Lipp, the art department coordinator.

By the end of her first day in the office the place looked like she had been there for months. Bookshelves were full. Fiberboard walls were pinned with samples. Office supplies were organized. A giant color-copier churned in the corner. Only the vague smell of the machine and new paint gave it away. It was a stunning transformation given that a week earlier the offices had been lined with rubble.

Lipp's desk, which anchored the room that would serve as art department bullpen, faced the hallway entrance. There was a full work-station on the other end of the space, and a table under the window. The door led to the first of the warehouses, this one considered flex space, and an exterior exit to the parking lot. While that area was dark and empty, with time it would serve as the space for catering to feed crew, contain cages for the Costume department, serve as a holding area for extras, and operate as overflow space for the Art Department.

It was Lipp's kit that had provided much of the décor. The bookcase shelves included a hundred different catalogues: signage companies, plastics materials, ironworks and stock photos. It was both mainstream and specialty retailers like Restoration Hardware. It held wrap books from other productions, which were full of information about vendors and set decorations used in the past. "It's a wrap" is a familiar movie set term that comes with the last shot on the last day of principal photography, but wrap was its own process. It referred to the period of time when a production shut down, when they dismantled everything they had spent months putting together. Wrap books documented everything from vendors to where furnishings from the show were stored, handy for reshoots or the next show.

It was a staggering transformation for a single day.

"Oh, this is normal," explained Lipp, who shared a rolling chair with her 32-pound French bulldog, Rocko. "There isn't time for me to go to the office supply store when a show starts. I have to be up and running right away."

Badalato had ordained that *Last Vegas* would be a dog show, where people could bring well-behaved pets to work. Lipp was pleased. A thick, white-bodied guy with the face of a Boston terrier, he took up the bigger share of the chair. She and Rocko looked comfortable despite the space on the chair, and after a time he jumped to the floor. Rocko had been in her life for two years, she said, the last of his litter. She said he had a medical condition where his testicles wouldn't drop but he seemed fine now.

In her mid-20s, Lipp had long blond-highlighted hair and was dressed like an artist, cottony light clothes and handmade jewelry. Her educational path had begun at a "name" college but she got the creative bug and transferred to SCAD, the Savannah College of Art and Design. Her first job on a big movie was as an accounting assistant on *The Conspirator*. It was there that she met Badalato and Samuels, ultimately landing another accounting assistant role on *Big Momma's House*. From there she moved to art departments and a couple of smaller jobs.

Her most recent movie, and the first one where she worked as art department coordinator, was *Parental Guidance*. It was shot in Georgia and starred Billy Crystal and Bette Midler. David Bomba had been the production designer. Lipp knew Mark Garner, the art director for *Last Vegas*, from *Big Momma's House*, although not as well as she knew Bomba, since they had been in different departments. Garner's office would be next to hers and Bomba's, the nicest, next to his.

Bomba arrived from his horse farm in Mississippi. He looked like a contemporary cowboy, ball cap on his head and visible stubble. Somewhere near 6'2," he wore jeans, boots and a pinstriped, short-sleeve shirt fit snugly about the gut. He checked out the furnished offices, happy with what he saw. Among other things, his office had a couch, which would be useful for meetings.

Bomba's office wasn't yet as finished as Lipp's, since he was out of the office a lot. The scouts, where they looked at various spaces to shoot scenes, would be ongoing until locations were locked. It wasn't just about helping the director decide where to shoot scenes. For Bomba it was also about understanding the director's vision for the movie. At this junction it was coming up with options.

What did it mean to say the production designer created "the look" of the movie? The best answer stems from the origin of the job, which happened during the making of *Gone With the Wind*. Famed producer David O. Selznick took note of the extensive contribution of the person responsible for art direction. "I would probably give him some such credit as 'Production Designed by William Cameron Menzies...'" Selznick wrote in a memo. Menzies is considered the first production designer. The production designer credit took hold very slowly from there. By the 1960s it was still a rare designation. For most movies, an art director was enough. With something like *My Fair Lady* (1964), where a "visual style" was created, the credit was given. Gradually, it became beneficial for most major movie productions to have someone in that role.

Garner's office had come to life as Lipp's had. As art director, he was responsible for implementing Bomba's plans, ensuring every detail was included, but there was a bigger picture, too. He would shepherd personnel, interact with management day-to-day, oversee the department's budget and paperwork. The Set Decorating was independent but still part of the Art department. The Props department, while in separate offices down the hall, also fit under the department umbrella. Then there was the construction department, which would build it all. There were literally thousands of details, from big-ticket things like the "backing" -- the photo backdrop of the Las Vegas skyline behind the penthouse set -- to the small sparkles that would dangle in long strings in front to create the twinkling appearance of a lighted city.

In most industries it's normal to start a permanent new job with people you don't know. There's time to get to know them. With a movie production time is at a premium, particularly on projects with tight budgets. There was tension in the air because Garner and Bomba had never worked together before.

It was that much harder on Bomba, who'd had the same art director for nearly two decades. Never mind shorthand, they had their own language. The duo had won awards, including for *Walk the Line*, the highly acclaimed Johnny Cash biopic. With *Last Vegas*, Bomba wasn't consulted about Garner's hire. Bomba himself had come on board after an interview with Larry Mark and Turteltaub in Los Angeles, the first creative hire of the movie. His deal, worked out later, didn't specify choices in hires. Here he would work with Garner, someone Badalato and Samuels had hired on both of the Georgia movies, as well as *Dear John*. Bomba's unhappiness about it had nothing to do with Garner's skill.

Garner had 30 years of experience in the industry and his own impressive resume. He'd got into the business as a fluke after studying to be a landscape architect at the University of Florida. He worked as a set designer for more than a decade before taking the role of art director and over the years had done nearly every job in the Art department. That included working as production designer on a number of movies, so he understood Bomba's job.

Samuels and Badalato had wanted to hire locally for several reasons. It was part of the production's agreement with the state regarding tax credits and other mandates but it also was a lot cheaper. L.A. crew was expensive plus they were outside hires, which meant they were paid per diem at the highest rates. The details were determined by various unions' requirements that *Last Vegas* had agreed to as a signatory in exchange for using the labor pools. Garner was based in Florida, so a relatively close hire, where Bomba's guy would have been an LA. hire.

There was another factor at hand that Badalato readily admitted. He wanted to know what was happening in the Art department and he liked having a known quantity inside. The Art department had a large budget and having his own man made him feel more comfortable. It also put Garner at a bit of disadvantage with Bomba, which he understood. "A production designer will bring his own art director or interview someone he knows," Garner said. "On this one, I was forced, in a nice way, upon him." He resolved to talk to Bomba about it later.

The PA was pleased. He'd found a good price on 34 tall two-headed floor lamps and for a time the bullpen turned into a lighting forest. There was a minor issue in that the different lamp heads required different size bulbs, one a standard issue and the other smaller size. He'd opted not to buy the bulbs at the store where he got the lamps because the price was too high and would cut into the savings, and vowed to find them elsewhere.

By now Badalato was completely moved in, occupying the first two-thirds of the corner office. Two clocks were affixed to the wall, one for Atlanta the other for L.A. There were some decorations, such as a lightweight cane prop used in a movie, a stuffed animal slingshot toy, and a monkey that could be sent screeching and flying across the room. He'd also hung a cross behind his desk reflecting his identity as a born-again Christian.

A list of his favorite sayings and expectations was displayed, "Excellence is non-negotiable." "Speak truth to power." "Always go to the king, not the warrior."

A white board hung on the far wall, a to-do list on it and some drawings. One was of a bus. Underneath its wheels was a stick figure and the words, "This is You." It had appeared after a conversation with a studio executive. She'd told him that if something happened, she wasn't going to cover for him.

It wasn't clear what had been said, but Badalato liked her for it. She was a straight shooter and he appreciated that.

It was the back third of his office that stood out. Badalato had cordoned it off for Buddy, his Golden retriever. It was prime square footage, glass windows on two sides, a big tree just outside as a backdrop. A pet fence blocked it off and a thick pad protected the carpeted floor while being soft on the paws. It was all about comfort, with a big new dog bed, a couple of bones, several balls and a giant stainless steel water bowl. Buddy had gone through some expensive training, and Badalato was a diligent parent. That meant Buddy was able to overcome his nature much of the time. But not always.

Buddy's main corrupting force was Rocko. The bowlegged canine who lived in the Art department had taken an interest in his counterpart in the production department. Rocko was an able escape artist. He would wait by the door of the art wing for someone out of the loop to open the door and then bolt out. The thick, white Frenchie had surprising speed for his stout legs and would barrel down the hall, through the bullpen and across the short hall to Badalato's office. Buddy barked in delight and the two enjoyed the 30 seconds before Lipp, in close pursuit, was there to retrieve him. Soon an oversized picture of Rocko was posted on the door of the Art department warning visitors not to let him out. It helped a little.

Badalato also had taken over an oversized deck off an exit door down the hall on the rear side of the property. He and Kamishin began a regular back and forth down the hallway from their offices to the various activities, past the bullpen entrances and the other offices and through the door on the far side of the costume department. That hallway door included an exterior exit.

That side of the Mailing Avenue facility faced the Beltline and an as-yet undeveloped portion of the 22-mile former railroad corridor that circled Atlanta. It was already up and running as a network of parks, trails and transit lines in other parts of the city. This portion was still remarkably quiet and private, the non-working railroad tracks down a hill outside the fence. Even in summer-hot Georgia it was lovely, at least for a while. The canines went crazy over it, particularly Buddy. A perpendicular segment of fence had been added from the building wall to the existing fence, creating a big dog run. Badalato had a stick that easily tossed a ball to the end of it, so Buddy got his share of exercise. It wasn't just a hangout spot. Badalato took his laptop out there and worked, did phone interviews and held meetings, depending on the heat. Bullpen crew knew to come get them immediately if a call to the landline warranted it.

Badalato and Kamishin were never far, whether inside or out. They popped in with news or to change priorities and announce meetings. There were dozens of happenings, big and small. Plans were under way for the offices in Vegas, which would open in a couple of weeks. They continuously worked on crew deals and the more people hired, the more there was to do. The production department was nearly crewed up. A new production PA was starting Monday. She would fill in as Samuels' assistant but just until the person hired for the job arrived. The studio had recommended someone and he was coming in from out of town.

There was still work being done just to ready the Mailing Avenue offices. This week the focus had been on finalizing the executive suites. The director and executive producer had been steadily working whether from the scout van, the Ritz-Carlton, Buckhead, a tony part of Atlanta, or Los Angeles. Starting the new week they would be based on Mailing Avenue. Each suite now featured an assistant's office in front and the exec's office in back, except for Turteltaub's, which had a third room.

The only things missing were the posters. What seemed like a simple project took surprising effort, given they had to be specific. Some of them were obscure. This time Stephens took no heat. She found them by the deadline -- nothing would have stopped her -- but it would come with a premium. It was Badalato who balked at the price. The beauty of movie posters wasn't just the personal connections but that they were a relatively inexpensive way to decorate the office. The place needed to look professional, given the people who would come and go. But he wasn't going to pay too much for "art" either. He had her pare back the order and eliminated the rush status. They would arrive next week.

Inroads had been made on De Niro's request for special paper but it was also proving more challenging -- and expensive -- than expected. They could find the different colored paper, but finding it with reinforced ends was a different story. They considered whether it made sense for a PA to personally add reinforcement to each sheet.

They had purchased almost nothing lightly, even when pressed for time. Every item of any size or volume had been researched to assure the best price. Whether it was paper in bulk or in a ream, office supplies in general, trash pickup, or furniture, they consistently had reviewed options.

The focus on the bottom line could backfire. The two-headed lamps now in place around the building had only one light bulb in them. It turned out that the second bulb was exceedingly rare. The retailer who'd sold the lamps made up the difference in the cut-rate price with the high-end bulb. The PA assumed he'd pick them up elsewhere at a better price but so far, despite significant effort, he had come up short. The young man was frustrated and vowed to continue the search in the new week.

CHAPTER THREE
8 Weeks Out
Aug. 27-31

O N MONDAY MORNING, Jeremiah Samuels made his way through the halls that squared off the production bullpen in search of Badalato. The chatter of the crew inside subsided a little more each time he passed one of the entrances and was seen by the occupants from a different angle. The big boss to everyone there, he had stayed in L.A. the previous week. While on the phone constantly it was his first time in person at the fully operational Mailing Avenue and a lot of new people had been hired.

He found Badalato coming out of the accountant's offices.

"And so it begins!" exclaimed Samuels, as they man-hugged in sight of bullpen crew. "And so it does," agreed Badalato. They dipped back into the accountant's office.

A youthful mid-50s, Samuels was tan with gray-white hair, black T-shirt, jeans and black Nikes. His title was executive producer, but to people in the industry "line producer" was the more telling job description. He'd been the first movie marine to parachute in, to snare Badalato's description, and also the general planning the assault.

The men returned to the bullpen. "I think most of you know Jeremiah?" Badalato leaned against the bullpen doorway wall as a grinning Samuels made the rounds. He soon connected names given to him on the phone with their faces.

Badalato and Samuels eventually moved to the hallway outside two offices. Samuels liked his office in the executive suites, and would keep it, but at the same time, he wanted to be closer to production. They talked about the details as Bomba entered the bullpen. The production designer was headed toward the fax machine with paperwork in his hand but changed directions to greet them. Bomba dragged a smile across his face as Samuels initiated a backslap. There was still tension between them over hires but it would not get in the way of work. After some chitchat Samuels and Badalato disappeared down the hall to the executive offices.

Bomba went over to the fax. He was already known to the bullpen crew. He was consistently polite and soft spoken, even overly so. It seemed incongruous on a man that tall with those boots, never mind that he was the production designer. They liked him for it. He took his turn at the quirky, older model machine. A list of steps next to a diagram and the instructions were taped to the table next to it, courtesy of Stephens, who worked quietly at her desk but was taking it all in.

He stood there and read the instructions, then looked at the paper in his hand and the fax machine. Within minutes Badalato and Samuels returned to Bomba's side. After some brief chitchat, Samuels got to the point. "How's it going with Turteltaub?"

Bomba became animated, any sign of discomfort vanished. This was a subject he liked. "I'm really excited about how he approaches things," he answered. "When he goes into a place he starts blocking, looking from one direction and then another. His mind is really in it."

Blocking was a way of determining where the actors would be on set. It may seem reminiscent of Fellini, a director holding two thumbs perpendicular with index fingers skyward to imitate a screen shot, but that was the process at play.

Bomba told a story about scouting locations for the home of Morgan Freeman's character, Archie Clayton. They had looked at five places before Turteltaub gravitated toward one. He had stood quietly in the house for several minutes, turning occasionally. The scene called for Clayton to hold his grandbaby, which his son takes from his arms. Where would Freeman stand with the baby? What direction would the son come from?

"He likes to wait to pull the trigger, and I'm like that," said Bomba.

"Good, good," said Samuels, noting that the downside to working from L.A. was missing the scouting trips.

"I have a lot of information about what he wants already," Bomba continued. "We're going to go through the script. He's going to give me notes and be more specific." Turteltaub was working from L.A. so they would talk on the phone.

As the men walked across the bullpen toward the exit, Samuels asked about a new scene Turteltaub wanted to add. The snippets of conversation were vague: what it would take to make it happen, how big a change was it from the current script, the bottom line.

"Would it average between five and six seconds?"

"Would it mean a new set?"

"How elaborate…"

"Depending on the footprint…"

They came to a stop where Bomba's path would diverge.

"That's what I hope to glean from the meeting," Bomba concluded.

"It's a lot for five seconds," Samuels said. Bomba agreed. "We'd need cars and clothes and…"

"No," said Badalato.

Badalato had been silent to that point and everyone laughed. His tone made it clear it was a joke. The script wasn't locked yet. Of course there would be changes, scenes added, and others cut. At the same time, he was making a point. It's about the money. Even accidental, it was also a fine display of good-cop, bad-cop. That was the end of the conversation. Bomba, looking relieved, headed briskly toward the safety of the Art department.

The EP headed to his office in the executive suite while Badalato went to his to call the building owners about the changes for Samuels' space closer to the bullpen. He would keep the executive office space while having a presence close to the center of action. Within hours workers were back cutting a door in the wall between two unoccupied offices off the bullpen. The phone man returned to add a line. By the next day, the casual new two-room office was delivered complete, debris gone, paint touched up and a steady dial tone on the landline. One side had a couch and the other a circular table for meetings. A new sign was posted outside that read "Jer's Lair."

Garner was on the phone in his organized office, neatly labeled binders on the bookcase next to his desk, folders aligned in racks. The conversation had to do with the backing for the penthouse set. They needed two versions of the photo backdrop of the Las Vegas skyline, day and night. It was the actual view from Aria they were recreating. The two images would hang side by side like two curtains with the time of day needed visible. Given the cost, which seemed in the neighborhood of $60,000, he was checking in.

Garner had the physical appearance of an organized man, clean shaven with clear skin. Meticulously groomed, dressed in khakis and a button-down striped shirt, he moved back and forth between the Art department and the production office getting things done. Always upbeat, he frequently had a quip or would share a smart-aleck thought. It was he who had secured the office space conference room for the Art department. He also named it the "Boom Boom Room," after a similar space on his last show. The name stuck just as fast.

With Garner in place, the art wing had quickly pulled together. A set decorator was coming in later in the week to meet with Badalato and Samuels. An interview with the likely prop master, whose job it was to gather and manage all props used in the movie, was also on the schedule. Independent departments, set decoration and props, would fall under Bomba's purview. Assuming they made it past Badalato and Samuels.

There was still some tension in the Art department. Part of it was that Bomba and Garner hadn't yet spent much time together. Given the distance was likely to continue with the prep process, Garner decided to broach the subject. Departments are extremely loyal, in general, in movies. The pressure each department faces grows every week and they learn to rely on each other, particularly if an issue arises with another department. Bomba was especially well-liked by people who worked for him. Most of them had worked with him before and enjoyed it. It was about trust. Garner waited for the right moment at the end of a meeting with Bomba to broach the subject.

Garner said he knew he wasn't Bomba's choice but that of the UPM and executive producer, but it didn't change the fact that he was loyal to the Art department and to Bomba. The production designer smiled and nodded politely and told him there wasn't a problem. Then he got up to leave but Garner continued. "I'm not their boy," he said, "not a mole."

Bomba stood there looking at him.

Garner said it wasn't a bad thing for the Art department that he knew them, either. It gave him the basis to make whatever case needed making, whether an additional hire or more money for set decorating, whatever it might be. Bomba nodded and left. Garner saw it as a positive and hoped for the best.

Several interviews were scheduled for new art department crew. Sean Ryan Jennings, who would serve as assistant art director, was the most recent official hire. At 26, he was a bit of a wunderkind with an impressive list of credits. He had impressed Bomba, who had worked with him before and sought him out. Jennings would start work next week and immediately leave for Las Vegas with Garner. Garner, who didn't know him, looked forward to the time to bond. An intense work cycle lay ahead and he wanted to get started.

The Aria Resort and Casino was integral to the movie and came with contractual requirements that it be depicted accurately. The men would be getting measurements and a lot of photographs, among other things, during their visit. Jennings' various skills included proficiency in computer-assisted design. The detail info they got at the Aria would enable him to create architectural blueprints for the sets they would build.

Crewing up other departments was becoming the big focus on the production side of the building. There were dozens of hires in process, candidates still being sought, interviews scheduled, snippets of conversations around the building or on speakerphones.

"I've always been insulted by the idea that people think they don't even have to read the script to get the job."

"You should see the agent who made the deal."

"How many days have we been talking about this contract? I'm starting to worry about the legal bills, having them on it every day."

"He's fast and he's funny. My only disclaimer is that he's a real right-wing chomper and he won't shut the fuck up." This comment met with raucous laughter.

Kamishin and Badalato remained focused on hiring. They divided work on deal memos, him handling upper echelon. While *Last Vegas* still needed a cinematographer, it was the costume department that was becoming a priority. That department needed a lot of prep time, while the Camera department came on later in the process. They had a costume designer but something was holding it up.

Word around the bullpen was that it was the same issue that stumped Bomba: She wanted to hire her own people from Los Angeles, including an assistant costume designer. An assistant designer did everything from research to collaborating on creative decisions and working directly with the actors. Not all movie productions have an assistant costume designer. This one, with the number of high caliber actors and otherwise large cast, seemed to call for it.

It wasn't the same thing as the costumer supervisor, who managed the department, and a mandatory hire. The costume supervisor was the main contact with other departments and had dominion over staff. They supervised the acquisitions of costumes, whether made for the movie or pulled from costume houses as loans. They organized mountains of wardrobe to fill actors "closets" and racks for background actors. In the case of *Last*

Vegas, they also would manage the department budget, which could be a separate position depending on the size of the movie.

Kamishin had a sizeable workload. They had someone in mind for the position of APOC, who would be her second in the department and take some of the pressure off. Also high on the list was a travel coordinator since all requests came to the bullpen. *Last Vegas*, being shot in Atlanta and Las Vegas, and having crew and executives coming from Los Angeles would require a lot of travel.

Kamishin was frequently in the bullpen with a new assignment to hand out. Generally businesslike but easygoing, she could also get tough fast. Midweek she came into the bullpen to see who was available to rustle up resumes. They wanted a fresh stack of qualified cinematographers and costume supervisors who were local or at least in the region. The task involved calling the unions and various agents.

After a few minutes Kamishin overheard a PA calling an agent to ask for CVs. In the course of the conversation the PA described *Last Vegas* as a "big movie." She was desk-side within seconds of the PA hanging up the call. "Do not tell them it's a big movie -- it isn't." she admonished. "That's going to make them think we have a big budget for this project. And we don't." With that she strode out of the bullpen as the stricken worker looked after her.

But by the end of the day they had made a good start on collecting resumes for costume supervisors and cinematographers. Relatively few were in the Atlanta market although there were a number in the region. It turned out there was a side goal of collecting resumes of costume supervisors to show talent could be found outside of Los Angeles. The idea that Atlanta's talent wasn't as good as L.A.'s was enough to ruffle any feather boa in town but it had to do with numbers. Georgia was a new production center. That was changing, quickly, as Georgia grew into its own but it didn't have the same base and resources of an L.A. or New York, which had been operating for decades.

Badalato said the pool of experienced talent in the Georgia was much wider than three years earlier when he last worked there. Many new people had been trained and the phenomenon of "migrant film workers," where people relocated to Atlanta for work, was real. By his count, Georgia's talent base could accommodate four major productions before it was tapped out.

There were at least that many movies in process in the area. Big movies. The biggest one by budget was *The Hunger Games: Catching Fire*. It had an estimated $100 million budget, three times that of *Last Vegas*, which meant it would get top-tier crew. Then there was *The Internship*, a comedy starring Vince Vaughn and Owen Wilson, which was in the midst of principal photography. Two other large movies were in prep and about to start shooting, both with bigger budgets than *Last Vegas*. One was *Scary Movie 5*, with its biggest cast yet. The other was *Motor City*, a revenge movie starring Gerard Butler. Then there were television shows in production, including the wildly successful "Walking Dead," with its elaborate sets and long production schedule.

Over two days, dozens of qualifying resumes for costume supervisors came in. They found few in Georgia. The bulk were regional, including Florida, Illinois and North Carolina.

First assistant director Gary Rake's arrival, one day ahead of Turteltaub's, brought a different kind of momentum. He signaled the right side of the movie brain, the creative side, coming to life. It all felt electric, more people milling around, multiple phones ringing, a well-stocked craft services in place.

Rake was about to turn 40, a detail provided to the production office by his wife. There had already been another crew birthday celebrated and a going-away party was planned for later in the week. Celebrations were another thing shepherded by Stephens, who added a surprise birthday party to the plan for Rake next week.

Rake could have been closer to 30 with his boyish good looks and a choice in clothes that conveyed youthfulness. He dressed with a flair for hip hop, long shorts and good sneakers. His thick brown hair was cut in a popular shorter style, turned up just slightly at the front. It was a package conveying a sense he would fit in comfortably at any country club. The 1st AD met everyone quickly and settled down in his office on the far side of the bullpen, the schedule open on his laptop.

Scheduling the movie was like putting together a multi-dimensional puzzle with pieces that changed. Principal photography contained 38 shooting days, the first 11 in Las Vegas. The breakdown at this point showed 117 scenes that happened in 45 different places that would become sets. Would they shoot scenes on location or on soundstages? What scenes involved what actors? What actors had what blackout dates? This movie was challenging in the sheer number of actors' schedules to be considered.

Rake couldn't imagine how ADs had done it in the days before computer software helped manage it. There was so much to it! Just one challenge, albeit a big one, was De Niro, who had the largest number of dates when he couldn't work. A newly added feature to the software made it possible for him to input blackout dates. Scheduling an actor by accident was the kind of hair-tearing mistake that had been too easy to make before. Imagine planning a whole day of shooting around an actor who wasn't available to work and then having to re-do it. Given the kinds of actors he was scheduling, the improvement came at no better time.

His job involved a lot more than just scheduling the movie. Anything Rake knew Turteltaub was thinking about, he was thinking about. His goal was to solve problems and keep as much off Turteltaub's plate as possible, so the director could focus on the creative.

The script for *Last Vegas* circulated to everyone working on the movie, remained in draft form. The underlying story was set but there still would be changes. Not everything Dan Fogelman had envisioned would translate to the screen, and the script was in the hands of two additional writers, Kyle Pennekamp and Scott Turpel.

There was some question about how to open the movie. Fogelman's version relied on historic photos to show the main characters' friendship over the decades preceding the jaunt to Las Vegas. That could be tricky to pull together. It was doable but Turteltaub had another idea. It involved a new scene entirely.

Another scene on a back burner was a three-way conversation in which the characters played by Douglas, Freeman and Kline would speak. Those scenes would be shot in a particular way, all of them separate, but Turteltaub was considering shooting it at once. That would impact how they were scheduled.

Rake had the El Cortez Hotel & Casino in old Las Vegas to consider. The famous hotel, opened in 1941, had marketed itself over the years as the place "where locals come to play." It had a colorful history, particularly around its ownership by gangsters Bugsy Siegel and Meyer Lansky. Fogelman had written it as the place where the main characters first land in Sin City and it appeared on page nine of the script. It was where they would meet Diana (Mary Steenburgen), the female catalyst for the plot, and be home to several lounge scenes.

Most important for Rake, Turteltaub loved the El Cortez for the scenes. It had the right look, with piano, red velvet curtain backdrop and dark, smoky atmosphere. The director could see Diana there. The character was a class act, retired from a professional job in another city, a newcomer to Vegas pursuing a lifelong dream of being a singer. It would be great contrast to have her singing there, standing out in the smoky environment.

But the current owners of the facility weren't so sure. One look at how the script depicted their place provided some insight: "Imagine the most decrepit Vegas hotel of all time. There's something about seeing it during the day that makes it extra depressing. The simple sign out front read, literally: GAMBLING – El CORTEZ – FLOOR SHOWS."

"They might be a bit put off by the script," was how Eddie Fickett put it. The Vegas-based location and production manager had met with executives at the El Cortez. They'd talked money and gone over some logistics like where the base camp and extras holding would be set up, as well as security issues and the use of casino staff. But then there had been a pause. And a pause is never good.

Samuels and Badalato were apprised of the situation. Samuels, who also knew Turteltaub wanted the location, was working above the line to see if they could "soften" the script to make it more palatable to the El Cortez. Fickett set up a conversation with the key decision maker and Samuels. Meanwhile, Fickett started to look for backup hotels.

Vegas wasn't like Atlanta, which was still immersed in the novelty of the movie business. The southern city was happy to cater to it. Vegas had a booming business and it wasn't movies. Movies came to shoot in the gambling mecca because plot lines demanded it. It was like that with Washington, D.C., as well.

Samuels came into Rake's office to talk about scheduling. They needed establishing shots of Sin City and were negotiating helicopter rates for a weekend. That made sense to Rake, who had a different scheduling issue. Something had come up with the date they talked about for shooting the airport scenes. The main characters arrive and depart from McCarran International Airport. The date of Oct. 24 had been bandied about. But the airport executive handling it said she had a mandatory federal disaster exercise scheduled that day so he needed to adjust the schedule.

There were hundreds of reasons why things couldn't happen on one day or another. Good reasons, too, actors' schedules and weather concerns and previous location commitments. It was the sheer number of things, greatly enhanced with the large cast, which made it hard to fit all the puzzle pieces into the same puzzle.

Gary Rake had moved up the AD ladder quickly given he didn't start in the industry until his late 20s. His early path had been learning about the financial world. After he earned a BA in economics from the University of Arizona and moved to New York for a career on Wall Street, he worked diligently to become a stockbroker, hunkering down through the lengthy hazing process. But once he had his paper, he realized it wasn't for him. His true calling, he'd discovered by then, was the movie business. To do it, he had to start over -- at the bottom.

Rake moved to L.A. to pursue the goal of being an assistant director just as methodically as he had being a stockbroker. They don't make it easy to join the Directors Guild of America. To earn a 2nd AD credential requires 400 days of work as a second AD or better on signatory projects. At least three-quarters of those have to be with an actual shooting company. No more than a quarter could be in prep or office work.

Any application to the DGA is carefully reviewed. It isn't unusual to have days disqualified or to have the mix not match up. The result is that it could take many years to accumulate the days needed to become a second AD. It was a tough enough process that it limited the makeup of the union, prompting the creation of a fast track program aimed at improving diversity.

Rake did it the old-fashioned way. He deduced that the best way for him to fast track an AD role was to focus on television jobs. He could accumulate more days more quickly that way. "It's easier to get on for 150 days with one job than piece together a bunch of commercial stuff and 40 days here, 50 days there with features. For me, that made a lot of sense." It also set him apart from a lot of people, who held out for work on movies.

It wasn't just landing a PA job -- it was to get called back. Rake worked hard to become regular crew. It paid off. He worked on 26 episodes of "Sex and the City" between 2002 and 2004 as either a production assistant or production staff, gaining experience and collecting days. His bulk credits -- where he worked at least one season -- read like flipping network channels: "Law and Order," "Fringe," "Ugly Betty," "Criminal Minds: Suspect Behavior." It was on "Common Law" that he met Turteltaub, a producer on the show for a time.

"I made a lot of contacts," Rake recalled. "When I became an AD those are the people who hired me." He worked as a 1st AD in television for four years and had worked on two movies before *Last Vegas* brought him to Atlanta. He loved his job but he noticed one thing had shifted. When he made the decision to work in the movie industry, the idea of traveling and long hours were welcome. Now that he was married with two kids he liked that part less.

The next good news: The search for a 2nd AD for the movie was over.

The third candidate was the charm. She had worked in LA. and had plenty of experience but was now based in Atlanta, which Badalato loved. She came in for an interview the same day they called and her deal was easily negotiated. She would start next week.

Jon Turteltaub arrived in Atlanta midweek with a fresh haircut. He looked serious but he was naturally funny, and he cussed a lot, which endeared him to the crew right away. Word about the first-week impression he had left on crew had been thoroughly circulated. Crew talked among themselves, not just on the show, with friends on other shows. They looked up his movies and scanned the crew lists to find out more about him, and details were fed back. Turteltaub was a good director, smart and at times entertaining, but he didn't suffer fools gladly. He had a biting wit that could take anyone down a peg so best not to get in his way. On the positive side, he wasn't a yeller.

Compared with some directors, he sounded like a dream but there was a natural apprehension. Any director has a lot of power, perhaps more than the CEO at a big company. A company executive has a longer lifespan and a lot of people watching him or her, including a board of directors. When a movie director is hired, he is handed the reins of the movie. The fact the studios or whoever had financed it have entrusted that person carries a lot of weight.

It was a lot of pressure for anyone. It came with a lot of responsibility and it wasn't just about making a good movie. Those days were long gone. This was about a return on the investment. If the movie failed for whatever reason it was on the director. But the director also had carte blanche, even if it came with budget strings, to run whatever kind of movie he saw fit. He could be a card-carrying personality disorder -- tabloids were full of crazy directors -- and the studios wouldn't make a change except in extremely rare circumstances.

Turteltaub won the crew over quickly. His first visit to the bullpen involved a search for craft service. That term, used generically, meant kitchen.

He wanted a snack of some sort and there were plenty there, everything from cereal and bagels with various spreads and frozen breakfast burritos, fixings for sandwiches, chips and nuts, fresh and dried fruit and yogurt, and plenty of different kinds of non-alcoholic drinks.

His request for directions might have been answered with a nod toward the hallway with the kitchen except he was the director. The PA, the young man who had been there from the start, happened to have a shopping list in front of him. It included a craft service run. What could he get him? Turteltaub said he didn't need anything but the PA pressed on. Was he sure? What about this or that? He was going to be out anyway.

"What kind of ice cream do we have?" Turteltaub asked. He said it in an expansive way, since the room was already following the discussion. He might have been an actor, the way he centered the room, comfortable in front of an audience and almost inviting a conversation. Badalato and Kamishin were nearby. Hearing a commotion that involved the director, they joined the room.

"I had some ice cream recently that was unreal it was so good, but I don't know what it was," said Turteltaub. It was a natural lead in that prompted a host of suggestions from the observers.

"Ben & Jerry's?"

"Breyers?"

"No, no," he said. Turteltaub held his hands like he had a snow globe in them. "It was a cone -- with cookies in it!" By now everyone was pulled in. It would be good to be the person with the right answer.

"Good Humor?"

"I don't know what it was," he said. "But it was so good I had to ask how much it cost!"

The crew watched him.

"They told me it was like, a dollar, and I said, 'No way!'" Turteltaub continued. "One dollar? That's crazy. This thing should have cost eighty bucks!"

He seemed so serious everyone laughed.

"I mean it! That's how good it was."

The conversation widened to other kinds of ice cream sold in individual servings and then general snacks. Turteltaub was winding down with the fun and insisted he was fine. Now that he knew where the kitchen was he could help himself. The excitement subsided when he left the bullpen, but not the discussion.

The PA had been taking notes the whole time, gleaning what kinds of things the director liked. He told Kamishin he was going to go on the craft service run now, rather than wait, and would make a special effort to find ice cream for Turteltaub. She nodded emphatically in support.

The job description of anyone working as a production assistant might include aptitude in the art of ass kissing, the institutionalized version of sucking up to people in power. It was part of the culture. Even the next person up on the ladder rung could be due a smooch. There was some justification for it at Turteltaub's level. Nobody wanted the director to go for ice cream. They wanted him to be thinking about the movie, all the time. It was the reason for assistants.

When the PA returned from the run, he had one box of ice cream cones with pieces of Oreo-style cookie, which seemed closest to what Turteltaub had described, along with two other brands. Kamishin gave the go-ahead to deliver it to Turteltaub. The young man first opened up the box of cones, so he had one exposed, and then was off for the executive suites.

He was back two minutes later. This time he went right to Stephens' desk and whispered in her ear. She burst out laughing. They were laughing, sharing the private joke as he took his seat at the table.

"Oh, no. You have to tell us what happened," said Jordan Anderson, the newest production assistant to be hired. She had arrived in a car with Arkansas plates but seemed to know a lot of people.

The others chimed in, including Kamishin, who had stayed in the room while he was gone. He was not going to get out of it without telling everyone.

"His door was open but I didn't want to bother him, so I stopped at the entrance and he waved me in."

"Got that part. What did he say?"

The young man started laughing again. "He took the cone and looked at it. Then he looked at me and said, 'Oh, you are one bad-ass muthafucker!'"

The room busted out. This was a director who could talk to the little people.

Kamishin took the remaining box of ice cream cones for safekeeping. There was a private fridge in her office that she and Badalato shared. Food might get pilfered from the main kitchen but few people would have the guts to remove anything from her office. The director's stash would be kept in the freezer.

Later in the day, Turteltaub came into the bullpen again, this time looking for a ride. Rake was off somewhere or he wouldn't have needed one. His assistant was not on the payroll yet. Maybe one of the PAs could drive him?

Kamishin and Badalato, who were at Stephens' desk when he came in, looked at each other and then back at the director. They were thinking the same thing. Not every PA drives a decent car. They didn't want to put the director in a dented car without air conditioning. Turteltaub picked up on it just as fast.

"I'd like to ride in an older vehicle," he said. "I would enjoy that." He had his ride in no time, although it wasn't an old vehicle.

Turteltaub seemed approachable, like a regular guy. Most directors of his caliber don't give off that vibe. They deal with department heads while the 1st AD manages the larger crew. Turteltaub remembered names but he also seemed to take note of who did what. His memory was remarkable.

"Jon's an experienced director and he's very, very smart," was how Rake summed him up. "Scary smart. He knows everything about everything and anything. It's a little bit to his own detriment, because it can be frustrating." It wasn't clear if Rake was saying it with irony and it didn't sound cynical. It wasn't reverence, either, more matter-of-fact.

He added that Turteltaub always made him think of a scene in "Broadcast News," the 1987 movie, where a boss speaks to the young, all-knowing television producer played by Holly Hunter. "It must be nice to always believe you know better, to always think you're the smartest person in the room?"

"No," she replies. "It's awful."

Badalato and Kamishin fed on spreadsheets. Anything of sizeable expense should be evaluated in that context. The fastest growing spreadsheet involved room nights at the Aria Resort & Casino. They had begun detailing planning for the location work in Las Vegas.

The Aria barter was expected to cover the lion's share of cast and crew location expenses but the spreadsheet set out to prove it. Could production fit the crew and cast into 1,000 room nights? The rooms weren't all created equal. How would they divide it up? What was covered, what wasn't? If they exceeded the maximum, what would the impact be to the budget? And what about food? How would they feed everyone? It was already clear that food in Vegas would be a monster to manage.

There had been numerous scouting trips to Vegas on the creative side and they began planning for the production trip. Where would the production offices be, where would they house the department, where would they park trucks. Where would they store equipment or keep extras -- background actors -- between scenes. Just the pool scenes at Aria had a list of things to be reviewed.

The studio called in the middle of the meeting. What hotel would Mary Steenburgen be staying in when photography began in Atlanta? It was two months away -- after principal photography in Vegas -- but they needed the information now. The actress had officially joined the cast more than a week earlier, with news of it making it to the entertainment news wire. Now the studio was negotiating her perk package and trying to determine actual costs.

In addition to negotiated pay, actors get a "perk package." The two deals are generally negotiated separately. That seems counterintuitive, but few perk packages end up killing deals. Somebody was trying to sort out total costs, including her stay in Atlanta, before they signed off.

The call changed the priorities of the day for Kamishin. It didn't sound hard to book a luxury suite, but this wasn't reserving something for a honeymoon. A larger negotiation was in the works. The hotel didn't necessarily want to commit right away because it was possible it could get full price for it. Minimally someone higher up would have to sign off. It was another spreadsheet entirely.

They were consulting with a local accommodation specialist who regularly worked with the hotels. She'd been helping Badalato since he arrived. Her main focus was on finding crew housing, since it was the immediate need. She and Kamishin had planned hotel site visits but suddenly the priority moved up. Kamishin wanted to see the space.

Before numbers could be firmed up there were other questions on both sides of the equation. Would there be other actors needing other suites? The more rooms booked, the better the deal. They talked to different high-end hotels to get an answer before they landed on the Ritz.

There was one other thing that Kamishin needed to know first. Did the Ritz accept pets? Steenburgen wanted to bring her dog.

Midday Friday, Badalato came into the bullpen to ask for a crew list for *Motor City*. The movie had just been shut down and he wanted it ASAP. This could help bridge the gap with a new supply of local, available crew. Several people had friends on the show and a list was delivered to Kamishin in short order. She would make one of the calls but returned to the bullpen a minute later with four names highlighted. They hoped to interview all of them.

It had been a good week and this made it better. They were sorry the show was shutting down, but it helped address the need to hire skilled crew. It made the mood even lighter for a going-away party for the PA.

He seemed genuinely surprised by the party. He was reluctant to leave the movie, but he also liked the fact that the teaching position he'd just been hired to do would continue after this movie wrapped. That also would give him more time to work on his screenplay. He'd been working on it his first week on the job but admitted he had been too tired after that to continue on it. They teased him some more about the light bulbs, which had since been found.

It felt like an open house with more than 20 people convening in the bullpen for cake and ice cream, the numbers proof the crew had expanded. Turteltaub had a later flight to L.A. and joined the fracas. He had been there a few minutes before there was a break in chatting. A woman sitting on the couch piped up.

"The last time I saw you, you were fourteen." It was the payroll accountant, a stout red-haired woman nearing her golden years. "You look exactly the same."

Given Turteltaub's energy it had a ring of truth. He laughed.

"'What's Happening?'" he asked, referring to the 1976-1979 sitcom that followed three African American teens living in Watts.

"'Carter Country,'" she said, another sitcom from the same time period, this one based on characters who lived in Georgia. Jimmy Carter was president at the time. "Look at us now," said Turteltaub. "So successful we're both in Atlanta." Everyone was paying attention by now.

The director had grown up around television sets. His father, Saul Turteltaub, got his big break after Bud Yorkin and Norman Lear disbanded their partnership. That well-known pairing had brought classics to the small screen like "All in the Family," "Maude," "Good Times" and "Sanford & Son." The senior Turteltaub and Bernie Orenstein, both writers on "Sanford & Son," had teamed with Yorkin in his new company. A year or so later, Turteltaub-Orenstein-Yorkin Productions, also known as Toy Productions, was created. That was the company that produced "What's Happening" and "Carter Country." The conversation lasted until Turteltaub looked at his watch. He had to catch the flight home to LA. and his wife and kids.

49

The party continued from there. Eventually the conversation turned to *Motor City*.

Details were coming in about what had happened to the movie. In the meantime, talk turned to how often movies get shut down, more often than non-industry people realized. The best story was about *Crisis in the Hot Zone*, circa 1994, which was to star Jodie Foster. Its failure was almost folklore in movie business circles. It was in development at the same time as *Outbreak*. Both were dramas about viruses let loose on the world and the two respective studios waged battle. Eventually Foster backed out of *Crisis* citing issues with the script. *Outbreak* went on to do well, netting an estimated $188 million, a reasonable return on the estimated $50 million it took to make it.

Meanwhile, *Crisis* had nearly finished prep with shooting days away when the axe fell, according to the storyteller. They'd hired dozens of crew, built elaborate sets and spent millions of dollars -- $7 million, by this account. Not only were all of those people laid off, they had to restore the space, which involved removing a large amount of cured concrete poured for the main set. This was along with the cost of breaking contracts and leases and assorted legal fees. All of it for a movie that didn't have the lead actress locked in.

Two people vowed to talk to friends on *Motor City* over the weekend to see what had happened.

CHAPTER FOUR
7 Weeks Out
Sept. 4-7

MAILING AVENUE STAGEWORKS could have easily fit into North Hollywood by now. It looked and felt like a movie studio, from the departments coming to life to the sign on the facility – a new business in itself. The coup de grace was the framed posters in the lobby, front halls and executive offices. The 13 movie advertisements were all connected to someone in power behind the scenes of *Last Vegas*.

The first posters in the lobby were for *National Treasure* and *Phenomenon*, a logical nod to Turteltaub, the creative head of *Last Vegas*. In the corner it was *Jerry McGuire* and *Dream Girls*, the handiwork of power producer Larry Mark. A little farther down the hall were *House of Sand and Fog* and *The Conspirator*, both projects of Samuels. *The Conspirator*, filmed in Savannah, had Badalato as unit production manager. Samuels' office had a framed poster of *Dear John*, another movie he and Badalato worked on together.

Badalato's office had *Top Gun*, homage to director Tony Scott, whom he had referenced several times since his death. It hung in the corner of his office, slightly over the trim of the window so it would fit, as he ushered the production staff into his office. A large whiteboard centered the wall, adorned with various notes and drawings. In the center was a drawing of a bus with a stick-figure body under it and two words "bus," and "under," and an arrow pointing to the body. The caption: "Where are you?" It was Badalato's handwriting.

It was the Tuesday after Labor Day but there wasn't an ounce of summer malaise as the Production department funneled into his office for a staff meeting. He was fully entrenched by now. Clipboards hung on the wall with various schedules. His desk had a series of file display-holders, one of which held folders for Construction, SPFX (special effects), Set Dec, Cranes, Grip, Camera Package, Costumes and Logo.

Even in the midst of the vast technological revolution that has enabled the business world to cut down on or even eliminate paper, it still offers the best utility to movie productions. People are on foot a lot so they cannot easily stop to flip through a phone to retrieve a document, much less carry a laptop. This is even more true when shooting, during which the crew uses the closed-loop walkie as the primary mode of communication.

Badalato and Kamishin held regular staff meetings but this was the first one for the "crewed up" Production department, which included four new hires. In the mix were the assistant production coordinator, a production assistant and a staff concierge, who had come in as a PA but had been knighted into the role of concierge for the larger cast. One had been on *Motor City* on Friday when it shut down.

It was a diverse group, half of them African American, one Asian American, three Euro Americans, and one canine. Buddy tried to hold court in the penned-off area that encompassed the back third of Badalato's office. He barked occasionally as the group dragged in chairs. A small canvas couch had been scavenged for him a day earlier. As the group crowded the room he barked more, prompting Badalato to shush him. He offered a single bark in response.

Badalato, one of two men in the group, ignored the laughter and gave a brief introduction about who he was and the expectations he and Kamishin had for them. It sounded ominous enough that there was some squirming but overall it was a happy, attentive room.

"Production is a service department," he began. The movie was now seven weeks into prep and only a few weeks remained before the start of principal photography. Each one would build in intensity. Production would be open at least 12 hours a day. If another department was open, Production would be open, so it could just as easily be longer. The hours are long for everyone on a movie, but for the bulk of the crew that was during principal photography. The Production department was there in prep, photography and wrap, the period when they would shut it all down.

Attitude was important, he said. The staff should try to accommodate everyone, be consistently professional, and avoid conflict. He wanted them to avoid swearing and dress nicely, although he didn't say what that meant and no one asked. Movie and television sets don't generally have that stated but if that occurred to any of them it was not detectable.

As far as the staff was concerned, he continued, the actors could have whatever they wanted. Telling them no, if that were to happen, would be left to higher-ups.

"If someone comes in asking for something unreasonable, hand it off to me or Damiana," he said, Kamishin looking on silently. "We'll decide if it's something that's going to take too much of Production's time or if their personal assistant should handle it."

Tensions would run high at points when they were shooting. That was normal given the stress of principal photography. "Crew will come in with issues and put their frustration on the production staff," he said. "Some of them may be rude."

The production staff should not respond in kind. Hand it up rather than engaging.

"Let me know what's going on and if I need to, I'll give them a tune-up."

The Production department was now crewed-up, as the full room showed. Nikki Simpson was the APOC, the second in the department, and with her a PA from her last job. It was common practice to recommend people, and he had experience for the job. Then came Wendy Calloway, who had gone to work on *Motor City* Friday morning, been laid off and then rehired the same day on *Last Vegas*. It had been a good weekend, she said.

Everyone knew the search for APOC had been in the works but Kamishin said she'd also spent time looking for someone with experience for the travel coordinator job. It was a job that demanded experience, yet people often moved on to other jobs quickly.

The studio hadn't considered *Last Vegas* a high-travel show when Samuels and Badalato were working on the budget for the movie. They initially planned a two-person office. This movie production had more than just the normal comings and goings, which was generally enough to keep a one-person office busy for a production this size. The movie was shooting in two cities and would have a big cross-country move. In the end, they went with one position.

Badalato turned to personnel matters and complaints of inappropriate behavior, a topic that would have been handled by the human resources department in a conventional business. Without any HR people on site it fell to him, and to some degree the accountant, to enforce standards. Badalato recited a list of people to talk to regarding issues or complaints, basically a walk up the hierarchy leading to him.

"And if you have a problem with me," he paused, "find another job."

Badalato's tone had gradually lightened and this came with the timing of a seasoned comedian, everyone bursting into laughter at the same instant. It woke Buddy, who had grown weary of the meeting a minute after his owner started talking. He again offered a single bark.

Everyone knew that Badalato had a boss in Samuels, and that the executive producer was present and approachable. And there was the studio from there. Everyone also knew where a conflict with either man was likely to lead, and it wasn't good for crew. It was unheard of to go to the studio, at least with any positive result.

Earlier Badalato had said he'd had occasion to speak directly to a famous actor about a sexual harassment complaint from crew. "More likely it's a producer" to be called out, he said, adding that also was rare. "It's a conversation but you need to have it."

Turteltaub and Rake had both gone to LA. for the holiday weekend to be with their families, the director to his Malibu beach house and Rake to his home in North Hollywood. With fewer days in the work week there was more to accomplish in both cities. They were only in Atlanta for a couple of days and would leave for Las Vegas to scout later in the week.

Turteltaub's week started with meetings, first the casting director, Mark Fincannon, then a locations review set for noon, followed by more scouting.

Fincannon & Associates was one of the best-known locations casting groups in the region. It was founded in Charlotte, N.C., in the early 80s as a family business and it remained one. They had some work before but got off the ground in 1983 when Frank Capra Jr. arrived in the state to scout locations for *FireStarter* (1984), a movie backed by Dino De Laurentiis. De Laurentiis ended up so enamored of the state that he opened a studio in Wilmington, where the casting company soon established a presence. That studio became EUE/ Screen Gems in 1996.

The casting firm, which included Mark Fincannon's brother Craig Fincannon and sister-in-law Lisa Mae Fincannon, had thrived. It won its first Emmy for *Bastard Out of Carolina* in 1997 and another in 1998 for *From Earth to the Moon*. The next year they opened an office in New Orleans. Atlanta was added in 2009. Fincannon & Associates was about to win another Emmy for casting on "Homeland," a drama about a bipolar CIA agent who specializes in Middle East operations. The first season of the original series, primarily shot in North Carolina, had been a big hit for Showtime. The second season was in production and would air in the fall.

Gary Rake came into the bullpen looking for Fincannon and they talked about another project they had in common. A few minutes later Turteltaub entered from the other hallway, fresh cup of coffee in hand. He thought of something and detoured to Badalato's office. The ink was dry on the cinematographer's deal and he would start Monday. Turteltaub wanted to make sure he and the cinematographer were seated together on the flight from LA. to Atlanta. Badalato said he would see to it.

By then Rake and Fincannon had come to the other side of the room to wait for Turteltaub, who entered the bullpen a little too quickly, splashing coffee out of his cup.

"Oh shit," the director said, looking down, a grin on his face. "Did I get my shirt? Because I can't meet one of the Fincannons like this." He extended his hand to Fincannon as everyone laughed.

They exchanged pleasantries and walked toward the hall.

"We have three people for . . . ," said Fincannon, trailing off as they exited the bullpen.

Fincannon's job was location casting, which meant coming up with actors in or near Georgia. He had plenty of ideas already, given his relationships with casting specialists and agents and actors in the Eastern third of the country. The cast would hover around 50 for *Last Vegas*, which had nothing to do with the thousands of background actors needed. A different company handled extras casting, and interviews had been scheduled.

The casting director told Turteltaub his thoughts. The director had several people he liked for certain roles, including for the wife of Sam, Kevin Kline's character. From there, Fincannon would hold auditions. Once a decision was made on a hire, it was the casting director's job to negotiate deals based on the budget. Sometimes they even managed the hire throughout the movie.

As Turteltaub met with Fincannon regarding casting, the production designer and location manager were meeting elsewhere to prep for Turteltaub's next meeting. John H. Findley III arrived early morning, his face red, his gray hair and goatee a little damp. He was dressed in Georgia-professional summer wear, light khaki shorts and a blue short-sleeve shirt, and hurried through the bullpen to his office. As location manager, he spent much of his time on the road looking at places, inside and out. He was seen regularly at Mailing Avenue, just not for long periods. September had started but it was still hot, which made his footwork tiring.

Findley had been one of the earliest hires. He was responsible for finding places for every non-studio scene shot in Georgia. His goal was to get as many places checked off the list as soon as possible. Turteltaub's goal was to find a perfect match for every single scene. The process wasn't in perfect alignment, even if the two endpoints were the same.

Today's meeting, an overview, was the biggest one to date. He needed to summarize where they were in the process, a reminder of what had been decided, what was under review, and what was left. A lot was left.

So far they had decided on the house to shoot scenes with "Archie," Morgan Freeman's character. Where they would shoot scenes with "Paddy" (De Niro), "Billy" (Douglas), and "Sam" (Kline) was still undecided. They had looked at a lot of options and it was likely Turteltaub would greenlight at least one at the meeting. But he wasn't one to put a check mark down if he thought they could do better. Details about the characters would be reflected in their homes, and in his mind, there was still plenty of time.

Findley, logically, was hoping for decisions so he could lock things in. There were still a lot of other scenes to be shot in Atlanta. The good news was that his assistant location manager would start later in the week, so at least he'd have help.

The Art department conference room -- now universally referred to as the Boom Boom Room -- was a museum of possibilities. Four large conference tables were pushed together in the center of the room, surrounded by a dozen chairs. A couch with throw pillows centered the far wall.

If not for the decorations it could have been a giant den out of one of downtown Atlanta's trendy loft buildings. The ceiling was open with darkly painted HVAC ductwork and pipes aloft. The white walls were covered with what amounted to giant bulletin boards, black-painted fiberboard. Lights were aimed at them.

The Boom Boom Room served many purposes. It was workspace, meeting space and display space. But it was also a gathering place for the Art department. They had lunch there as a group, the only department that would break from their desks for a meal. That was by design. Bomba always joined them at the giant conference table if he was on site. His department was a team and this kept them connected. It was a relaxing time but they also worked.

Many movies use storyboards, a series of drawings that show various scenes planned for the movie. Bomba was using images. In the past week, hundreds of photographs had gone up around the rectangular room. It was an organized *Last Vegas* display of options with the feel of a one-room exhibition. Ultimately the display was set up for one patron and that was Turteltaub, who would point to the things he liked best.

The detail was remarkable. It showed the production designer's process with a feel for era and place, his ideas about where the movie could go spread out over 360 degrees. It was organized like a clock of locations, starting from the beginning of the script to the end. Big labels with place names and smaller labels under those with subgroups blocked out entire walls, each with groups of photos. Much of it was labeled "research."

The sign over the left side of the biggest wall read "Flatbush, NY, 1955." This was where the movie opened and where the main characters grew up. Dozens of shots covered the early years. A number of smaller labels from the scene were affixed to the fiberboard with clumps of pictures: exterior liquor store, interior liquor store, and a smaller area labeled "Baltimore 1955."

Several of the pictures featured boys playing, since that's what the actors would be doing in the scene. All of the images in the section were black and white or sepia tone. There were streets with shops and without, some with old cars and signs, some just of signs. There was an industrial shot for a 'big picture' look at the place.

Present day Las Vegas was next, a huge area that stretched across two and half walls, a breakdown that reflected where most of the movie took place. It wasn't full but still held hundreds of photos, including images of the city and various streets, and then smaller sub categories. The section mapped off for the Aria hotel was the largest group broken out, although there was still plenty of blank area for more images. It was both interior and exterior shots. A lot were of the penthouse, including hallways, bathroom, kitchen, a large staircase. Then exterior shots focused on the pool, where a couple of big scenes would be filmed.

The Aria presented a special challenge because some of the work was subject to approval. Bomba needed to get it right. It was a big part of the reason Garner and the new assistant art director were in Las Vegas right now, getting more photos, measuring rooms and getting more images. The numbers would be dropped into a computer-assisted design program to further plan the sets.

Then there were exterior shots, Old Vegas, McCarran airport, a couple of the sidewalks in front of larger casinos for outdoor scenes. One scene was set atop the Stratosphere Casino Hotel & Tower, at the X-Scream, which called for a ride by Douglas ("Billy Gherson") and Steenburgen ("Diana Boyle"), or more likely their stunt doubles. There were other images from Atlanta, including a nightclub and funeral home, for other scenes. They would shoot exteriors on location in Las Vegas but scenes that take place inside could be built as sets.

One corner was blocked out with a series of specific towns that would be home to the heroes: Demarest, N.J.; Brooklyn, N.Y.; Naples, Fla.; and Malibu, Calif. "Diana," Steenburgen's character, wouldn't arrive in the movie until the characters were in Vegas so there weren't any sets to be built around her home base.

Bomba planned to put a lot of effort in those scenes. "It's the only time people will see them in their homes," he explained. "We have to establish who they are as individuals." It was a short amount of time, which made it even more important to get it right.

"It has to go a long way toward getting people to invest in the characters, so a lot of information has to be transmitted quickly," he said. He wanted people to buy in to characters and providing background on them aided in delivering surprises later. Even punch lines were better when a moviegoer had more detail about the character making the joke. The buy-in was important for the success of the movie: The more people can emotionally invest or enjoy a movie, the more they recommend it to friends.

In the case of *Last Vegas*, the homes were especially important, Bomba continued. "Once they leave for Vegas it's going to be much harder to provide information about them as people."

More images would go up in the next week or so, especially from the Aria since Garner and the assistant art director were getting more shots from there. As elaborate as the walls were of the Boom Boom Room, it was all temporary.

Four Fellas was up and running at Warner Bros Costume Department in Los Angeles, Dayna Pink officially on board as costume designer. She had been on the phone often but there was tension between her and Badalato and Samuels that centered on hires. Turteltaub and the producers liked Pink, a lot. The proverbial devil was in the details, which they had worked out.

It was a parallel to the story to the one playing out in the Art department. Pink wanted a comfortable budget and people she knew, and that meant people from LA. Badalato and Samuels wanted local hires and to keep a thumb on expenses. The irony was that, like the production designer, the tight schedule and budget constraints made them even more intent on hiring someone they knew to help them manage the challenges. The fact she hired Jennifer Jobst, a well-respected costume supervisor out of Chicago, went a long way with Badalato and Samuels. They supported Pink's hire of an L.A. based assistant costume designer -- on a part-time basis. So it was a happy holding pattern, with all three women working away in Burbank.

Saying that a costume designer decides what the actor wears on screen is like saying linen is a fiber. They design the overall look as well as specific costumes based on thought and interaction with the director and the actors. That means deciding how they are created to begin with, whether renting them from a costume house, purchasing them from retailers, or hiring tailors to make them from scratch, or some variation. But designers are also responsible for delivery, although they have a costume supervisor to oversee that.

Part of what Pink brought to the job as costumer designer were her connections. She knew people at the costume houses, trades people but also top-end clothiers who could make the costumes for the lead actors. Knowing their talent was key because she had to trust they could turn around that many clothes competently.

Everything a principal actor wears in a major movie is thoroughly considered. With an ensemble cast, particularly of this caliber, that attention to detail was quintupled. There were another dozen significant roles in the movie, and another tier beyond that, and all of them needed attention. Then there were thousands of extras.

Each of the five actors would have their own look but their costumes also had to be considered in relation to the other actors. It was an aspect to the job that few people outside the industry knew about. It was entirely too easy to have one of them clash, even mildly, with another. Unless it was intended, it was a mistake. A lot of the forethought that went into costumes was to ensure they didn't stand out unless they were supposed to be noticed. Clothes helped to understand the character, which in turn advanced the story.

Most of the costume prep would be done at Warner Bros. in Burbank, CA. Pink had easily made the case for that to Samuels and Badalato. Atlanta was a precocious child in the world of movie production but it had not yet sprouted costume houses. Given they wanted to rent a lot of clothes to keep costs down, it made sense to work from California. The facility provided dedicated workspace for productions. "LAST VEGAS" went up on the door.

Why the Warner Bros. lot, since that studio had nothing to do with this movie? It had a huge costume facility, an impressive business in its own right even if it wasn't linked to the parent corporation. The facility had racks and shelves of costumes and everything related, along with workspace for costumers -- and at 60,000-square-feet it would fill an American football field. There were also seamstresses and tailors and artisans who could make or alter just about anything.

The seemingly endless aisles of frocks were organized by "era, decade, style." The categories were both specific and general, with something for everyone. One category was "ethnic" and another "all periods through modern." It was everything from formal bridal to uniforms and sci-fi to western frontier. It had historic costumes and hats and belts and slippers along with shoes and masks and decades of jewelry. It had 30 variations of the same kind of sweater.

Last Vegas would need contemporary attire along with uniforms, bridal wear, selections from the "casino/dance/showgirl," and some formal party wear. It also needed a Vegas feel for the hundreds of extras at the party. Then there were the period scenes, a special challenge. The movie opened in 1955 Brooklyn, with child actors portraying the main characters as children. Warner Bros. Costume Dept. rented prep cages and design suites or offices with direct phone lines. It was in one of the bigger offices that the women set up shop, pulling costumes and storing them in the designated cages. Cages got their name from being chainlink fence partitioned off space, although not all of them were wire mesh. Commonly used on soundstages, they provide storage areas near the stages.

The facilities had standard fitting rooms and those more appropriate for stars. The fancier fitting rooms have lighted, mirrored platforms, separate dressing areas and seating areas for viewing. Mary Steenburgen and Morgan Freeman were likely to have fittings there, since it was close to where they lived. Freeman also lived in Mississippi, so they would have to sort that out.

Part of Jobst's responsibility was organizing the shipment that would go to New York for fittings. Costume boxes may be the strongest cardboard creations in the world. They come in different sizes but all hold their weight. Just the one E box marked "Paddy," could carry up to 600 pounds.

A "pull" is costumer jargon for getting clothes off the racks of a larger collection. Jobst oversaw that process that all told, amounted to hundreds of items of clothing, most of which was slated for background. Pink and the assistant designer were locking in on specific costumes. They shopped for clothes and talked to designers. In the process, the costume team would build a "closet" for each actor.

They worked late all week to get as much done as possible before each of them traveled. Pink and the assistant designer were flying to New York to meet with De Niro, Douglas and Kline over the weekend. Jobst was heading to Atlanta to open its office. Pink would meet Jobst there while the assistant designer returned to LA.

Some of Jobst's kit from Chicago had already arrived at Mailing Avenue. Three oversized boxes emblazoned with the Western Costume logo of the Greek comedy/tragedy masks, had landed in the bullpen. It took two PAs to move one, each person on opposite sides.

Getting the offices in Atlanta ready was essential for the Costume department because they would be working elsewhere until right up to when the company moved to Atlanta for the stage work. First up was the location work in Vegas. Once they returned to LA., where they were prepping, there were four weeks before principal photography kicked off there. That meant getting it decided, organized and packed in two weeks, and then unpacking perhaps a thousand costumes for it to be organized and ready, timely fittings completed, in time for the first shooting day.

Each day they set up for the following day. Once they finished shooting in Vegas, the production moved to Atlanta. The costume offices had to be operational when they returned because there would be no time to set up. They'd be shooting.

Movie buffs following the failure of *Motor City* knew it was a revenge flick starring Gerard Butler as a newly released felon out to settle a score. They might have known it was to be directed by Albert Hughes, who did *The Book of Eli*. Some might also have known that Mickey Rourke and Adrien Brody had recently been added to the roster.

What they might not have known was that it was unlikely any of those actors had set foot on the soundstages at that point, yet Hughes and some of the actors might get paychecks anyway, thanks to "pay or play" provisions in contracts.

The crew on Mailing Avenue had followed it closely. What they knew a week earlier was that the *Motor City* project had laid off 138 people. By now they had talked to their friends, and several of the former crew were now at work on *Last Vegas*. Now, a week later, a story about what happened emerged.

The crew of *Motor City* went to work on Friday at the Atlantic Civic Center, which had been operating as a stage/warehouse. They were told to attend a mandatory 11 a.m. meeting, where they learned it was their last day.

It came as a surprise to some of them because of the money spent. The movie had been in pre-production for two months in Atlanta and was weeks away from the Sept. 17 start of principal photography. Expensive commercial space had been leased, office supplies purchased, contracts for services signed. Not only had sets been designed, they were being constructed and about one-third of them were nearly completed. Costs were already in the millions of dollars, although still a fraction of the estimated $30 million budget.

The word-from-the-set put the main issues with the script, which had little dialogue. The concept of an action drama with little use of the spoken language was potentially groundbreaking terrain. Making a contemporary silent movie proved successful in the case of The Artist, which fared well in the 2011 Oscars, but that film was about silent pictures.

Shutting the production of *Motor City* down wouldn't be cheap. Just tearing down one of the sets which had involved pouring a significant amount of concrete was going to be expensive. Producers and financiers released a professional, tightly worded explanation stating that a firm delivery date compromised their ability to make a quality movie. Some stories said the producers on *Motor City* hadn't realized it was a "drop dead" date where they had to deliver.

It was a blip in local news, noteworthy for how different it would have been if it were a permanent business with a similar number of employees closing in town. A movie folding makes for a different kind of a news story than a factory closing its doors. The factory story ends up being about the workers, the loss of jobs, it's effect on the community. The movie entertainment stories were about the people above the line.

The inside take was that it was unlikely producers didn't know about an ironclad date in a contract, although they might have assumed they had more wiggle room from Warner Bros. More importantly, contracts, including post-production schedules, can be amended.

It could have been as simple as someone with control of the bank strings, or at least one of them, deciding the potential for *Motor City* to be a flop was greater than its chances of being a groundbreaker and they saw an insurable reason to exit. However it played out, it would be pricey.

"Lawsuits to follow," offered one passerby.

As freelancers, the possibility it could end suddenly was always a fact of life for the crew. They just hoped it didn't happen here.

The presence of Simpson, the APOC, gave the bullpen a different feel. A giant whiteboard -- this one dwarfing the others around the building, including Badalato's -- had been offered up by the owners of the building. She made it the centerpiece of production, a way to keep track of everyone as well as a way to have fun.

As the assistant production coordinator, or APOC as it is more commonly known, Simpson was Kamishin's second and Stephens' immediate boss. Stephens, whom she had worked with on "Teen Wolf," had recommended her for *Last Vegas*. In the end, Simpson was selected over the other strong candidates because of it.

An attractive, 30-something African American from New Jersey, Simpson had been in Atlanta several years. She had come from the corporate world and while somewhat new to the movie business, the experience translated well. She learned the business fast by working in different production jobs, including production secretary on *For Colored Girls* and travel coordinator on *Good Deeds*, both Tyler Perry projects.

Simpson handled big-ticket items and higher-up production issues. She dealt with the primary actors' assistants, such as scheduling their physicals, as required under their contracts. As the Locations department secures places to shoot, Production prepared and managed certificates of insurance. The Art department was trying to get photos of the actors as younger men to be used as props on sets of their characters and she was trying to assist them. Robert De Niro wanted special paper for his scripts and she was figuring out exactly what that would entail.

The white board, with its numerous elements, was common in production departments around the country. It made it easier for everyone to keep track of everything. It was a daily check-in board that contained a lot of information along with lighter elements. Simpson had each person in the bullpen create a cartoon character avatar, which was taped to the board. Next to it they would update what they were doing, various errands and so forth. One look could spot check whether someone was available for a bigger project or eliminate the need to ask where a PA had gone.

Simpson added elements that changed with the date, like the "Fun Fact of the Day" and "Word of the Day." The word of the day wasn't just any word. It needed to be from the urban dictionary. And it had to be used in a sentence. The first one blazed across the board: "Tool: 1. Fool, idiot, useless individual; 2. One prone to manipulation by others; 3. A student who does nothing but study." And, "I was quite a TOOL in my youth but sensitivity training made me a man." The daily fact was to be movie related. As in, "In 1939, 1,400 actresses were interviewed to play the role of Scarlett O'Hara in *Gone with the Wind.*" The bullpen crew would alternate daily responsibility for filling it in.

The bullpen crew nimbly straddled a small gulf between their immediate bosses and the one inhabited by other members of the crew. Production department staff was loyal to Badalato and Kamishin, and Samuels, although he wasn't there as much. They had hired them, whether one of them or all three, but it was more than that. The bullpen crew liked the bosses.

That wasn't true everywhere on Mailing Avenue. A growing number of people were feeling pinched. Grumbling had grown just four weeks in, and most of it was budget-related.

Money was tighter on most movie productions these days, not just *Last Vegas.* Crew was being paid less relative to what they used to earn. They had seen perks cut and rental fees for their kits reduced, at the same time they were asked to do more. They felt the way a lot of middle-class Americans had in the recent years. They were also earning less in pay and benefits while being asked to do more. Most mid-level workers took work home, if only in the form of their email, which often required a response after hours.

Working in the movie industry, despite all the glamour associated with it, came with grueling schedules and conditions that were uniquely demanding. Most crew ruled out any effort to do anything but work Monday to Friday. There was no scheduling a doctor's appointment if it could possibly be avoided. You or your spouse got your kid to daycare without being late to work. There was no taking your lunch break to run an errand; lunch was on site.

But it was also pride in ownership. Their work would be on display. For department heads, in particular, it wasn't a case of being able to do the job with the budget provided. It was whether they could do it with appropriate quality. They were judged by how well their work looked on screen.

From the crew's vantage point, many of the so-called savings just cost them elsewhere. Devising shortcuts was time consuming and had potential to backfire when there wasn't time to fix it. If the set or the costumes or the camerawork or the props came off poorly, it was on them. In some sense, it seemed like a fear of embarrassment similar to having the copier quit at the wrong moment.

A naïve question was bounced through the bullpen about the big pay for above-the-liners relative to the salaries and perks for people below the line.

"Do the actors know how much they pinch the crew?"

"Would they care?"

"Some would. Maybe some would take less to ensure crew got what it needs."

"It doesn't work that way. It's more about the producers and the studio. If they can negotiate the actors for less, then it stays with the studio. So, why should the actors take less?"

"So, it's not like De Niro could say, 'I'll reduce my fee by $200,000 to make sure more stays with the people below the line?'"

"Exactly."

What about the concept of the international 'fair trade' movement, which advocated the payment of higher prices to workers? In that case it amounted to paying more to exporters to ensure workers were paid better and environmental standards met in other parts of the world, but was there a parallel? Not in this America. These aren't migrant farm workers. They had choices and most had union representation. Being paid scale was a decent salary. The market law of supply and demand was in effect: If they didn't want to do the movie for scale, with fewer perks, others could and would.

CHAPTER FIVE
6 Weeks Out
Sept. 10-14

A FAKE NEWS REPORT was unleashed from the petri dish of an Internet troll over the weekend. It claimed Morgan Freeman had died, and it bounced through social media upsetting fans all over the world. It concerned anybody involved in the movie who saw it, but it stopped Badalato in his tracks. He immediately went online to research. Debunked, he passed the information on and resumed his day. Freeman was alive and well.

Badalato was standing in the bullpen early Monday morning as the production staff processed the thought of a world without Freeman. Someone asked about the impact to the movie if it had been true.

"There's probably a clause that's triggered that says we all go home," said Badalato.

Then the bullpen discussion shifted to how the show could go on.

"Who could replace Freeman?" Kamishin said, posing it as a question, though it wasn't.

"I don't think you could do it," Badalato agreed.

"Not in six weeks," she said. "No way."

One of the newer PAs, the same one who asked whether the movie would be impacted, chimed in. "There has to be a lot of guys of that caliber in that age group. What about Al Pacino?" The actor had been in the news recently. He was going to star in Glengarry Glen Ross on Broadway and was also a candidate for a movie about Joe Paterno, the football coach.

Badalato and Kamishin looked at each other the way parents might if their three-year-old said the preschool teacher was going to take the class on a field trip -- when pigs flew. But they didn't laugh.

Not just any significant actor in the age group could fit the bill. It had to be the right match, and to draw the way the producers wanted, it needed to be the right demographic. An African American would be ideal, but at least a minority to broaden the appeal. But there also had to be chemistry or balance with the others in the cast. Then there was the matter of scheduling. There were quality actors who could fit the bill but the calendar was stubborn. Who was available full time for two months beginning in six weeks?

It was a stark reminder of how tenuous it all was. *Last Vegas* was about the older set and the actors were age-appropriate: De Niro 68, Douglas 69, Freeman 75, Kline 65. If something happened to Freeman, or to Douglas, who had been sick in recent years, or to De Niro, it was likely the production would be shuttered. Kline also would be very difficult to replace, if not impossible. That something could conceivably happen to one of the stars had been thoroughly considered by producers, financiers and attorneys long before now. With the millions of dollars on the line to make *Last Vegas*, expensive insurance policies were in place to cover game-changing events along with other merely inconvenient delays.

The bullpen had scheduled several appointments with doctors for the actors, something required by the insurance companies to assess their health before taking on the risk. The insurance wager was more than just deciding the likelihood the actors could withstand the rigors of the movie. It was also a bet that life would not otherwise intervene. Whoever would make the decision to pull the plug, should something like that happen, wasn't in Atlanta.

"That's way beyond my pay grade," said Badalato.

By then, two people had emerged from the hall to the kitchen. They were finalists for the craft service job and had prepared an assortment of food for sampling by the crew. Their interview was being termed an audition and the crew would vote on which of two finalists they liked best, although it was clear veto power lay with Badalato and Kamishin.

Food is primarily delivered in two ways to movie sets. Both are generically termed "craft services," though they differ. Craft Services was a department of the movie. Its crew provided lighter fare between meals, both simple and ramped up snacks, along with coffee and beverages. A catering company provided breakfast, lunch and dinner buffet-style for hundreds of employees when the movie was in full swing.

Food wasn't a luxury but a part of life on a movie set. Its role had been defined over decades and detailed in union contracts because no one was leaving to get lunch. A movie crew was essentially caught on set. Union rules required food be provided every six hours. If they missed the mandatory time, a meal penalty fee would accrue in six-minute increments.

The money spent on food and beverage was worth every penny of return in productivity. It was not an area where Badalato and Samuels sought to save money. They'd even spend more for a higher grade of food. For instance, the caterer would provide a juicing bar with fresh fruit and vegetables, along with ginger and other ingredients.

"You can ask people to do a lot if you feed them well," said Badalato.

Given the rumored passing of Freeman, the bullpen discussion about the actors continued long after the group disappeared into the office for the meeting. Being in touch with well-known actors was part of the job and they were used to celebrity. Yet a shift had also occurred. Now the cast had transitioned into "our actors."

Initial opinions of the actors were guided by their public personas. Freeman was beloved, a national treasure. Douglas was a legend, a Hollywood icon. De Niro was revered, "the greatest living actor," a repeated sentiment. Kline was both a screen and stage actor with a couple of Tony Awards on the shelf. Steenburgen was still new to the fold, the least known among the crew. But she was a veteran actress, and well respected.

De Niro, Douglas and Freeman would bring full entourages, each composed of the same number of people under the contract. Each group included a personal assistant, drivers, hair, makeup, and in at least two cases, standins. They work for the actors on a regular basis and are hired as part of the movie, at the direction of the actor. The movie would provide Kline and Steenburgen with assistants, as well, along with hair and makeup professionals. Interviews were under way for those hires.

That was in addition to whatever else an actor's particular perk package dictated. Producers and studios had learned it was better to cap it. In addition to being paid the same, the top three actors in *Last Vegas* each had up to $100,000 in perks. They could spend it how they wanted, but when it was gone, it was gone.

The opinions evolved as new information came in from people who had worked with the actors. De Niro garnered the most crew discussion. One woman told a story about being on the set of 1996's *Cape Fear*. She said she made the mistake of getting in De Niro's sight line, which is an actor's line of vision when they are in character. Anything that can distract them from the scene isn't a good idea but when an actor is playing a murderous sex offender seeking revenge, it's especially problematic. She had been reprimanded and still recalled it vividly.

"I wasn't anywhere near him," she said.

"He's not usually like that," replied Katrina Rice, the assistant prop master.

The Props department had arrived earlier in the week, led by prop master Dwight Benjamin-Creel. Props are anything that an actor touches in a scene. It is up to the prop master to purchase, build or otherwise acquire those things in prep, and then to manage them during principal photography, doling them out and securing them. They are also responsible for the look of those things on set. For instance, one scene would have an actor packing a suitcase, and between every take, the Props department would unpack it so he could do it again. Another example would be if the director suddenly decided someone needed to wear blue hat. The Props department would find one, hopefully in the props truck.

Though Benjamin-Creel was the prop master for *Last Vegas*, he had been upstaged almost immediately by Rice, which didn't seem to bother him in the least. She had arrived in the bullpen in grand fashion. Everyone was fairly casual on Mailing Avenue, many in T-shirts and jeans, but she wore a bright skirt with a bow-like backside, a blouse with revealing neckline and high heels. She was a natural beauty possessed of self-confidence and a striking personality.

Rice had no problem jumping in to clear something up: "It's not easy being De Niro." She and Benjamin-Creel had just finished *Killing Season*, which starred De Niro and John Travolta. If De Niro didn't take care of himself, the world would have eaten him alive a long time ago, she added.

She told of a scene in *Killing Season* that involved De Niro's character carrying a weapon. The scene was shot first with a stunt man. When De Niro got before the camera, he carried the weapon with a different arm. Rice was called on the walkie to ask the actor to switch arms, which she did. He didn't do it, so they radioed her again. When she was asked again, he didn't reply. She relayed the information back. It was clear he'd heard her and she wasn't going to ask him a third time.

But she also understood why he hadn't done it.

"It's his character," she continued. "He doesn't follow the stuntman's lead. The stuntman follows him. It's up to De Niro to decide what arm he wants to use to carry the gun," she explained.

The craft service meeting concluded, Badalato emerged from the office and into the bullpen, taking in Rice, who was center stage. Generally he met crew before they were hired and she was a rare exception.

"Billy Badalato," she said, extending her hand before he could speak. "I met you on *Conspirator*." She had been a day player on the movie and he didn't recognize her, but it probably didn't hurt that she had recognized him.

He looked mildly entertained as they chatted for a few minutes about the movie, which was made in Savannah. Badalato recalled the show's "mulch ninjas," production assistants whose jobs were to cover the streets with the substance and to make them more appropriate for 1865. It was a distinction that made it into credits as the "mulch division."

Rice asked about the production scout planned for Las Vegas. While the creative side had steadily gone on scouts and would return to Nevada later in the week, Badalato and Kamishin were planning a one-time production scout. The Props department also needed to suss things out. Badalato said they were working on the details and he would get back to her.

Turteltaub and the others were scouting Atlanta with the goal of finalizing a couple of things before they left for scouts in Vegas. It was Rake and Bomba, and Samuels on the business side. Newly hired cinematographer, David Hennings was also added to the mix. There had been a couple of names bandied about for the role of director of photography and someone at the studio pushed for him. He and Turteltaub covered a lot of territory on the flight from L.A. to Atlanta but the DP still had a lot to catch up on.

One of the benefits of using Hennings was that he was on top of changing technology. *Last Vegas* would be shot in digital. The use of film to make movies was trending down while digital was still trending up. It was a near split between the two mediums in 2012. Given that the movie business had always been about film, it amounted to a sea change. Many lamented it as the ruination of Hollywood. In the end, it was a business decision. It was going to be less expensive. The upfront costs might be higher, but the savings in distribution would be pronounced.

Hennings arrived at Mailing Avenue Tuesday morning with a lens-laden suitcase and a sheepish grin. His face was slightly chiseled, his dark hair on the longish side. He didn't have just a twinge of rock star; he looked like he might have been one back in the day. He disappeared quickly into his office and began the standard back and forth. Then he took time to talk to people in the bullpen, offering advice about a camera on a desk, and was generally approachable and friendly.

"We're lucky with him," one of the supervisors said when Hennings was out of earshot. "So far," someone said, to laughter. "DPs can be offputting, even prima donnas."

The notion was that all departments on a movie were expendable except camera. Technically, you could make a movie without a director or a production designer or a producer, but you could not make it without a camera. It was a point that rubbed some the wrong way.

By now the first assistant director knew the script like Badalato knew the budget. The difference was that most of his details were still in motion whereas Badalato's were about to get locked. Movies aren't shot in the order they appear in a script. They are shot for financial efficiency, weather, the availability of key actors and any number of other variables. The timeline of the story is sewn together later in editing.

In a month the production would move to Las Vegas for the final weeks of prep. Rake spent most of his time with Turteltaub with the ongoing scouts and various meetings. He also spent time in the office working on the shooting schedule. He would sit behind his desk with his head in his laptop, adding and manipulating information.

Rake purposely left some out. "It's too early to enter all the details," he said. "If history speaks, the script will change and I don't want to be married to all the details." Scripts don't come with numbered scenes, that happened on his watch. At this point he had well over 100 scenes, several of which had already changed and would change again.

Rake praised the software, a standard in the industry. It didn't just create the shooting schedule for the movie, but ultimately other key production documents. How the assistant directors of the past used to schedule movies without it, he said, was beyond him.

He had added a summary to each scene, something short. Each scene was its own entity, including the characters in it, and it built from there to include the location, set dressing, the number of extras, props, vehicles, sound and visual effects, and whether there were stunts.

The first scene in the script, "Flatbush Corner," involved the main characters as children. The synopsis read: "A young gang huddles outside a store." It was the first script day and would follow the scene throughout the entire production, as would the timeframe.

The story of *Last Vegas* happened over six script days, which created a timeline. The opening scene, the first script day, took place in 1955 while the second jumped 50 or more years into the future. Script days were essential to the Costume department, which had to have clothes ready for every scene, regardless of the order in which the scene happened in the story. It was possible they would shoot scenes from several different script days on a single day, and that helped keep it straight.

"A script doesn't generally say, 'next day,' so sometimes you have to figure that out," said Rake. Eventually the schedule would include seeming minutia like whether the character had bruised knuckles from a melee a day earlier in the plot or whether there were vehicles in the scenes. It was whether a crane would be used, and they already knew they would use several throughout the movie. It was a colossal amount of slicing and dicing. Navigating it was a skill developed over time.

Right now, Rake's focus was on dates that the actors couldn't work during production. A "red flag" feature sent a warning if an AD tried to schedule an actor on a blackout date. Before it had been entirely too easy to schedule a scene with a number of actors when one wasn't working. Before the red flag, a lot of time was spent double-checking to prevent mistakes.

Scheduling all the players in this movie, given the actors involved, had to be a puzzle. Did they have a lot of blackout dates?

"At this point it's mostly De Niro," he said.

Kristina Peterson stuck her head in the office. As second AD, and because they had room, she had been assigned a private office but she didn't want it. It was on the other side of the bullpen from Rake and that was too far away. She said she planned to move into his office. It wasn't quite a question, although she paused for a response. He nodded in agreement.

They needed to be in close proximity, particularly with the relatively short prep time. Too much would happen too fast.

Peterson's presence changed the dynamic for everyone, but especially Rake. It took pressure off and freed him to do other things. His primary job was to manage Turteltaub and make sure the director's plans were being implemented. Her primary job was to assist Rake, although being 2nd AD also came with very distinct responsibilities. All of the paperwork spawned by the scheduling software ultimately would run through Peterson. She would manage cast movement, oversee extras and approve paychecks, although ultimately it was Badalato who would sign off.

Peterson, who was on the tall side with long hair, had arrived with a confident stride. She engaged immediately and she remembered names. By the end of her second day she had purchased everyone in the bullpen a round of specialty Starbucks drinks. They knew she was currying favor and they didn't mind one bit. They had to work with her whether she bought coffee or not.

She was into yoga, which she said helped her manage stress and connect to some of the staff. But mostly she was fast on her feet and not afraid to say what other people wouldn't. A conversation about the competition between craft service companies vying for the job was under way on one of her first visits to the printer in the bullpen. She sipped a soft drink and listened to the conversation while she waited for the paper. That in hand, she turned to the group.

"Oh yeah. They'll come in with lobster tails and shrimp etouffee. Then when they get on the show it will be Tootsie Rolls and Kool-Aid," she said, "not this fancy Fresca I'm drinking right now." The bullpen roared with laughter.

Peterson took the desk on the right of what had been Rake's office and soon had the place festooned. A black silhouette of a tree filled the wall behind Rake's desk. Birds in various types of motion flew around the room. It was a simple design made of black material that adhered to the wall, easy to affix. A lot of the crew added decorations to their work areas but hers was the most elaborate. She'd done it all in an hour.

Peterson knew her way around the business. She was launched into the industry in the mid-1990s via the Assistant Directors Training Program. The competitive program, co-sponsored by the DGA and the Alliance of Motion Picture and Television Producers, began in the 1960s. Initially created to give better access to people who weren't connected to the industry, it went a long way toward adding diversity behind the camera. Peterson, who is Asian American, did well in the program, which included education, training and paid experience on movies and productions. Trainees who completed 350 or 400 days of paid, hands-on work experience on film and television projects end up second ADs.

Rake and Peterson were both at their desks the next day when Samuels came into the office. They were ready for him.

"Update?"

"The swing set replaces a driving scene with Archie," Rake said.

The end of a script included a scene where the actors are home and on the phone, an epilogue to their Vegas adventure. The original version had called for Morgan Freeman's character to be driving. Driving and talking on the phone was a problem. The new scene would have the same lines but have him at a swing set with his grandchild.

"Good," said Samuels.

Turteltaub had a television actor he liked for the role of Todd, a sidekick to the four main characters. It should be finalized this week, Rake said, before he transitioned to the next topic. "We're adding a scene with Cirque du Soleil that replaces Blue Man," he said.

The Blue Man Group, a theatrical group known for its blue hue, comedy and experimental music, was in the original script in three places. Cirque du Soleil, the $3 billion entertainment company that created its niche merging circus arts with Broadway-quality theatrics, was about to open a new show with a permanent berth at the 1,840-seat theater at the Aria. The show was called "Zarkana."

Samuels nodded, then gave his own update. The El Cortez Hotel & Casino was officially out of the script. They didn't want to be part of the movie. Someone in management told him a multi-million dollar renovation was in the works and they didn't want to be depicted with an old look.

Samuels said another classic casino-hotel in the area, Binions, had accepted. The scenes that called for a seedy casino would be shot there. Apparently some still believed all publicity was good publicity.

Jobst stopped at Stephens' desk to pick up additional resumes of local costumers submitted to the production. The *Last Vegas* email account had received 1,053 emails for work across all departments. Sometimes people eager for work would also wander into the bullpen, although the ads expressly said not to do that.

Next she went to Simpson's desk to check on the purchase of the washer dryer. Jobst had said she didn't care if it was new, as long as it had multiple settings to clean different kinds of fabrics. Simpson reported success. She'd found a washer dryer at the studio where they shot *The Internship*, which was in wrap and disposing of assets. In the mix was a multi-option, four-cycle, three-temperature Whirlpool washing machine and multi-option dryer, and for just a few hundred dollars. She also had secured a dry cleaning service for the Costume department. Crew could use it at cost.

The costume supervisor requested 25 industrial-grade garment racks to hang costumes. Known as Z racks, they had a 400-pound load capacity and correspondingly strong wheels. The wheels enabled the racks to move easily when loaded while the Z design of the base enabled them to fit together to move in bulk. Jobst also needed three-way mirrors and a slap sink, the big square sinks used with washer-dryers.

Then there were the cages. As a new facility, Mailing Avenue didn't have cages yet, but they were about to hire a company to install them. The partitioned areas, accessible to the stages, would be assigned to each department. The Costume department would have the largest area, in the first of the warehouse spaces, and Set Decorating, the next in size, would have one in the next warehouse.

The next time she came to the bullpen it was in search of a lamp. She stopped in front of the desk of a PA who had a two-headed floor lamp. Could she have one just like it? It was a generic request but Jobst's eyes had affixed to the lamp in a way that made it specific.

The PA stood up, unplugged the lamp and handed it to her, which made Jobst laugh. She gratefully accepted but there was something else, she said. She needed someone to help her move furniture. The PA duly followed her out of the bullpen and down the hall.

In her early 50s, Jobst might have been 10 years younger. She was cute in a way that seemed both effortless and polished. Her styled hair was above her shoulders, a darkish red with a dab of hair product so it stood up a little. But the clothes made it. She wore a comfortable and balanced ensemble, a black summer dress, silver flats and a jazzy sweater with jagged stripes of pink, olive and black and white.

The Costume department had four interior offices assigned to the department. That meant one for her and one each for the costume designer, and the assistant costume designer, whoever it turned out to be. The fourth would be the costume bullpen with a couple of desks for costumers.

Jobst went directly to the end office, plugged in the lamp and turned off the fluorescent lights. Then she shook her head, turned the lights back on and announced the furniture needed to be moved. It turned out her mission was more focused than just getting the Costume department space up before the costume designer arrived. Dayna Pink was now en route from New York.

Jobst' goal was to make the end office good enough that the costume designer would want it, since the designer had first choice. Her ulterior motive soon became clear; she wanted the other office. It was across the hall from what would be the costume bullpen. That would make it easier for her to communicate with costumers at work. As with Kamishin and Badalato, she wanted eye contact if possible.

The room Jobst wanted was slightly larger but if anything, the end office she wanted to appeal to Pink was the natural pick. It was on the end near the exit and hall rather than being sandwiched between two offices. Besides, Pink and the assistant costume designer wouldn't spend that much time in the offices once shooting began.

As costume supervisor, Jobst would practically live in the offices, whether here or Las Vegas or in one of the costume trailers that would go on location. Those trailers were semis designed for costume departments, with built-in racks for clothes, a washer dryer and workstations on one end. If anything, Jobst would spend more time in the offices on *Last Vegas*, because she had responsibility for managing and documenting the department budget, something she normally relegated to someone else.

Jobst and the PA shifted furniture around for a while, improving a little each time. Finally Jobst stood back, satisfied.

"It's better. Not great, but better."

The lids were off her Western Costume boxes, two in the hallway and one in the other office. The giant cardboard boxes bore the insignia of one of the greatest costume houses in the world. The Hollywood company was in its 100th year and still did extensive business. *Last Vegas* also planned to cull from its collection for the movie.

The concept of a kit, where extensive and specific work supplies were brought to every job, was in full display with Jobst. A traditional tool kit was open on the desk. It contained the usual hammer, pliers, screwdrivers and the like. It was vaguely feminine, a lot cleaner and brighter than the average, with colored handles on several of the tools.

The thick-cardboard costume boxes were filled with a variety of other items. It was tags, labels, multiple pincushions, safety pins, a big bag of rubber bands. A lot of items were in baggies. Then there were paper clips, a chalkboard eraser and archival quality bags, for storage. There were desk racks for paper, a calculator, sterile wipes and rubber stamps with ink pads. The final box had clothing items, an assortment of fabrics, a lot of scarves and a pair of pink, blue and fluorescent yellow tennis shoes.

Jobst had worked on many movies and television shows since her first credit on *Blues Brothers* in 1980 with Dan Akroyd and John Belushi. Chicago was abuzz with the production. Belushi was a favorite native, if wild, son and here she was with a job in the middle of the movie.

With a reported budget of $17.5 million -- a lot in 1979 -- the good times rolled to the extent it was almost legendary. If comedies lend themselves to pleasant production environments, this was a full-blown party. Akroyd and Belushi sponsored the Blues Club, a private bar for cast and crew alike.

The movie had plenty of on-screen talent, including Ray Charles, Aretha Franklin, James Brown and Cab Calloway, each of whom does a song with Jake and Elwood. Each went through the Costume department as part of the process. Then there were famous friends of the blues brothers; Carrie Fisher, who was then involved with Akroyd, was a regular, as were numerous others.

It was an exciting time for Jobst, who loved the work. She'd stuck with it ever since, including involvement with the union and owning her own shop. Her credits included *Dark Knight*, *Public Enemies*, and *Contagion*, along with a lot of TV shows.

Dayna Pink and the assistant designer worked in New York over the weekend, holding the first meetings with Douglas, De Niro and Kline. Pink arrived on Mailing Avenue directly from the Atlanta airport. She dragged her luggage behind her, sunglasses affixed to her face until she got to the bullpen. She looked fashionable, tall with long hair and the slightest air of rock star.

The bullpen crew had talked to her on the phone when she was less than happy so no one knew what to expect. The discussions with Badalato and Samuels had been stressful. But this woman was charming, personable and funny.

She had left the bullpen to go to her office. She returned a minute later and stood at Simpson's desk. They chatted for a second but Simpson could tell the designer was on a mission.

"Yes?'

"There's a large bug on the floor of my office," she said.

"Dead or alive?" Simpson asked like it mattered, because it did.

"Dead."

"Asante?" Everyone laughed, including Pink, as Simpson punted the problem to a production assistant.

The young PA, who had most recently worked at Tyler Perry Studios, occupied the desk closest to the main entrance of the bullpen. He was good looking with great skin and a gorgeous grin. He was handsome enough that someone asked him earlier if he had considered being an actor. He replied that he would, but only if someone approached him first.

Pink looked at him with a warm smile as he got up to help her.

"Thank you," she said. "The bug is the size of a Louis Vuitton bag."

He returned from the Costume department a few minutes later, a big grin on his face.

"It was the size of a nickel," he said.

Pink was a relative latecomer to movies, her first credit coming just seven years earlier. But she came from the fashion industry and she knew style and clothes. She was behind the '70s outfits in *Hot Tub Time Machine*, which garnered attention. The big splash for her followed the success of *Crazy, Stupid, Love*. GQ.com did a short on Pink's work on that movie when it hit the charts that put her age at "40 something" which seemed about right. Above-the-line talent often selects creative hires and Pink had a fan in Steve Carell. She worked with him on *The Incredible Burt Wonderstone* and *Seeking a Friend for the End of the World*.

The meetings with the actors had gone well, she said. Some might find it interesting to go to the homes of the actors but that wasn't the case here. She hadn't minded but it was time-consuming.

First they met with Kline, who had plenty of ideas about Sam, his character. He wanted him to be on the youngish side, as Kline was, although he'd already agreed with Turteltaub that Sam would be gray.

De Niro, who was on a movie outside of Paris tentatively called *Malavita*, had flown to New York for the weekend. The dark comedy, which co-stars Tommy Lee Jones and Michelle Pfeiffer, is about a retired American gangster who relocates his family to Normandy to live under witness protection. That meeting was Saturday. Then, on Sunday, Pink went to Douglas' home in Bedford while the assistant flew home.

The first meetings with the actors were pegged "meet and greets." There were technical aspects. It is possible to get sizes from actors' assistants or even other costume designers, but they still needed to check them. It was also a meeting of the minds. Actors logically had ideas about what their characters should wear, but some more than others. Part of Pink's challenge was to get everyone on the same creative page.

It was the business page, at least at this juncture, that was most taxing. The costume budget meeting in Samuels' office in the executive suites was polite, Pink and Jobst pressing on the needs of the department. Jobst had taken up the cause of advocating for more resources for the department before she even got to LA. *Last Vegas* was a big costume show. It wasn't just the cast but that the story took place in high-end Vegas. There was also the huge opening scene from 1955, which would be very expensive.

In different ways at different times, Badalato or Samuels said no, generally repeating their belief the job could be done on the existing budget. They were happy to shift things around within the department's budget. And if changes were made to the show and what was needed, they would be happy to talk about more money.

When the meeting was over, the women cut through the bullpen, Pink looked somewhat flustered. "They're very nice," Pink said to Jobst, as they hastened through. "But you're not getting any more money." The supervisor nodded in agreement but didn't say anything.

Jobst and Pink hadn't worked together before but it wasn't evident. They easily spoke the same language. It helped that the respective roles as designer and supervisor were clearly defined, something that had happened over decades. They both loved their jobs, budget tension not withstanding. The meeting with Badalato and Samuels behind them, they turned to planning and interviews with costumers. Jobst organized it so Pink could meet as many candidates as possible. With costume prep happening on the West Coast, and Pink on her way back to L.A., there wouldn't be a lot of other opportunities.

Pink and Turteltaub had breakfast at the Ritz the next morning. They discussed the meetings with the actors, and went over the look of each character. They also touched on extras. They would look good as a group, upscale, but he also wanted to add in some "weird" characters. But the director liked what he was hearing from Pink and didn't feel need to push. She left from there for the airport.

While near opposites, the production and accounting offices frequently interacted. They teamed up daily on meal orders and coffee runs, although accounting never did the pickups. The numbers people, with two offices parallel to the bullpen, were buttoned down. The people in the bullpen might fit in a practical joke here and there. Not the accountants. Aside from tapping on keyboards, their offices were quiet.

Being next to each other meant the noise of the production bullpen, which ebbed and flowed with the tide of visitors and crew, could flow into the space of the numbers people. The accountant had a private office and shut his door several times a day. He certainly did that if it got too noisy but more typically it was for privacy. Most of what he was doing involved confidential information. He was frequently on the phone with the studio or representatives of the actors. The accountants' role was to follow the rules and there were a lot of them. Just meeting the requirements of the unions was time consuming. Each union -- WGA, SAG-AFTRA, IATSE and the Teamsters -- had a book of rules. They didn't all parallel and they shifted with each new contract. To grasp all the nuances of each union took years of experience, and even the accountants double-checked the books. The payroll person had them all neatly lined up in bookends where she could see them. It was everything from rates and safety guidelines to per diem and rest periods.

This week the union was personified. A man with the IATSE local called the production office. He demanded to know the address of the studio and sounded "aggressive," according to the PA who took the call. It was striking enough that she had put him on hold, lest she make a mistake. Was it okay to give it to him?

"Sure," said Badalato. "Give it to him."

Later in the day, Michael Akin, the business agent from IATSE 479 came into production and walked around, looking into offices and asking crew questions. Akin did not stop in the bullpen, although crew immediately told Badalato he was walking around. Badalato nodded but he didn't get up. It wasn't the normal process for a visitor but then as the union rep, he was more than a visitor.

The full name of IATSE extends past the five-letter acronym: The International Alliance of Theatrical Stage Employees, Moving Picture Technicians, Artists and Allied Crafts of the United States, its Territories and Canada. It included many different movie departments, from costume to construction to craft services, props and set dressing, grips and electricians, even special effects and schoolteachers. The 479 local encompassed all of Georgia, except Savannah and vicinity, and all of Alabama.

Unions were in decline in a lot of parts in the country, but not Georgia. IATSE had done its part but so had the state. Local 479 had 300 members in 2005, when tax credits were first instituted by Georgia. By 2012, it had grown to 1,300 members, a number that rose to 1,800 in mid-2013. The paced slowed somewhat but it was still growing. By August 2016, Local 479 would have more than 2,100 members.

Akin had received a tip he felt he needed to investigate, although it wasn't clear what. He was there to look out for his people. Once he finished his self-guided tour, he came back to the bullpen and stopped at Badalato's door. The accountant had joined Badalato in his office by then to discuss something and their conversation stopped. There was a raised voice and the meeting quickly disbanded, the accountant walking down the hall toward his office and shaking his head. He took a seat at his desk but left the door open.

Akin, who had walked into the bullpen from the hall in front of Badalato's door, said something in the direction of the accountant. It seemed somewhat aggressive. The accountant stood up from his desk and came to his door to look at him. "Just what kind of jurisdiction do you think you have?" he asked, a look of disbelief on his face.

"I have a helluva lot of jurisdiction!" replied Akin.

"Not with the 871," said the accountant, who wouldn't have been in the role if it were up to Central Casting. "You don't have jurisdiction over me." IATSE 871 was another branch of the union. It represented production accountants, script supervisors, production and art department coordinators and the respective department assistants, among others.

There was nervous silence in the bullpen, all heads in laptops, as the accountant went back into his office and sat down, again leaving the door open. Akin continued into the interior of the building, stopping in one of the unused offices to use the phone. He patrolled a little longer and then left. Someone watched him drive away and reported back.

Then everyone started talking at once. What just happened? What had Akin said to the accountant? Had everyone heard that? Was that normal? Over time, crew was asked the same question: Are Unions good or bad for the industry? Everyone agreed they were good, to a person, including Badalato. Collective bargaining gave crew a voice they would not have otherwise and it established rules, which meant everyone knew what to expect. It also did a lot to ensure safety on set. Most believed the unions deserved a lot of credit for the strength and stability of the industry.

Badalato said Akin was trying to do his job. The UPM's maternal grandfather had been a well-known union man. Steve D'Inzillo led efforts to unionize projectionists in New York City in the 1930s. He became business agent of New York Projectionists Local 306 in 1945. Movies were taking off in popularity and there were thousands of positions in screening rooms. It wasn't just movie houses, but museums and libraries, producer-distributors, film laboratories. In the late '40s there were more than 2,400 trained projectionists. By 1999, there were fewer than 500. D'Inzillo remained active in the union until shortly before his death at 90 in 2000.

The better question for Badalato was whether he found it ironic that he took fire from all sides. Half the department heads were angry because he wouldn't let them hire from LA. Now he had the guy from the union, a man who paid close attention to local hires and was well-acquainted with state employees who oversaw the use of tax credits, aiming for him, as well.

"The UPM makes people mad on both sides of a lot of issues," he shrugged. "It's that kind of job."

While the production office had come to grips with Badalato's attitude about saving money, other departments hadn't come to it as readily. The most vocal point of contention had been limiting whom department heads could hire from where. The general consensus was broader. Grumbling that the budget was too lean for the caliber of the cast and the ambitiousness of the project continued to build. Most creative managers had been open about that.

"It's top heavy with some of the biggest actors in the world. Does it make sense to have a cheap-looking movie?"

"Wait 'til he sees what it costs to light that. He's going to be pissed."

"There are 4,000 extras. That isn't a small movie."

The last comment came after Turteltaub had added more extras to the mix. Background actors weren't paid a lot but it added up. On top of that, additional crew was needed to manage them, and all of them had to be fed. Samuels and Badalato worked numbers and found a way to give Turteltaub what he wanted.

In the bullpen the craft service challenge was coming to a conclusion. Both vendors went all out for the gig. The second one had more variety and quality vegetarian fare. A lot of people passed in and out of the kitchen during their display. One of the accountants picked up two plates of food, passing a small group gathered in the hall between the kitchen and bullpen.

Rake, Peterson and Samuels had stopped to graze on samples when the topic of background actors in the movie came up, and the increase to the total number of extras. Badalato and Samuels were still interviewing people for the extras casting job.

Peterson, who ultimately had to manage background actors, noted that was a lot of extras, particularly since Turteltaub wanted them to look good.

"We want the extras to have a high-end look," agreed Samuels, adding there were always a lot of background actors planned.

"Have you seen the people at the really nice Vegas resorts?" she replied. "They're all beautiful. It's like they're genetically perfect."

"That's true," said Samuels.

"Atlanta extras will not come with the look of Vegas extras," pressed Peterson.

"I'm confident we'll be fine," said Samuels.

Rake finished chomping on a Bird's Nest, a veggie appetizer with shredded hash browns that was the crowd favorite from the tryout. But he didn't say anything.

There wasn't much wiggle room as far as Samuels was concerned. The penthouse scenes that took up a big part of the movie would be shot in Atlanta. There would be challenges that came with that, one of them being ensuring Atlanta extras could pass as high-end Vegas party goers, but they weren't making a change. Everything in Atlanta was less expensive than Vegas. That was the point. Now they had to make it work.

It would be up to the extras casting people -- and the Costume department -- to make the human props in the penthouse scene look like they were in upscale Sin City.

The group disbanded and Rake and Peterson resumed work in the AD office. Rake and Turteltaub would leave for Las Vegas the following day to scout and he and Peterson had a lot to coordinate before he left. For one thing, they had scouted Barnesville, Ga., a town about an hour from Atlanta, earlier in the week. It was on for storefront location for the 1955 opening, "at least for now," Rake said. The actors in the opening scene would be teenagers, a little older than first planned, to strengthen the scene that established the history and relationship of the four heroes.

Simpson would get to work on that and otherwise hold down the fort in Atlanta.

An issue arose around Pink's next meeting with the actors in New York. She wanted to hold them in the more typical fashion, by setting up a space at a hotel for formal fittings. Production thought it would save money if they held the fittings at the actors' homes. Jobst and Peterson were in the bullpen talking about it. Crew, even department heads, didn't just call the actors unless they had established contact. There were too many departments working to have all of them reaching out. Peterson was in touch with them and on occasion served as liaison.

"I am calling Kevin Kline next," the 2nd AD said. "I'll see if he's available Friday the 21st. Michael Douglas is available, at least he said he's not planning anything else. He's in Bedford that day but probably going to be in the city on the afternoon of the 21st. That means he could be in earlier for this and available mid-morning?"

"If she can do a fitting for those two on that day, that would work," said Jobst. "The question remains for Morgan. Is he going to be around?"

"Morgan is in Shreveport but I don't know where he's going from this point forward," said Peterson, who was about to walk into her office. "Jeremiah talked to his agent about Dayna calling, and the agent said it's okay to call him directly."

"Oh, they've talked, they're buddies," Jobst said. "He's going to be in L.A. The only thing I was hoping for was some help from production."

Peterson stopped to look at Jobst, who delicately continued on. It didn't make sense for Pink to travel to Freeman. "That throws us off with money and time and everything." This was a large cast and meeting with each of the major actors at their homes wasn't practical.

"What would you like me to do?" Peterson, who had a way with tone, asked with sincerity.

"I just think we need help when they say, 'come to my house,'" she said. "What if production called and said they'd like to schedule it?' It gives Dayna an out with these guys. Then she can say, 'I'll be in east Rutherford N.J. Let me check with the ADs, since they are handling logistics.'"

Peterson said she didn't mind that. There were budget limits that weren't up to her.

Jobst knew exactly where that was going. She said the Costume department knew how they would like to do it. The best option was to create temporary fitting rooms at a hotel in New York that was used to accommodating such requests. They had suites for it. They'd bring Freeman in to the fitting rooms at Warner Bros. Costume Dept. in Los Angeles, since that was convenient for him.

Jobst said she met with Badalato, who told her to come up with a price. With Warner Bros. shipping, the hotel rooms and other space needed, along with other assorted expenses, the total would probably be about $25,000. He had naturally resisted and final word was still out. Jobst continued with her pitch. Peterson wasn't the decision maker but it wouldn't hurt to have her on board.

There were significant costs involved no matter what. Personal meetings involved shipping costumes to the homes of each of the actors. Then there was transporting Pink and the assistant designer to those locations and housing them. Then it all had to be undone and shipped back. But the real cost was the time it took to do it all, particularly flying Pink around. With a condensed prep period, there wasn't time to spare.

Jobst could see that made sense to Peterson.

"The thing is, none of us are authorized to approve that kind of expense," said Peterson. "It's the size of the expense. It wipes you out," she said.

"It is the least attractive," Jobst said, seemingly in agreement that the hotel was too pricey. "I mean, other than not having a fitting."

That much was out of the question. They had to have fittings. Peterson said she would help pull it together.

The next topic was the updated script, which had just been released. The script still had a wet T-shirt scene, part of a big pool party. The crew had discussed the scene before and none of them were fans.

"JESSICA, sinfully hot in white T-shirt and nothing underneath, gets hosed down as she grinds and bounces in front of ..." The name was uppercased in the script because the character was appearing for the first time.

Jobst had not been around for the earlier discussion. What did she think?

She laughed. "When I read it the first time I thought, 'Check. There's the obligatory Vegas bathing suit scene.'" Her bigger concern was spraying down the character. That meant the Costume department had to provide a dry wardrobe changes for each take.

Peterson had gone over to the fax machine to send something but she was listening.

"Oh, there's not going to be a wet T-shirt contest in this movie," she said.

Everyone looked at her expectantly. Maybe she knew something they didn't.

"It's still in the script," Stephens offered.

But Peterson said she knew that. It was more just a sense she had. The scene was problematic and they didn't need it for story. There are other ways to get a sense of hot women without hosing them down. It wasn't just that running water on a movie set is a pain, she said, Jobst nodding in agreement. There were ratings to consider.

"Watch," Peterson said, with conviction. "There will not be a wet T-shirt contest in this movie."

CHAPTER SIX
5 Weeks Out
Sept. 17-21

TURTELTAUB WAS IN THE AIR so much there might have been contrails in the sky. After the weekend in L.A. with his family and one day of work he returned to Vegas for a scout Tuesday. He flew back to Burbank that night and made the quick trip to the Warner Bros. costume offices for the 8:30 p.m. "Wardrobe Show and Tell." Pink's formal presentation also included Amy Baer, the key creative producer. It was an opportunity for everyone to give input.

Pink and the assistant designer spent the day setting up for it, although in effect they had been preparing all along. Clothing racks held some individual costumes but the real focus was on the black display boards. The presentation boards depicted every costume planned for each major actor in the movie.

Costume designers don't just pick clothes for the actors to wear. Their job is to help tell the story. "Billy Gherson," the character to be played by Michael Douglas, was a rich, successful attorney. Morgan Freeman's character, "Archie," was a laid back grandfather with health issues. Robert De Niro would play "Paddy," a still-grieving widower who wasn't getting out of the house much. Kevin Kline was "Sam," a youthful retiree in Florida bored with his life with permission from his wife to cheat.

Pink designed the costumes to reveal the characters, something she and Turteltaub had batted around most recently at their breakfast in Atlanta. Billy's look would be tailored while Paddy's a little disorganized, given his wife had helped dress him and she was gone. Archie would wear comfortable clothes appropriate for a grandfather and a man content in his place in life while Sam's look would reflect a man trying to look younger than his age.

Another group of presentation boards depicted the actors as a group. It wasn't just what Billy, the rich lawyer, would wear. It was also how it looked next to Paddy, a former pub owner, Sam the accountant and Archie, the retired cop.

Given the number of ensemble scenes, it was important to see how the costumes looked in relation to others. It was entirely too easy to have the costumes of two actors clash on camera.

Turteltaub and the producers liked what they saw and happily signed off. He would stay the rest of the week in L.A. for the first time since he had started prep, meeting with potential music supervisors and interviewing cast for a key role, a young sidekick to the retirement-age character. It was almost a reverse of the previous week, when he started in Atlanta, went to Vegas, and then to L.A.

But the blueprint for *Last Vegas* was coming to life. Turteltaub liked the MGM Grand sidewalk for a frolic with all the principal actors, which was good given the relationship with MGM. It was the same thing for a set on top of the Stratosphere Hotel & Casino, which would be the scene of a date for characters played by Douglas and Steenburgen. It also looked good for shooting the airport scenes at McCarran Airport, which would be ideal. Airports weren't always up for the movie business. Finally, there was the Neon Museum, a graveyard of old Vegas signs, which wasn't in the original script but promised to be great visually.

Those plans took the movie through principal photography but Turteltaub was also considering post-production. If the crew on the front end were the miners, and the director the alchemist, the people in the darkened offices six months or more down the road were the metallurgists.

Just as crew was being hired to manage all the details needed to tell the story from Atlanta and Las Vegas, the creative producers were starting to drill down on post-production talent. That was a different set of plans all together. Post wouldn't start until mid-January but they needed to get key players scheduled.

"It's as important as anything that happens in production," said Turteltaub. You could get the best actors, and coax the best performances from them. You could hire inventive minds to run departments, and the best crew to mine the creative material. You could have brilliant producers who planned distribution and marketing and then execute well. But if the post-production team didn't transform it all into a reasonably good story, you had nothing.

Two editors would start when photography began, working from afar but involved day-to-day. Everyone else wouldn't come on board until after wrap. They would handle color grading and visual effects and sound mixing and design, sound effects, foley and automated dialog replacement, or ADR. Foley created sounds that audio didn't pick up, like the rustling of a jacket or footsteps, while ADR -- looping -- synced sound with the actors. Even music -- a composer to write the score for the movie, studio musicians to play certain parts and then an orchestra to fill it out -- was a thought gaining momentum and that was one of the last things that happened. And for the producers, it wasn't too soon to think about any of it.

Amy Baer focused the week on music supervisors, whose job it was to coordinate the work of the composer, editor and sound mixers. Three interviews were scheduled at Gidden Media, her company. All of the candidates, two of them duos, were powerhouse players who worked almost constantly. All had long credits, one going back decades. Collectively the candidates had been behind the scenes on projects as diverse as *Black Swan*, *Fright Night* and *My Week With Marilyn*. There was also a duo actively at work on Quentin Tarantino's current project, *Django Unchained*.

The audio and visual data were collected and managed separately. The raw visual data captured each day would be sent to a lab, which would process it and send out dailies. Picture editors would be in the background, reviewing the dailies and organizing them. They had a picture editor in mind, one in particular. It was someone Turteltaub had worked with before.

When principal photography began the director would be absorbed in every shot, pushing the actors to do more, getting every angle, trying different options. But time was of the essence and he had scheduled shots he had to make. Being able to trust the person in the background reviewing dailies for content took a layer of stress away.

Back in Atlanta they were finalizing the hire of a script supervisor, who was also someone Turteltaub had used before. The script supervisor sat next to the director in the course of photography, helping with continuity and keeping track of the work done. At the end of each shooting day, they produced a production report. It documented the number of scenes shot, number of camera sets ups, and number of script pages contained in the completed work. It reflected the total work done and what remained, broken down by the same measures. And it contained other details, like the film roll or card numbers associated with the material.

The script coordinator worked most closely with the director, tracking which takes were the best, talking to actors if they missed lines, getting information from the Camera department that identified codes for film rolls or digital cards that matched up to the work done for the day. They coordinated with the video assist who controlled playback, and helped anyone who had a question about continuity.

Occasionally, the script supervisor also worked with the editor. Editing didn't start until post-production but that person would be on board during principal photography, reviewing dailies. It was a new trend in the digital age. Turteltaub planned to use the same editor he'd worked with on several projects.

While the creative team had been scouting Las Vegas on a nearly weekly basis since prep began, another type of scout was in the works. Badalato and Kamishin were planning the Production department scout, which would be a one-time event where they drilled down on the things they specifically had to manage. There would also be an Art department scout at the same time and they would join efforts at certain points.

All of it was happening on a condensed time period, which would include them working on the weekend. Badalato, in true form, didn't want to spend any more money than necessary. The rooms booked for crew weren't going to be comped like the ones during principal photography and he didn't want to spend the money. They needed a production scout but the more efficiently they could get it done, the better.

The Production and Art department scouts included Badalato and Kamishin, 2nd AD Peterson, and the art director, assistant art director, set decorator and prop master. The four days included travel time, flying on Saturday, working on Sunday and returning Tuesday. They would meet with the locations manager and a production manager there. They would also meet with Bomba and Rake to talk details. Meetings and consultations with Aria officials, since most of it would be shot at the resort, were planned in advance.

Sorting out how they would use the 3,000 room nights provided by MGM as part of its exchange with Four Fellas was just the start. Aria Casino and Resort was a huge facility with 4 million square feet in City Center on the Vegas strip, a highly congested area. They had to figure out where offices would go, where they were in relation to everything else, where to park trucks and trailers, where to store equipment, where to hold extras, and how and where to feed everyone. The Locations department would coordinate permits and get police and other government permissions, but it had to be supported by production. Then there was security.

Food presented the biggest challenge to production because it wasn't included in the agreement with the Aria. Thousands of meals would be served over the course of the month of production. There were two groups to be fed, crew and extras, and each had to be managed differently. The strict rules governing what food could be brought into the resort made all of it a gauntlet. Crew could be fed in the cafeteria, provided the movie reimbursed the Aria, but was it workable? Figuring out where to hold and feed extras was another layer of complexity.

Housing required a lot of organization and not just because of the number of people. The more they had it planned, the less they'd have to hear complaints. To some degree status would be based on floor. The higher the floor, the better the view. Plenty of rooms on the fourth floor, where the offices would be, overlooked casino roof. Those would be less than desirable.

But the priority was the actors, who would be provided the 6,000-square-foot Sky Suites at Aria. Douglas, Freeman, Kline and Steenburgen would stay there. It was a good example of the "Most Favored Nations" agreement, where the actors were entitled to the same treatment. These suites were fabulous and comparable.

De Niro preferred the villas atop Caesar's Palace. Those residences were closer to 10,000 square feet, the size of the soon-to-be auctioned home of famed Hollywood producer Richard Zanuck, who died in June. The villas were considered by many to be the nicest of all extreme luxury accommodations in Sin City. The one slated for De Niro had four bedrooms, a living room with working marble fireplace, formal dining room, exercise room, media room with 10-foot television, and rooftop area par excellence. Caesar's Palace offered other amenities, including a private jet service for its high rollers and a private hangar facility for VIPs, like De Niro, who wanted to bring their own planes.

The reason the production cared about where De Niro stayed was because they had to get him to set. A portal-to-portal agreement meant the actors' days began when they left their accommodations, not when they arrived at work. While they were in Las Vegas they clocked the transportation time to Aria from Caesar's Palace. It was probably just a five or 10-minute commute time to get the actor back and forth.

All of the main actors had the choice of opting out of the suites provided to them at Aria, but that didn't mean the movie production would pay the bill. De Niro had an ongoing relationship with Caesar's Palace, the Roman Empire-themed casino resort, which first opened in 1966 and consistently kept up with the times. A plan was on the table to create the first Nobu Hotel within Caesars Palace, following the huge success of the Nobu restaurant chain, although it hadn't been announced yet.

The actor was approaching his 30 year anniversary as a principal in the chain of high-quality Japanese-style restaurants and adding a second Vegas location made sense, particularly if they were going to link it to the brand new enterprise, Nobu Hospitality. The hotel, slated for 180 rooms, would replace what was currently Centurion Towers.

Chef and proprietor Nobuyuki Matsuhisa had opened his first U.S. restaurant in Beverly Hills in January 1987. That's where he met De Niro, who was so impressed by the caliber of food he sought out the chef. Story has it that it took several years of urging on the part of the actor, but in 1994 they opened the first Nobu in New York City in 1994. Now there were dozens of the restaurants on six continents.

De Niro's love of New York was well known although the past few months had been bumpy. He and wife Grace Hightower had recently been displaced from their penthouse at the Brentmore at 88 Central Park on the Upper West Side. A fire in their clothes dryer significantly damaged their home along with others in the building. They had temporarily rented the penthouse on the 35th floor at 15th Central Park West once occupied by Yankee Alex Rodriguez. When De Niro was in New York, that is. The actor worked voraciously. *Last Vegas* wasn't the only movie he had slated for release in 2013. There was also *The Big Wedding*, *Killing Season* and *American Hustle*. He was currently working in France on *The Family*.

Douglas and Freeman were at the pinnacle of long careers, as well, and could work as much as they wanted. The same could be said of Kline, who was more inclined to the theater stage than the others. Steenburgen was also in high demand. None of them worked with the appetite of De Niro. Like De Niro, Freeman would fly to Vegas by personal jet.

Freeman spent a lot of time at his 124-acre ranch outside of Charleston, Miss. The property was centered by a hacienda-style mansion with gabled roofs. It had a pond large enough to be a lake, and a barn with horses. It was a gorgeous place dotted with magnolia trees that he purchased from his parents in 1991. He had hired people to work on in it over the years but he'd also done a lot of the work himself. At one time the actor also had an interest in a blues club about an hour from his home. That was the extent of his non-movie or television projects, in terms of what was publicly known.

Douglas spent a lot of time at his country estate in Bedford, N.Y., with wife Catherine Zeta Jones. There were tabloid rumors of some marital trouble but they still shared the 6,600-square-foot mansion on five or six acres with their two children. The country estate had stables and horses, a swimming pool and spa and workout area, but was modest enough to fit in with upper class Bedford.

Kline lived in New York City with wife, actress Phoebe Cates, and their two children.

So many people out of the Mailing Avenue offices meant the phones rang less and there were fewer people to make requests of the production crew in the bullpen. That meant many items on its list were getting scratched through. One was a decision on De Niro's reinforced paper.

Various documents, whether the script, the call sheet, or anything else shared, changed colors when revised to ensure everyone worked from the same version. Signs posted on the wall made sure everyone knew the colors and the order: "*Last Vegas* Script Color Revisions: White, Blue, Pink, Yellow, Green, Goldenrod, Buff, Salmon, Cherry, Tan, Grey, Ivory, Orchid, Revision Blue." By now the copier room was neatly organized, stacks of colored paper organized on the back end of the table with hole-punchers and staplers. But not a single sheet was reinforced.

It had taken some effort but Simpson found reinforced paper that was available in the colors needed and abundant enough to fit the demand. She needed all the colors in the hierarchy up front if possible as there wouldn't be time to look for them later. The price was somewhere near $300 for 1,200 sheets. "It could be worse," someone offered. Simpson looked aghast. "Do you know how much paper I can buy for $300?"

Assuming the numbers were right, the colored paper with reinforced edge for De Niro's script would cost 25 cents a sheet. Basic white paper came in at less than a penny.

Simpson's process included a rough estimate of what a PA's time would be to periodically sit for a couple of hours to add 348 circles to the script but one factor couldn't be quantified. Having to siphon off a PA in the midst of shooting to affix the reinforcements could present problems if they were slammed.

"It isn't a good use of their time," she said.

Next there were camera rental quotes and certificates of insurance for locations, since several spots had been confirmed in Atlanta. The timing of the camera quotes had come with Hennings. He had a relationship with Panavision in Los Angeles, where he generally got equipment, but Simpson was comparing other options ala Badalato. The certificates provided owners of property leased to shoot scenes proof of $2 million coverage in the event of damage.

Stephens had overseen the creation of the paperwork bookcase, which had 20 different areas labeled. It was becoming more full with things like the crew information sheet, office supply order form, directions to various places. Many others, like the daily call sheet, would be added when photography started. There were constant projects under way and she kept the PAs organized.

She also had an extensive file system, folders and other organization tools in place. It looked like it could be overkill but for one important thing. She wasn't just planning the framework for document flow and other paperwork needed during production. She was doing it in a way to make it easier when it came time for wrap, when the movie shut down. The better organized she was now, the easier that would be.

"This is why they call it 'prep,'" she said.

Stephens balanced it with good humor. She was almost always upbeat. That day she'd gone to the Art department and when she returned to the bullpen she saw someone shooting photos. She approached stealthily through the hall and then leaped into the room, squarely into the frame. It was an exceptional photo bomb, Stephens at her best, lightweight and energized. It had been quiet in the bullpen at that moment and that jarred the room loose.

Jordan Anderson coordinated signage. In addition to updating interior office doors they were personalizing signs for parking spaces. The system ensured premium spaces were reserved for higher ups and key crew. There were plenty of parking spaces in front of Mailing Avenue at this point, but they would become increasingly scarce as the production grew. Badalato had leased a neighboring lot for the eventual overflow for people who didn't get a spot.

Anderson had quickly turned into one of the most nimble and engaged of the production assistants. She was resourceful and listened for an opportunity to help, before a request came in. Generally dressed in a white T-shirt with her hair pulled back in a ponytail, she didn't shy away from jobs that required lifting or carrying.

It was a normal bullpen day, if subdued, when word came from Las Vegas that there had been a conflict. Someone on the crew had pissed off a studio executive. A call that two studio executives would be coming to town Thursday -- weeks ahead of schedule -- set the place abuzz. Later, Badalato called from Vegas with a memo he needed prepared for each department. It arrived later in the day along with a note that he wanted signed confirmation of receipt.

MEMO
From the desk of Billy Badalato
Last Vegas
TO BE HAND DELIVERED
To: <u>All Department Heads and Supervisors</u>
David Bomba
Mark Garner
Dayna Pink
Jennifer Jobst
Patrick Cassidy
John Findley
Dwight Benjamin
CC: Jeremiah Samuels
Accountant
Damiana Kamishin

RE: Department Budget Meetings
Date: Friday, Sept. 14

All department budgets were due on Thursday (9/20) for in-person meetings with Jeremiah Samuels, me, David Ruben [CBS Films] and Matt Leonetti [Good Universe], who will be visiting from Los Angeles for this purpose.

<u>Budgets Outstanding Currently</u>
Wardrobe
Set Dressing
Locations
Props

Please acknowledge receipt and contents of this memo by signing below.

Print Name
Signature
Thank you for your cooperation in this matter, BB

It was rare that studio brass wanted to meet with individual crew, particularly a lot of them. No one could remember it happening.

Badalato noticed that offices in the executive suites had not been updated with the names of the visiting executives. Anderson had two each on her desk, one for the office and one for the parking space. Given one of the men had a driver, the sign for the parking space wouldn't be needed.

Someone said it looked like production got new equipment while other departments got used equipment, but it wasn't true. Almost all the equipment was used. The Production department had internalized the Badalato budget mentality early on. Restraint had been a steady undercurrent -- from limits on lunch to precision paper orders to used refrigerators.

There had been cases where Four Fellas bought brand-new big-ticket items. The top-of-the-line copier machine that Badalato had ordered early on was a good example. It had been heavily used. The Art department had its own printers but still would send jobs to the top-of-the-line copier because of its capabilities. Its biggest responsibility would be collating and printing scripts at a rapid rate.

Badalato had his reasons. "An older washing machine or refrigerator rarely breaks and it's unlikely to embarrass you if it does," he said. Too much goes wrong with older copiers and the risk of one breaking down at the wrong time far outweighed any potential savings. The thought of waiting for a technician to arrive to repair an older machine while 100-plus cast and crew wait for revised scripts -- on the time clock -- was more than he could stand.

Samuels arrived on Mailing Avenue first thing Tuesday morning and went right to the accountant's office.

"Is everything good? I want to make sure we have everything but-toned down for these guys."

"We're good," said the accountant.

Badalato and Kamishin returned Tuesday night and were in early Wednesday. A meeting on the production scout soon filled the office, this one with Samuels present, since he hadn't seen them much in Vegas. Buddy was in his large pen in the back and delighted to see everyone.

Despite the volume of questions answered during the scout in Vegas numerous logistical issues remained. There was space set aside inside the

Aria's giant hotel that would house the Accounting, Production and AD departments, as well as the director and producers. That still left all the other departments. Aria had offered up a space off-site that at one time had been a sales office but wasn't being used. They didn't know until they saw it that it would work.

The remote office space for departments was called the Annex. It had a kitchen and was more than big enough to contain the Art, Costumes, Transportation, Set Decorating and Props departments. Each would have private offices and room for storage aside from Transportation, which didn't need it.

"It's a huge building," said Badalato. "They have room to unload in front of it. There's plenty of space for wardrobe, same with the Art department, plenty of room for storage."

Better, he said, it was big enough that there was no need to rent space. "That saves us money we don't have."

Samuels nodded his approval, and asked, "Is it fenced?"

"Yes. It's well lit, but we'll still want security," Kamishin answered. "Just one guy, sitting on the camera truck with a machete. That should be it." It garnered a laugh.

There was a distance between the Annex and the offices for the rest of the production within the Aria. It took about 15 minutes to go between the two, by foot or shuttle. It was a longish walk from the hotel past retail and restaurants and bars to get to it down the block. Taking one of the van shuttles the Teamsters would be operating would be just as long, given it had to wind around city streets and past pedestrians and street lights.

Then there were the technical needs of the movie.

"We identified where the generators will go," said Badalato. "We can have the camera and generator out front. We put the cable on it, do our business, and we're done."

"Good. What about the footprint for the condors?" asked Samuels. "I'm worried about cracking concrete."

Turteltaub wanted certain kinds of shots that required cranes, which could hoist lighting and camera equipment. He and the cinematographer were going over the details as part of their prep. Now production was trying to make it happen.

"We can fit a technocrane but we cannot use a condor. We can use scissor lifts, but nothing big," Badalato said. "Big silks are not going to happen unless we use scissor lifts. That's all we can do." The silks diffuse light, making it softer.

Samuels asked about the pool. The script called for a large pool party and a lot of extras. It would be late October by then. What about weather? What about light? They looked at Peterson.

"The pool is a special nightmare," she said. "6:30 is sun up and it's dark by 5, but it's unshootable by late afternoon. We could go toward the boys for close-ups but that's about it."

They had talked to Aria's property manager about changing the opacity of the water and had been given the go-ahead. "We can make it a darker blue, if we're worried about reflection."

Then the topic turned to hotel rooms. The agreement with Aria would comfortably cover everything needed in terms of housing. Whoever had struck that deal had been right on the money. "There are three for ADs, four PA rooms, other operational rooms. There are actors' assistants rooms, plus one for hair and makeup," said Kamishin. There were others for personal assistants. There were the people above the line, Turteltaub and the producers, as well as the studio executives.

"Not everyone is going to be staying at the hotel," said Peterson. "Morgan Freeman's assistant said he wants to stay at the Mandarin."

The sky villas and other suites at Aria were high-quality and perfect for the primary actors' accommodations.

"De Niro is definitely going to stay at Caesar's Palace, which could add another 30 minutes," said Peterson. That was the worst-case scenario and including traffic for his commute to and from Aria.

"What about Mary Steenburgen? She doesn't work every single day we're there."

"She'll have a suite."

Badalato said they didn't need to figure it out now, given variables at play, as long as they had the broad strokes right. Each actor still could decide, as De Niro had, to stay somewhere else.

"Let's plan to have their rooms anyway, including De Niro," said Samuels. "That way we're covered."

"Absolutely," said Badalato. "I'm getting a floor plan. We will be assigning rooms. It should work fine."

The last item on the list was food. Understanding the rules of Aria and how to work with and around them would be key. The limitations on what could be brought inside were firm. Refrigerators were only allowed in some rooms. It still wasn't clear whether microwaves would be permitted. But they had discovered another twist when they were there: No food could be taken outside of the cafeteria. That meant crew couldn't go down before call and get something to eat later when they had more time.

It was the distance to the cafeteria that made that challenging. It was far away to go on break just to pick something up, much less to have to sit down and eat it. It took about 15 minutes to get from the hotel rooms to the cafeteria for employees, which was on the other side and below the giant casino floor. To get there required going down the elevators from the hotel, through the casino and the employees-only doors, through a series of hallways and then down an underground escalator.

Managing the extras was another matter entirely. Peterson said they had identified an adequate holding area where they could stay -- if Aria signed off. But feeding them was another challenge entirely. The agreement with the resort casino only allowed the crew to use the cafeteria.

"We'll do a one-hour walk away lunch for the crew, with access to the dining room," answered Badalato, couching the answer in union terms. "Extras feeding ... not sure. Let's put a tbd on that."

Samuels nodded in agreement and the meeting disbanded.

An assortment of Art department people took chairs around the large table in the middle of the Boom Boom Room to get ready for the conference call about product placement. Lipp set up the call on the speakerphone in the center, while people from the Costume and Production departments signed in from their respective offices elsewhere on Mailing Avenue.

Product placement would happen on two levels. The top level was the studio, including a vice president at CBS Films who would be on the call. The other was Movie Mogul Inc., an entertainment marketing company that specialized in product placement, which had organized the meeting. On the highest level, a product could be added into the script provided the producers agreed to the deal.

Deborah Harpur, CEO of Movie Mogul, introduced herself and noted others on her team, and then settled in. "We're going to create an email integration team to help us decide if we're a Coors versus Miller movie," she said brightly. It was a light segue to what sounded like a pitch about what her company could do to help the Set decorating, Props and Costume departments.

Movie Mogul had relationships with 700 brands, "a shopping list," that ran from bathrobes to craft services, automobiles to appliances. Whether that was a precise figure or just to demonstrate connections didn't matter. She said the company also could get items not on the list. They understood deadlines, she continued, and would get things delivered to departments when agreed. And in this case, it would also be to the right place, whether Vegas or Atlanta. The pitch showed a thorough understanding of the script and the production, as well as common frustrations in dealing with third parties providing goods.

The timing was right. Departments were actively making decisions about what was needed for a scene or character. With tight budgets this was helpful. "You let us know what you need. We'll do all the outreach. We work with Ashley to make sure there are no issues with clearance," she said, a reference to Ashley Kravitz, who was already contracted to work with *Last Vegas*. Her company, Cleared By Ashley Inc., obtained and documented the legal permission needed to use a product on screen.

What did they need? Benjamin-Creel asked about eyeglasses, sunglasses and watches. Someone on the Movie Mogul side named a high-end watchmaker that seemed ideal but lamented that despite logic, wasn't interested. "They want to be seen on younger actors. Not that they don't adore the cast, they do," she said. "But they're thinking about the demo that's going to see this film." The frustration, she added, was that it was an older demographic that purchased high-end watches.

With eyeglasses there were a number of options, including several companies Movie Mogul routinely worked with, but there was a pause. "A larger retailer, like LensCrafter -- there may be another level of deal there," she said. Higher end deals would be coordinated through the studio.

The executive from CBS Films said the airline deal, or at least the proposal for one, was in. That would involve a specific airline being featured in the movie. There were two airport scenes and another two scenes inside a plane, although it wasn't clear the same airline would be seen in all four.

Patrick Cassidy, the set director, weighed in on slot machines. Someone had sent an email to MGM about using its trademarked one-arm bandits. It appeared they would be available for use in the set they were recreating in Atlanta, but the production company would have to cover shipping to and from Vegas. He also gave the name of the new set decorating coordinator who had just been hired and would soon start. She would be handling a lot of the details.

It was already established that Pink wasn't on the call and Jobst had stayed quiet, prompting Movie Mogul to seek her out. "Question for Jennifer, 'Have you made any decisions about shoes?'" "We haven't yet," Jobst replied. "We are reaching out to talent reps." Costume designers work closely with the actors and the best practice was to ask their people, first, if they had a preferred shoemaker or clothing designer. In some cases it was part of the actor's package that they use their own people, although Jobst didn't go into that.

Another topic diverted the discussion but it soon circled back. "Jennifer, another wardrobe question. What will they be wearing into the party? Shooting the scene where they're being fitted, will you need multiples of those?" The story had the actors buying new suits for the party they planned. One scene in particular promised to be a fashion display. It was after the characters have new suits and walk alongside one another showing them off. Several of the crew at the table in the Boom Boom Room looked at each other as they waited for Jobst to answer the question from her office in the Costume department.

"Dayna's already working on that," Jobst said. "That's one of our main priorities. It's through a custom tailor." The voice on the other end said she understood a specific shop was being used as part of product placement. The costume supervisor said that was the first she had heard of it. "Dayna would need to be involved," she answered, with what was turning out to be customary understatement. "I'll let her know."

Gradually the meeting wound down and it was back to Harpur. At this point the movie was in the process of determining whether a particular brand would be product integration or a product statement, she said. "That will determine whether it's a fee-based or a backend promotional program."

It was a lovely bouquet of corporate language. What it meant to the crew in simple language was whether or not they had to use the product. A brand that got into the script -- say, Aria -- was assured of being on screen. That meant departments included it as they planned. To that end, the Art department had an earlier conference call regarding Sky Villa furnishings for the penthouse set they were including. Since that deal was already inked, the call included people from Aria, people from Aria/MGM, which was the corporate side, and CBS Films.

There was another layer where a product would be seen on camera. It wasn't a full "statement," to use the marketing vernacular, more of a mention. Ultimately whether something was provided and even integrated didn't guarantee it ended up on camera. Some deals only paid if it did. Regardless, it could still be useful to the company who provided the product because it could be stated in marketing.

The departments involved, Costumes, Set Decorating and Props, had plenty of things they needed. They were more than happy to tap the resources offered by Movie Mogul.

There would be regular group emails to keep them all in touch. "We will send status reports, what's been offered, what is still pending, who has declined." The spreadsheet would highlight anything new. It was easy and fast to read, she promised. "Check it to see if what you want has potentially been found," she said. If not, they should reach out. Movie Mogul was "super friendly."

After the call they resumed their regular work. By day's end members of the crew had pieced together a story about what had happened in Vegas that hadn't stayed in Vegas. The production designer had spoken truth to power, to paraphrase one of Badalato's wall sayings.

It had happened at a work dinner with eight people including Turteltaub, Samuels, studio executives, and key crew. The goal was to have a relaxed dinner and go over some of the locations. Studio executives aren't generally part of the movie prep process although they can be if they want. With Vegas close, and a relatively fun place, the production was seeing its share of visits from LA.

In the course of the get-together, the CBS Films production exec asked what he probably thought was a benign question or at least one in which he expected a benign answer.

"So, how's the show going?"

The production designer answered honestly.

"It would be going a lot better if you gave us the money we need to make it."

The echo of a knife clinking on a plate might have been heard for miles.

Bomba figured he was asked a direct question and he gave a direct answer. Never mind that this was Prickly Guy, who had run off an early second AD with tone at not having been personally notified of his hire. It was anti-climactic from there. The meetings between the executives and department heads, along with Badalato, Samuels and Kamishin, went off without a hitch

Wednesday afternoon. Each department meeting was slated for 90 minutes, although none of them took anywhere near that long.

By all accounts it amounted to a show of muscle. The executives reinforced that departments were not to exceed their budgets. It was a very loud reply to a comment a guy made at a dinner after a very long day but it did have the desired effect of silencing the topic.

Ironically, Prickly Guy slept a lot during the day. He arrived on Mailing Avenue feeling sick, and awhile later needed to lie down. Production showed him to the couch in the Boom Boom Room. The Art department conference room was windowless and aside from the light that seeped in through the rafters, it was fairly dark. The open-air ceiling meant some sound wafted in but otherwise it was a nice place to rest with air conditioning that blew through like Alaska. They tried to make him comfortable and then left him alone while he fended off some kind of stomach bug.

The executives were gone the next day, mission accomplished. Meanwhile, the invisible stress current that had pulsed through Mailing Avenue was gone like the flip of a switch.

A conversation was under way in the Props department about the studio executives' visit. Katrina Rice sat behind her desk on the left, her Pomeranian "Mango" in a dog bed at her feet. Propmaster Dwight Benjamin-Creel was in the desk on the right, the office small enough that the two desks met in the middle leaving room for a single chair for a visitor from the Art department. Props used its second office next door to store items.

Benjamin-Creel wore shorts and an orange button-down shirt and leaned back in his chair, his fingers laced behind his head. He had the look of a man who had been working in the movie business since 1985, most of that time in Georgia but not always. One of his best memories was from Minnesota when he worked on *Fargo* (1996).

The Coen brothers had sought his input with the famed wood chipper, more than any director before or since. Benjamin-Creel said they were so nice to work with that when a strike loomed, he went out of the way to help them in advance. That way, when the strike went into effect and he was required to stop work, what they needed was already in place. The prop master had come out of pocket for it and when he got to his car, he saw they had reimbursed him by leaving cash inside.

Fargo went on to win two Academy Awards, the Coens for Best Screenplay and Frances McDormand for best actress while the wood chipper went onto its own fame. In 2011, it went on permanent display at the Fargo Moorehead Convention and Visitors Bureau. But you don't know when you work on a movie that it will become iconic. Most of the time, it's just hard work, Benjamin-Creel said.

When Rice met him she was a new graduate of SCAD, the Savannah College of Art and Design. That was in 2007 on *Three Can Play That Game*. She told him right away she wanted to be a prop master, and he was delighted. In all the years he's worked on movies, he'd never heard a woman say that. Since then they had worked on *Zombieland*, *Footloose* and *Killing Season*, among other movies and television shows.

Last Vegas was typical in most ways. They agreed there was new acceptance, or at least resignation, to the budget limitations. Samuels and Badalato had gone over Benjamin-Creel's proposed budget again ahead of the meetings, shaving it by about 10 percent. It was now down to $70,000 where he initially requested $87,000. He said Samuels followed up with him later one-on-one.

"He wanted to know if I was sure I could make the smaller budget work," he said. "I said I thought I probably could."

Samuels told him he knew it was a pinch. His first budget proposal to do the movie, based on extensive number crunching, had been larger. It wasn't a dramatic difference, but the studio declined. It was clear, he told Benjamin-Creel, that if Samuels wanted to make the movie he had one option, and that was to make it at the smaller sum.

"Let me know if you run into trouble," Samuels told him. "I'll see what I can do."

Benjamin-Creel seemed to appreciate that offer. They reiterated they weren't going to add any money to the mix and Benjamin-Creel didn't ask for any. But he didn't mince words about the studio executives.

"They don't care about the movie," he said. "They care about how much money the movie can make." It wasn't said with disdain, more matter of fact. They were about business, he said, which lead to another point.

His pet peeve with journalistic accounts of the movie business was how often they referred to studio executives as "filmmakers."

"They are not filmmakers. They're film financiers," said Benjamin-Creel.

104

"What's the definition of a filmmaker?"

"It's someone actually involved in the making of a film."

Jon Turteltaub was a filmmaker, so was 1st AD Gary Rake. So was David Bomba and the entire Art department. The crew who made up the Props department, the Camera department, even the Production department although they weren't often on set -- all of them were filmmakers.

But you can't fly in from L.A. for a day and act as muscle to the bottom line and claim to be a filmmaker, he continued. "Then, you're a movie executive. Maybe you're really important and maybe you're even richer than you are important," he said. "But you aren't a filmmaker."

Rocko suddenly appeared at the door to see Mango. He and the smaller dog had a moment of play before Chloe Lipp arrived to claim her Frenchie. They were all friends. She asked Rice and Benjamin-Creel about lunch, since Props were technically part of the Art department and they ate together. That decided, the art department coordinator looked around the crowded office.

"Where's Triscuit?" she asked. The heritage of Rice's other dog was less certain than puffy Mango's, although she looked like she could be part Dingo.

"I left her at home," said Rice. "We're going to Inserection and I didn't want to leave her here."

Lipp laughed. "Have fun," she said, as she and Rocko departed.

Inserection was Atlanta's biggest sex store. Benjamin-Creel and Rice needed props for the bridesmaid scene in the movie, specifically penis hats as called for in the script. In Rice's view, penis hats were inauthentic and hence patently wrong for the scene. "I'm 29 and that's the age people get married," she said. "I've regularly gone to bachelorette parties for the past few years. And I can tell you women at bachelorette parties don't wear penis hats."

But the script called for penis hats and they would find them. Turteltaub had touched on it in their meeting but his point had been more expansive. The director said he didn't want to garner an R rating. So, they should find penis hats but also look for other items that weren't as risqué. He had a lot of ideas for the scene, noting its potential to be very funny. He specifically wanted them to keep their eyes out for human angel wings.

Their conversation had drilled down on luggage. The Props department had flagged something in reading the script that no one else had noticed. The hero actors arrive in Vegas with suitcases and move between hotels, but at no point did the script have them put the bags down. Turteltaub thought about it and said where they would lose the bags.

As with the Costume department, Props was mindful the bags the hero actors pulled in the early scenes needed to be true to their characters and they asked the director. They talked about them as if they were real people. The director said Billy and Sam would have newer luggage, Billy in particular something up market. Meanwhile Paddy and Archie would carry older, more worn suitcases.

The Props department needed to accumulate a fair amount of luggage given the airport and travel scenes. Some bags would come through product placement agreements, in bundles or perhaps as specialty pieces for specific characters, but they still needed to be prepared. It was also important that luggage didn't look alike, so they kept an eye out for suitcases with good prices.

A short time later they pulled up in front of the Inserection, parking in a prime spot in front, which was in full view of Cheshire Bridge Road and steady traffic. There was no competition for the few places there. Most of the patrons continued down the drive, under and behind the building to park out of sight.

The Inserection website explained its clientele. "Our customers rent or purchase the latest and hottest products in the market to enjoy in the privacy of their home, or at our stores."

"Let's see what the pervs are doing today," said Benjamin-Creel, laughing as he got out of the car into brighter sun and his transitional glasses automatically tinted a darker shade. There were thousands of items. Given the store's motif was "penis," they were confident they would find penis hats but it didn't happen immediately. There were the glow-in-the-dark penises and penis straws, penis cake pans, penis pasta, a big inflatable penis ring toss and a penis tiara. They stopped there, since the penis tiara was at least headwear, if not a hat, but rejected it. Finally, there it was. It had to be inflated, and the penis hat would be larger than most heads by half. But it could sit atop of the head of whoever wore.

The props team collected a few additional items in the meantime, including penis straws, but the bulk of the items were more demure bachelorette party favors such as sashes and a hair band featuring heart-shaped antennas.

They were at the counter to check out inside of 20 minutes. A very weary looking but very attractive woman in her 30s rang it up while a man with a greedy number of tattoos and piercings sized them up from behind the counter. The bill came to $130.37.

106

The next stop was Richard's Variety, a G-rated store. By now they were keen on finding Turteltaub's human angel wings. They were in luck. Not only did Richard's Variety have angel wings, it had handkerchiefs for use in two funeral scenes.

The mission a success, they returned to Mailing Avenue. Rocko was seated outside the props office, Lipp nowhere in sight.

The next day a new sign had been put on the door of the Art Department: "Please Keep Door Shut Wandering Canines." Lipp sipped a bright green chlorophyll beverage through a straw while an assistant worked at the other desk. The assistant had her Chihuahua, who sat in one of two dog beds, side-by-side under the table between their desks. The little dog watched Rocko as he practiced yoga in the middle of the floor.

The department offices had filled out. In an office at the other end of the U-shaped office corridor graphic artist Lisa Yeiser worked on a multi-part computer system the size of something on a broker's desk on Wall Street. Two 30-inch screens stood upright on her desk in a wide V, a keyboard in front of them and a large electronic drawing tablet in front of that. She wrote on the pad with her right hand while her left hand extended forward to work the keyboard. The machine on the table in front of her had a bright red logo that read *Last Vegas*. The large screen on the left displayed numerous variations.

"It's a drawing table. Don't leave home without it," she said as she looked up from her large, faux black-leather rolling chair. Yeiser, who had a grin on her face, was clad in black with a black-and-white sweater, her arms sleeved in art. Tattoos extended from her arms to her hands and fingers on the keyboard. Her long blond hair, pulled into a ponytail by a black scrunchie, revealed another tattoo on her neck.

As the graphic artist on the movie, she was responsible for creating material with graphic elements. That covered a wide range of things, from labels to store signage to fabricated photographs, a faux logo for a character's business or a real one that would serve as the show logo or mark.

The logo wasn't something to market the movie, although it has happened that studios pick them up for wider use. This mark would go on various items used in production of the movie. It included artists' renderings and other drawings, blueprints and eventually the daily reports. It would also be the back of the directors' chairs and crew T-shirts.

She offered a quick visual tour of the development of the in-house *Last Vegas* logo. The foundation for the graphic had been the shape of the famous "Vegas" sign, the sideways vintage-looking diamond, and she built from there. A trump card from each suit in a deck of cards made up the background of each letter in "LAST." The "L" is a Jack, the "A" is a Queen, the "S" a King and the "T" an Ace. "VEGAS" brought up the bottom deck.

"We have four primary actors, and each card represents an actor," she explained. "It's more complicated from there." She clicked on a button to show it in mathematical detail and then with barely detectable movement began clicking through different logos. There were nine, all similarly themed but with more variety.

She had given them to Bomba when she was finished. As production designer, he pared the group down and took the best to Turteltaub, who picked two. The final concept merged them. She went back to the first screen, where she had started, and the winner.

Yeiser worked a lot. She had just come from working on *Devil's Knot* starring Reese Witherspoon. Before that she did *Trouble with the Curve*, a Clint Eastwood movie that was currently in theaters. She had worked with Bomba and Lipp on *Parental Guidance*.

She laughed when asked how she liked *Last Vegas*. *Devil's Knot* was a dark drama about the murders of three children. "It's a nice change," she said laughing. "A comedy is a good contrast."

Yeiser's next task was working on a photo that would be part of set decoration in the home of Robert De Niro's character. She put a copy of it on the desk. It was a young couple in front of a pub and a closer look revealed a much younger De Niro. The woman wasn't recognizable. The actress was still to be determined. She wouldn't be in the movie, except in the photos. But they had to have all permissions to do that, and that was still to be determined. Sometimes they used crew or their family for images used in set decoration. It was easy to get approval and all the signatures required.

Yeiser was working out the sign. She put the options up on the left screen, showing seven variations of "Paddy's." It seemed a lot of work for just one image. It was possible the Costume department also would use the logo to create a T-shirt for De Niro's character to wear in a scene. There was artistry to it, no doubt about that, but she was also managing the practicality of copyright laws. This make-believe pub owned by a fictional character couldn't look like any actual "Paddy's" pub on the planet, so she would design it from scratch.

Badalato looked relaxed as he talked on his cell phone at the table set up on the outdoor deck. A big tree provided shade and a degree of comfort in August. Now that September had kicked in cooler weather the deck was getting more use.

He was negotiating a deal with either hair or makeup and alternately referred to his laptop and a folder spread out on the table as he talked. De Niro, Douglas and Freeman had entourages that included hair and makeup. Production hired hair and makeup for Kline and Steenburgen. They were the priorities, but there was a large cast from there. The department would add help on days when there were a lot of extras.

Badalato would lean back to listen and swig on his water bottle while Buddy stood in wait. The Golden Retriever had a tennis ball and was waiting his turn for a game of fetch in the de facto dog run. A fence surrounded Mailing Avenue. The back of the building also had perpendicular sections of fence that ran between the building and the larger fence. It wasn't just for the Golden Retriever, although he used it the most. By now there were a half-dozen dogs on site. "Geez," Turteltaub said one day, "I'm going to need to get a dog for the show!"

Badalato hung up the phone, the deal done. It had been a long week, given they had worked the previous weekend in Las Vegas with no respite. He and Samuels and Kamishin had also met with the business agent for Teamsters Local 728, which represents transportation, to decidedly less fanfare than the visit from the agent from the IATSE local. There had been interviews with extras casting companies as well.

But the big accomplishment of the week was getting past the executive visits. The good news was that it had shut down any expectation by department heads that they might get more money.

Someone asked whether making the department heads sign for the memo was necessary. Aside from Pink and Jobst in LA, offices were a minute from the bullpen.

"It seemed like a simple email would have done it."

Badalato grinned.

"I did it on purpose," he said. "That way no one could say they didn't see it."

"Would any of these people have done that -- pretended not to get it?"

"Probably not," he agreed. "The larger point was that everyone needed to come to grips with this budget. It had gone on long enough. They took it to a higher level and they got their answer."

"Did it piss you off that someone went to the studio?"

"No. That's a good thing," he said. "It forced the whole issue forward. Now, it's handled. Everyone has had their say and we can move on."

"It's true that some things have been added that are really expensive."

"Like what?"

"Like the additional extras. That's a lot of people. It does seem to contradict whether the budget is that tight."

"That's Jon. The director wanted more extras."

"Was it in the budget?" This was a paraphrase of his own words but there was no sting.

"No. We had to make some changes. We cut in other areas."

"So, the director gets anything he wants?"

"If we can make it happen, yes."

"It would seem to send a message to the crew that more money is available somewhere. You say you're holding the line on expenses but then adding things that aren't cheap."

"We've said all along it's a tight budget. Starting in interviews. Would it be better if it were bigger? Yes. It isn't. We need to make it work."

"Hardball?"

He shrugged. "Sure."

"Is there potential for quality to be impacted if the budget is too lean?"

"Of course. We work hard not to let that happen. But the studio's position is that people are coming to see this movie because of these actors. They aren't going to notice or care what the set looks like or what the actors are wearing."

CHAPTER SEVEN
4 Weeks Out
Sept. 24-28

THE COSTUMERS PREVAILED in the request to hold the fittings in one central location in New York, rather than traveling to the actors' homes again. Ultimately it was the only thing that made sense. Pink and the assistant designer went over the weekend for fittings with Kline, Douglas and De Niro, who all had primary residences there. Freeman and Steenburgen were scheduled for L.A. later in the month.

Production booked a queen room, a bedroom suite and a fitting room at Trump International Hotel & Tower at 1 Central Park West. It was an expensive bit of square footage on the West Side with space for a changing room and a fitting area with multiple mirrors and comfortable seating. They contained costs where they could.

There were no frills. While Pink stayed at the more expensive Trump property, the assistant designer stayed at the Hudson Hotel a quarter mile away on West 58th. Its quoted rates were about a third of those at Trump Tower and the Hudson was just a five-minute walk around Columbus Circle. Union rules governed accommodations as well as how crew flew based on job titles so it wasn't Badalato's doing, although he certainly embraced the rule.

The staff at Trump Tower was accustomed to famous people and business, including movie industry needs like fittings. There were back doors and halls if anyone needed to be kept out of sight but truth be told, they rarely had a problem. New Yorkers in general were used to celebrities and anyone who could afford to stay at Trump Tower probably didn't have time to focus on anyone but themselves or the reasons that had brought them there.

Pink and the assistant were harried given all they had to do. They arrived Thursday night and their first meeting, with Kline, was 10 a.m. Friday. The good news was that most of what they needed to set up was there. The racks were available and all but one of the boxes shipped by Jobst had arrived. There was a lot of work to do to be organized and ensure the right feel for a comfortable, low-pressure meeting.

They began by using the boxes marked "Sam" to organize Kline's character's closet, since they were meeting with him first. That term, "closet," had been used for decades to refer to the collection of clothes and accessories for each actor.

Of the leading actors, Kline could most easily escape recognition. It helped that he was letting his hair turn a grayish white for the role of Sam, since fans knew him with dark hair. Kline arrived in need of coffee, which they quickly accommodated. Pink tweeted the image of gourmet coffee delivered by room service, although she didn't identify the actor. "Does this cappuccino look good? It should, $44.00 to deliver it to my room in NY" with the hashtag "#Doesthiscoffeecomewithahandbag?"

Turteltaub had agreed to a youthful look for Sam, a character bucking his true age balanced by the gray hair. Pink worked with it. There were longish surfer shorts for the pool party, unusual on someone in their mid-60s, and other clothes you would find in Florida, where Sam lived, or in another semi-tropical locale.

Pink saw the character of Sam as having a "comfy, happy golfer essence." He would wear high-waisted pants, buttoned-up shirts and white sneakers, perhaps looking a little goofy. Kline liked the concept and added a couple of thoughts that shifted it slightly. His character was pining away for his lost youth. Perhaps something ridiculously young looking? Pink handed him a hat and glasses to try on. "He took a minute to absorb the look and started to laugh," she said. They both knew they had found Sam.

That meeting concluded, Pink and the assistant focused on Michael Douglas, who was scheduled for 3 p.m. He played Billy, a high-powered attorney.

Douglas, who had just wrapped *Behind the Candelabra*, an HBO movie about Liberace, wore his trademark red ball cap to travel. Keeping his head down and the cap snug had been effective at masking him over the years. The general rule of thumb, not just for him but any high profile celebrity, was not to make eye contact. Keeping your head down was the key.

Billy would have an executive look, wearing the most expensive clothes of the male characters. Pink had tailors she knew, trusted and relied upon. They had not disappointed with this early demonstration. The clothes fit the actor, needing only minor modifications. As with Kline, the additional details gleaned from the meeting were helpful in filling in clothes for other scenes.

By the end of the day they were tired but happy. Both of the meetings had gone well, sure, but there was also some breathing room. De Niro wasn't due until Monday. There was time to meet with clothiers and to shop. They focused on Paddy's character, given the upcoming meeting, but they also picked up other clothes and accessories. A fanny pack for Morgan Freeman's character Archie, a down-to-earth guy, was one thought.

Meanwhile, De Niro was flying to New York from Paris with his trainer. He was still shooting Malavita, which had been renamed *The Family* just outside the French city. As a rule he traveled on his private jet but with a transatlantic flight and a trip of a few days it made sense to fly commercial.

Once they wrapped *The Family*, he would turn full efforts to his role in *Last Vegas*. De Niro could usually blend into any environment, despite his fame, and he had done so easily at Trump Tower. As a native New Yorker he knew his way around but it was deeper than that. Several people who had worked with him over the years, not fans, but people who had seen him work the camera, had a similar comment. His skill lay in his ability to be a blank slate. He didn't insert himself into the role. He had an ease in which he could free himself of himself and disappear into character. There was no De Niro, the thinking went.

The actor temporarily transported himself into the role of Paddy at the 11:30 a.m. meeting Monday. Monica Ruiz-Zieglar, his personal costumer, was there to help. She had been part of De Niro's regular working entourage, having helped dress him in eight movies since 2011. The actor had ideas about Paddy, all of which made sense to Pink.

It had all been by the book, easy and relaxed. As soon as De Niro and Ruiz-Zieglar were out the door, Pink and the assistant designer flew into motion. Kline and Douglas' closets were already packed. They hurried to pack De Niro's closet for shipment, so they could get to the airport. By then the one missing box had arrived, and it was turned around for return to L.A. They parted at the airport for different flights an hour apart, Pink in first class and the assistant designer in coach.

It was a hugely successful trip for Pink. She had crossed a big hurdle. She was past the concept part of the creative process with three of the primary actors and into specific costumes. Better yet, the actors' meetings had provided a degree of calm. Each had been delightful to work with. That wasn't always the case.

There was another element that eased the strain for Pink. Badalato and Samuels had reversed their decision that the assistant costume designer be hired locally. While she had been there from the first meetings with the actors, it was thought then that she was a temporary hire. Now she was on for the run of the show. It was a good thing to have out of the way. They could focus on the rest of the costumes for De Niro, Douglas and Kline and the primary fittings for Freeman and Steenburgen. There were at least a half-dozen actors with significant roles to consider, and two-dozen more that also needed to be thought out. And then there were the thousands of extras. Jobst was working on that in Los Angeles.

"I'm baaaack!"

Turteltaub surged through the bullpen, announcing his presence on his way to Rake's office. The director had been away from Mailing Avenue for more than a week, the longest since production began. The bullpen crew had looked forward to his return, a sharp contrast to the visit from the studio executives.

"Did you miss us?" Simpson asked.

"Not only didn't I miss you ..." replied Turteltaub to a burst of laughter, as he continued with a grin to the 1st AD's office.

The crew had continued their homework on Turteltaub, talking with contacts who had worked with him. What was he like? Word was mostly good, that he was smart and funny, but one report came in the form of cliché: Turteltaub did not suffer fools gladly. Do your job and hope he doesn't decide you haven't and you'll be fine.

So far no one had seen anything but Turteltaub the funny man. He talked to everyone and remembered names. Department heads described him as a collaborator. Badalato called him "congenial." Samuels, in his bullpen office on the phone, was heard talking about the show. "Jon?" he said to the caller. "Jon's great."

Turteltaub left Rake's office, cutting back across the bullpen.

"Important question," someone asked him.

"I know the answers to some important questions."

"*Phenomenon*?" The question was about the 1996 movie he directed starring John Travolta, Kyra Sedgwick and Forest Whitaker. Travolta played George Malley, a regular guy until he's struck by a light from the sky and adds IQ points by the dozens.

"I definitely know the answer."

"How did you get the book to move like that?"

In one scene, Malley demonstrated his newfound telekinetic powers by waving a pencil to open a book from across the room. It's 17 years later but Turteltaub knows exactly.

"Today it would be much more expensive to do it," he said, animatedly. "They'd spend a fortune on it! You'd CGI the pencil." (Computer-generated imagery is used to create special effects in movies, a standard part of contemporary movie making.)

"You'd have him doing all this powerful stuff," Turteltaub continued. "And it wouldn't be as good," he said, matter-of-factly.

"How did you get the book to open?"

"Fishing line," he said.

He reached onto a desk, grabbing a three-ring binder to demonstrate. He held the top open slightly and held an imaginary line over it. Then he closed the binder and opened it again.

"Fishing line!" He repeated, dropping the cover of the notebook with a shrug. "That's it."

"You can't see it."

"I know! Brilliant!" He was joking again yet not, given the cost-benefit ratio of fishing line to CGI.

"Jon? We're ready if you are." Rake, now on the other side of the hallway with the rest of the scouting team hovering nearby, was there to rescue him.

"Can we confirm Grip and Electric?" Kamishin asked.

The crowded production meeting felt like a squad room before cops hit the street. There had been a big influx of hires. The largest group, the Construction department, had taken over the middle warehouse. But there were still plenty of crew to be hired.

Badalato said early on that 40 percent of the crew would come on the two weeks before photography started and proof was materializing. Badalato said he thought it would be soon, since Hennings was meeting with the two locally based camera crew Production had found. The hires had been bandied about for several days.

What he didn't talk about was the tension between him and Hennings. The same scenario experienced with a couple of other department heads was playing out: The DP wanted to hire crew he knew. They were L.A.-based, as were most camera crew. There would be two cameras at work, each with its own dedicated crew. One of them could be based locally, Badalato figured.

He turned to Simpson. "Where are we with bids from the camera houses?"

"We're still waiting on one," she said.

"It's probably Panavision," said Badalato, "because that's the way Hennings and the studio like it. But we want to do our homework."

"At least Panavision is in Atlanta now," offered Kamishin. "They weren't here before." Panavision had opened a local office 18 months earlier (March 2011) when it became clear that the production work happening in Atlanta would continue.

Panavision's presence was important for another reason. Operating in Georgia meant movie productions could use those expenditures toward tax credits. Even if they rented the equipment from Panavision in L.A. it would transfer to Georgia when work began there. The cinematographer for *Last Vegas* preferred to use Panavision Woodland Hills in L.A. He had a relationship with them and a history. It also made sense because of its proximity to Las Vegas, where photography began.

They rattled off several confirmed hires. There had already been much talk about the soundman, who was at work on "Walking Dead." Samuels and Badalato knew him and liked him but someone high up had resisted. Now, he was officially on board and they were putting the finishing touches on the boom operator position. That person held the mic over the actors and otherwise assisted with sound on set.

One dolly grip was on board, a man based in Chicago. To an outsider watching a movie shoot it would look like that person was part of the camera crew, since the job was about moving the camera on a dolly. They had to pull or push the camera -- often with a camera operator and camera assistant on it -- with fluid motion. Setting up the dolly, leveling and balancing the rails, could be challenging.

Also, they were going to need an assistant for De Niro in Vegas after all.

"His regular guy isn't there. Let me know if you have any ideas."

"I could do it," said the concierge, a specially created position. Given the high profile nature of the cast, Samuels liked the idea of having one of the PAs designated to assist with any special needs that arose.

The woman, who had long hair and wore huge hoop earrings and a purple scarf, had interviewed as a production assistant and been bumped up to the concierge role, somewhat by chance. It paid better than a straight PA job and it seemed to have gone to her head quickly.

Kamishin was taking it all in. She said there would be plenty for her to do as concierge. Her fallback was to help the bullpen with anything that came up. Kamishin paused a half a beat to let that sink in. "De Niro will need a full-time assistant."

The young woman blinked her eyes rapidly and nodded yes.

"Let us know any ideas and we'll check it out," said Badalato, moving on. "Bristie, can you check for any new resumes for video assists?" A video assist operator handled playback, keeping track of what had been shot for whoever needed to see it. Not every show could afford one but it was essential for a movie like this. A video assist could help the script supervisor in checking a continuity issue or the director who wanted to see a particular take.

"We're planning to bring in a guy from Carolina, but let's make sure we haven't missed something locally."

Stephens nodded in agreement and he asked her how many applications had come into the email address she had set up for the movie.

"As of yesterday it was 1,507," she said. Resumes also flowed to the Production department via more traditional methods. People regularly dropped off resumes of friends or people they'd worked with in the past that they knew were good. Stephens had organized folders for the best resumes by position. She would check for any new emails and get back to him.

"Just give me any you think meet the caliber of this show," said Badalato. That meant he wanted her to cull through the various applications for people with experience, and more specifically, the right kind of experience.

Next they went through what was happening in Las Vegas. The Costume department, at work at its temporary offices at Warner Bros, would be among the first to move to the Annex. The Transportation department was also getting into place. Among other duties, they coordinated getting various trailers set up, including the costume trailer, which would be parked outside the Annex and used for location work. The Vegas production office, now open on the fourth floor of the Aria, had two people working.

Kamishin asked for an update on the move. It had been part of the collective consciousness from the beginning. There had been phone calls and emails and meetings to plan and more meetings to check progress and of course spreadsheets to detail it all. The first spreadsheet, the Badalato way, was a basic cost comparison to see if he could save significant money by using one shipping method more than another. It had broadened from there.

Now the group drilled down on what was the spreadsheet that tracked the move, whether breaking down individual crew kits or departments or shipping companies. Some would go by FedEx, the rest by Santini or Panavision. Still other items would move by truck, including propmaster Dwight Benjamin-Creel's 18-wheeler prop trailer, which a Teamster would drive. All of it had to be tracked to be reconciled later.

As things moved, the spreadsheet would be updated to log tracking numbers and weight, dates and times shipped. Insurance was also tracked, with the starting point for each at $2,500 in coverage, many of them for far more than that. What type of container was used? Was it a pallet, box or suitcase? How many were there? What were the measurements? Which company would move them? What was the cost of shipping?

Badalato wanted an updated projection of the bill. That was a daunting task, since it was all estimates. The bulk of items would move from Atlanta, but there were also things shipping from New Orleans, Chicago and New Mexico. That didn't include costumes or camera equipment, which would go direct from LA. to Vegas. The bill would be in the tens of thousands of dollars.

They had begun shipping last week but a problem had arisen. For some reason, a couple of boxes had been turned away in Las Vegas. Simpson said she had called her counterpart in the production office there to double-check the address. The boxes had been labeled correctly. She said she would report back if there was an issue.

Simpson moved on to bids for the HVAC installation needed for the warehouse space. This was no ordinary air conditioning. It had to cool the soundstages in what amounted to about 58,000 square feet of space. The machinery would go on the roof and be attached to giant, moveable duct tunnels that could be fed onto different stages, depending on which place they were shooting. Although it would be November when production started in Atlanta, and relatively cool outside, stages warm up quickly with the lights and all the people working.

Right now it was good the warehouse space stayed cool. Jerry Henery, the construction coordinator, and his two foremen, had just moved in. With them had come the largest kit of all contained in two large tractor-trailers. It took a lot of effort just to unload the trucks and what came out seemed like more goods than you could have in just two semis.

The 10,133-square-foot mill shop filled as hundreds of large containers were unloaded, including giant wooden boxes and carts and rolling flats and pallets. There were at least two just dedicated to sawhorses, containing 60 or more. There were worktables and racks of plywood and other wood and general supplies, entire pallets with shrink-wrapped goods on them. A lot of the wood crates had drawers to them that opened like old library card catalogues.

Then there were the metal tools, some of them giant, and some of them unidentifiable to anyone who didn't work in construction. Just the array of saws was staggering, with circular saws and table saws and electric miter saws and pendulum saws. They even brought their own industrial-strength trash containers.

Then there were the smaller containers and a huge assortment of handcrafted boxes. They were bigger than traditional toolboxes, although there were plenty of those as well. Some had generic "Construction" labels while others were marked "Screws" and "Lags." One large, homemade wooden box contained thousands of screws. Inside were 12 compartments with different sizes and types. Several of them were the size of fishing lure boxes but with more compartments.

It took a full week for the mill shop to take final form. Work started in the back warehouse on the foundation of the Aria penthouse set while they customized the rest of the space to maximize efficiency. At the beginning of the week, it looked like a colossal move with crates and pallets and wooden boxes and machinery. By the end of the week, it would have been easy to assume the mill shop had been in operation a long time.

Both of the warehouse spaces had small offices sticking out of their walls like boxes. The one in the mill shop itself had a big framed door in the middle, although it opened at the top like a country door. They had added a strandboard room in front of it and then attached hooks. Now they held 100 different kinds of hoses. Industrial strength shelving made up the exterior walls of the new extra room. Those were filled with families of things, like construction glue in a host of sizes and varieties, as with caulk, duct and other tape, cleaning supplies.

It seemed the space wasn't quite enough to contain them and the department had spilled out into the large stage. That pre-existing office against the wall in that space was bigger, with several rooms that opened into it. Henery needed the small office but not the entire space. So they built a wall that partitioned off the end with Henery's office and then built an extension on his desk to the wall. The end result was two different private spaces with separate entrances.

Henery's side also provided a foyer into the construction office, where they installed chest-high drawing tables, which now held architectural drawings. They were building other platform tables outside the office space for more blueprints. Better to have them readily available.

They had a lot to do fast. The biggest job facing Henery was the recreation of the Aria penthouse suite. It would have two floors, with two small swimming pools on the main floor, and a wall of windows on one side that would overlook a faux Las Vegas skyline. It also would have smaller rooms, including a bedroom suite and a bathroom. As expensive and as fancy as that all sounded, it was still significantly less expensive than shooting it in Las Vegas. That much had been determined months earlier by Badalato and Samuels.

First, they had to build a huge platform foundation, lifting the first floor off the ground by seven feet. There were two reasons. For one, as a penthouse, it needed the feel of height for its vantage point above the city. The swimming pools in the living room of the penthouse were the other reason. They were dipping pools, so on the smaller side, but they still needed a place to hold all that water.

Any movie lover could close their eyes and visualize some of set decorator Patrick Cassidy's work. It was the college in *The Great Debaters* (2007), the country club in *Secretariat* (2010), the barroom in *Book of Eli* (2010), the beach house in *Safe Haven* (2013/14). He did *The Great Debaters* with Bomba. That movie received a lot of critical praise, including for its production design and set decorating. The two men had worked together several times since.

The walls of the corridor outside of Set Dec, the other side of the Art department hallway, had filled-in with samples. It was swatches of paint colors and wallpaper and types of fabrics. The next corridor wall had a little more of the same, along with the Art department calendar and a colorful, large chart of sets planned for the movie. The calendar showed each day of photography based on sets to be used, each color-coded. That meant that you could see all the pool days, and what were single-scene locations.

The crew had filled in as well. Cassidy was on the phone at his desk at the far end of the room, one of the rare times he'd been in the office long enough to sit down. As set decorator, he was in charge of all set dressing, from furniture to curtains, lampshades to artwork. His first hire had been a buyer, a woman based in Atlanta who knew her way around everything from flea markets to standard retail.

Now the leadman was also working. He would operate as the foreman of the department. He would oversee operations when they were shooting as well as keep track of the moving parts. Ultimately, it was his responsibility to ensure that everything that had been leased or borrowed for the show had been returned, and that items that hadn't been leased or borrowed had been disposed of otherwise. He was young with white hair and brought with him a striking dog named Zelda. She was a match for the Target store mascot.

The Set Dec department coordinator was at the desk closer to the entrance. Her job paralleled that of Chloe Lipp in the Art department, a mix of keeping track of where people were, paperwork and anything else the department needed. The window between their two offices made sense now, although they were also within loud talking distance of each other.

Cassidy was on the slender side and serious-looking. He had brown hair cut relatively short and wore horn-rimmed glasses, an Izod-styled navy blue, shortsleeve shirt and khakis. He talked quietly on the phone with someone about the challenges of getting slot machines in Atlanta. It wasn't that they couldn't be found locally but whether they could be found without trademarked logos.

Because of its breadth, the biggest artistic challenge for him as the set decorator on *Last Vegas* was the Aria penthouse, with its multiple sets. The penthouse structure was some 9,000 feet, all of it built to specs. The assistant art director had measured on site in Las Vegas so they could recreate it with precision.

It would have six rooms. Because it was based on a real place, they knew what it looked like, but that came with unique challenges: It had to be approved by the Aria under terms of the barter agreement. The most intricate of sets to be built wasn't the massive, gleaming penthouse. That was the store they would bring to life from the middle of the last century. The 1955 Brooklyn set would need a soda fountain and stools, shelving for dried goods and liquor and other appropriate furniture. Then they had to have the cash registers, signage and thousands of era-appropriate products.

The biggest overall challenge he faced, however, was the same as the others. The financial limitations were an issue given the types of sets needed for the movie. They wanted to depict high-end Vegas. *Last Vegas* was a good show, he said, even with the challenges. On the up side was a solid crew and director, whom he had met with several times, and working for Bomba. Especially working for Bomba, he repeated. Cassidy had teamed with him in *Parental Guidance* and *Race to Witch Mountain*.

If Cassidy had a secret to how he brought a set to life, it was that he took time to get to know the characters. An interior designer figured out what their clients wanted and worked from there. A set designer had to figure out how the space helped explain the character. Cassidy had learned to think of them as real people. That helped him sort out how to convey meaning to the places on camera that would represent them. The more he understood the characters, the easier it was to visualize the sets in his mind and then to put them together.

It required some digging. "It's about depth of character," Cassidy explained. "And it's not something that's always in the script." Who were Billy, Paddy, Archie and Sam as people? Where did they live? Where had they worked? What were their statuses in life? Were they happy or depressed? The script gave a lot of clues. Paddy had a great love and now she was gone. Billy was wealthy and liked younger women. Archie was a steady character bouncing back after a stroke and living with his son.

Cassidy also had to consider them as a group. The sets shouldn't overlap unless that was the intention. The characters in *Last Vegas* shared the emotional challenges of aging, although each character handled it differently.

Screenplays aren't like books. They don't provide a lot of detail about characters. What did the script actually say about Paddy? He was a suffering widower. They decided the character and his wife ran a pub before retirement, and he would do something with that. But did they have children, and how many? The set decorator thought perhaps three, and he ran it by Turteltaub during one of their meetings.

"They're his people, more than mine," explained Cassidy. "It's just that I'm buying their drapes." He described the meetings with the director as "an exchange -- more of this, less of that." The director was engaged but he wasn't a micromanager.

Turteltaub thought there had been one child of the union. Paddy's emotional challenge was the loss of his wife, and too many children might deter from that. That helped Cassidy in planning decisions about furniture, art, knick-knacks: Heavy on the pictures of the wife, maybe just one or two images that included one child.

Freeman's character, Archie, conducted himself in a measured way in the script, almost with a sense of protocol. That indicated he might have been in the military. He had also suffered a stroke, and lived in his son's home, but there wasn't a lot more about him in the script.

"I asked Jon for more details about Archie, and did he mind if I talked to Morgan?" said Cassidy. "If his character was in the Army, was he non-com? What was his rank?" Paddy had a whole apartment to show who he was, while this character had a room in his son's house. Cassidy was considering a trophy or trophies, or perhaps a shadowbox of medals. It would say a lot about Archie in a small amount of space and an instant of screen time. Turteltaub said it was fine with him to reach out to Morgan. It wasn't something the director needed to authorize but it was good for him to know.

Freeman had a reputation for being easygoing and approachable so no one feared blowback. It was more than reputation, although it had preceded him. Anyone on *Last Vegas* who interacted with Freeman, or his entourage, had thus far had a pleasant experience.

Cassidy said the conversation with the actor had gone well. Freeman said he thought Archie was military but added a shift. His character had served in the Air Force, just as Freeman had. Better still for Cassidy, the actor had photos from his time in the service. He would send them along with the others that had been requested by the second AD.

There had been a personal side to it for Cassidy. He had watched Freeman on The Electric Co. To the set designer it had been "a more urban version of Sesame Street." "Morgan taught me how to read when I was 12," Cassidy laughed.

The Production department checked in with the assistants to see if the respective actors preferred to use aliases, otherwise they would use their character's name for accommodations. Some actors used the same pseudonym over time, while others changed it up. For this show, Morgan Freeman was "Jacob Revere." It went a good distance in terms of protecting privacy, however they did it.

Quentin Pierre, Freeman's personal assistant, and Robert Gaskill, his driver/security person, won over everyone in the Production department just as easily as Freeman had. Both men were consistently polite and friendly.

Pierre started as an actor in the '70s. That included regular work on the cult classic "Space 1999." He also served in various capacities on the first three

Star Wars movies, and as a stand-in or double on other projects. He occasionally attended events around the trilogy. But he has found his place with Freeman, whom he met on the set of *Glory* in 1989. At the time, he was working as a double to Denzel Washington, who ultimately earned an Oscar for best supporting actor for his work on *Glory*.

One of the PAs tasked with organizing creature comforts for the actors asked Pierre what Freeman liked. Pierre's English accent piped over the air from London where he lived. He said he would send a list but stressed that they not go overboard.

"None of that star crap. He don't go in for that bullshit," said Pierre. With the accent, the PA couldn't tell if he said "We" or "He" but it was very nearly the same.

Best of all, the list was manageable.

Items for Mr. Freeman's Trailer

This is a general guide to items that should be kept stocked in the trailer by whomever drives the Trailer on this show. We understand some of these items might not be possible to get here and know that a lot of this might seem redundant.

*Coffee maker with/ fresh coffee – regular and decaf – (semi strong blend) Sumatra blend will be ok, raw sugar, regular white sugar, yellow packet Splenda, half and half & plain Vitamin D milk...

*Electric water kettle with/ assorted teas – honey and lemon – hot chocolate...

*Wide slice toaster with/ assorted breads – wheat or seven grain and white – bagels and soft/spread butter (Healthy Start or I can't believe it's not butter)...

*Blender, large plastic cups for smoothies...

*Fresh orange, pineapple and cranberry juices...

*Bottled water for coffee and regular drinking...

*Coke, Diet Coke, Sprite or 7-up, Ginger Ale, Lemonade...

*Fresh fruit, bananas, oranges, grapes, mango, papaya...

*Salad Dressings, Zesty Italian & Creamy Caesar...

*Crystals Brand Hot Sauce, if possible...

*Large package of mini snickers bars...

*Plates, glasses, cutlery (forks, spoons, knives, etc.), one good large sharp knife...

*Air fresheners, hand soaps, towels, paper towels, Kleenex, toilet paper, large dinner napkins...etc.

*TV, DVD & CD players, Satellite TV with Sports Channels – most Important is the GOLF Channel.

Temperature of personal / make-up trailer must be kept very warm... "78 degrees" – please preheat trailer prior to our arrival/call time

Thanks in advance for helping us take care of Mr. Freeman. We will purchase any other items we have forgotten or have special needs of...

Robert & Quentin.

Rake hurried into Mailing Avenue from the scouting van, returned from its near-daily tour of Atlanta. The creative team was going back to Vegas tomorrow and he needed to work on the schedule.

Creating the shooting schedule was as core to his job as it was to making the movie. It was the roadmap that showed everything happening during principal photography; what they were shooting when and where, what scenes, what actors, etc. Numerous other documents sprung from it. He wanted to get an officially updated "One Liner" out to the crew. That was the short version of the shooting script, which laid out the scenes in the order in which they would be shot. It left off details such as cast and location but it would be enough for now.

It was the nature of the beast that the schedule changed constantly at this stage. The natural dilemma for an AD, any AD, was when to release it. The longer they kept the schedule, the more accurate it would be. At the same time, crew needed information.

Some of it was part of where they were in prep. Until Turteltaub signed off on specific locations, they couldn't be "locked." It was only then, when a lease and contract were signed, that the Locations department could guarantee the space. Until then the Art department was hamstrung. They could barely design a set conceptually without the space, since the physical location could change everything.

There were plenty of other variables. One new blackout date from an actor -- and there was at least one -- could be completely disruptive. Given that so many scenes were ensemble, one actor being unavailable on a given date could throw off the entire schedule. Rake had to sort it all out, although it helped that he had Peterson working.

Several key roles still had to be filled, including the character who would be the chief sidekick to the lead characters. The director had settled on an actor for the role but it wasn't official until his deal was inked. There were a host of other important, albeit smaller, roles from there. Amy Baer, the creative producer, was working to get Kanye West in for a cameo.

Rake's mind was swirling when he got to the office. Peterson was there with a visitor. He greeted them quickly as he hurried to his desk, noting his commitment to getting the One Liner out.

The visitor said she thought it was finished.

"Billy and Jeremiah kicked it back," Rake said with a smile.

"There's a surprise," said Peterson.

He laughed. "Yeah. Not a total surprise," he said. "Jon wanted to put it through anyway."

When savings in the neighborhood of $100,000 were realized elsewhere in the budget, Turteltaub figured it should translate to another shooting day in Vegas. The schedule Rake submitted reflected the added day. In the meantime, the studio reclaimed the money and allocated it elsewhere. Without that money in the budget, the added expense of another day of production was out of the question.

"It was a good effort," Peterson said. She had created a workstation along one wall and added decorations to the room.

Rake nodded but focused on his laptop instead. He turned it to show a chart, which filled the screen. The document was currently eight pages, every scene of the movie detailed. It showed that the first day of photography would start high atop the Stratosphere. That involved a scene where Michael Douglas and Mary Steenburgen have a play date to the scary ride in Vegas. It sounded like a heck of a first day.

"It probably will change," said Rake.

Samuels appeared at the door. "So, helicopter," he said, looking at Rake.

"Helicopter," Rake answered.

The 1st AD penciled in the aerial shots but it needed Samuels' okay and he was eager to get it off his list. They would get establishing shots from the sky during the day and at night, since they would go in the afternoon. They would get a sunset, which could double as a sunrise, crowd shots, traffic, and the Stratosphere from 5,000 feet.

Samuels had firm numbers for leasing the helicopter and could confirm dates. Badalato had handled the bid process, a task he enjoyed because of his earlier incarnation in the movie business. He had owned a company that specialized in aerial logistics and safety planning. A "one-stop" aviation resource, it offered everything from support services to full coordination of aerial units. Badalato had also worked in underwater safety, most notably on *Double Jeopardy*.

They would shoot the helicopter scenes on a Saturday during the three and half weeks that the production was in Vegas. That was by design, since most of the crew would be off that day. They would only need a handful of crew.

For the most part weekends were sacrosanct, credit for which went to the unions. It was entirely possible for movie or television crew to work through a Friday night and well into Saturday. Considered an extension of Friday, with corresponding pay increases, that was permitted under union rules. Bringing someone in to work on Saturday was different. In any event, overnighters were unlikely to occur on *Last Vegas*. The 12-hour maximum workdays of the main actors didn't prevent it but would limit its need.

Samuels also told Rake work was scheduled for the roof on Mailing Avenue. A week earlier Rake had returned to the studio while it was raining. He had flagged Kamishin and they hurried out to the back warehouses, where the main sound stages would be built, to listen to the rain. It was loud enough to disturb shooting. Badalato had talked to the owners of Mailing Avenue and they were installing material on the roof that would quiet any rainfall. It wasn't cheap but it would prevent any disruption should it rain during photography.

There was a situation in the bullpen. All of the packages that had been shipped from Atlanta to location in Las Vegas had been inexplicably re-routed. Given that some 2,000 pounds were somewhere in process, it might even rise to a problem.

Simpson had followed up when there was first mention of a problem days earlier. Now, she double-checked everything again and began trouble-shooting in earnest. Kamishin stood by her desk.

"What happened, exactly?" Kamishin asked. She had been aware of the earlier problem but thought it was resolved. Simpson thought so, too.

"I asked her, can we send this here? And she said, 'Just use the address I gave you."

"Did she check?"

"I assumed so. I asked her to."

The boxes had been redirected to the Annex, the building near Aria that would house most of the movie production departments. But that also presented issues, Simpson explained, because it was an unused building. Aria had shuttered it and apparently it hadn't been reopened yet. She said she was about to call. Kamishin left to update Badalato.

The company would move on Wednesday next week. The goal was to have their kits waiting for them. The Mailing Avenue production office had been open 16 hours a day, taking care of regular business while also steadily shipping boxes, trunks, pallets and more than a few odd-sized kits. It was an issue before but the problem had now increased ten-fold. It was the last thing they needed.

Kamishin returned to Simpson, who by then was on the phone with the woman in Vegas.

"We did exactly what you said. I checked it against your email and I called you to double-check," Simpson said into the phone. "It's not a deliverable address. They are refusing it; Everything is being rerouted."

Simpson's tone became more pronounced as the conversation continued. When she hung up, she looked at Kamishin and then the rest of the bullpen, who of course had been listening in.

"It wasn't her problem?" Kamishin asked, prompting her.

"When I told her they are refusing delivery she said it wasn't her problem. She literally said that: 'That is not my problem. I sent you the email and I was very clear. If you didn't follow the directions that's your problem and you're going to have to figure it out.' "

Kamishin stared back. Now the rest of what Simpson said was in context.

"Before I could explain it to you fully, you were telling me it wasn't your problem," she said, calmly. "We have provided this to everyone, company-wide." She said the last two words separately. "Company. Wide."

At that point, the conversation had turned.

"How did you leave it?"

"I asked her to get me a new address, one she had confirmed."

"What did she say to that," asked Kamishin.

"She said yes. And that she hadn't thought of that."

Kamishin shook her in disbelief. "Keep me posted."

Despite the added pressure, and a buildup of new boxes over the rest of the day, the overall mood in the bullpen was light. They would wait until things were sorted out in Vegas to resume shipping. Meanwhile, smaller things on the list were getting handled.

Kamishin sent out queries to find out if and what aliases the actors used. Most of them used fake names on hotel suites to ensure privacy on location. She also reviewed the crew list, which Production created and maintained. It now had 90 names on it but there were still dozens of positions to be filled. With all the new people on board, it had taken longer. She wanted to make sure it was right before it went out company-wide.

Even in stressful conditions, there was levity in the bullpen. Stephens was a big part of that. She worked hard but also loved a good prank, generally with assistance. One afternoon everyone waited until Kamishin was out on the deck on break. Then, when they heard her coming back up the hall, Stephens folded herself into a rubber crate. It was the same type Badalato used, black with yellow top. It looked way too small for a person. As soon as Stephens heard her come into the office she popped out, startling Kamishin into the air several inches. The jump delighted everyone. Even Kamishin laughed.

Simpson's giant wallboard had been kept up and changed daily, everyone taking turns filling in the quotes and word of the day. "Down" was the word of the day, meaning to be knowledgeable about something or to give respect and recognition for something.

The stars of *Last Vegas*, or movies they had worked on, were the most often used subject matters for the Fact of the Day. This one was about Morgan Freeman, who had since been fitted in L.A. "Morgan Freeman enacted the lead role in his school play at 8 and won a statewide drama competition at age 12. "

It was also a place to list things that production needed to pick up. It read "White Paper! TSA, Toaster, Card Stock, D. of Labor" by one name. Another had "Cast List, Minor's permits, AD Printer." An up-dated cast list was already in the works. It also was a way to keep up on each person in the bullpen. Icons had gone up for each person who worked there and it was possible to look to those to find the person needed.

Wendy Calloway, a miracle of modern travel arrangements, cut through the bullpen and stuck her head in Rake's office. The core creative team -- Turteltaub, Rake, Hennings and Bomba -- were scheduled to go to Vegas on a

5:40 p.m. flight. She had booked the trip, flights and other aspects of it, days earlier. She had just heard they might want to catch an earlier flight. Rake was a calm voice of reason, and the boss. Did he know about that?

Rake looked at his watch and thought for a minute. He was already a veteran of Hartsfield-Jackson Atlanta International Airport. Changing the flights this late didn't make sense, particularly with traffic. While close enough to Mailing Avenue, it was still the busiest airport in America.

A few minutes later, Calloway returned to his office. Turteltaub had decided they should fly earlier. She had checked and there were seats available in business class, so all them could fly in the manner commanded by their respective unions.

"Well okay then," said Rake, standing up. "Let's go to Vegas."

Kamishin joined them in the hallway. If they were going to catch that plane, they'd better get a move on. The bullpen could help. She instructed the concierge to get in the scout van and wait in the parking lot, since she would be driving the men to the airport. Jordan Anderson was to contact everyone to make sure all the travelers knew their departures had been pushed up.

Hennings heard the news and soon took perch in the lobby of the main entrance of Mailing Avenue. He had a rolling suitcase, an over-shoulder bag and a heavy rectangular case. He opened the case up on one of the tables. Inside was a foam-cushioned collection of at least three lenses and light meters and cords.

There were different labels, D-H, which were his initials and then a series of three lenses that began N-1, his Nikon camera wedged at the top. A pouch covered another area of the interior, which presumably held a fourth. While the other people got organized, he pulled out one of the lenses. It had infrared capabilities, the latest addition to his collection. He didn't say he loved it but you could tell he did.

Turteltaub suddenly appeared in the lobby and took one look at Hennings' luggage.

"You are not bringing all of that for an overnight to Vegas."

Turteltaub was carrying a black Tumi duffel bag, which held everything he needed. It hung loosely over his left shoulder, a water bottle and banana in his right hand.

"Seriously. That's ridiculous."

Hennings by then had the case closed and lowered to the ground. He laughed, although he was indeed serious. More people arrived in the lobby, the flow pushing the two men out the door together, one hauling perhaps 50 pounds of goods, the other less than 20.

Rake and Peterson were already outside, exchanging details at startling speed about what needed to happen in the next day, since she was staying on Mailing Avenue. Samuels and Badalato soon joined them, along with Badalato's wife, Anne, who was visiting. She had their other dog, Bisou. Buddy remained inside, barking occasionally at his exclusion.

Kamishin, who was standing near Badalato, shared something quietly into the ear of Stephens, who then sprinted toward the door. Calloway, who was just outside the door on the cellphone, stepped out of her way.

Meanwhile, Simpson, who had been inside, walked up.

"Where's Bomba?" Kamishin asked, revealing the likely subject of the whisper. Anderson had found the production designer, who had gone to his hotel to get something, Calloway said. She had her keys and was on her way to get him to take him to the airport. Kamishin nodded.

Soon they were all loaded in the van, Turteltaub in the center in the seat just behind the driver. Everyone was laughing both inside the van and out, optimistic traffic would cooperate so they could make their flight. The ground crew headed back inside Mailing Avenue as the van pulled out.

A few minutes later, Rake called. In the chaos he had left his phone charger. They alerted Calloway, who was then en route to the airport with Bomba. They were close enough to turn back. Someone from Production went out to the parking lot to hand off the charger and save time.

The machine was officially well-oiled. All of them made the flight, the charger returned to its owner. The driver returned with one item: Hennings' camera case. He had removed what was essential and sent it back.

CHAPTER EIGHT
3 Weeks Out
Oct. 1-5

CALLOWAY HAD BEEN AN IMPRESSIVE one-woman travel office. Just the volume of paperwork coming from her office during prep was evidence enough. It wasn't just plane tickets. She also oversaw the rental cars that had been used in prep, 25 a week on average as it heated up, although the bullpen assisted. She handled things like the Costume department trips to New York as well. She also handled arrangements for studio execs, producers and even job candidates.

Then there were the Atlanta hotels for crew and longer-term arrangements. A local consultant worked on contracts with hotels and larger housing needs, including short-term rentals that had everything needed, from trash pick up to cable.

Thus far they had used four hotels in Atlanta, the Ritz Carlton downtown and Buckhead, the Westin and the Hilton. There were underlying guidelines that governed who stayed at the Ritz or the Westin. Above-the-liners, Turteltaub and Laurence "Larry" Mark -- the producer coming in later in the week -- naturally went to the Ritz. It was more amorphous from there as to accommodation and what crew traveled by what class of travel. The distinctions were determined by any number of factors, starting with union agreements but also deal memos.

Everyone above-the-line flew first class, as did studio execs. Some department heads flew first class as well, but not all. Bomba and Pink, the production and costume designers, respectively, sat up front while the heads of the smaller departments, Set Decorating and Props, flew coach. The seconds or lead managers in all of those departments, some with big management roles like the costume supervisor, flew coach, as did the script supervisor. Meanwhile, the entire assistant director team, including the 2nd AD and the 2nd 2nd AD, flew first class. For that, they could thank the Directors Guild of America.

With the looming move to Las Vegas, Calloway had hundreds of flights to arrange, all of which had to be closely tracked. Each itinerary appeared as a line item on Calloway's core spreadsheet to that end. Each trip required an individual memo. Travel memos went out widely via email. It was something that saved time, because it enabled people to check schedules on their own.

The spreadsheet contained travel details like the person's name, title, and class of travel. From there it was the airline, flight number, confirmation number, departure city, time, transportation, arrival city, time, hotel.

Handling the travel requirements of prep was manageable but the workload had intensified. The hope was that it would lighten when principal photography began, given the Transportation department would be operating, and they could handle ground travel.

Calloway had increased her hours and often stayed later than the rest of Production. A week earlier she had gone too far and had stayed overnight. It hadn't been planned but she needed to get paperwork done and it was easier to finish.

When Kamishin found out the next day, she insisted Calloway stay home and rest. Calloway worked from home in the morning but still showed up on Mailing Avenue later in the day. Kamishin also assigned the concierge to assist in the travel office, although it wasn't clear how much she helped, since she was the first to say she didn't have any experience.

Then something fell through the cracks regarding one of the airport pickups. It wasn't clear exactly what had happened or if it was even Calloway responsible. But Prickly Guy, via his assistant, called to complain, this time with particular venom.

Any calls from his office were answered gingerly. Kamishin, who was within earshot when the call came in, grimaced and nodded toward her office, indicating she would take the call there. She listened quietly until the caller suggested the travel coordinator should be fired.

She promised to check into it while coming to the defense of the travel office. Kamishin was tough and not afraid to lean on staff but she was also fair. All kinds of mistakes happen, she said with a calm tone, including limo companies that agree to make a pick up and don't tell drivers. That had already happened once, so she wasn't going to jump to conclusions now.

Kamishin knew exactly what the travel coordinator job entailed. She also knew that anyone in the role took heat, even though they had no control over airlines, hotels or drivers, which generally was where a problem originated. It paid more than other production jobs for a reason – no one wanted to do it. If you could do the job, you could also be the APOC or production coordinator, positions that had great ability to control outcomes.

Calloway was doing a great job, Kamishin said. There certainly wasn't anyone available who could do it better. Firing her was out of the question; they'd be lucky if she didn't quit.

Ironically, the fact the travel coordinator was overworked pointed back to the studio. Badalato and Samuels initially budgeted two people for the office. The studio had insisted *Last Vegas* wasn't a high-travel show, despite two locations 2,000 miles apart, so they reduced the line item.

There was one other wrinkle. Part of the workload involved re-doing finished work when the traveler decided to make a change. There were no rules that limited the scope of changes on *Last Vegas*. Sometimes there was a business reason for it, as with the creative team needing to see an additional location, which required an earlier flight.

The bulk of the changes seemed to be for personal convenience. If it were occasional it wouldn't have mattered but some people were changing the same flight twice. At the same time, a rule wouldn't have applied to producers or studio executives anyway, and they were the main culprits.

The changes were frequent enough, and unusual enough, that crew had already noticed. They all got the travel memos and could see the same ones going out. More than one discussion had taken place about how much the frequent changes to non-refundable fares cost the production. It was a tight budget after all.

Badalato had shrugged off the criticism. The budget was in order. Complaints about the travel office were another matter. Kamishin handled it well, and his silence meant the studio could take concerns to another level if they felt it warranted. He would deal with it then if needed.

He also knew Calloway was doing a good job. A few weeks earlier he had asked her to price the cost of chartering an entire aircraft to move the company to Vegas. He once saved $100,000 that way as line producer on *Around the World in Eighty Days*. She had done research that impressed him, although it showed no meaningful savings with chartering aircraft in this case.

Getting people to Vegas was in some ways the easiest part of the move. The core production team would remain in Atlanta, along with much of the Art department and the construction team, since they were building the stages and creating the sets. But roughly 80 percent of crew -- and their kits -- needed to be in Las Vegas by next Wednesday.

The boxes in the bullpen were back down to a steady flow. The shipping problem had been worked out with a confirmed address. There apparently was still some issue, but the backlogged goods had been delivered.

Someone asked Simpson if the woman had apologized for the mishap and she laughed out loud, a genuine from-the-gut laugh.

"No. She did not apologize."

The main thing was that the problem seemed resolved. The move was remarkably well organized from the Atlanta side. Based on detailed, orderly records, they could answer a question about any box or pallet or suitcase they had shipped.

All along, Badalato and Kamishin had kept tight controls of the FedEx account numbers. The policy caused some strain with departments because it added another layer of bureaucracy. Most people were used to providing numbers to vendors to ship things directly and this required going through Production for approval. Some people had special arrangements for the account but Production did not give the number out readily.

Props, in particular, experienced it as a hardship, since they ordered things on an almost daily basis, some of them quite small. Providing vendors the account number made it easy and fast for them. Instead they had vendors use their own accounts to ship things, which added a premium to the cost.

Now it made sense why Production kept control of the account number. The volume of what had to move amounted to a big line item in the budget, particularly with the move. Kamishin had learned the hard way that giving the number out freely could lead to unexpected bills as crew used it to ship things on their own that might not be approved otherwise. On a show where the budget was tight, it could be sizeable enough to push them over budget. No one in the bullpen forgot the name of this game, which was still to bring this movie in on -- or under -- budget, least of all Kamishin.

This was all on top of the normal workload involved with prepping the movie. The decision to fit moving day in the middle of two tech-scouts had come later. Both of those coordinated events, which were needed to finalize all aspects of locations, also had to be organized. Among other things, the scouts would bring studio executives to Mailing Avenue. Prickly Guy, alone, was guaranteed to add stress.

It was conceivable that Larry Mark's arrival in Atlanta would generate a sense of foreboding similar to the first visit of the studio execs. As one of two top creative producers on *Last Vegas*, he could impact any of them. Instead it was nearly the opposite as crew, none of whom had met him before, prepared for his arrival.

Mark, 63, had produced or executive-produced a long line of significant movies across all genres. While his name wasn't recognizable to the average movie-goer, he was nearly as iconic in his field as were De Niro, Douglas and Freeman in theirs. In the past decade he'd been behind the scenes on *Julia & Julia* with Meryl Streep, *I, Robot* with Will Smith and the megahit *Dreamgirls*, with Beyoncé, Jamie Foxx and Jennifer Hudson. Scanning back another decade the high-caliber list continued: *As Good As It Gets*, *Jerry Maguire*, *Working Girl* and *Black Widow*. And that was just a sampler.

Mark started out with publicity and marketing posts at Paramount Pictures, eventually becoming vice president of marketing. From there he became vice president of production at Paramount and then executive vice president of production at Twentieth Century Fox. Along the way he worked on a lot of very successful movies, including *Terms of Endearment*, *Trading Places* and *Broadcast News*.

The bullpen crew was discussing Mark when Samuels came into the bullpen. Calloway had handled his plane ticket as part of her job as travel coordinator but Production would organize his transportation to the Ritz and then to Mailing Avenue. Samuels, there to drop off paperwork, picked up on the conversation.

"If there's a movie I wish I'd made, it's *Jerry Maguire*," he offered. The 1996 hit about a sports agent whose moral epiphany gets him fired was nominated for five Academy Awards and garnered an acting win for Cuba Gooding Jr. Included was a nomination for Best Picture, which would have meant a statue for Mark. It also made a lot of money, but most of his movies did.

Somebody asked Samuels why he liked it. As line producer, he was generally in a hurry when he came through the bullpen. He would chit-chat but this seemed deeper than a passing nod to the conversation at hand. "I just really think it's a great movie -- on so many levels," he said, coming to a stop. "Larry Mark is the real thing," he added. "And he's a nice guy, too."

It was a rare side of Samuels. Simpson used the opportunity to ask him about *Love Jones*, which is on the list of top films made by black directors. It's known as a love story with strong acting, great sensibility and solid dialogue. Samuels had executive produced the 1997 movie, which meant it was being made the same year *Jerry Maguire* came out.

"That was my first producing -- producing role," Samuels said. "Can you believe they made it for $7 million?" They chatted about Love Jones, various actors and a pivotal scene where there had been too much fog when they were shooting to suit the director. Simpson knew a lot about the movie. She had produced two black-genre projects of her own, *Breaking Up Is Hard To Do* and *Probable Cause*. The conversation wound down with talk of the wrap party for *Love Jones*, which included an anecdote about a tattoo.

Samuels had a more recent tattoo story of his own. He pulled his collar back slightly to show a "reboot" button. He had gotten it after his divorce.

After Samuels left, Simpson returned to details of Mark's arrival.

"Asante." The PA was seated at his table working on something.

"Yes?"

"You are going to pick up Larry Mark."

"Sure," he grinned. "When?"

"Tomorrow," said Simpson. "You'll pick him up at the Ritz Carlton and bring him here tomorrow." Her voice trailed off slightly as she looked at his clothes. "Is that all you have?"

That took the grin away. He was wearing jeans and a nice, untucked, white button-down long sleeve shirt. He tilted his head, just a little, and looked back at her.

"You need to dress appropriately," said Simpson.

"Okay," he said, looking puzzled as he lifted up his arms and looked at his shirt. He looked good. He had driven other famous people before dressed the same. He'd even been the one to pick up Prickly Guy, reporting that not only had he been nice, he had asked the PA about himself.

"You'll need to go into the lobby with a sign," she said, pausing. "And wear a cap." She turned her attention back to her desk. Asante looked at Stephens, who was his immediate boss. She quickly looked away.

"I do not need to wear a cap!" Asante said it with just the slightest lift at the end of the sentence as to be a question.

"A cap," said Simpson, firmly.

Stephens looked up at Asante, who was looking back and forth between them. She gave him a compassionate look that said she knew it would be hard. But she nodded. Yes, he did.

"A cap? You're kidding," he said. "No way."

Simpson looked up from her desk, this time slightly annoyed.

"Asante, yes. This is Larry Mark. Larry. Mark."

He kept looking at her, the grin returning.

"I don't believe you," he said, looking at her intently. Simpson joked a fair amount, that was true, but she seemed extremely serious.

"Fine," Simpson said, sounding annoyed. "Then you can ask Damiana." She again turned her gaze to her desk.

Asante sat there another minute, mulling it all over. Then he headed to the travel office, the hallway in the other direction from Kamishin's office. He'd ask Calloway. The travel coordinator would tell him the truth and it would be safer than going to the production coordinator.

Everyone giggled after he left the room and Simpson shushed them. A minute later Kamishin came into the bullpen to hand something to Stephens. Simpson whispered loudly that Asante soon would ask her whether he had to wear a cap to pick up Larry Mark.

"Tell him yes, okay?" Simpson asked.

Kamishin laughed.

Asante returned a few minutes later with a *Last Vegas* logo sign to make it easy for Mark to identify him. A short time later, Kamishin, who had continued going back and forth from her office, was back in the bullpen. Simpson prompted him.

"Asante. Do you have a question for Damiana?"

Kamishin stopped and looked at him.

Asante smiled broadly.

"They're telling me I need to wear a cap to pick up Larry Mark."

"A driver's hat," Simpson clarified. "Yes."

Kamishin nodded yes to him, rather solemnly, and turned around to the bookcase near where she was standing.

Asante looked crestfallen for the two seconds it took for Kamishin to pivot back around. No, she said. He did not have to wear a cap.

The room burst into laughter.

"I knew it!" said Asante.

"You did not know," said Stephens, who was laughing so hard she could barely get the words out. When she had stopped laughing and could take a breath she said it again. "You did not!"

"Yes, I did," he replied, matter-of-factly, a look of relief on his face.

When Rake had updated the One Liner a week earlier, he also put out an unofficial version of the "Day out of Days," which detailed the actors' schedules. It showed why he wanted to wait. The main shift was an additional blackout date for De Niro, and the corresponding ripple effect. The actor had initially listed the date as one he was available, but by the time it was scheduled, he no longer had it available.

The first version of the DOOD had shown Michael Douglas and Robert De Niro on for 40 days, Morgan Freeman and Kevin Kline 39, and Mary Steenburgen 22. The version out this week now had De Niro, Freeman and Kline to 37 days, Steenburgen 20, while Douglas stayed the same at 40. His character was at the center of the story, so that made sense.

The DOOD was a three-page chart with a small font best viewed with a magnifying glass. It contained a wealth of detail that enabled shooting days and other fractions that could be looked at like the slices of an MRI. The characters' names comprised the left column: Billy, Paddy, Archie, Sam, Diane and so on for hundreds of slots. The columns across the top of the chart represented each shooting day followed by columns for work, hold, travel and holiday, along with the time each actor would start and finish. "Hold" meant they were available to work if needed. Looked at vertically, one row showed everyone due on a particular day.

The names were numbered in order to 55 to cover the entire cast with a couple extra blanks for room to grow. After the A List began the large group of secondary roles. The mystery television actor that Turteltaub had been considering for the role was revealed there.

Jerry Ferrara, who would play the role of "Todd," a young sidekick to the lead characters once they teach him a lesson, was on for 25 days. Only they were going to change his name to "Dean." Clearance, the lawyers in LA, decided "Todd" shouldn't be used, although nobody was sure exactly why it represented a conflict.

Ferrara was a television actor best known for his role as Turtle on "Entourage," which ran on HBO from 2004 to 2011. A television actress, Bre Blair, would play "Lisa," the fiancé of Michael Douglas' character. She had a long list of one-episode roles on various television shows and more than few short but recurring roles, most recently on "90210" and "Make It or Break It." She had also been cast in several TV movies. Her scheduled work on *Last Vegas* was originally planned over 14 days but had since been winnowed down to 11 days. Her role was a small but important one. It was Lisa and Billy's wedding that brought the foursome to Vegas.

Though most of the significant roles had been cast and finalized there were still two that needed to be filled. The biggest was Roger/Madonna, a female impersonator, who was at the center of a smaller but still strong plot point. It needed an actor who could portray a regular guy and do a reasonable -- or funny and unreasonable -- version of a Madonna imper-sonator. The other role, Lonnie, the Aria's high-roller concierge whose job was to make sure key guests are properly entertained, was also key, but not as tough to cast.

Whichever actors landed those roles would work about 20 days. From there the DOOD moved to less significant roles similar to how credits of a movie read: "Pretty young clerk," "Danny the Greaser," or "Cabbie No. 1." In the mix was a cameo of Carrot Top, the comedian also known as Scott Thompson.

After number 55, the chart skipped to the 100s and four holding places for stunt actors. Then it skipped again to the number 200 with the lone entry: Kanye West. The hip hop musician and artist, whose relationship with Kim Kardashian currently filled entertainment news, was still on there but probably not for long. The scene he was scheduled for would be shot on Dec. 11, and he had a scheduling conflict. Given the schedules of all the other actors working that day, changing it would be nearly impossible. The creative producers were working on replace-ments.

Meanwhile, the scouting trips had increased in intensity. There is worse work than getting into a van with a group of guys -- and it was all guys -- to review potential locations for movie sets, even in summer heat of Atlanta and Las Vegas. But with the pressure on the forays were no longer laid back, as they had been in the early weeks.

One anecdote from the scouts emerged above all others. For the most part it had been the same creative team, along with Samuels as line producer. But this one included Prickly Guy, who joined the group when he was in Atlanta. Any new person to a small group changes its dynamic but this was something else entirely.

Prickly Guy said what he thought and made suggestions about what should happen. It sounded strangely like he was telling the director what to do. That wasn't wise with Turteltaub. It had the effect of silencing the others unless they had to address something. The director kept quiet for a while, longer than anyone would have expected. Finally the studio exec pushed too hard, citing a movie he had worked as a basis for whatever recommendation he offered.

"Yeah?" Turteltaub said, turning his head to look at him. "How did that movie do?"

It hadn't done very well. The director knew it, they all knew it. If there was one thing the guys in the van knew at that point it was who else was in the van. If there were two things they knew, it was what each of the others had done in their careers in the movie business.

The studio exec could exert influence in getting someone on the crew fired, or at least let them think so, or have his assistant browbeat PAs who answered the phone. But he couldn't fire the director. The man comfortable stepping on toes had finally landed on boots. Prickly Guy was quieter from there, at least for a while.

Turteltaub still had a lot of decisions to make based on the chart on the wall at the Locations office at Mailing Avenue. It laid out current progress. The left side was a list of 12 locations needed in Atlanta, while the top column was a checklist: Insurance certificates, W-9, Contract, Check Request, Permit, Base Camp, Crew Parking, Extras Parking, Catering, Extras Holding, Police, Security, Rest Rooms, Dumpsters, HVAC, Release.

Just six locations, half of them, had "x" marks by insurance certificates, which meant they were locked, since that was one of the last things to happen. That had them a little worried although Turteltaub not so much. He was holding out for the best options, and when he had to, he'd pull the trigger. One of his options was not to pick a location at all, which would require they instead build it on the soundstages.

At the same time, every day that went by without confirmed locations added a little pressure to creative crew working on Mailing Avenue. Their work couldn't begin until the director signed off. A new set would have to be designed, built and decorated, for instance.

The Locations department still felt pressure to find new places. By this point they had looked at hundreds of locations. Kai Thorup, the assistant location manager teaming with Findley, said 44 churches alone had been visited, photographed and cleared. Then there were storefronts under consideration, an indoor pool scene, club scenes. Thorup thought the department had come up with very good options, although he knew not to press that point.

"Even if it's perfect, the director will want to see what else was out there, in case there was something out there that's more perfect," he said. "That isn't just Jon. It's most directors."

It wasn't always smart for the Locations department to show a director the best stuff first. Most wanted to see other things, only to then come back and select the first one shown. It was better to build up to it, show a few secondary options before going to the primo one. The other issue was whether another director had ever used the same location in a different movie. That was a turnoff for a lot of directors. They wanted an original look. There were no examples of Turteltaub rejecting a location because it had been in another movie.

But the end was in sight, even with five weeks before principal photography kicked off in Atlanta. Once Turteltaub left for Vegas next week he would not return to Atlanta until they were shooting. All his effort would then be on Vegas, teeing up the first days of principal photography.

The Art department had stayed every bit as busy as the bullpen. The table under the window between the two desks of Lipp and the assistant now featured two dog beds. Rocko and the Chihuahua were fast friends by now and their pattern was established. The little dog stayed in its bed to watch the art world. Rocko lay on the floor closer to Lipp. Sometimes he sat in the chair.

Lipp had helped organize the Art department's tech scout, although they would stay on Mailing Avenue. By getting the others to the location together, Bomba could ensure they were all aware of changes for the sets that would be built or adapted there. It also helped prepare him for next week's formal tech scout. He needed to be able to answer any questions that would come up and to make a case if any of the changes would create budget issues.

The first two stops, a funeral home and a nightclub, had been approved by Turteltaub and locked by the Locations department. A third site, this one under consideration for a wedding chapel scene, would be the last stop in the day. Turteltaub and Mark, who were out at another meeting, would join them there.

Bomba had worked closely with Turteltaub. The production designer had a clear idea what needed to be done and assumed most of his people did as well. The work of the day ensured the rest of the department shared the vision. Now it was a matter of making it all sync.

There were nine people in the mix and they arrived in separate vehicles. Patrick Cassidy, the set decorator, and two others from his department were there, as were Garner, the assistant art director and another artist.

As art director, Garner had the additional goal of filling in whatever blanks remained in his "director's plans." That was something very specific, a prepared document that summarized all the sets that would be distributed during the tech scout. It added creative flesh to the bones of the shooting schedule and all its offshoots.

Four vehicles converged on the defunct Candler Funeral Home in Decatur from different directions at almost precisely the same time. It was easy to see why Turteltaub and the others made such intense effort to get the right locations.

The funeral home was literally right out of the script and befitting the character of Maurice. He was the cross-dressing performer befriended by Sam, Kevin Kline's character. Maurice, ne Madonna, would dance himself to death, a turning point in the plot. The funeral home scene would be filled with most of the cast.

Despite it being in the middle of incorporated DeKalb County, the place felt like old-style Vegas. Although perhaps not tacky, it made up for it by being vacant and dated. Built in 1960, the facility had viewing rooms and storage areas and furnished sitting areas and a large basement where corpses had been prepared for viewing for decades. It smelled like rotten eggs stored with mothballs.

It was a big piece of real estate, five acres of land and about 25,000 square feet of building. Listed at $1.7 million that January, it was now down to $1.4 million. The main section to be used for the movie, the church area, was a relatively small portion of the facility. Four scenes would be shot at the funeral home over the course of a single day, according to Rake's schedule.

Findley, the head of the Locations department, had discovered the funeral home while doing work for the movie *Motor City* a couple of months earlier. That script hadn't called for a funeral home but he made note of it. A short time later he was reading *Last Vegas* to prep for an interview with Badalato and Samuels. When he read the funeral scene he knew he had a prime candidate. It was a detail that also played well in the interview.

The seven people from the Art department on the scout fanned out, measuring things, lifting drapes and examining pews. Garner walked with the assistant art director through one lobby toward the one on the other end, the smell of place still strong.

143

"What is that?" The assistant art director wrinkled his nose. It wasn't as pronounced there as in other parts of the building but still strong. It was weirdly musty with a thin coating of potpourri, neither of them the dominant odor.

"Don't worry, you won't be able to smell it in the movie," answered Garner. He had come to a stop at a wall and looked at it sideways. The paint was a soft, tan color. "Paint it Pepto pink and call it a day," he joked, as he resumed walking. The assistant looked at him askance but stopped short of an eye roll.

"What? It is a drag queen's wedding," Garner said. The younger man laughed.

With the director's plans on his plate, Garner's focus was less on aesthetics. Bomba and Cassidy had that down. Director's plans are a compilation of detailed notes about each set. He prepared a standard three-ring binder in advance of the tech scout to be used by everyone. He needed to prepare a description of the place but also to make notes on what the set needed. It was his job to track it from there. He would make sure the work got done and handle final tweaks to the budget if it cost more -- or less -- than planned.

The binder would break down each set on *Last Vegas*. It would contain a list of things needed by each segment, construction, scenic, signs/graphics, set dressing, greens, props, special effects and any other ancillary material, like aerial shots of the location or layouts of the sets. It also comes in an electronic version. Garner allowed that with time it was likely to move in that direction. As with some other kinds of paperwork in movie production, it still made sense to have a hardcopy. In this case, people on the tech scout were on foot going from place to place, and having something in hand was easier.

Garner had made a lot of director's plans over the years. Someone asked if one stood out and he answered immediately.

"*Conspirator*. Robert Redford," he said. He was art director on the movie about the prosecution of people accused in Abraham Lincoln's assassination. Shot in Savannah, Ga., it starred Robin Wright as Mary Surratt. The director's plans were particularly detailed, he said, given the movie was a period piece with a lot of specialized elements.

He was proud of the result and confidently handed the notebook to Redford, who didn't extend his hand to get it.

"I don't want that thing," said Redford. Garner laughed as he recalled it, although it didn't sound funny.

His efforts as art director on *Last Vegas* had widened with the start of the construction coordinator. Henery, who was with them on the scout, had hired a dozen crew in just a week. Henery was independent, with his own moving construction business, but Garner would track process.

Findley and the two real estate agents listing the sprawling, ranch-style building had been standing in the biggest of the foyers while the crew meandered around the place on distinct missions. Gradually, they all collected nearby. Bomba joined Findley, Cassidy not far behind, and nodded for them all to join. They listened as Bomba explained to the two women what he wanted to do.

The scene would use a different entrance than the one everyone had come through. He walked toward the entrance of the smaller of the lobbies and opened the double doors. Bomba and Cassidy looked at the entrance from different angles, Cassidy noting a minor structural flaw. Bomba had seen a mark in the trim that required touch-up paint inside as well as a bubble in the varnish of the exterior door. Those things could be repaired; it didn't need a fresh paint job.

Next were the windows on either side of the 14-foot entrance. How to dress them, curtains or drapes? And what colors? They decided on sheers as Bomba helped Cassidy measure the windows. Garner took notes and would check later that it all got done.

That finished, Bomba walked to the 500-seat chapel without a word. The rest of them pulled behind him as if by magnet. This was where the giant funeral scene would take place.

The real estate agents had quietly followed along. "There's special peach-toned lighting over the stage," one of the women offered. "It helps with the color of flesh on bodies."

"At least we hope everyone will be alive when we're shooting," Garner said quietly.

"She knows it's not a real funeral, right?" someone replied.

The group talked about lighting and furniture and whether the windows needed draperies and where the casket would go on the stage. Bomba and Cassidy again looked at various things on the wall and decided against any major alterations. One change was needed, however: The valance in the hallway should be re-hung over the coffin, he said. Then the discussion turned to flowers.

Slowly, the crew had settled into pews. As soon as Bomba was finished, they were up. The entire visit had lasted less than 30 minutes.

"C'mon," said Bomba, giving a last look over his shoulder at the chapel as he headed out. "I don't want to be here anymore." He stopped and thanked the building owner on his way out.

Within moments the vehicles were all on the road going in the same direction, much as they had converged on the funeral home. The next stop was a popular nightclub in Midtown Atlanta.

"The next one isn't going to be as easy," Garner said.

Two nightclub sets were being created for *Last Vegas*. Both of them would be named after bars in the Aria but would be shot in Atlanta. Unlike the penthouse set being built on the soundstages to precise measurements taken at the Aria there was room for variation.

The Velvet Room in Tucker, Ga., would be the site of the biggest of the bar sets, fashioned after the HAZE Nightclub at the Aria. That scene would include hundreds of extras. At the center were the lead actors, having fun at the high-end club and flirting with young women, when a younger guy creates a scuffle. De Niro's Paddy would deck him.

The second stop focused on scenes that would represent a different, smaller club at the Aria, this one called the Deuce Lounge. That's where Kevin Kline's character, Sam, would encounter a female impersonator named Maurice/Madonna. Someone noted they were going back in time, starting at the place where Maurice would be eulogized and then to where he was introduced in the movie. That was a normal part of any shooting schedule.

The Vanquish Lounge, at 1029 Peachtree Street, would serve as the place where the naïve Sam would hit on Madonna, not realizing it was actually Maurice. With 6,000 square feet of space, it was too big. But it had the right decor. The club featured huge billboard-sized images of exotic animals and sexy women. It also had alligator leather booths and sofas. Except for its size, the club was a good fit.

The location nearly didn't happen. Once Turteltaub gave the greenlight for the location negotiations began. The nightclub's management wanted somewhere in the neighborhood of $10,000 to rent it for two days. Badalato and Samuels had balked. Samuels tried to negotiate with the nightclub's management directly but they held firm. In the end, with time pressing in, they agreed.

The urban hot spot was large and needed to be converted to a cozier nightclub. Cassidy, the buyer and leadman conferred by a giant leopard graphic on the wall while the rest of the Art department fanned out, measuring couches and tables and taking photographs. Bomba arrived a few minutes later, cradling a giant Starbucks.

A huge graphic mural ran the length of the largest bar. It had two images of women, one of them taking up 60 percent of the space, and two tigers. The woman in the larger image seemed to be all flesh but no actual body parts were visible. The angle looked down on her head one side, her hand covering her breast, while the rest of her body bent seductively with a tiger head nearby. The other image showed the long back of a woman in a low cut dress and just a hint of the crack of her buttocks. Bomba liked the look of the place for the scene and the images were big enough to be easily lost in the background.

Bomba and Cassidy stopped at another graphic near the entrance on Peachtree Street. It was the only place in the nightclub where a lot of light got through. They would need curtains to match the décor to block out daylight.

Soon it became clear how they would make the place cozy. Screens, with fabric to match established designs and to fit the décor, would go up to block portions of the large space. Bomba moved to the middle of the room, again with magnetic effect. He walked the line where the first screen was to go while somebody else measured.

The group listened in as he and Cassidy talked about changes, Garner taking notes. Adding slipcovers to the bar stools would give them a classier look. The couches would work, Bomba said, as long as they made some repairs. The set designer, this man on the Art department staff rather than set decorating, carried CAD-designed architectural plans in one hand and a measuring tape in the other. As they talked, he measured the table or couches with a lot of detail. In the end, he would have precise details to turn his drawings into a very close approximation of the set.

Cassidy mentioned a high-stakes gaming area in the back booths, in keeping with the Aria. The production designer liked that idea. They needed casino atmosphere. The Atlanta set had to have an authentic Vegas feel. Slot machines were also in the works. There was a question about whether they needed to add loop-and-playback to the TV monitors.

One of the crew called out the time, reminding Bomba they had to meet Turteltaub at a church on the other side of town. The last stop was under consideration for a smaller chapel scene, this one where the characters played by Michael Douglas and Mary Steenburgen would briefly interact. None of the churches they had visited for this scene had fit with Turteltaub's imagination. He didn't like this one, either. Instead of putting an "x" mark on the chart in the location office, meaning a location had been selected and locked, they could wipe it off entirely. They would build the set on Mailing Avenue.

It was one more thing for the Art department but they had assumed the list of sets would grow. They had time for this one, since it was scheduled for later anyway.

Cassidy now turned his attention back to the sets in Las Vegas. Traveling back and forth had required balancing, since he had so much to do in Atlanta. It helped that Vegas had its own leadman and buyer.

Vegas was a lot of location work but that didn't always make it easier. It was rare that the Art department wouldn't make changes, no matter how perfect a place seemed on the surface. Things in real life don't necessarily translate to the screen. A wall with a stain barely visible to the eye would be accentuated on camera. A couch that stands out when you enter a room could be striking but on camera it's distracting. Then there are technical considerations.

Cassidy said many changes were in the works for the scenes in Las Vegas that were designed expressly so they wouldn't be noticed. It was new seat covers for some of the casino shots. They were doing that for the bar scenes to be shot in Atlanta and they needed to match. They would also add greenery, different cab signs, signage for the airport. The biggest effort involved the scenes by the pool, since they were building a large stage there. Other things weren't as big but still time-consuming.

One thing that remained on his desk was a scene in the casino that required a giant upright wheel. Once spun it would make a number of turns before stopping at a prize. He could easily make it in Atlanta, but given they needed it in Vegas it made more sense to have it made there. There wasn't a production-controlled mill shop in Vegas but he would work on that when he got there.

As planned, the Costume department had spent the bulk of prep at Warner Bros. Aside from grumbling about the size of the first bill that came in -- met with a comment from Samuels that if costumes went over budget they would risk a cut elsewhere, perhaps the loss of a costumer position -- things had calmed down between them. Distance hadn't hurt one bit and neither had Jobst. The costume supervisor had a personality that enabled her to get along with most people. Like many good costume supervisors, she was adept at the middle-child role and skilled at the art of subtle negotiation, something occasionally needed between factions of the movie family.

Just driving to the Warner Bros lot meant a tour through traditional Hollywood. It was a beacon to the industry, entrenched in Burbank, as were others, the same way the Malt-O-Meal Co. was in Northfield, Minn.

Once past security the history of it opened up. The term "lot" itself seemed deceptively small to anyone outside California. Located on the edge of Burbank next to the Hollywood Hills, the Warner Bros compound spread over 162 acres. It was split between its 110-acre main studio lot, a 32-acre ranch, and a 20-acre backlot that could be rain forest or city.

Virtually everything needed to make a movie or television show was contained there, from prep through post-production, most of it on the main lot. There were 30 sound stages and a river of rental and service departments from grip and electric to mill and craft shops to special effects, sound and audio mastering. The tributaries were a drapery specialist, a sign shop and scenic art department.

The costume department building loomed large in the mix with its seamstresses, colorists and costumers. The *Last Vegas* Costume department, along with people working on other movies and television shows, worked from the largely windowless floor that had the cages. Jobst had continued to pull clothes from Warner Bros. but she and the others also had Western Costume to cull from. All of it was done with an eye toward organizing it for the move to Las Vegas and principal photography.

Pink had returned from New York with clear vision for Billy, Paddy and Sam. Her process had been a blend of logic and creativity. What clothes would these characters wear before they got to Vegas? What clothes would they wear as part of the transformation that occurred there?

The meeting with Kline had gone well enough that Sam was essentially finished. Billy, the wealthy Malibu lawyer, needed nice clothes but also to be fit well, so added attention was placed there. Michael Douglas had a particular clothier he worked with who they were happy to use.

Paddy's wardrobe was an extension of the clothes he wore in the first scene. Logically, that was a bathrobe, since he didn't get out much. That spoke to a character who probably didn't shop for clothes much. Paddy would still have the same jeans and polo shirts he had when he tended bar at his pub, say a faded, logoed pub T-shirt. The graphic artist had finished the logo for it back on Mailing Avenue.

While dapper in his youth, Archie's wardrobe would be comfortable and comforting because of his stroke. He would wear a patchwork coat that gave off that vibe. The character would also have a baseball cap.

She also considered the clothes the characters would wear as a group. They would all undergo a transformation. Each outfit -- every accessory -- needed to reflect where they were in that timeline as well as their unique styles. A scene in the movie included them in a fitting room as they planned for a big party. The physical transformation on camera would be the characters in their new suits walking along a busy corridor in Aria. How would they fit together?

Pink decided that Paddy, the most black-and-white in demeanor of the characters, would wear a white dinner jacket, and sport a "Rat Pack look." That helped with the gruff personality of the character, who wasn't afraid to take a swing at somebody. Archie's attire, a red suit with open collar, would reflect his flamboyant youth, which came through in the script when he wins big at the gaming tables. The others would be in different colors, but not too dramatic a contrast.

Morgan Freeman and Mary Steenburgen's costume fittings were on the calendar and the same preparations were under way as for the others. Only this was much easier. A floor above where the *Last Vegas* costumers worked were "star" dressing rooms with lighted mirrored platforms, separate dressing areas. Anything they might need for the meetings was probably in the building.

Steenburgen's character, Diana Boyle, involved the same thought process on the part of Pink, just more of it. As the sole female lead, she needed to command the screen, but she also had a lot of costume changes. The character's background as a lawyer was important in planning. As a lounge singer, she needed a series of gorgeous dresses and a casual-professional appearance for her other scenes, including jumpsuits, leather jackets, and "modern looks accented by great jewelry."

Finalizing the looks for the other two lead actors was the biggest task on the calendar but there were other fittings in the mix. There were numerous other costumes to consider for characters. Fittings would continue throughout on an almost tiered basis, getting the most important finished first. The movie had a lot of "specialty background," people who would wear unusual costumes. For that matter, the department was responsible for approving the costumes of all background actors. Some could be advised to bring costumes but that didn't guarantee they would be appropriate. Minimally they had to be checked.

All of that was happening in the midst of their last week at Warner Bros. Jobst had been organizing the costume move all along. The facility had a checkout process that was detailed. Then all of it had to be packaged appropriately for shipping. The actors' closets were organized separately.

Costume boxes -- generally called containers -- were their own breed, distinct from other cardboard boxes. These were particularly durable and specifically sized. E Containers measured a hefty 42" by 29" by 27," D Containers a more demure 27" by 19" by 19." The WCC brand on many of them meant they were sold by Western Costume Co.

Boxes were labeled by character name. There would be a lot of them, given that all primary costumes needed duplicate versions, more if they would be damaged in shooting as with the pool scenes. Then there were the racks and boxes of clothes for extras. Everything was catalogued and organized for the move.

That accomplished, the Costume department would fly to Vegas on Monday, as would the assistant art director. He would get the space in the Annex opened up for his department and arrive Monday. Cassidy had local set decorating people there. The Vegas-based Locations department had been at work for some time. The satellite production office, by now ensconced in offices on the fourth floor of the Aria, was there to help them settle in. Almost all of the rest of the crew would arrive on Wednesday.

CHAPTER NINE
2 Weeks Out
Oct. 8-12, 2012

B Y 7:30 A.M. MONDAY the Mailing Avenue bullpen was nearing full throttle. The Atlanta tech scout would take place over the next two days and with it an influx of people from the studios, including Prickly Guy. Then there was the company move to Las Vegas on Wednesday, followed by two days of tech scouts there. Then one final week of prep before principal photography kicked off in the heart of Sin City.

Surely two, two-day tech scouts 2,000 miles apart was more than anybody could do in one week? It was a question for Badalato, who was fast-walking in and out of the bullpen, to Kamishin's office, to Rake's, to Samuels's.

"Wait until we start shooting," he replied, with a grin.

It was either a great mask or real confidence, and with Badalato most people assumed the latter, but the pressure was on. It was up to the Production department to make sure the tech scout ran smoothly and that all the people, and all their kits, made it to Las Vegas on time. It presumed its satellite office in Vegas could handle the crowd of crew moving into the hotel, and that the scouts there had enough support.

The Production department had rented the short buses, or "people movers" in the sales vernacular, to take the group around to review locations. The department also had organized food, and provided whatever other support was needed. They coordinated the out-of-town visitors visa vis Calloway.

Crew in the Mailing Avenue bullpen would stay in Atlanta to continue prepping for their return after the location work. All they had to do was make it through the current stress to the end of Wednesday. Then the place would be emptied out and relatively calm, at least for a month.

Simpson returned to the bullpen after checking the buses. They had arrived early and were clean but something was missing. Asante was sitting at the table unoccupied when she returned. He smiled.

"Where are the coolers?" she asked. A cooler generally went on the regular scouts but not always.

"Findley said he didn't want a cooler," he answered, referring to the locations manager.

Simpson looked at him for a second. That seemed unlikely. If the head of the Locations department had said that, it probably had been at an earlier scout. The Production department had purchased Artesian water and higher-end snacks for the brass on the tech scout. Had he been out when that happened? She skipped all that and got to the point.

"Jon Turteltaub does want a cooler," she said. "And he's the director." Turteltaub was in office in the executive suite, door open and on the phone, completely oblivious of attempts to ensure his comfort.

Asante's grin had disappeared by the end of her first sentence. He was on his way to craft services by the end of the second.

The Atlanta Locations department had organized the itinerary for the local scout, ensuring each place was ready to receive the group. There were more than a dozen location visits, each coordinated with landlords or real estate agents. The tech scouts presumed all locations had been approved, but with the elimination of the remote Barnesville location for the 1955 scenes at least one was up in the air. That was another issue entirely. At the same time, the Locations department in Vegas was finalizing efforts for the tech scout there.

The Atlanta group consisted of more than 20 people, including Turteltaub and the ADs, Badalato and Samuels, all locations department crew, other department heads and respective crew, along with any studio executives or producers who wanted to attend. It was normal for the final tech scout to have studio presence. Budget estimates would be firmed up and potential problems would be identified with plenty of time to fix them.

The buses were scheduled to leave at 8:00 a.m. but 15 minutes into the hour both were less than half full. There were two reasons. The first was that the buses couldn't leave without the director. As long as Turteltaub remained in his office, crew knew they could keep working, because buses weren't going anywhere without him.

The other reason was Prickly Guy. A couple of crew held back surreptitiously until he boarded so they could get on the other bus. A few minutes later Turteltaub appeared, leaping up the steps of the bus Prickly Guy was on. He stopped in his tracks and looked around, and nodded pleasantly at the junior studio executive. Then he exited and boarded the other bus. Meanwhile, word that the director was out front circulated and soon stragglers were on board. The buses pulled out a short time later.

Not everyone disliked Prickly Guy, and there were crew oblivious to the conflict. The camera crew, two of whom were officially on the clock this week, thought he was great. The negative sentiment was centered in the creative departments on Mailing Avenue. Prickly Guy had run off an early hire for the AD office. He had called all departments out on the carpet for the comment of one department head. He or his assistant had steadily insulted or offended people on the phone. And he had gone after a member of the crew. That it was a popular member of the crew who did work for all departments hadn't helped.

There had been ongoing discussions about Prickly Guy.

"What exactly does he do?"

"He's here to get the attention he lacked as a child," was the first reply, to raucous laughter.

"He's as useless as the G in lasagna."

"Seriously."

"Nobody really knows."

"He represents the studio's interest."

"He's here to check up on Samuels and Badalato."

It was fear. There had been enough unpleasant interactions that no one wanted to be next. Yet, in a weird way he had strengthened the crew. It wasn't new that crew looked out for its own. There was a strong sense of loyalty, particularly within departments. But he had made it stronger and bolstered the bond between departments.

It didn't mean there weren't conflicts among crew or departments -- there were. It was just that as a rule they handled problems among themselves. It was one way that movie production differed from most corporate experiences. Within corporate America, if one department was slacking, or there were issues between departments, it was accepted that an upper-level manager would intervene. The collective experience of movie crew was that introducing an outside force into department dynamics -- even an UPM or line producer, much less someone from the studio -- made it worse. Even getting poor-performing crew fired wasn't a good idea, because the position was likely to go unfilled.

Prickly Guy had in effect united them against a common adversary. While Badalato and Samuels were viewed somewhat critically, it wasn't the same. A line producer and UPM were part of normal framework, there day-in, day-out. Crew understood they were doing their jobs, even if they didn't like it or them, depending on the movie. The studio intervening on the level of crew was different because it didn't happen much. In being aggressive, Prickly Guy played into a dynamic that thrived with a villain anyway.

Not only was he more hands-on than anyone was used to from a studio, he didn't seem to make things better. It didn't seemed like he saved any money or added any expertise. Crew said he was more of a distraction. Every studio executive had questions and occasional issues. Prickly Guy had complaints. He needed to be accommodated promptly and gingerly and it was draining. The best way to manage him was to avoid him.

Studios develop projects, pull together financing, market and release movies, generally through established distribution channels. They have a lot riding on a production running smoothly. So, naturally they pay attention and intervene if needed. But studios hire a veteran line producers like Samuels to manage the day-to-day process of making a movie on or under budget for a reason. He has a track record and doesn't mind being the bad guy.

Job descriptions of studio positions vary greatly between companies. Some are revealed in titles, such as an 'executive in charge of marketing,' or publicity or distribution, or some combination. An executive in charge of physical production might oversee several movies in the pipeline at one time. Once one begins, they can track progress, watch expenditures and generally monitor what happens. If anomalies occur, they step up but otherwise the goal is to hire people good enough to do their jobs.

Baer and Mark, the creative producers, were a different breed entirely. Mark, in Atlanta the week before, had returned to L.A. Neither of them planned to attend the tech scouts. They didn't have time or inclination to micromanage the details of various sets, particularly given what was on their calendars. "They aren't tech-scouty producers, although it's certainly theirs to do if they want," said Badalato.

Instead their gaze was on the quality and salability of the movie. That meant items above the line or beside it. Baer was wrangling talent while Mark monitored script changes, although both participated in each. It was official that Kanye West could not do the cameo. Word was that Baer had organized another rapper for it. T.I. would attend the cast read-through in Las Vegas, an audition of sorts.

Changes were still being made to the script, which would soon be "locked" or finalized, although tweaks were a normal part of the process. The table read was on the schedule, the last big event leading up to principal photography. It was an organized reading of the screenplay by all actors with speaking parts, along with Turteltaub and producers. Other actors would attend to read parts that hadn't been filled, hoping for those roles or simply to stand in.

The pool scenes, and the outcome of a scene that initially centered on a wet T-shirt contest, were still in flux but coming together. Peterson reiterated it would not be on screen but so far it remained in the script. Turteltaub had landed on hiring a popular DJ to anchor the pool party scene and Baer and Mark liked the idea.

The cameo initially slated for Kanye, as well as the expanded role of the DJ and the sexy pool party, had a bigger mission. The producers and Turteltaub wanted to add appeal to the movie to entice more young moviegoers, particularly males. Movie producers talk about projects in terms of the "four quadrants," meaning male, female, young and old. *Last Vegas* had natural appeal with three. This got them closer to the fourth group.

Chad Rivetti and Chris Flurry, 1st Assist and 2nd Assist on A Camera, went to work at Panavision in Woodland Hills, Calif. The company designed and manufactured film and digital cameras and lenses. It also leased them to the movie and television industry around the world. While Panavision had offices all over the world, including Atlanta, it didn't have one in Las Vegas. There wasn't the demand to justify a separate office at that point, particular with its headquarters and the mother lode of equipment just four hours away in LA. It had operated in Sin City before in the past though and wouldn't rule it out in the future.

A camera-shop owner and several partners founded Panavision in 1954. Their initial focus was on projectors, since the business demand at that point was coming from theater owners. They needed lenses to accommodate a widescreen format because that was what was being delivered by the studios of the day. Without it, the big-screen picture suffered. That work led them to camera optics and the development of anamorphic, or cylindrical, lenses.

The effect was to compress a wide image into a standard frame that could then be expanded when projected. That generated a screen image that was about 2.5 times as wide as it was high. More importantly, it greatly improved the experience of moviegoers used to a more distorted picture. The Academy of Motion Picture Sciences gave Panavision a Scientific or Technical Award in 1958, a plaque, for the anamorphic lens. The company has earned 18 other citations since then, including an Academy Award statuette in 2002.

Panavision filed for its first patent in 1954, the same year it opened, and had applied for many since. It worked hard to keep at the forefront of the technology, including the seismic shift to digital. Its first big effort along those lines was in 1999 but the real game changer was Genesis, which came in 2004. Others were also working on it. Not even a decade later, nearly half of the movies being produced in the U.S. were shot in digital. That would only increase.

Now, the company employed 1,200 people around the world, about a quarter of them at the headquarters. In addition to servicing and leasing cameras and lenses and related equipment, offices there housed executives as well as its research, development and design staff. There also were dozens of mechanical, quality, optical and digital-imaging engineers, as well as machinists, technicians and salespeople at the facility.

Rivetti and Flurry had three days of paid prep to get camera equipment checked out, scrutinized, and ready for shipment to Las Vegas. It had already taken longer than that. Paid prep had declined over recent years for camera departments, as it had for others. It was part of the trend in cost cutting within the movie industry. Plenty of people considered it counterproductive. Panavision, for its part, expressly asked its clients to be thorough in checking out equipment.

The theory among Camera department crew and Panavision execs alike was that studio executives, producers and UPMs didn't understand well enough what happened in camera prep. If they did, they would understand that the downside of a hurried prep process far outweighed a couple of extra days of prep. It could be costly to fix something in post-production but at least it could be done. Then there were problems that were harder to remedy, like a miniscule scratch on a lens, undetectable to the human eye. Presumably someone would catch something like that along the way but things happen. At the camera level, where a problem could shut down principal photography for a day or worse, shortcutting the prep process was particularly high risk for little reward.

The decision to go Panavision surprised no one. Hennings had a relationship with the company. He knew exactly what he was getting, both figuratively and literally, and the producers supported it. He told Rivetti and Flurry to pull the camera package they had used for Horrible Bosses. It was a good starting point, since the camera needs of Last Vegas were similar. A

Panavision tech was assigned to assist the two men as they tested the equipment. The tech would pull replacement parts or equipment, exchange lenses or whatever else the camera operators needed.

As a private company, Panavision didn't disclose balance sheet details but keeping things close to the camera vest was part of the corporate culture. The company was behind the biggest innovations in motion picture cameras over decades and it kept details of its technology proprietary as long as it could. Rather than sell motion picture equipment to costumers, its business model was based on leasing. Even when it came time to retire a camera, it dismantled it for parts rather than sell it. It also spent heavily on research and development to stay on top.

Over the years, Panavision had accumulated debt. Faced with increasing competition, and controlled by corporate raider Ron Perelman since 1998, it had gone through a series of chief executives. The last couple of years had been tough, as revenues declined amid the economic downturn, making the payments harder to manage. But the dust had settled, the debt was restructured, and the company stabilized. Its revenues, estimated at more than $260 million a year, were growing again.

Panavision's history, as deep as almost any in the movie industry in Los Angeles, was on display throughout the headquarters building. There were enough artifacts to wow anyone fond of museums, and it wasn't open to the public. Employees and costumers walked past windowed display cases with notable equipment and awards. A big marketing slogan spread across one wall, four antique movie cameras under it: "Panavision: Unparalleled Optics. Optimized Cameras Systems. Inspired Engineering. Worldwide Presence."

Around another corner was an inverted 35mm underwater camera on display. It had been developed and built in 1964 for the James Bond movie Thunderball. It looked like a Panavision camera of the day, the logo atop an amorphous shape of the film reels inside, with early Scuba bubble suit masks on the front. A plaque on it noted its roles in the swimming pool scene in *The Graduate*, and later on Jaws, Steven Spielberg's confirmation to the world that had come to Hollywood to stay. A scaled down version of the camera, that one used years later by James Cameron to shoot *Titanic*, was on display elsewhere. Its specs were different: Cameron wanted real footage from the grave of the Titanic itself, so it had to be built to withstand the pressure in order to operate in the deep ocean.

The displays were wallpaper to Flurry and Rivetti, given how many times they had been to the Panavision compound. Then they settled in on the main prep floor. There was a checklist of parts to go through to ensure everything listed on the order was actually there. That was just the start. Just because they had used the same equipment before on another movie was no guarantee it was okay. The opposite could be true depending on where it had been between.

"If it's something we used on a show a year and a half ago, they may have the same batch of sensors on it. That could become a problem," Flurry said. They had to look at everything. Was each camera fitted with the right sized aperture matte?

The big, open room had work areas, or rental bays, on either side of it, and they settled in to the one assigned to them, which had a sign that read "Last Vegas." Resolution analysis charts hung in many of the work areas, several of which were also in use. The large black-and-white charts, which hung in most of the bays, featured grey scales and multi-lined circles and Siemens stars, which they could use to test the back focus on lenses. The stars were more recognizable to the mainstream population from psychedelic posters that had re-emerged in recent years from their heyday during the psychedelic 1960s and 1970s.

There were other tools and aids to test the equipment, color charts and grey scales and scratch tests for the lenses. Color charts enabled them to make sure the cameras they leased aligned to pick up the exact same red, for example. Doing that on the front end prevented a lot of headache for editors in post-production. They found several things they didn't like and changed them. But they didn't blame Panavision or any of the other companies that leased equipment. "Something that's in range of tolerance for a manufacturer may be on the edge of the tolerance for us," Flurry said. That's why everything had to be checked. Everything.

The cameramen were in regular contact with Hennings. He had an impressive personal collection of lenses so they conferred on which lenses to get to have on hand. There was some versatility but it could come down to needing one lens for one shot. "Things change. You'll prep a lens. Then it will turn out we don't want to use it. Or we'll add one."

It could be they would only use the lens for one shot, say shooting inside a doorway. The physical size of the lens in that case would be important because of space limitations. "Lenses do different things and with certain shots we need a specific piece of equipment. There's a big difference between a foot and six inches when you've got to get a lens in a doorway." All of it required a lot of thought and planning.

When Rivetti and Flurry had finished the process it moved to the shipping department, where the equipment was packed for the move to Las Vegas. Panavision techs knew better than anyone how to ensure that equipment arrived safely. Once they finished shooting in Las Vegas, the same camera equipment would then be transported to Atlanta for shooting there. Since Panavision had an Atlanta office, the rental would transfer to a Georgia business at that time, cutting costs to the production money as part of the tax breaks.

Hennings had been on the phone with them regularly. The Camera department was one of three he headed as cinematographer. The Grip and Electric departments, the other two, were also officially on payroll. The gaffer, the key grip and best boy were on the tech scouts in Atlanta. Rivetti and Flurry would join them in Las Vegas for the tech scouts there later in the week.

The Grip department was in charge of maintaining, installing or removing equipment in support of the Camera and Electric departments. The key grip was the department head while the best boy was the second. They looked at what changes they would need to make to enable others to do their jobs. Would they need to cover windows? Would they need to design and build a lighting grid or erect a single light? And how much prep time was needed? A grip supply company would provide the equipment.

The Grip department stopped when equipment carried a volt, which is where the Electric department picked up. Stephen Crowley was on board as the gaffer, also known as the chief electrician or lighting technician. He determined power sources and where cables would run. Did they have enough power? If the location needed a generator, how far would it need to be from the stage so it didn't impact sound? There were layers to his job, but to Crowley the most important was the risk assessment. Were there any potential safety issues? Did the location have a sprinkler system? Was all required safety equipment present? Were expiration dates good?

There was another type of gaffer, a rigging gaffer, who operated as a technician at the gaffer or DP's direction. There could also be two best boys. The term "best boy" came online in the movie industry at some point in the 1930s. Folklore has it the term was born when a key grip asked a gaffer if he could "borrow his best boy."

Nowhere is the history of the movie industry more evident than in titles like "gaffer" and "best boy." The terms had been used long enough that there was mild debate as to etymology. Most said they thought "gaffer" came from the use of a gaff hook used on ships. Dockworkers and mariners were hired in the early days of movies, the explanation went, and they brought tools of the trade. A gaff hook, used in fishing, could be used to manipulate natural light by pulling canvas over giant windows in some of the warehouses that were used as sound stages.

There is some question whether that is correct. A "gaffer" in the United Kingdom still referred to an old man, and had as far back as the mid-1500s. Some etymologists believe the term stemmed from a contraction of godfather and gammer, a name for an old woman. An 1841 census identified a gaffer as a foreman of a work crew, and it likewise was defined in Webster's second edition that year as a foreman. It's also noteworthy that at the same time, a "Penny Gaff," a theatrical performance that cost a penny or two to get in, was gaining in popularity in Victorian England. That would have put a foreman backstage on a Penny Gaff, although they wouldn't have been electricians any more than the men manipulating canvas with gaff hooks to control light.

Whether it evolved directly from either place or was an amalgamation of both, by the 1920s "gaffer" was the boss of the Electric department in Hollywood.

Peterson saw Chloe Lipp enter the bullpen from her desk in the AD office and got up to meet her in the middle. The art department coordinator was carrying something and the 2nd AD hoped it might be photos. It wasn't.

"Still waiting on De Niro," said Lipp. "The story of my life."

A momentary lull in the bullpen meant the line was delivered to the whole room, garnering a laugh. Lipp was popular across departments. Part of it was social, as she organized social events and tended to include everyone. Generally she was laid back at work, too. She would be staying in Atlanta along with most of the Art department to prep the stages while Bomba, the assistant art director and set decorator, went to Las Vegas. Bomba and Cassidy would go back and forth given how much work remained in Atlanta.

Peterson laughed, but just a little. She was feeling the stress of the tech scouts and the list of things that was incredibly long with the amount of time she had before her flight to Las Vegas. The photos had been challenging from the start and they were nearly done. Rounding them up had involved communications with all of the lead male actors, since they needed images of them at various stages of their lives. Most were props around the homes of their characters but one was a "hero prop," given it was held by an actor and part of a plot point.

All had been resolved, save for De Niro. Given it was his character clutching the hero prop a resolution was needed. The fact it wasn't already handled is why it had landed on her desk.

Freeman had been first, sending a bundle of photos in the mail. Peterson handled those pictures like gold. Once copied by art department crew she personally handled their return. Lipp had handled images from Kevin Kline, who had delivered a loaded jump drive, which the graphic artist loved. Douglas had been similarly responsive.

De Niro had been harder to reach or at least get a response from. He was out of the country but he also controlled his image to some degree. In 2006, he donated career materials from the 1960s through 2005 to the University of Texas at Austin. The collection contained more than 1,300 boxes of papers, film, movie props and costumes. Someone thought it had cost money to use it when they worked on another movie with him, although no one verified that. Graphics had worked around it, making his prop images tiny.

The added complexity was that in addition to Paddy, the image was to include Sophie, his widow. Since there was no adult Sophie in the cast, they needed an actress whose likeness could be in the image.

The challenge of getting actor photos was part of the reason for reshaping the original script. The opening had called for a montage of photos of the characters to show the passage of time, boyhood through their Vegas reunion. The new opening scene had child actors portraying the characters. It was their images, taken in a camera machine in the 1955 scene that would become the creative device linking the characters. That saved a lot of trouble, although it didn't eliminate the need for photos of the actors for set decorating or the hero prop. Peterson said she'd follow up with De Niro's assistant.

Next she sought out Badalato to talk about the child actors. The photos of the kids would be shot in Las Vegas. Their images were needed for another prop in the scenes in the corner store. But they needed the images for the 1955 scenes, which would be shot on the Atlanta stages. Various scenarios were considered on how to schedule it. Ultimately they decided to move the photo booth prop to Vegas for the stills, since trucks were going anyway, and then they would bring the child actors to Nevada for the shoot. Most of the kids were from L.A. so getting them to Nevada was relatively easy.

But having child actors work in two states added to the complexity of managing them. There were special union rules governing children, as well as strict state and federal laws. That meant coordinating two sets of rules, one in Nevada and the other in Georgia. Production had applied for the required work permits and would hire certified teachers.

This particular issue had come from a staffer at one of the state labor departments who had read the script. The 1955 scenes had been addressed. This question was about whether the pool scenes, which would be shot in Las Vegas, had any children in them. It had been easy to resolve, Badalato said. "In this case, it was just a process of saying, 'There will be no kids.'" Why were they getting the child actors from out of state? Didn't they have kids in Atlanta? "Somebody wanted those actors," he said, "presumably Jon."

More had come to light with the shipping issue in Vegas. By now most of the rerouted equipment and assorted packages, boxes and suitcases had been delivered, although occasional problems kept popping up. There were several layers to the cluster. First, things couldn't just be sent to the Aria. There was a fee associated with deliveries but the place was also so big it would be easy to lose things. The best solution was for goods to go to the Annex, the unoccupied building going back in service to accommodate the movie production.

The building was a two-block walk to Aria, through the casino and up the elevators to the fourth floor to get to the bullpen, where deliveries were usually managed. Given the Annex had ceased to be a working building, the U.S. Post Office had stopped delivering mail there. Getting letter carriers on board to delivery there again was challenging, given the facility had a gate around it. That was also an issue for shipping companies, FedEx and the like, who didn't recognize it as a live location and couldn't get in anyway. Now that some departments were operating they could reroute things to the Annex, although that didn't eliminate security issues with leaving the gate open.

By the time the tech scout buses had returned all of it was handled. The first day of the tour had gone well. "It was fine," said Turteltaub, when they all filed in. "At this point it's all about cables and buckles and shit."

This time Garner's Director's Plans came in handy. The detail contained in the three-ring binder saved time because it answered questions before they were asked. Detailed information was broken down for each location. Basic notes included which scenes would be shot at each location, signs or graphics, set dressing, greens, props, special effects. Some locations also had site maps or architectural layouts.

The group started at Georgia World Congress Center, the convention center in Atlanta. A section of it would be refashioned as an airport in Florida where Sam, Kevin Kline's character, has a plot-point chat with his wife before he takes off. From there the buses went to the Candler Park Funeral Home. Then it was on to the Bethesda Park Aquatic Center in Lawrenceville, Ga. That was another Sam scene, again with his wife.

After the lunch break at a Dunwoody deli, the tour continued to the homes of Archie, Paddy and Billy. First was Archie's house, a nice suburban residence not far from the deli. The character had a stroke and lived with his son and family but it also featured a window low to the ground, part of a joke in the script.

From there it was back into the city for the location that would house Paddy the widower. It was an older building in downtown Atlanta but it could easily blend into Brooklyn. Turteltaub liked the apartment enough that they were using a lot of the furniture, which was somewhat unusual. Billy, the wealthy character getting hitched, lived in a Malibu beach house. The location for that scene was a home in the Buckhead section of the city, which was at least four hours from the Atlantic Ocean. Thanks to the use of a green screen, which enabled the integration of two video streams, they would add the Pacific Ocean in post-production.

There was one big shift by the end of the day. Turteltaub had decided against the Barnesville location for the 1955 scenes. He liked the location, just not enough to move the entire company there, especially given his other option. He would go with a storefront they'd reviewed in East Atlanta. The shift was fine with Badalato and Samuels. Since it eliminated the need to shoot an hour away for the day, it was likely to represent a cost savings.

The immediate result was that it cut the tech scout for the second day in half since they no longer had to go to Barnesville. So the group went to Vanquish, the Midtown nightclub that would double as one Aria hotel. It had plenty of gold for a bar scene with celebrity lookalikes. Next they went to the Velvet Room, in Tucker, a close-in suburb of Atlanta. That's where they planned the larger bar scene. Both prevented lighting challenges to Hennings. The last stop was a church chosen for another funeral, an early scene where Michael Douglas' character eulogizes a friend.

They were done and back to Mailing Avenue by midday. Turteltaub left on a 7:20 p.m. flight Tuesday night to Vegas, along with Hennings, Rake,

Bomba, Samuels, and a couple of assistants. The prickly studio executive was with them. Shuttles ran back-and-forth between the airport and Mailing Avenue as crew flew to Vegas.

For the past two weeks as soon as shipping companies came to pick up boxes and other items it seemed more soon appeared to replace them. For every member of the crew ready to leave for a month, there was another who needed something. Then, just like that, they were gone.

The schedule for Wednesday was brief: "TRAVEL DAY -- Tech Crew travels from Atlanta to Las Vegas. *Please review individual itineraries or travel movement for details."

There was paperwork to manage on Mailing Avenue, rental cars to be returned, and an overloaded fax machine that threatened to quit permanently before it was resuscitated by Stephens. But the crew that remained in Atlanta was of two minds. Most had wanted to go to Vegas, but if they couldn't, getting everyone out of Atlanta for a while was a good alternative.

Aria loomed 51 stories over the Las Vegas Strip, higher from a different angle. It was shaped like a giant chromosome, an X of hotel rooms, with giant casino and massive retail space leading to the convention center. It was still new, part of the City Center development announced by MGM Resorts International in 2004. That 76-acre project included other resort hotels and a people-mover that carried people to other MGM properties, like the Bellagio.

Aria featured 4 million square feet with 16 restaurants, 10 bars and nightclubs and a big theater. Inside it buzzed with intensity. It had a high-end lobby and a beckoning dark casino with flashing lights and cacophonous sounds. Like any gambling establishment, most money that changed hands went in one direction. There were thousands of people there who didn't mind and even if you couldn't see but a hundred at a time you could feel them.

Aria was so big that it swallowed up the production of *Last Vegas* like a vitamin. With 4,004 rooms and suites, it could have absorbed all 3,000 room nights -- the core barter agreement with the movie production -- in a single night and still rented out 1,000 rooms. Aside from the days it took over the lobby or pool or gaming areas, the movie production would blend.

Four Fellas had taken over one corner of the fourth floor X, occupying a dozen rooms or suites. The Production department took the suite at the left far end of the hall. It consisted of three rooms, along with a large master bath, small entrance foyer and half bath. The back walls of each of the rooms were lined with windows that overlooked a rooftop.

A small foyer opened to the bullpen, which generally functioned as the living room of the suite. It was set up as an office with tables for desks. The kitchenette was set up with craft services; a waist-high refrigerator on the wall on the other side had additional snacks and beverages.

To the left of the bullpen was the master bedroom, which had been deeded over to the ADs for their office. To the right, the corner of the building, was a room centered with a conference table. The room had two copiers as well as an ID machine to make crew passes. Boxes were stacked beyond that against the wall, curtains drawn against the end windows behind the table.

A production manager was on the phone talking about shipping issues, which apparently were still a problem. Her frustration level was high. She turned and faced the windows to the rooftop, which reflected the bright Nevada sun. "That's why I get bitchy," she said into the phone. "When I say clearly to do something and you don't listen, I have to take a tone. I don't like to take a tone," she said. She listened briefly. "I'm just telling you so you know how I work." It was the same woman who had clashed with the Atlanta office.

Seeing her on the phone meant anyone entering the bullpen turned toward Celeste Pawol, who sat working at a table on the other side of the room. The Aria rooms that had been bartered for use by the movie were handed over in bulk for the production to manage and it had fallen to her to check in crew. Room assignments had been done in advance. Her job was to provide room keys and packets, then photograph the crew, prepare their security badges and enter them into the system.

One of the crew she had checked returned a short time later looking very tired. His room card had been demagnetized or for whatever other reason was not working. He asked her if she was the production secretary as he handed it back to her.

"No, I'm a PA. And I'm temporary," said Pawol. "They asked me to help out until they could find people." There was no production secretary, at least not yet. She was a driver, she said, and would stay until her job started in transportation. Based in Las Vegas and standing about 5'2 she smashed any stereotype of a Teamster.

Pawol organized all room keys with problems and picked up a clipboard with her notes to go to the front desk. Phone calls weren't doing it. She needed to talk to a real person with a card machine. Just as she stood up to deal with it, the manager, who had been on the phone the entire time, hung up.

"I'm off to key hell," said Pawol, holding up her stack of room keys. "I need to talk to someone face-to-face."

"I'm in my own hell," the woman replied. "I'll come down to help you in Aria key hell when my hell is complete."

Somehow packages were still being rerouted, she explained, including some to a nearby casino resort. Pawol, who had moved to the door, nodded and shook her head, listening patiently.

"Let the awe of Aria seduce you," she said, using the resort slogan.

It was some much needed levity.

There was good reason to be frustrated. While most packages were arriving as they were addressed, there continued to be regular strays. Beyond that, the bullpen was understaffed. Despite all of its entertainment businesses, Las Vegas did not have a large base of skilled movie crew. It could go a movie deep, and with *Hangover III* shooting in town, they were gone. That movie had a much bigger budget so there was no luring anyone away.

The office had gone through a couple of PAs already. The most recent hire had been asked to put together a small bookcase for use in Badalato's office. It had taken the young man several hours and when he was finished, he proudly brought it in and left it there. Several parts had been put on backwards, one shelf upside down, and it was just slightly wobbly.

A short time later a small group had joined Badalato to look at the bookcase. The woman in charge of production for the Las Vegas portion of the movie heard the commotion from her office next door and came in to see what was up.

Badalato had his phone out and was getting ready to take a picture of a shelving unit, which leaned just slightly left, the underside of a shelf face-up. Someone started to fill her in on what had happened but she already knew.

"It's awesome!" said Badalato, snapping away delightedly. Everyone laughed, except the woman whose office had hired the young man. She frowned and left the room.

The young man did not come back the next day.

The first day of the Vegas tech scouts focused on locations on Aria property. With 23 scenes they divided the tour into three categories, the front of the building, the giant casino, and the pool area. Five of the scenes were in front of the resort, where the biggest challenge was creating cab and valet lines since Aria was using its own.

It was a smaller group than had been on the Atlanta scout, although not by much. There didn't seem to be any producers or studio executives along, save Samuels, who was en route. Some of the faces were different, like the Vegas locations crew and an Aria rep, or new, like the production sound mixer. The core was the same, Turteltaub and Rake, Hennings and camera, grip and electric, Bomba and Cassidy.

Samuels arrived a minute later and the group moved outside to the main entrance of Aria. It was a huge area with people all over. Just the overhang at the main entrance was big enough for a hundred cars to load people in or out. There were multiple traffic lanes just for Aria and a spectacular water feature in the middle.

The longest scene had Billy and Diana on a walk but the shorter scenes required the discussion. All signage that directed passengers had to be created and approved and Bomba confirmed graphics were in the works. They were adding a bench for seating, as well as stanchions where a row of passengers would wait for cabs. What about the cab tops and their advertisements or anything else that would appear in the background that had to be cleared? That was in the works.

The group moved on to the lobby and front desk area. It was huge with high ceilings, perhaps 40 feet or more. The top 10 feet were windows on either side, which added a lot of light to an already well-lighted place. Hennings planned to use a crane to lift the camera in order to get the grandeur of the place. Samuels noted the sparkling lobby floors were marble and needed to be protected. Floors weren't necessarily designed to withstand the weight of a crane and repairing a crushed marble floor could be expensive.

The lobby opened to the cavernous casino floor, which was much darker. At 150,000 square feet, the casino was the starter size of a Walmart Supercenter. It was quiet at that hour relative to other times of day and night, but even at that it was a dull roar of sound. It was like a wall of noise punctuated by a thousand tiny stabs of sound. The energy of it registered somewhere between excitement and dysphoria.

The production sound mixer had a scanner in his hand and he ran it every place they stopped, at the slot machines, the blackjack tables, outside the bar. As the head of the Sound department, David Kelson's job was to capture all dialogue and ambient sound on location or the soundstages. It wasn't the noise that concerned him, at least not at that point.

He was checking interference on various frequencies. Aside from Manhattan, Las Vegas was "ground zero for mike usage," he said. In big cities, particularly those with a lot of entertainment, finding open frequencies was part of the process. Each actor would be miked individually, which meant Kelson needed a lot of channels. What was available would be different depending on the time of day but it still provided needed insight.

Hennings also was concerned about frequencies, just in a different way. He took in the gaming monitors and did some camera math. The machines operated at a different frequency than the cameras and in his case they needed to synchronize. It was only a slight change but lining them up would avoid camera interference. He had seen occasions where an undetectable flash of light ended up in footage because of it. Nothing like that would happen on his watch.

Bomba was looking at the small monitors on the blackjack tables that featured advertisements. They could only reflect shows that were approved and he didn't want to get there and find there was something on a set that wasn't cleared. He was going to add two blackjack tables. He and Cassidy were mindful that one of the scenes had a drink spill on the gaming table, which meant it had to be replaced or at least recovered between takes. They were also putting in different chairs and additional foliage to soften things. Logos and signage were an even bigger factor inside than out, he said, but it was under control. Then there was the scene where De Niro and Steenburgen spin a game wheel and win a prize. There was no such game but set decorating had efforts under way to find or create it.

For the Art department overall, the biggest single effort in Las Vegas was transforming one of the pools at Aria into a stage. They needed a place for the scene where the four actors judge the wet T-shirt contest. Regardless of whether that scene remained there would still be a pool party. Aria had three outdoor pools. Each was named after a planting theme. The Palm Pool had been ceded over to the movie. It was late in the season, so it was relatively painless for the hotel to lose access to one of its pools for a few days.

The challenge was finding a place for the stage in the Palm Pool area, since there wasn't one. The Art department designed a stage that would straddle the Palm Pool, complete with catwalks and rock and roll truss. It needed to be fairly large, with room for all four actors and plenty of contestants. The set would feature pipe decking and pool jets for effect. It also needed a DJ booth, platform and catwalk. That would need to be decorated, although exactly how would be determined later. Then there were the finer details, like adding a leading edge or stripes to the cabana curtains, replacing or adding 20 colored umbrellas and installing four mini lifeguard chairs. All of this would be topped off with banners and flags with approved graphics or advertising. They also would need plenty of orange Aria towels.

A lot of work had gone into it already. Detailed drawings had been done and a contractor hired to build it. Vegas had a good number of companies that could build stages. Kim Houser-Amaral, who handled the Locations department in Vegas, helped with the process. Turning the pool area into a finished set of that proportion was a logistical nightmare. There was only one way in and one way out for contractors. They would have to use an elevator on the west side of the property. "One elevator," she said. "One loading zone." The loading zone could barely fit two trusses and there were at least a dozen. That meant a lot of heavy stuff had to be physically moved.

Houser-Amaral was also working on Aria's requirement that everything be packed up and moved overnight. All equipment would have to be loaded up and moved at night and brought back early the next morning. While the resort was standing firm on things inside the casino, at least for now, she got an agreement from the hotel that the production could store things by the pool. The production would hire security to watch it.

The second day of the tech scout focused on external locations. This was where a Locations department really earned its coin. The Nevada Film Commission oversees the permitting process and all applications to each jurisdiction where photography was scheduled, in this case both county and city. Then there were individual government departments that needed to sign off. Police, transportation and public works departments all had to weigh in before a permit was issued. Permits outlined special production needs that had been approved, such as traffic closures. There were security issues that had to be addressed with each one, none more than crowded locations. There were plenty of those planned for the movie.

Turteltaub initially wanted to shoot in front of Showcase Mall near Gameworks, which was across from New York-New York. It was easy to see why, given the visuals. It felt like the Vegas version of Times Square, a huge bag of M&M's and a giant bottle of Coca-Cola. The problem was that they had wanted $20,000 for a four hour window -- to start at 5 a.m. There was no such headache with shooting at an MGM property.

The Bellagio and Mirage were both MGM properties. While the costs were relatively low by comparison, each came with its own set of unique logistical and infrastructure challenges. The group on the tech scout routed around to all of those places.

There was the matter of closing off the sidewalks in front of both the Bellagio and the Mirage. They decided where they could put director's village -- where monitors for the director and others would be -- as well as the video playback and other monitors. They also would need a place for the craft services and the props cart and other crew paraphernalia. Also, all of the major actors were involved and they would need to park trailers. Their drivers would need to be able to park as well.

Just moving the tech scout around to review locations was a reminder of the challenge ahead. All of it was happening on one of the busiest places along the famed 4.2 mile Las Vegas Boulevard, better known as The Strip. Another scene called for a traffic jam, which required stopping traffic. Houser-Amaral believed she could get a lane closed if it happened early enough in the morning -- but just one lane. It was almost unheard of to get multiple lanes shut down. That made shooting a traffic jam, which they needed, challenging. Then there was Binions and the other shots around Old Vegas to peruse, including the lively Fremont Street corridor.

The tech scout wound through the sites chosen for a play date around Vegas between Michael Douglas and Mary Steenburgen's characters. Initially the scene involved them going to Mastro's Restaurant, which in the script had a fabulous view of the 109th floor overlooking the Strip. The new script scrapped Mastro's. Now the characters would be at the Neon Boneyard. That location, a new outdoor museum that featured classic Vegas signs, would be relatively easy. The production would go in early and have the run of the place.

Shooting at the X-Scream was a little more exacting for the people on the tech scout. The scene had two characters taking the ride over the edge of the Stratosphere Casino, Hotel & Tower. The ride started 866 feet off the ground and plummeted 27 feet off the side of the building. The actors would have stunt doubles if they didn't want to do the scene, although neither had said one way or the next.

The production company wasn't concerned about the safety of the ride, since that was established. More than 200,000 people rode on each year without incident. But getting all that equipment up there? How would they shoot it? All of it involved lights and cameras but this also was a space issue. How much room was there for equipment and people? Just to get the full flavor, Rake and several others got on the ride to test it during the tech scout. In the end it was decided they would affix a camera to the front of the ride to get the full effect.

The tech scout also included McCarran Airport. That they were going there at all was fortunate, because most airports didn't have the room to accommodate movies or the inclination, since it was removed from its purpose. McCarran had just shifted a lot of its foot traffic to a new wing, leaving the old wing and hence availability. It was a given that there was nothing negative in the script about flying. That it was likely to promote tourism rather than deter it was an added bonus.

The wing was still in use but lightly traveled and perfect for a one-day shoot. The tech scout firmed up what had to happen. They would need to spruce up some signs, which had needed it until now, and install others. They would be adding specialty advertising art and generic slot machines, among other things. Slot machines without trademarked logos on them were easier to come by in Vegas than Atlanta but were still needed.

The Annex was a separate building on fenced property and relatively quiet, despite its close proximity to the Vegas Strip. It was a big space and it felt wide open, especially in contrast to the fourth-floor offices in the Aria. Once home to development offices for Aria, its mission was fulfilled when the project was completed, so it had been shuttered and slated for demolition. But there wasn't anything wrong with it, and it was easily restored for use by the creative departments.

There was a circular driveway and a front door with a coded lock opened to the lobby, which gave way to a large, roundish atrium. The Costume department took up the left side of the building while the Transportation department, on the other side of the atrium, was in a much smaller place.

Dusty Saunders was on the phone inside while a driver sat in a chair outside waiting to talk to him. As transportation coordinator he managed the Teamsters who would move cast and crew around town. He orchestrated the vehicles that moved them as well as the trucks and trailers that would make up base camp at any location.

There were also "picture cars," vehicles to be used in the movie, to pull together. It might be a car, bus, truck or van, but any vehicle seen in a movie is a "picture car." In this case, it was cabs that needed consideration. The movie needed a number of them with the heroes coming and going around town. One would need to be large enough to hold all five of the main characters. That scene was a traffic jam, which likely would require yet more picture cars.

He had been prepping Las Vegas for a couple of weeks by then. It could be a challenging job with a lot of moving parts but Saunders had done it for decades. He had benefit of knowing his way around Vegas, since he had worked there several times over the years. So far, all was going as expected for *Last Vegas*. The crew had been transported from the airport to Aria. The shuttle that ran from Aria to the Annex and would for the rest of the time they were there was operational. Part of the deal with the Aria involved some limo service, as well, although the Travel department had the lion's share of responsibility for it.

Badalato and Samuels had worked with Saunders before and offered him the whole show, which would have meant working the Atlanta portion of the production, as well. He had declined so they hired another coordinator, this one based in South Carolina.

Saunders had good reason to decline. He had run transportation on Newsroom, an HBO drama created by Aaron Sorkin, and the new season was starting soon. The last thing he was going to do was let go of that gig to take a couple of months of work in Atlanta. Given that Newsroom was a strong series and likely to be renewed again, he stood a good chance of getting the job back yet again. The six or seven weeks of work in Sin City timed out perfectly for him to do both jobs.

Saunders liked working for Sorkin, the creator of Newsroom and one of the best-known Hollywood screenwriters actively working. He was easy to work for and a genuinely nice guy. Sorkin had worked his way up, writing for television shows over the years. He had broken out with *Social Network* and *Moneyball*. Both earned him Oscar nominations for Best Writing/Adaptation and he won for *Social Network*.

Saunders had another reason to hold on to the gig. He liked to be able to work in Los Angeles, where he lived, and that's where "Newsroom" was shot. It was harder to find work there all the time. The movie industry in southern California had felt the pinch of movie tax credits in other states. It didn't happen right away but over time, it increased how often movie crew had to travel for studio work, not just to work on location. California legislators had approved some incentives in 2009 to counteract the exodus but it wasn't enough. Leaving home was a fact of life for most California-based movie and television crew. Now states that offered sweeter tax breaks -- and stuck with them -- were on their way to being full production centers. They would build their own crew bases in the process.

But he also saw *Last Vegas* as an easy gig compared to some others. The location work would be done early in principal photography. There were base camps to set up and lots of crew and cast movement. But then they would settle into Aria. Then the most regular run would be picking up crew from the North Valet side of the giant resort and casino and getting them to the Annex or vice versa. The main entrance was too crazy, the casino just inside, too many people, busy cab lines, commerce, shops. The side entrance was smaller, although it would dwarf most resorts.

The other side of the atrium had glass-walled offices that revealed Jobst and the assistant designer at work. The Costume department had the most real estate of any of the departments and there was no mistaking its place in the movie. There were three, large interconnected rooms, each larger than the next, and an alcove in the back that might easily be considered a fourth.

The first room faced the entrance area and parking lot with floor-to-ceiling glass. The largest of the rooms, it was filled with rows of clothes for background actors. The racks were organized by gender and size. A partition split off the next room, which had a giant square table in the middle. The next space down had racks of some of the hero clothes that were being labeled. The next room had a giant waste-high table in the middle. Around the edges of the room were actors' lines and closets, labeled with cryptic letter-number combinations, all in various stages of progress. There were sewing machines and other tools for alterations in the alcove area beyond that.

It was an impressive operation for something that would only exist a couple of weeks. It had been a big move, Jobst said, but it had pulled together quickly. She was her chipper self although she looked tired. Dayna Pink had been there for the first two days of the week and had then flown to New York for final fittings with De Niro and Douglas. She had gone without the assistant and was staying at Trump Towers again. She would return to Las Vegas on Saturday. Jobst picked up one of the printed out sheets of coded numbers and a box of ball caps on her desk. The hats read, "U.S. Air Force" across the top and "Retired" at the bottom. She carried them to the table in the middle room where Kate Duke was working. As the key costumer, she would be on set with the actors but in prep she could help out. She stood at the table with a printout of tags. It looked like secret code, squares and rectangles of various sizes filling a sheet of 8-by-11 inch self-adhesive paper.

Now the number letter coding started to make sense as part of Costume department software used by many in the industry. The system enabled them to track what the actors needed based on scenes to be shot that day. They referred to Lines, which were each character's change of clothes. They went in order, as in Change 1, Change 2, Change 3.

On the top left side of the page in front of Duke it reads, "1 BILLY, 1, D2, 6,7" in various boxes. Each character has been assigned a number that is used in all paperwork. Billy, the Michael Douglas character, is 1. The next n numeral, "1," refers to the change number. D2 is the second script day. The 6,7 are the scenes the costumes will be worn in. The tags are then put on various costumes using tape, safety pin or rubber band.

They were used to organize costumes based on script days. When the Costume department did its breakdown, it determined the lapse of time over the course of *Last Vegas* was actually seven script days, more than an earlier count of six. Really, it was eight script days if you included the 1955 scenes where the main characters were introduced as boys.

Scenes are not shot chronologically but for efficiency. Somehow the Costume department had to make sense of what script day it was in relation to what clothes they needed to prepare. It was essential for keeping track of it all, given they could be shooting scenes from script Day 5 on shooting days 2, 11 and 27. That could then be matched to the shooting schedule. That meant Scene 6 could be shot in Las Vegas in October while Scene 7 was shot in Atlanta in November and nobody would miss a beat. That in turn linked to the shooting schedule. Several departments used script days to organize the show, but they needed it most.

The ball caps she had picked up were for Morgan Freeman's closet. Pink had decided on them for Archie, who had served in the Air Force. It was a done deal, but they would have them handy if Freeman liked them. There were several, as was practice, in case they used it and one was lost or damaged.

All costumes had backups. How else could you ensure Billy looked the same in Scene 7 as he had in Scene 6 if they were shot weeks apart?

Knowing where each costume would be used or re-used was just a start. Most had multiple pieces but then there were duplicates. In cases where they will likely be destroyed -- as in scenes where De Niro's and Douglas' characters push each other into pools -- there were four of them. Two were for the actor, one for a stunt double and then a backup saved in case they needed it for reshoots.

In the meantime they were building a continuity book for reference. The book included details about each character's outfit in each scene. It also covered what costumes were needed for each scene and how many changes were required in a shooting day. It might have fabric content and weaves or any number of other things as well. Once established during photography, a photo and written description would also be added. The book would grow with time.

On the other side of the atrium was another reception area and a hallway that lead to much larger area. The middle was a large room. Temporary crew offices had sprung up in the offices that surrounded it. The Costume department had one more room there. It was set up for fittings and had the feel of the dressing rooms at the costume houses in Los Angeles. It had long mirrors and a nice throw rug, comfortable chairs and a private area for changing. The final fittings for the main actors were spaced apart on the schedule in the coming days.

The remaining offices were occupied by the Art, Set Decorating and Props departments. Bomba and Cassidy would stay in Las Vegas into the first week of shooting and then return to Atlanta to focus on the locations and sets being built on the soundstages. Garner had stayed in Atlanta for the same reason. The assistant art director would stay and manage the location work once they left. His office was set up for the duration, his CAD system in full display.

Most of the hires for the Art department work in Las Vegas were local. A temporary art coordinator was handling day-to-day requirements. Cassidy had hired local set decorating crew, and a buyer sat in the department offices. Next to it was a storage room with set dressing, primarily large letters used in neon signs at that point.

Benjamin-Creel and Rice were at work a couple of offices down. All the luggage they had collected, including a good influx of product placement, was in the far back room. The third room had various props spread out on desks, generic or fake-brand coffee cups, cigarettes and condoms. The most variety had been reserved for the condoms, given the plot point in the movie. The middle of the three rooms held their desks and a table, which they huddled over. In front of them was a list of luggage.

A product placement deal had been inked with TravelPro. That provided them with a number of options for suitcases for the lead characters, as well as the character "Lisa," fiancé to Billy Gherson. One of her scenes prominently included luggage.

The Props department had earlier sent their requests in for Travelpro, Atlantic, National Geographic luggage/bags, and Austin House accessories. Douglas' character, Billy, was to get the premium, Travelpro Platinum 7 luggage. The brand had promised to provide extra luggage for the background of hotel lobbies and airport scenes. Even the director's wish that Paddy and Archie have older, distressed luggage had been passed along. Travelpro sent photos of distressed luggage and options for the fiancé, and decisions had been made.

Now Benjamin-Creel and Rice had to sort out exactly what had arrived and organize it.

A printed-out email on one of the desks had two sentences high-lighted. "NO OTHER luggage brands can be used by the 4 male leads, and no other supporting cast or background extra's luggage logos should be prominent. If you choose something else for Lisa, please let Eddie know so he can give feedback."

CHAPTER TEN
1 Week Out
Oct. 15-19

GARY RAKE SAT ALONE in the Lockwood 1, clear-framed eye-glasses strapped to his head. The script was splayed out in front of him. Highlighter in hand, he pored over it one more time. In a little over an hour the meeting room would be filled with the entire *Last Vegas* crew, as well as producers and studio executives. As 1st AD he would lead the pre-photography production meeting that involved a group review of every scene in *Last Vegas*. All departments would be able to ask questions -- and be asked questions -- to tie up any loose ends.

The windowless room was part of the 300,000-square-foot convention center at the Aria. The room was centered by a giant square of conference tables, each with brown fabric slipcovers. Bowls of candy and Aria-logoed paper and pens were spread around the 50-plus seats. More tables lined the wall on the right and two empty self-serve lunch buffets were ready for setup in the back.

It was all neat and orderly but for the noise coming from the other side of one of the membrane walls. Lockwood 1 was one folding-wall away from another event. It wasn't even 9:30 in the morning and a party next door punctuated the room with bursts of singing and clapping. Loud bursts. Rake continued to pace through the script, seemingly oblivious to the ruckus.

The Vegas Production department supervisor appeared in the entrance of the room, a large stack of scripts in her arms. She had just returned from a trek to the fourth-floor production offices back to Lockwood, a solid 10-minute walk. Confronted by the singing, she stopped dead in her tracks, slack-jawed.

"What is that?" she asked, resuming her stride to the table at the far wall to add her stack of scripts to others collecting there.

"Sounds like karaoke," Rake replied.

"That's not going to work," she said.

"I know," he said. He turned the microphone on in front of him and tapped it as a test. That worked.

"I'll find out what's going on," she said, turning toward the door. She noted the irony of the convention center booking morning events side-by-side, given that the rest of the 38 meeting spaces were vacant.

It had been a late night in the bullpen. The studio had approved the revised script late in the day. Part of the holdup was that the scriptwriter, Dan Fogelman hadn't been given much time to review the changes. Two writers had worked on it over the past weeks, a normal part of finalizing a script before photography begins, but Fogelman had balked. There were still issues but they vowed to make it right when he got to Las Vegas. The revised script would be distributed in the meantime.

The printer, apparently annoyed by the volume, had also balked. It was already accommodating a heavy workload but the scripts were 117 pages each. They had soldiered through. Now they had printed scripts, staggered in alternating directions in stacks, but they weren't fastened together. The PA sent to purchase brads came back with the wrong size and was sent back. By the time he returned with the right size, reinforcements had arrived in Lockwood 1 and a brad-fastening brigade finished the job. Soon each place setting, now with nametags, also had a script.

The nametags were key to room organization and identifying crew. Rake and Turteltaub's seats were at the center of the far side of the square of tables. That row also included producers and the two studio executives. Various departments were set up on both sides of the square to their right and left, while the one ahead held Badalato and the other production leadership among others. A group of PAs set up a table parallel to the wall and facing into the room within earshot of Rake and Turteltaub. Hotel staff set up a buffet along the back wall.

Alicia Accardo was the first member of the crew to arrive who wasn't either an AD or in the Production department. After a quick exchange with Rake, the script supervisor found her seat and dug in just as he had.

The first people to do the job began appearing on sets in the 1920s and were called "continuity clerks." It was their job to make sure scenes matched. The present-day job still involved overseeing continuity, although it was much more elaborate, along with responsibility for tracking and keeping records and notes on the creative progress of the movie.

The local production supervisor returned from the karaoke check and walked toward Rake. "They will be wrapping up soon," she said.

"Good," he said. "What is it anyway?" It was weird, the level of noise at that hour.

"It's some kind of awards banquet or something," she said, as she turned back toward the rear of the room. "Who knows."

Accardo looked up from the script to ask her for an email version. The production supervisor promised her one and apologized that it wasn't already out.

Other people began to trickle in representing all aspects of the movie. Ashley Kravitz was there, of "Cleared by Ashley." She had been an active part of prep, handling legal clearances for the movie. It was an under-recognized job but key, since it involved getting permission to use anything visible on screen that had third-party rights. A T-shirt with a logo, a magazine on a table, a branded slot machine were just some examples of things that either had to be cleared or recreated before they could appear on screen.

Rake picked up his cell phone, which was on the table in front of him, as he had several times. This time he took the call. It was Chase, De Niro's executive assistant. The actor had requested a schedule change and this was a follow up.

"One thing, it probably means he's going to work in Atlanta earlier, maybe Nov. 8," Rake said. "We're trying to make that work. I have that he has to leave on the 9th at night but at this point, Jon needs him in the scene. "

Rake listened as he scanned the room, which was rapidly filling with people.

"Let me do this," he said. "Let me look at some options. It may be a creative decision, like whether we can take Bob out of the scene. If that's a problem let me know." He listened some more. "Is it Nov. 6 you're talking about? Those are travel days. There is no work on the 6 or 7, no shooting days. Because the best days for us were the 8th and 9ᵗʰ, I thought? And, on the 13ᵗʰ... that would be the second day. The location is two days." More listening.

"The 13th begins a two-day sequence at a nightclub," Rake said. "I'd have to move a lot of things around, but it's possible. On the 14th... The 16th could work, because Bob's only in one of the two scenes, but I'm not sure it's going to work for the location. I don't want to say that it's unlikely, so let me check."

There was another pause. The room was getting noisy and he had to listen harder to hear. "Okay," he said, finally. "I just have to ask Jon how badly he needs him in that scene. It's low impact on the 8th and 9th. The 14th is a really big switch. Not saying it's impossible, but a lot of phone calls have to be made that involve all the things we're prepping, all the locations would have to be rescheduled, almost. We'll see where Jon's at." He listened some more and said goodbye.

The room was now full. A fabric-faced folding wall was doing little to soften the din of voices. Some people were in line at the buffet, some took plates to their seats while others mingled. There were a good number of reunions as crew saw people they had worked with in the past. Turteltaub appeared and began making his way through the room.

It was a miniature and subdued version of the president of the United States entering the chamber of the House of Representatives for a major speech. Some turned to make contact with him while others migrated to their seats, all of them aware he was in the room. He lingered at Accardo's chair. She had worked with him on several of his movies. He showed her a photo on his iPhone. They laughed.

A minute later and he was at his chair for an exchange with Rake. The 1st AD told him he was ready for the meeting and that he'd talked to Robinson and would update him later. Turteltaub sat down and leaned back behind Rake to talk to Amy Baer, who had taken her seat and was on Rake's right.

A minute later Rake tapped on the mike and the room, which had continued in high volume, fell silent immediately, regardless of where sentences were in conversation. Rake introduced himself, gave a quick overview of what the meeting would entail, which would include going around the room. He handed it off to the director.

"My name is Jon Turteltaub and I am the second and hopefully last director of this movie." There was a burst of laughter that felt like a lot tension being released at once. "It's a great story -- ask me sometime." He didn't go into it, but Peter Chelsom, best known for *Hannah Montana: The Movie* had initially been tapped for leadership. When Turteltaub got the first script of *Last Vegas* it still had Chelsom's name on it. As often is the case in Hollywood, things changed.

"I actually feel we're pretty well prepared, compared to a lot of movies," Turteltaub continued. "I don't feel like anyone is panicked. It's given me a lot of confidence in everyone."

Baer was next. She talked about buying the script when she was president of CBS Films and being honored it would be her first producing credit. Then it moved to Samuels, who punted quickly. Next Bomba introduced himself as someone who worked in the Art department, a modesty Turteltaub took issue with.

"You do not just work in the Art department. You're the production designer!" Everyone laughed. Hennings introduced himself and said if anyone saw him at a roulette table they should feel free to stop him.

And so it went, somewhat lightly and fairly quickly around the room. The introductions had stayed in the center square. When it got to Badalato, he suggested the rest of the crew introduce themselves. These were the smaller players, the production assistants and personal assistants making up the perimeter of the room.

Then the meeting was in full swing and they went through each scene in order. Rake was at the helm but Turteltaub pushed it along. There were relatively few questions, despite it being opened up to anyone. Then it got to the Props department, and Benjamin-Creel asked a question. The director answered and then said, "Anything else I can do for you?" There were even fewer questions after that.

Rake said the meeting would take several hours but it finished sooner and disbanded quickly. Perhaps it was a good sign there were so few questions. "Oh, they have questions alright," he said. "They just didn't ask them here. They're afraid of Jon. They'll just ask me -- later."

Turteltaub didn't mind the meeting ending early. Unlike the CEO of a corporation who has all year to manage a company, review small issues and step back quarterly for big-picture progress, he had six days before the big clock started ticking. Then there were 38 days of principal photography, most of them jammed. Millions of dollars would be spent. And whether it all succeeded was ultimately on him.

But pressure was building for everyone. All of the actors were arriving the next day and the cast read-through was the following day. There was one key role still to fill and a rap star coming in to read for it with the group. Decisions had to be made about everything from what cars to choose to how to choreograph a scene with Cirque du Soleil. There were costumes and props to sign off on, sets to review, and cameras to test.

And De Niro wanted a schedule change.

The ADs fastened a sign to the entrance of their cramped office: "Door closed for noise control. Welcome." Inside two mini-conference tables had been pushed together in the middle of the hotel room. Peterson and Lillian

Awa, the 2nd 2nd AD, sat directly across from each other. Two PAs, one a veteran with nearly enough hours to be an AD and another on his first show, were at work in the bathroom. A third PA had parked herself at one end of a thinner table pushed up under the window.

The room was smaller than a regular Aria hotel room because as part of a suite, a big portion had been ceded over to a grand bathroom. The good news was that it was a big bathroom with room for storage, which they had put to full use. It had a large walled stall with heated toilet, a walled shower, and a big bathtub anchoring the main room.

The PAs had filled the bathtub and the wall behind it with boxes. A table was wedged into the other side under the his-and-her sinks and against the wall of the bathroom stall and its heated toilet. There they spread out 40 commercial-grade Motorola radios contained in the first delivery. Valued at about $300 each, more if you asked Badalato, they needed to be tested, inventoried and assigned.

The Vegas Production department offices had been laid out differently than in Atlanta. Department heads in Atlanta had wanted, to a person, to be in close proximity to staff, even within eye contact. The Vegas production department chief had set up her office in the next hotel room down the hall. Instead, the AD's office, which was a separate department, took over the bedroom in the production suite.

They were making it work. Matt Fortino, an experienced production assistant on the cusp of becoming a 2nd 2nd AD, talked about how important it was to keep the handheld two-way radios organized.

"We ordered the walkies in time for the camera test," he explained. "You want to hand out as many as they can hand out before you shoot. The worst part about the first day is if you have people who can't communicate with your guys." This way the departments had a chance to get used to them.

"Now we're making sure that they all work and that they are all charged and labeled," said Fortino. He had worked with Peterson before in L.A. and then reconnected in Atlanta. She knew he was good crew and pushed to hire him.

Awa was making sure the suites were organized for the actors. Production handled some of it but with photography starting more would fall to the ADs. It was a matter of making sure that what the actors wanted had been picked up and ensuring it made it to their suites. The four main actors would arrive on Thursday, so there was some time. Kline had wanted coffee and other easy-to-get items, which had already been picked up. Somebody asked about the Freeman list, which they knew was nearby. It was already established that De Niro wasn't staying at Aria, but they would save his suite for him just in case he changed his mind.

Mary Steenburgen was arriving a day ahead of the others to get acclimated. Could she have a piano put in her suite and a vocal teacher on her last weekend? She would be singing in the movie and wanted to prepare. They told her they thought they could make it happen and would run it by Samuels. In the meantime, someone needed to meet her and show her to the suite.

"I hope Ayesha is back in time so I don't have to meet Mary," said Awa, referring to the PA who had been at the end of the window table and had since gone on an errand. All reports were that Steenburgen was delightful to deal with.

"Oh, Mary's great. It's nothing personal. I just don't like to deal with the actors like that," she said. This was now a common thread. Unlike half of America, which is enamored of celebrity for no reason, many crew would just as soon not do the one-on-ones.

"My stuff happens on set," explained Awa. It's prep, so she was there to help in any way she could. But when it came time to shoot, she might need to relay a request of Turteltaub's directly to the actress, perhaps an unpleasant one, and it would be easier if she hadn't facilitated her personal needs. Not that she couldn't, and wouldn't, as needed.

Awa was forthright and obviously smart. She also looked much younger than her 32 years, so it was like a newly minted college graduate talking at a post-doctorate level. Like Peterson, her entry into the movie business was through the DGA training program. Her segue to *Last Vegas* had been through Rake, who she had worked with before. Her other passions included flying helicopters. Part of the motivation for getting her pilot's license, she said, was so she could talk to people about something besides the movie business.

A common way to look at the split in duties between the 1st AD and the 2nd is along time lines. The 1st AD's focus is on the current shooting day while the 2nd AD's is on the next day or days. Rake was out with Turteltaub making sure shots were lining up the way they wanted them in a schedule that worked. Peterson had to make sure everything that came out of those decisions was in place when they needed them. Awa's role as Second 2nd AD involved supporting them both but exactly how that played out was different on different shows. At this point it was filling in as needed, and organizing the actors was just the start.

Peterson left a message on the voicemail of Jerry Ferrara's agent. "The cast read-through is at 10:30 a.m. in Vegas, Oct. 18. So we would be flying Jerry out on the morning, probably on an 8 a.m. out of LAX or Burbank, then returning that afternoon."

She scribbled something on a yellow notepad as she talked.

"I'm figuring he could easily make a 3 or 3:30 flight back. We would pop him back on a flight with the lovely Bre Blair, who plays Lisa. I think he's been in touch with travel but we hadn't heard back, so I thought I'd call."

A voicemail had come in while she was on the phone, so she listened to it. "Okay, who wants to talk to Beach Bunny Betty?" she asked when she hung up.

An issue had arisen with the extras casting director in Atlanta, not to be confused with the casting director, and some of the work, or more of it, had ended up on Peterson's desk. "Yes!" The PA who had taken over the walkies for Fortino was ready for something new, although he might have been picturing a different kind of bunny. Real Playboy bunnies had been hired from Playboy Enterprises but that was in the works and in any case a different scene. This scene involved retirement-age people in a water aerobics class. Betty was their geriatric aerobics instructor.

"She needs to know the shoot is still Nov. 9," said Peterson, as she wrote down the number and handed it to him. "She also said she knew of a place that was very 70s that we could use for the scene. She's very sweet but all the locations are locked, so tell her thanks but no thanks."

"What's her name?"

"Beach Bunny Betty," said Peterson. "That's her name."

"Okay," he said, slowly.

Peterson was already on to the next task, and this one involved escort cards. In the movie, Sam hands out flyers for the penthouse party and is given one in return. It's an encounter that tees up a later scene, where a high-end call girl appears at the party. Although the party scene with the escort wouldn't be shot until Atlanta, the scene where Sam gets the card was scheduled for Day 3. The Art department would make the cards, and props would manage them. But without an image, things had slowed. Peterson wanted to get it handled.

Men in bright orange shirts that read "Girls! Direct to Your Room in Minutes!" are a fact of life in Vegas. The risqué cards they hand out are as plentiful as venereal disease. But Peterson didn't need just any card. She needed one that could be cleared, ideally with the image of the actress on it.

Peterson called the actress that would be playing the floozy to check her availability in case they wanted to fly her to Vegas to be photographed. Another photo shoot was scheduled for a scene with the child actors who play the main characters as young men. She could add the actress in the mix. She got her on the phone.

Gary Rake came in and went right to his bag in the corner. He and Turteltaub had a series of meetings, one of them a casting call. In the meantime he was looking for something he needed for Hennings.

Badalato opened the door and looked around the room.

"Hi. Kristina, can you come in with the cast list? You're the person who knows the most about it."

"Sure," she said.

Badalato was gone as quickly and Peterson looked at Rake.

"Excuse me while I go talk to the producers about who we booked for casting" she said with just the slightest tone. "Can I get an upgrade to casting director?"

There was a pause slightly over a beat.

"Sure," said Rake. "Put in for that."

Everyone laughed, Peterson most of all. She would no more get a bump for the extra duty than ask Badalato about it, and everyone knew it.

She printed something to take with her to his office and noticed there were only a few sheets of paper in the printer. Awa could read her mind.

"We're out again," she said.

"You have got to be kidding me," Peterson said, dumbfounded. "We're out of paper again? Did you check that box of fun she came in here with so proudly a little while ago? I thought it was filled with supplies."

"Yes," said Awa. "Just not paper. I asked her and she said she's getting some. The PA forgot it."

"The PA? The same one who got too little paper last week?"

She had a small pad on her desk with a list of things on the top, and several more pages under it. Many of them would require paper. This was ridiculous.

"We're going to need to buy it ourselves and expense it," said Peterson, clearly annoyed. She grabbed the paper needed for the extras meeting from the printer in a swift, fluid motion.

186

It might be a car, bus, truck or van, but any vehicle seen in a movie is a "picture car." In this case, it was cabs that needed consideration. The movie needed a lot of them with the heroes coming and going around town. Then there was a scene in which the main actors were stuck in a traffic jam, which would require other vehicles.

Turteltaub and a group of crew collected in the lobby for a 2:45 p.m. pick-up time for the picture car meeting at 3 p.m. That gave time for the van to wind around City Center traffic to the Annex building a couple of blocks away. The director stood near the Buddha statue surrounded by the others. There were nine people in total, the ADs, Turteltaub's personal assistant, Hennings and the heads of Grip and Electric departments. The rest of the Camera department, along with other crew, would meet them there.

The lobby was bustling with patrons. Most were dressed casually or in business attire. Occasionally, someone would stand out in the mix. The latest was a young man in hot pink shorts. Still, nobody in the group even noticed. The director was saying the statue didn't look like a Buddha to him, despite the fact its belly was rubbed into a different color by all the others who did.

"Really, it looks like Charles Olson," he said, which crew guessed was a reference to the poet, since there was a strong resemblance.

The nearby ADs were focused on specific tasks. After about 10 minutes and no van, Rake had stepped aside to call the Transportation department. Time was wasting.

Peterson, also on the periphery of the group, could have been at her desk upstairs the way she worked the phone. She had been on it most of the time they had been in the lobby.

"No," she said firmly into the phone. "Stacey is the hard body."

Rake returned from to the group looking slightly miffed. The van was going to be late.

"No kidding. How late?" asked Turteltaub.

"He said 10 minutes but they aren't sure."

"They aren't sure?" Now the director looked miffed.

"That's what he said." Rake, generally understated, said it with just enough tone to give the impression he had handled it.

Turteltaub looked at the Buddha, where tourists had again stopped. He seemed about to say something but shook his head. Then he turned to Hennings with a comment about the X-Scream.

One of the more challenging scenes to shoot in *Last Vegas* involved the ride, which sits atop the Stratosphere, the tallest structure in Vegas. The characters portrayed by Michael Douglas and Mary Steenburgen go there as part of a play date. The scene was scheduled to shoot the second day of photography.

"The ride itself is pretty lame," Hennings said. "It's just not that scary." Because the tech scout had included riding it he had first-hand knowledge.

The X-Scream was touted as the third highest thrill-ride in the world but it was also true it doesn't do much. It swung people in a car 27 feet over the side of the building and dangled them there. Once it started to bring them back it dropped them again, making them think it has failed. That was the height of its scare. Then it swung back around.

"We need to shoot above it, with double cameras, looking down. That's scary," answered Turteltaub. Hennings nodded.

The plan in place was to use a green screen and fill in the shots when they returned to Atlanta, Turteltaub continued. If it went that way, they could shoot the actors, put blowers on them, "and maybe you see slight horizon."

"Maybe it plays perfectly from the front," Hennings said.

He had his camera out and held it in front of the director. He flipped through shots he had taken on the tech scout of the Stratosphere and the X-Scream.

Turteltaub liked that idea much better. He peered into the viewer.

"Maybe we can shoot in a way that avoids the need for the green screen," the director agreed. "I'd rather go for it and get more of it finished. That would save a lot of money, and we still have the green screen as an option."

"If they could eliminate some shots, that would be a bonus," added Rake, who was looking at the camera viewer from the side. The helicopter shots, which would include a look at the Stratosphere, were booked on a Saturday.

"Who thinks of working on a Saturday as a bonus? Thanks!" Everyone laughed at the joke, except perhaps Rake, whose point may have been it would be a bonus not to work on Saturday.

Kerry Rawlins, the head of the Grip department, jumped in. Grips provide support for the Camera department by installing equipment needed to facilitate photography. They also support the Electric department in setting up equipment that holds lights.

"I can build two fly swatters and get a crane up on the Stratosphere," Rawlins said. "You don't need two fly swatters," replied Turteltaub. "Now we're down to one." "That's right," Rawlins answered. "One."

This had the echo of Badalato or Samuels to it. A fly swatter was a swath of heavy material put in front of the sun or light to diffuse it or create shade. It literally looked like a fly swatter, a rectangle on the end of an arm, material strung between a frame like a trampoline. The larger issue was the equipment needed to hoist it in the air. Cranes and other equipment to do it cost money. That one would work, instead of two, had the ring of a producer.

More time had passed and still no van. Not only was the director and this batch of crew standing idle, aside from the impromptu shot meeting, there were many others waiting for them at the Annex. Rake took out his phone as he walked outside to look for the van, which pulled up a minute later. It was just shy of 3:15.

He came in to alert the others.

"There's other stuff Jon could have been doing," he said. "Shit happens. We know that. You can't help that sometimes the van can't be here when it's supposed to be. But you can let us know that 2:45 isn't going to work."

Inside the van the mood was light. The Annex would be a very fast trip if you could fly it in a helicopter but it would be a solid 10 minute drive by vehicle given the intense foot and auto traffic along the way. The van headed out the driveway and down Harmon Avenue to the light at Las Vegas Boulevard. Now they were in the thick of City Center and Vegas life. Planet Hollywood, New York-New York and the Hawaiian Marketplace were all close at hand.

Somebody asked what was in the Hawaiian Marketplace, an 80,000-square-foot shopping center.

"There's King Kamehameha," said Turteltaub, referring to the giant statue at the international market, a large retail area. The king who united the Hawaiian Islands into one royal kingdom in 1810 after years of conflict is widely revered.

"And there's a ton of Japanese tourists," he added. "Now that's Hawaiian."

This was pure Turteltaub, where getting his full meaning often required an additional second to process. For every three Americans that visit the Pacific archipelago there is one Japanese, a significant portion of its tourist base.

The van pulled up at the Annex, where a much larger group was waiting. Dusty Saunders had orchestrated the gathering of cabs and drivers, who were huddled together about 40 feet away, where more taxis were parked.

Turteltaub walked over to where Saunders stood. They talked briefly, then the director started to make his way through the different cabs. Hennings, who had been surrounded by the camera guys as well as grip and electric, walked over. Rake was talking to Awa and Peterson.

Turteltaub stood in front of a Prius taxicab.

"I think that's funny, these four guys getting into a Prius," he said. He stood there for a second, his mind working the idea of retirement-age characters getting into a newer-age vehicle and being a little crowded in the process. The question was whether it would hold everyone.

Hennings climbed in the backseat with a detached 17.5-75mm lens, which can get a close focus shot with a minimum distance of 2 feet. He put it up to his eye for a few seconds. Panavision.

"Take a peek," he said, handing it to the director.

Turteltaub got in the front seat with the lens and leaned back against the wheel, squinting as he looked through the lens into the back seat. It gave him an idea of the room in the vehicle for what he wanted, among other things.

Then he got out of the car and came around the front. He looked through the windshield with the lens for all of a second.

"Can I get a 35?"

Hennings handed him one.

Turteltaub looked again. He climbed out of the car and stood there a minute just looking at it. As he turned away one of the cameramen said hello and extended his hand.

"Long time," said Chad Rivetti.

The director reached back.

"You're Tony's kid," he said.

Rivetti nodded.

"You were on *The Kid.*"

Rivetti nodded again.

Turteltaub had directed *The Kid* starring Bruce Willis in 2000. Crew included Tony Rivetti as first assistant on A Camera and Chad Rivetti as second assistant on B Camera. The traditional way up the ladder of the Camera department, a zig-zag between jobs on the B and A cameras, was evident. Now the younger Rivetti was first assistant on A Camera. Turteltaub asked after Tony Rivetti and was told he was wrapping another show.

The entire greeting had probably taken less than a minute. Then it was back to work, Turteltaub onto a taxi-minivan nearby. Rivetti took a few steps back to where Flurry stood with his cart. Hennings was already there, looking through a lens.

The van was emblazoned with the Desert Cab logo. It had pulled up from the group a short distance away after a prompt from Saunders. A driver from Flamingo watched from nearby, arms on his chest. Every driver wanted their vehicle to get a turn.

After a few minutes, Turteltaub was back at the Prius. He popped the hatchback and looked inside. He stood there for a long minute. Then he walked back to the other vehicle and had the driver pop that one, as well. Hennings stood nearby frowning.

Turteltaub said he liked the van for the one shot but for the other, his first choice was the Prius.

"You'd be happiest if it wasn't a white cab, is that correct?"

Turteltaub was looking at the DP without the hint of a joke. There was only one answer.

"Yes," said Hennings, smiling. "I would be happiest if it wasn't white." The human eye naturally balanced white as part of normal brain function. The camera sensor registered the exact amount of light it received, making it harder on the cinematographer to deliver clarity.

Turteltaub looked at Saunders, who had been standing nearby. The transportation coordinator, instrumental in organizing this meeting, had followed along.

"Can you see if there's a Prius that isn't white? Turteltaub asked. "For David's sake."

Saunders nodded.

"I would note that it's a Prius Mirage, which is in cahoots with MGM," someone said. MGM was the force behind the Aria and the movie production's corporate barter partner.

Still, there was concern about whether the Prius would be big enough for the scene with all the actors.

"It will work for what Diane gets into," said Turteltaub.

Hennings was wiggling the headrests. "We'd go over the shoulder. Do these come out?" He pulled his head out of the car to look for the operator.

"Can we remove the seat?" The driver nodded.

They conferred another minute. It remained to be seen if they could get a Prius that wasn't white, but they had identified another option if not. Picture cabs for the portions of the movie shot in Las Vegas decided, their work here was done. Turteltaub and Hennings talked about the technical camera test the next day as the group started to disband. The DP was testing the casino and various shots there, starting early morning. The director said he would stop by at some point.

That afternoon the fourth floor of the Aria hotel was filled with people. The doors of the bullpen and Accounting departments were always invitingly open, although the chief accountant had an office inside that stayed closed. The doors of the offices of Badalato and Kamishin were typically a foot ajar. It seemed to say they were available, but they wanted you to think about it. Then there were offices that weren't open as often, like those assigned to Turteltaub and Samuels, whose work didn't center there. But it was normally a quiet space regardless of who was working.

This time you could hear the noise generating from that corner of the X of the chromosome design halfway down the long corridor from the elevator. It was high energy, like a group in line for a concert waiting for the doors to open. It was a gaggle of young women milling about in the hallway chatting away as they awaited auditions.

This was the "hot girls" casting call for the pool scenes. The talent agency had delivered everything slender in its coffers. It was a good range of ethnicities, every one of the would-be starlets attractive. There were blondes and brunettes, two with jet-black hair and one with red hair. Most were tall but not all. They wore full makeup and had nicely if not beautifully done hair, long and short and curly or not.

A couple of them had the girl-next-door look, casually dressed and wholesome, but most of them had dressed for attention. The volume was misleading in the sense that there were only about a dozen of them. All of them had brought legs, lots of legs. They were perched on more kinds of heels than the average person could name. They were on stilettos and wedges, pumps and slingbacks. One woman teetered on a monumental pair of platforms. Another, in very short-shorts, kept pulling and tugging at them, trying in vain to cover her cheeks for more than 60 seconds at a time.

Two women wore very similar skin tight frocks. The fabric began at the same place on both of them, four inches past the start of the thigh, and ended at the same place up top, just past the chest. Recognizing they matched, they decided between themselves they should stand apart when they met the director. Others, listening in, compared their outfits. Perhaps they should stand separately, too, if their outfits were similar in color.

The young women settled into the hallway while work went on in the bullpen. Rake and Turteltaub came in separately on different tasks. Turteltaub was talking to someone on one side of the room while Rake was crouched in front of the supply cabinet. Other crew was there to pick up clean clothes, part of a wash-and-fold service the Production department set up for crew at cost.

A few minutes later the cinematographer came into the bullpen. He noted the beauties in the hall in for the casting call, who by then had made themselves comfortable for the wait. Some were sitting on the floor, others standing or propped up against the wall.

Hennings asked would the director need his help? He was in roguish form, deceptively casual in jeans and white T-shirt and quality tennis shoes. Not all T-shirts are created equal. This one was a John Varvatos design. It was a pleasant enough ensemble he might have been a model in a Viagra commercial.

"I can check skin tone and make sure it's right for lighting purposes," he said, a big grin on his face. Easily 20 years older than most of the women in the hall, he was handsome and doubtless would have found a welcoming committee.

The group in the bullpen laughed, Turteltaub smiling and shaking his head as he whisked by Hennings on his way out. The director wasn't gone a few seconds before he boomeranged back into the room. Seeing the women in the hallway had given him pause.

"Come on," he said to Rake, who by then was standing at a table in the front of the room gazing at a piece of paper. "I'm not going in there alone."

The First AD, an amused look on his face but otherwise silent, dutifully followed the director for the auditions.

The camera test the next morning made for a more tightly wound Hennings. Wendie Mosca, the public relations manager for MGM Resorts

International, stood outside the employee entrance of the side of the Aria casino floor at 7 a.m. to meet him, along with other members of the crew.

The Aria was just one of the hotels in Mosca's job description but this wasn't something she wanted to delegate. She needed to establish the perimeters of what the crew could do on the casino floor. She said twice there were a lot of rules, each time adding the Aria would do everything they could to assist.

With Hennings alongside, Mosca opened a different "Employees Only" door and the rest of the crew followed behind. Crew was familiar with some of the underbelly of the resort thanks to meals in the employee cafeteria, but this was new terrain. She moved briskly and veered off down another back hall as she wound through a wide hallway, down a narrow one, eventually arriving at large commercial elevators. The group filled two cars for the ride down. Then she lead them through another hallway past some more doors to the loading dock. That opening revealed a cavernous underground with roads and trucks dropping things off, others parked in the distance. It was a secure underground entrance like something out of Batman. This was where they had parked the camera truck.

The larger group stayed with Mosca while Hennings headed toward a row of trucks in the distance. There Rivetti and Flurry stood next to a cube truck and a couple of rolling carts. They had the back open and the electronic lift-gate down waiting for him.

The camera truck wasn't fully loaded, but what was there was expensive. The shelves on one side had boxes and various machinery and lens cases. Rolling carts like the one on the ground took up another large section of the truck bed. They were sturdy and looked more like something in an emergency room than a grocery store. Made of stainless steel, each had at least two shelves rimmed with two-inch lips. One featured a device that looked like a vice grip, which was a resting place for a camera not in use.

These could be thought of as the equivalent of desks for cameramen. Each was personalized, some labeled, as with "Flurry Cam." Rivetti's was also identifiable. As with other crew, their kits came with a fee. Hennings's cart was different. It wasn't labeled but it looked like him, tall and skinny and busy. The DP had it custom designed and was proud of it. The carts used in the industry were limited, particularly when he started. The wheels couldn't pivot and a lot of extra time was spent to move them as a result. He spent thousands to design this mobile DP cart, which was put together at Panavision before they shot *Horrible Bosses*.

It was worth the expense, which he said amounted to several thousand dollars. Just the monitors were roughly $30,000. It had six shelves and also featured the strong wheels on the bottom. It did more than pivot, moving easily in either direction. It had a system that locked the wheels in place when they were set. The monitors at the top looked expensive, but then so did all of it.

Flurry and Rivetti offloaded the rest of the camera equipment, riding up and down on the electronic gate of the truck as Hennings pointed out what he wanted. Some things they took off other rolling carts, each of which had several shelves and various control mechanisms. There was fluidity to it, like they'd done it before. It had taken less than 20 minutes to load the three carts by the time they locked the truck. "We're like a three-person married couple," Rivetti joked. Hennings looked at him with one eye, like "what did you just say?"

The camera staff, now with equipment, returned to the door where the rest of the crew and the casino executive had waited. They followed the same path back out to emerge on the casino floor. Hennings was gone in an instant, speed-walking past bleary looking patrons. He moved swiftly enough through the 100-yard maze of bells and whistles and lights to put distance between he and the crew. The key grip and gaffer kept up while Rivetti and Flurry were close behind with the equipment.

Rivetti and Flurry had checked the equipment, and Hennings trusted them. The technical camera test was to see how it functioned in the environment where it needed to work. Lighting was the big issue. It was okay where they settled but as they moved away from the lobby and into the casino it got darker. It wasn't just making it brighter but lighting it in the right way. Then there were challenges unique to the environment that had to be managed.

The DP came to a stop at the far end of the casino floor near the large check-in area of the Aria hotel, then turned back into the interior a few feet. There he paced back and forth deep in thought. Meanwhile, Flurry had locked the wheels on his cart and begun to assemble the camera near him. It happened in stages with an effort that belied the weight of the parts. First the giant tripod, then he attached a swivel, then he carefully detached the camera, which was secured to the cart, and reattached it to the parts on the ground.

The monitor at the top of the DP-mobile came to life with brilliant clarity, the slot machines on the screen more vibrant that the machines themselves. It was startlingly superior to any high definition television on the market. Now Rivetti, who as focus puller handled camera controls, went to work.

At the top of the DP's list was sorting out the flashing lights on the games of chance. Hennings knew they wouldn't be in sync with the camera. Because the lights operate at a different frame rate than the cameras they could cause problems. The camera operated at 24 frames per second. Video and other games operate at a different frequency. The result could be a flash or a pulsing. So he set about finding the precise rate in relation to the camera speed.

The DP had his glasses on, glasses off, throughout the entire process. He went back and forth between the camera trained on the slot machines and the monitor. After 10 to 15 seconds of staring at the monitor he went back and adjusted the camera and did it again. Then they moved to another location, camera assistants, grip and electric, and ADs in tow, and checked it again.

The afternoon was filled with meetings, starting with Cirque du Soleil. Turteltaub and Rake were meeting with reps of the Quebec-based mega-entertainment company near where they would shoot the scene, the DP and ADs all there in the background.

The script called for a montage of shots featuring the main characters of Zarkana, its most recent show to open. They would receive flyers for the party. The first rewrite had an acrobat run backstage after doing a "spectacular flip and tumble." Sam would hand him a flyer for the party. The updated script, the blue one that had just been released, also revealed other details: "The ZARKANA sign hangs over the staircase leading to the show. Paddy comes down the escalator handing flyers to the THREE SEXY ZARKANA PERFORMERS who are handing out their own programs." Uppercased letters indicated characters introduced for the first time.

The meeting was in front of the escalators and staircases under the bright blue Zarkana sign, where the scene would be shot. It was in open space, with chiming and ringing from slots and other machines on the casino floor to one side, wide hallways curving into two directions around it on the other. Next to the entrance to the stairs was the Race and Sports Book, where guests could bet on anything from NFL and NCAA games to motorsports, rodeo and dog racing. High-stakes poker wasn't far away.

A group was waiting there until Turteltaub and Rake arrived. It was the PR rep for the Quebec company, as well as other ADs, Hennings, and the Aria PR manager. Turteltaub and the Cirque manager, who had French as a first language, chatted a few minutes while they waited for a couple of other members of the troupe to join them.

The director said he was a fan of Cirque shows and took his kids. "My son thought the show was called 'Circus L.A.,'" he said. It took her a second to sound that out, the phonetically similar Cirque du Soliel and Circus L.A. She laughed mightily.

"He knows he lives in L.A., and that it's a circus," said Turteltaub. "So why not?"

"Smart boy," the woman said. The rest of the Cirque troupe had just walked up. She introduced them to the director and Rake using a mixture of French and English, mostly French. Then she turned it over to Turteltaub, who spoke in English but grew more animated with each word.

"We'll have a lot of people going down the escalator, people on the steps, people everywhere," said the director, pacing back and forth and waving his arms toward the staircase. They didn't need to understand his words to understand his movement. They nodded in agreement.

"Robert De Niro will hand flyers to the performers," said Turteltaub. "The performers just need to take them."

"Of course," she said. A couple of the performers standing by brightened at the mention of the actor's name, which did not need to be translated.

"How many performers could we have?"

"How many do you want?"

"Could we have several?" asked Turteltaub.

"Sure!" she said.

Someone handed him a glossy brochure of Zarkana, flipped open to the characters. The plot of the circus show has Zark, a magician who has lost his way, searching for a woman to get her back. Along the way there are the usual Cirque plethora of clowns, people on stilts, ring spinners, ball bouncers. He pointed out several he liked and she made note of it. It was all very easy, the meeting remarkably short.

All the while, Hennings had been walking around. He paused from various perspectives, finally perching halfway up the staircase looking down, thinking about shots. He joined the group as they were finishing. Rake was giving the date they were shooting the scene, which would be Monday, Oct. 29. Somebody would be in touch with more details but they should just plan to be here, by the escalator. She agreed and the party dispersed.

There was a little bit of time before the next meeting. Turteltaub stopped to play a hand of poker on his way back up. There had been a lot of talk about his poker-playing process. Reports were that he won more than he lost.

He pulled out his wallet as he took a seat at the poker table. Most of the crew had peeled away but there were still a few in the mix, including Rake and Hennings and a couple of production assistants. Turteltaub liked a good game of Pai Gow Poker. It involved one 52-card deck plus one Joker, which could be used only as an Ace or to complete a straight or flush.

Turteltaub took two crisp $100 bills out of his wallet and traded them in for chips. It was just the director and the dealer, no other players. The game didn't last long. With the house victorious and the $200 gone, Turteltaub was out of the chair. He and Rake headed across the floor toward the elevators, which were around the bend at the edge of the casino floor. The rest of the crew that had been tagging along to that point fell behind.

The topic turned to the director's command of poker. "He may be down $200 but he knows when to quit," someone said.

"Oh, Jon's not down," said Hennings. "He walked away with $700 last night." Someone else confirmed it, saying he'd been impressive to watch. "He definitely knows when to quit," he said. Hennings joked that he'd like to have had that same sense when he was at Roulette table the night before.

Steenburgen arrived a day ahead of the others to the delight of producers. Her role was challenging given that she had to sing and there was still talk of her playing the piano herself. The actress left a stellar impression on the PA there to greet her. The actress had been friendly and chatty, happy to be there. The PA asked what else she needed, prepared to find her a green bean smoothie if that's what she wanted. But all Steenburgen wanted was to make sure her family could find her suite. Her daughter and husband, actor Ted Danson, were arriving later in the day.

De Niro, Douglas and Freeman arrived in Vegas on Wednesday. De Niro and Freeman traveled by private jet, with entourages. Douglas and Allen Burry, his executive assistant, flew together on United Airlines. The rest of the actor's entourage would arrive in advance of his first day of on-screen work Tuesday. Kline also flew commercial, as Steenburgen had Tuesday. All of them were in suites at the Aria except De Niro, who went to Caesars Palace as expected.

The 'table read' or 'read through' was the next morning, They would all meet to read the script together as a cast. It was the last big thing to happen in prep for the Production department. They had reserved Copperleaf 3, a smaller space in the convention center. The goal was a more intimate space, big enough for cast, producers and studio officials, and perhaps some department heads, but not the entire crew. Now the list of people the room had to accommodate was at 28. It had grown each day of the week as more people from the studio decided to attend. Several of the names of the execs were heard for the first time. "Of course," said Badalato. "Who wouldn't want to watch this cast sitting at the same table to read a script?"

All the conditions were right, given proximity to L.A. and the general appeal of Las Vegas. Were the only option Atlanta, someone noted, some of them might have been able to stay in L.A. to meet obligations. It was one of the fringe benefits of working in the business that had seen a lot of such things eliminated.

People think successful actors are spoiled and that was true to some degree here. The major actors were checked in before they ever arrived, their rooms or suites pre-stocked with whatever they requested. The Production department did most of the stocking while it was up to the AD Department to provide the hands-on with actors. A driver would deliver them to the Aria, where a PA would greet them. The PA would have the keys to their suites. They would escort them and make sure they had what they needed.

Gift bags had been prepared and placed in their suites. Each suite was stocked with whatever they requested individually along with other comforts. PAs knew to seek out what else could be done to accommodate them. But there was also reason for it. It was in the interest of the project to make the actors comfortable. They wanted the best performance they could get out of them and if a case of Evian helped keep them in the suite preparing for their role, so be it.

Crew in Las Vegas had thus far echoed what people in the Atlanta bullpen said about dealing with the top actors and their entourages. They were pleasant and easy to deal with. The biggest headache was a driver for one of them who wanted kitchen amenities at Aria. It was something every member of the crew wanted. It had even been a sore point, since people who work on location are used to having a private food and beverage supply. In this case, the hotel specifically limited what could be kept in rooms so the production had little choice. Then the driver's job widened to include cooking for the actor, which likewise widened housing options for him.

It had all gone smoothly until they were getting Jerry Ferrara checked in. His suite wasn't ready when he first arrived. The PA there to greet him told him and they sat down on a couch to wait. He sat talking amiably to the PA, not the slightest bothered by the delay. Then Prickly Guy walked by and saw them sitting there. He changed direction immediately. Was there a problem? Why was the actor in the lobby? What happened? One of the assistant directors, who had been approaching from a distance, quickened their pace. That saved the PA, who was looking bewildered. Ferrara assured him he was fine and the executive moved on. Luckily for everyone, the actor's accommodations were soon available.

Actors lower on the totem pole checked in at the bullpen, just as crew did, rather than being met in the lobby. Toward the end of the evening an actor who had already checked in returned to the bullpen. He pretended to look at paperwork and then went to craft services. There were various snacks and a small refrigerator on one side, and he loaded up with them.

Then he went to the supersize cooler a few feet away. It had soft drinks and two kinds of bottled water, one of them high-end. He set the snacks down and scavenged through the cooler for the expensive water. He found several, shook off the cooler water and set them down. Then he resumed digging and found another bottle of the branded water. The supply picked clean, he loaded it all in his arms awkwardly and left the bullpen without a word.

"Typical actor," one of the bullpen veterans said as soon as he was out of earshot.

"Really?" A visitor working at a table had noticed him because he was vaguely familiar. He had the face of an actor who played the murder victim in different episodic television shows. She had watched with amusement as he scoured for the best snacks and water.

"It's not necessarily typical," someone else said. "But it certainly isn't unusual."

"Typical B-grade actor," the first woman said, correcting herself.

It was nearly 10 p.m. by then and they were tired. Finally the printer, which seemingly had been going for hours, came to a stop. Now they could get to the last work of the day, which was preparing the scripts for the table read the next morning. These scripts were different from the ones used at the crew production meeting. Now an official version, they were printed on blue paper. Each one had to be hole-punched and placed in 1.5-inch binders rather than fastened together with brads.

The top Las Vegas manager, the one who had frowned at the wobbly table, arrived a short time later to help them. She was back up and at Copperleaf 3 by 6 a.m. the next morning. The Production department had spent days preparing for the event. She would make sure it went off well.

The set-up in convention center space was more elegant than the one she put together for the production meeting with the whole crew. There were nicer tablecloths, water and glasses and wrapped breath mints. The food, which would be set up buffet style against one of the walls, was the highest-grade offering available. The issue now was making them all fit comfortably. The number of confirmations was now at 32. That didn't include the people who would just show up.

The room wasn't set up for that many people. A long table with rounded ends, made up of a series of tables with ends overlapped, was set for 18 people, with more tables on the sides of each wall. She expanded the cast table to 22 seats then shifted tables around the perimeter and got additional chairs. All told that would accommodate the influx.

By then, crew had shown up to help. The next step was to double-check each script, verifying pages were in order. The printer had continued to act up on them and they had worked late into the night. "It's easy to make mistakes that late," she said. To her point, several scripts were missing pages or otherwise out of alignment. They pulled out any that needed fixes and then distributed the blue scripts to each place setting, the best at the head of the table with the main actors.

Each place setting had a nametag. It looked logical but the precise placement had also been carefully considered. Turteltaub would be at the head of the table. De Niro would be seated to his left, Douglas to his right. Freeman was next to De Niro, and Kline next to him. On Douglas' side it was Steenburgen followed by Jerry Ferrara. De Niro's script was specially checked to ensure its pages reflected the reinforced punch holes and it did.

The Copperleaf 3 had a back entrance, as did the larger room used for the production meeting. It provided access for food and general deliveries but also private access for the movie stars to stay out of common areas. That would avoid word spreading in the hall about movie stars and keep them out of it if it did. So far it was quiet. There had been more people lurking around on Tuesday for the production meeting when there hadn't been any actors present.

201

Douglas and Burry, his executive assistant, arrived first, not just ahead of the big names but almost anyone else. The actor quickly found his place at the table while Burry approached the others in the room to introduce himself, in effect also introducing the actor. The two men have one of the longer relationships in the business, dating back to 1985. Burry began as a publicist and eventually opened his own agency in the U.K., Douglas one of his clients. He had been working exclusively for Douglas since 1996.

It was Burry who responded to inquiries about whether Douglas was promoting his Oscar chances in 1988. Four years later, Burry let them know the actor wasn't available to discuss controversy over the NC 17 rating for *Basic Instinct*. He answered questions about whether the actor was dating Catherine Zeta Jones in 1999 and about the birth of their children in 2000 and 2003 and anytime there was tabloid gossip, if they bothered to call. He'd been there to answer questions in 2010 when news was out that the actor had throat cancer.

That illness, now in remission, was something producers had considered when they hired Douglas for *Last Vegas*. The actor looked tired to several people, and producers were only human if it crossed their minds. They also knew he'd been to the doctor and the insurance company had signed off on his health. Moreover, the actor came with a solid track record over the long term and if he said he could play the role the better bet was that he could.

Burry continued to mingle with various people as the room started to fill. Douglas stayed in his seat until Bre Blair arrived at the table. He rose quickly to his feet to greet Blair, who was cast as his young and beautiful on-screen fiancé. "I'm a lucky man," said Douglas, gallantly kissing her on the cheek as she beamed. They talked for a moment before she took her seat on the other side of Kevin Kline's chair. Kline had arrived by then and chatted with actor Roger Bart. Blair sat between them, joining in the conversation.

Bart had landed the role of Maurice ne Madonna. Turteltaub had taken his time filling that role but now it was clear he'd gotten what he wanted. The role was for a heterosexual who earned a living as a crossdresser, so it couldn't be too flamboyant a character. At the same time, the actor had to pull off a reasonably funny Madonna.

Bart had a number of significant television credits. He was best known for his work on "Desperate Housewives." His background also included some singing roles, here a small detail in casting him as a performer, since he wouldn't be singing. Clearly the actor had a sense of humor. His first big break was a brief role as George Carlin's long lost son in the comedian's television series. Kline was also a funny guy and there was laughter from their triplex at the table.

Morgan Freeman had quietly arrived from the interior hallway and gone to the buffet. It featured substantive food along with coffees and assorted teas, fruits, breads and croissants. Freeman filled his plate before taking his seat across from Douglas. Soon they were engaged in a discussion about flying. Freeman had arrived in Vegas on his high-speed Emivest SJ30. The $7 million-plus jet had been his since 2009. While the actor earned a pilot's license at 65, he had a professional pilot to fly it for him.

Freeman had turned to his food when he looked up to see his assistant and his stand-in walk in the main entrance. "Hey, Q," he called to Quentin Pierre, who walked toward him. Then he and the stand-in took a seat on the sidelines.

The other actor chairs filled in. Rapper T.I. took his seat to the right of Ferrara. He was up for the cameo first anticipated for Kanye West. He had come with an entourage and the Production department provided them with a suite originally planned for De Niro. They kept it for cases like this or if the actor changed his mind and decided he wanted to be closer. T.I.'s entourage had gotten him into hot water with the production office by making short shrift of the liquor supply and leaving a mess.

The middle of the table, eight seats, four on either side, were readers. They were needed since all parts of the script had to be read aloud. Two of them were full time stand-ins for the actors. The rest had come from a local talent agency. The local talent aspired mightily for one of the minor roles that remained.

The far end of the table was set up for producers Laurence Mark and Amy Baer on one side and CBS Films president Terry Press, and Maria Faillace, executive vice president, on the other. Given space limitations, a side table was set up along the wall not far away for Samuels, and two other studio executives.

It was one of three tables production had set for overflow. The middle table included the writer of the screenplay, Dan Fogelman, his assistant, and Accardo. The last table had crew, including Gary Rake. Every one of the seats added along the wall was put to use. The place was full to its seams with some of the biggest names in Hollywood, except for De Niro. Where was he?

"He likes to arrive last, after everyone else has been seated," an assistant offered.

It had been a tight schedule earlier in the day for De Niro's camera test. Camera tests were about how the actors will look on these cameras in this movie given the entire package, wardrobe, makeup, and hair. Do the costumes work as expected for the character? Do the watches and jewelry selected fit or would others be better? If the characters wear glasses, do the frames work?

De Niro's costume fitting was on the schedule from 7 a.m. to 8 a.m. and he also needed hair and makeup, with the overall camera test set to conclude by 10:10. In the mix was also the props show-and-tell. But the end time was firm, given a lot of them had to get back to Aria in time for the 10:30 table read.

The Annex had filled with crew and producers there for the test, all of them waiting for De Niro. But 15 minutes later he still wasn't there. It was normal for some crew to stand around at any given time, because their jobs didn't all happen at the same time. But to see that many crew not working and being paid was enough to tax the nerves of any producer. A few more minutes passed.

The ADs, whose job includes tracking actors, came back quickly with an explanation. De Niro had stopped to get a haircut but things had been complicated by a late change in hair stylists. Michael Douglas' hairdresser was standing in for De Niro's regular stylist, who was attending to a loss in his family.

"Get used to it," Peterson said, without the slightest hint of snark. "He will get haircuts on a weekly basis." She said it as a matter of fact: The man had great hair and it grew fast. And he would, quite literally, get it trimmed most weeks if he kept to his pattern. Rice, the assistant prop master, offered up what she knew. De Niro was just back from reshoots in Sofia, Bulgaria, for *Killing Season*, which meant his hair was styled for another role and probably needed extra attention.

De Niro arrived a short time later with dark hair, although it would be grey in *Last Vegas*. He was waiting for his regular stylist to fix it. There were some quick introductions but it was Rice the actor recognized in the crowd.

"Oh, it's you!" De Niro grinned, obviously delighted to see her. He reached out and she came over to him to say hello, crew and producers taking it in. He gave her a hug and a chaste kiss. "I'm so glad you're here." Then De Niro hugged her a second time, both of them beaming.

"I knew you were going to be here," she said. "That's why I took this show."

That might have been stretching it a bit. Rice liked to work, period, and it was hard to imagine she would have turned *Last Vegas* down. But it sounded good, and the exchange lifted the mood in the room. Turteltaub and Rake made eye contact, both of them looking slightly bemused.

Rice went back to a nearby table, set up with a display of eyeglasses, including sunglasses. One scene had the characters of De Niro, Douglas, Freeman and Kline buying new suits in Vegas. There had been talk of them wearing sunglasses as they walked down an Aria hall sporting their new duds.

It was the second time props had set up the eyeglass selection kit. Glasses worn on camera had to be anti-reflective because otherwise they interacted with the camera. The first time props had pulled the big package, specially ordering dozens of glasses after researching what the actors liked. They knew Freeman liked Aviators, for example.

All of the actors had picked easily, including Freeman who had indeed grabbed a pair of Aviators. Douglas picked something befitting his fat cat character. Kline likewise saw what he wanted for Sam although he requested the glasses be polarized. His selection was approved, but there was a blip. He wanted the pair in grey and they only came in black. Once the actors picked the ones they liked, the costume designer weighed in.

Steenburgen had talked about Diana as she pored over the frames. "I'm not interested in my character pretending to be younger than she is." She picked up a pair and tried them on. "People my age wear glasses. So, if it's okay with the director, I can have them on as needed." She tried on a couple of pairs and settled on one. Pink, who had been watching, looked at her for a long second and then nodded enthusiastically in agreement.

Once the actors had selected glasses and the Props department had ordered their prescriptions, they sent the display back. Given that any glasses that didn't get returned were billed in full, the Props department made it a practice to return the kits promptly. They also knew that De Niro didn't like glasses so there was no reason to keep them out for him. But Pink had asked them to have the glasses sent back in time for the camera test, not just for De Niro but in case she needed to make a change, which is where they found themselves now.

De Niro glanced quickly at the trays of glasses on display. "I'm not going to wear sunglasses," he said, softening as he looked at the director.

"Okay," said Turteltaub.

"Well, okay then," Rake said, swinging into motion. "Let's do the camera test."

Once his test was done, the producers and Turteltaub headed back to the Aria for the table read. All of them were in place at the Copperleaf 3 by the time Niro arrived, chatting in their seats. He had been whisked in through an interior hallway the same way the other actors had been and took his seat. They began a few minutes later.

The read-through went well. It was a solid script and there was a lot of laughter. Kevin Kline read his character with a stutter, the others more mainstream. The rapper there for the cameo missed his cues a couple of times, prompting De Niro to point to his script. "It's right there. On the page."

Fogelman, who had written the screenplay to begin with, spoke up about the changes he didn't like. It was one of those moments that might have gone awry but for Turteltaub's response. He promised they would take care of it over the weekend, before shooting began.

When it was over, the actors dispersed through the back halls. The other lead actors were due for camera tests starting at 1:15. Everything was set up as it had been in the morning. The Costume department had switched out the racks for Paddy and replaced them with the racks for Billy, Archie, Sam and Diana. Camera was back early, the ADs arriving a little later, all well in advance of the actor's camera tests.

De Niro was finished for the day. His plane was parked in the private hangar owned by Caesar's Palace for use of its guests. The smart money was on the actor going home to New York for the weekend but he could go just about anywhere.

Michael Douglas and Mary Steenburgen decided to work over the weekend. They called the bullpen to see about setting up a visit for them to the X-Scream. They would be riding it together in a scene and wanted to have a look. The bullpen notified Turteltaub who asked to join them. It was a date.

Turteltaub had more than that to do over the weekend. He also needed to roll up his sleeves with the screenwriter and go over the script. No one wanted Dan Fogelman to be unhappy. If anything they loved his script. He made arrangements to meet with the writer. Producer Larry Mark would join them.

PART TWO: PRINCIPAL PHOTOGRAPHY
Weeks 11-19½

CHAPTER ELEVEN
Shoot Week 1
Principal Photography Begins
Oct. 22-26
Day 1, 2, 3, 4, 5

AFTER TEN WEEKS OF PREP, thousands of creative hours and millions of dollars, the spigot was finally about to open. The next 38 shooting days would be when the real money flowed. All the time and effort spent in prep on the production side had been to ensure the next seven weeks would run efficiently. Now all focus would be on the creative side.

The crew began arriving in downtown Las Vegas in the cold pre-dawn hours. The first shots were planned for Glitter Gulch, the nickname for the casino area along Fremont Street, which was also the name of a neighboring strip club. They might have started principal photography at Aria or someplace with a few controls. No. For a host of reasons, including tradition in doing the toughest scenes first and the reality of the approaching fall weather, they were kicking off in the oldest part of the city. The Fremont Street Experience drew tourists and downtrodden alike.

In two hours, give or take, they would plop De Niro and Steenburgen down in the middle of it all and turn on the cameras. The two scenes were scheduled to take the morning. After a lunch break, the crew would resume in front of the lavish Bellagio Las Vegas hotel and resort. There the actress would shoot a scene with Michael Douglas. De Niro would be done for the day.

The set was listed as Tasti D-Lite outside of Binions at 128 Fremont Street, an area that allowed only foot traffic. That put base camp and the 30 trucks and trailers that were part of the production two blocks away at the corner of 1st and Ogden. It was surprisingly dark given the giant wall of light emanating from the backside of Binions. The trucks blocked the light on the ground, throwing long shadows. At 5 a.m., loud music played in the distance, all of it creating a surreal effect.

The catering company started at 1 a.m. to prepare enough food for 100 people. The call time emblazoned on the top of the Call Sheet was 6 a.m., which reflected when Turteltaub was due on set, along with the cinematographer and camera crew, gaffer, script supervisor and props department. At 3:30, the rigging gaffer had the earliest call time, grips and the bulk of the ADs were on the 4:30 a.m. shuttle, the Costume department at 5 a.m. Turteltaub and Rake arrived early, shortly after 5 a.m.

"Happy First Day" was a common greeting accompanied by palpable excitement in the air. The requisite amount of cynicism that came with any well-seasoned movie crew had vanished, at least for the short term. Most of them, even the most jaded, still liked what they did for a living. It was the challenge of days like this, in places like this, with actors like De Niro and Steenburgen, that reminded them why they got into the business.

The star trailers for the actors had lights on. De Niro had a 7 a.m. call time with a 7:45 a.m. ready call, which put him on set earlier than Steenburgen. De Niro, Douglas and Freeman's equal treatment, and their five staff, meant dedicated hair and makeup, among other things. Their stylists went to them. De Niro could be readied at the penthouse at Caesar's Palace or at his trailer.

Steenburgen was due at 5:30 a.m. with a ready call of 8 a.m., the extra time for costumes, hair and makeup. Kline and Steenburgen had assistants but not a full entourage. The production had a Hair and Make-up department, each of which had two crew, who assisted them. As leads, Steenburgen and Kline were at the top of their lists, although they worked with the entire cast. The departments would hire additional crew based on what was needed on a particular shooting day, whether additional cast members on the large-cast show or extras.

But as the sole leading lady, Steenburgen had something even better. She had the full commitment of Dayna Pink. The costume designer's vision would be most visible on the actress and she was intent on making sure Steenburgen looked great. The scene on Fremont Street would have her character, Diana Boyle, in a jumpsuit. That afternoon Diana would spend time with Billy Gherson, the character played by Michael Douglas.

The call times created a staggered delivery of crew, who arrived in vans courtesy of the Transportation department. The dining area that catering had set up was impressive. There was seating in place and tables for food beyond that, including a hot breakfast buffet on one table and then cold food, fruits and cereal and a variety of muffins and croissants on the next. A man stood behind an omelet table on the side, hands in pockets as crew passed him on their way to the coffee truck.

Each time a new van pulled up, the same thing happened. Groggy crew headed to the coffee truck, getting brew from exterior machines. Or, they waited for someone inside the truck to prepare a coffee. Most of the ones who headed to the food tables did so to pick up a croissant or fruit or granola bar or some combo they could carry. Then they headed toward the fluorescent light to work, even if they were early.

"Just walk toward the sun," someone said, "and turn at the music."

It wasn't a long walk, two blocks at a right-angle, and the set was exceedingly easy to find with lights that grew brighter and music louder with each step. The speakers at the Fremont Street Experience blared from the night before, bizarrely incongruent given few people remained outside at that hour, and most of the few that remained were passed out.

The camera and light trucks were closer to set than base camp but still a half-block away or more and around a corner. The cameramen managed the movement of the cameras and their own carts, including the Hennings mobile. The video assist pushed his equipment, the soundman and his crew theirs. The dolly grips managed camera dollies, other grips pushed rolling carts with lights and stands and gobos and flags and boxes.

To anyone wandering up in the pre-dawn hour, it might have been a giant playing field with an unrecognizable game. Crew with walkie-talkie buds in their ears like FBI agents traversed the area between Binions and the Nugget in different directions and at varying paces. The Locations department had laid the framework for the area, the biggest part the contract for the space, which meant dealing with Binion's as well as the city. There were a lot of other details to manage now that they were on site. The first was finding the origin of the loud music to silence it, which they or someone did to scattered cheers.

In the foreground, the cinematographer walked around quickly, occasionally stopping to wave his wiry arms like a conductor. The existing light stirred emotion in Hennings, it may have even offended him. Key grip Kerry 8590 stayed close, as did the best boy. The gaffer wasn't far. As Hennings talked and pointed at lights, they listened and looked and nodded. The problem lights needed to be overcome. New light would be put in place and he called out exactly what he wanted and they understood.

Somebody said, "get the BFL," which turned out to be the "big fucking light" or "big fat light" depending on who was asked. The BFL, off to the side, was pushed to the middle of Fremont Street and lifted up. Electricians unrolled cables. Things came off the carts, stands and various boxes and cords and panels and gobos and flags and screens, and stands went up and lights on those. A gobo shaped light something like a stencil might, while a flag blocked it or threw a shadow, both tools of the trade. Hennings stood nearby as they installed lights and accessories, adding this and changing that. Eventually he grew calm.

Someone wandering up would have known the two men off to the side were important, even if they didn't know who they were. One wore sunglasses at 5:30 a.m., the other was dressed urban-stylish, long shorts, hip hop hat with the high-flat front and a walkie-talkie, Turteltaub and Rake, respectively. The shades would have been incongruous for the early hour except for the ridiculously bright lights. Rake wasn't still for long. He began a rotation of sorts, like a fast-moving moon with ear buds circling the set and returning to Turteltaub.

Crew communicated on one of the walkie channels. As with marine use, there was a primary channel everyone tuned in. If there were longer conversations they switched to another channel. Each department had a channel that applied to them, although most listened to the main channel dominated by Rake and switched over for discussion. Rake would dominate any shooting day, not in terms of how much he spoke but in how closely the crew listened and reacted.

2nd AD Peterson was inside with hundreds of extras. Lillian Awa, the second 2nd AD, was outside, working with production assistants to set up a perimeter that would control foot traffic. As the "second-second," Awa was next in command after Peterson but worked more closely with Rake on set.

In the midst of it all, a switch was flipped and the overpowering fluorescent lights that dominated the block disappeared. But by then the movies lights were so bright that not everyone noticed. The PAs also installed two white 10x10 festival tents with sides for Steenburgen and De Niro in case they needed privacy between takes. Director's chairs with their names were inside. There would be no going back to base camp. The goal was to set it all up, get a shot of De Niro walking, the scene of he and Steenburgen chatting away on a park bench amidst the chaos of old Vegas, and move on.

A different part of the process was playing out on the second floor of Binions. The movie production had taken over the Longhorn Room. By 5:45 a.m., they had taken over the hallway too. Extras casting, costumes and props were teamed to prepare some 158 background actors -- or "BG" -- planned for the scene. The extras would fill in and around the part of Fremont Street where characters played by De Niro and Steenburgen would chat on the park bench.

Peterson talked with an additional 2nd second AD hired for the day. That woman, a local, was there to help corral the extras. They talked about how to space them, who in the crowd to pull out, and how to keep it all orderly despite the crazy environment. The woman looked at Peterson and told her this was Vegas, and there would be no controlling it. The best they could do, she said, was try to steer it.

"We're going to have to do more than that," Peterson replied, although she didn't sound as confident as normal.

The main gaming floor of Binions still had a few hollow-eyed loyalists pinned to slot machines but it felt strangely empty, even for that hour. Word had quickly circulated that there was something going on upstairs and from the looks of some of the extras, at least some gamers had found their way to the Longhorn Room.

Two people from the local casting agency sat at a table checking them in. They had a list of people and not all of the people in line had their names on the list. One way or the next, it was an authentic-looking group that might reasonably be wandering around Fremont Street on a normal day, tourists and drunks, eccentric and zany locals, all in the mix.

After they checked in the BG, which involved them signing paperwork, the next stop for extras was the Costume department. The main goal that morning was to ensure none of them wore anything with copyrighted branding or anything white, which was less desirable on camera. Rice, nearby with a props cart filled with items for them to carry, was next. She had tall plastic glasses and short ones and shot glasses, and different colored beverages to fill them with, like bright blue Gatorade.

Outside, propmaster Dwight Benjamin-Creel sat at a table in front of the Tasti D-Lite focused on the paper coffee cups De Niro and Steenburgen would hold. He used an exacto knife to cut out generic logos to affix to the cups, lest they look too much like Starbucks. It was precision work done with the surgical skill of a propman who had been at it for decades.

Just as he finished, Rice appeared, her work temporarily completed upstairs at Binions. She brought with her the wallet De Niro would need for the scene. During the dialogue between Paddy and Diana, he would get out the wallet to show her a photo of his late wife. The Props department keeps track of every prop an actor uses. They hold it until it's needed and then retrieve it to keep until next time. In this case it would be Rice to give it to the actor. She had a relationship with De Niro, but beyond that Benjamin-Creel didn't care if she handled all of the actor interactions. He was happy in the background, where he could make sure everything was prepped for the next day.

Other crew was less obvious, standing off to the side near the Starbucks attached to the Nugget, which was now open and was doing a great business. Badalato, who carried a mammoth backpack, stood off to the side of video village with Samuels, Kamishin and the Vegas production supervisor, watching the action. In the same way, the work in the production offices moved to the sidelines, even as the bullpen workload picked up.

The production designer and set decorator weren't far away. The bulk of the work by the Art department was done in advance and now they stood by if anything came up. Turteltaub saw Bomba and Cassidy and zinged them for an exit sign next to the Tasti D-Lite, which would be in the shot. It was the only evidence the director might actually be nervous, since he otherwise looked in his element. It was easily covered.

Suddenly a new issue arose. A loud compressor had started to work, coming on and off in intervals. It was accompanied by whiffs of spray paint, lightly toxic and unmistakable even in short spurts. The young man who ran the spray art kiosk, a booth in the area, had been delighted to arrive at work and see such a large crowd so early. He got to work quickly, excited because that many people assured a healthy, commission-fueled payday.

The problem for the production, and the Locations department in particular, was that the kiosk was perhaps 60 feet from where they planned to put De Niro and Steenburgen. Someone from the department went to talk to the young man, who was understandably reluctant to shut down, given the windfall he anticipated. They came to an agreement. Whatever the sum, the young man was soon beaming. He put the "closed" sign up, secured the compressor and other tools, and settled in behind the counter of the kiosk for a front-row view of the movie set.

Someone noticed there were Halloween decorations in the air. That was an issue, since *Last Vegas* didn't take place during Halloween. The production had leased two cranes for the day. Cranes are used to get shots or light sets from higher levels. One of the rented cranes was an 80-foot articulating condor. The condor was a boom lift considered "articulate" because it had full range of motion. The platform had a rail and was stable enough for a grip or camera operator to work on it with a degree of safety.

Mackie Roberts, the best boy grip, was a compact man in good physical shape with reddish hair and glasses. He seemed perfectly at ease as he stepped aboard the platform and attached his brightly colored harness to the platform rail. They raised and articulated the platform 40 feet up and over to the offending decoration. The condor came to a stop at a ghoulish dead body, which he removed.

It was like a giant puzzle but by 6:45 a.m. all the pieces had been connected. It was getting light quickly, the sunrise just a few minutes off. The movie lights, tamed with screens and other accoutrement, had been aimed in the right direction. Turteltaub had taken off his sunglasses. The director hadn't stayed in the same place for long but now he settled into his director's chair in front of monitors, the script supervisor next to him. The two of them huddled over the script. Rake also had a chair in the mix and would swing by but not actually sit in it.

All of the crew had walkie-talkies but air traffic was dominated by ADs. All of them listened for individual instructions from Rake, who now hovered near Turteltaub. He passed on the word to bring in stand-ins, so the cameras could be tested. They tested the cameras on stand-ins, making adjustments, Hennings looking into his screens with intensity. And then it was time. Rake radioed for them to bring in first team. PAs near base camp alerted the actors they were ready on set.

A few minutes later, almost exactly on the 7 a.m. dot, word came back. "Paddy's walking!"

De Niro had left base camp and was en route to set. The call was repeated anywhere there was crew with walkies. The crew had ear buds so the crowd didn't hear what was on the walkie but they heard the call repeated like stereo.

"Paddy's walking!"

A similar call went out for "Diana," when she left the trailer for the walk to set.

Everyone in the crowd, which continued to swell, heard the announcements but none understood it referred to De Niro and Steenburgen. No actors' names appeared on the Call Sheet either, only their characters and the numbers associated with them. While they didn't pass out Call Sheets to anyone who wasn't involved in the production, it wasn't that hard to get a hold of one.

Within a few minutes the actors took their places on a park bench. The extras were spread out on two sides of the enclosed Fremont Street area, awaiting the cue from the second ADs to send them into the scene. Things grew more chaotic by the second as more people heard they were shooting a movie. It didn't help that Binions was wide open along one side, open for business and with multiple wide entrances, providing easy access to the makeshift movie set. Turteltaub zeroed in on the actor. He was in a different zone entirely, oblivious to the craziness around him. And it was insane. The casino wheel at one of the entrances continued to work despite the action, offering up a free coupon to play inside with each spin. That provided a reason to linger despite the best efforts of people trying to control the set. Who could blame them? It wasn't just any movie. This was De Niro -- Robert De Niro! -- not 25 feet away from the wheel.

Then it was all in motion. Rake, conductor of the crew orchestra, zeroed in on the director. What Turteltaub called, Rake repeated into his walkie. The crew, listening intently to ear buds as outside noise grew, repeated the commands to the larger crowd.

"Quiet!"

The surprising thing was that it actually worked. They knew what it meant. This was Hollywood, baby!

"Picture's Up! Background! Rolling! Action!"

They were rolling! Extras, lined up on either side of the open area, looked to their handlers. Guided by the ADs, they were sent into the crowd in fast but irregular intervals. The second 2nd AD hired in Vegas sent them from one side, and someone else from the other. A small number seemed to come from other directions entirely. For the ADs, who had all done this before, it was a mix of finesse and luck. Somehow it worked, extras merged into the background like real locals and tourists on a normal day, if perhaps a little busier.

There was little controlling the extras once they were dispersed from the waiting line. That was particularly true of anyone who didn't want to cooperate or had their own idea on how to improve the shot. One man stopped to light a cigarette 20 feet behind the actors with every take, unaware he was safely off camera.

"Cut!" The command reverberated through the crowd as crew repeated it, the spell of Hollywood silence that had descended over them gone instantaneously. They all began talking at once but they returned to their places like pros. As far as Turteltaub was concerned there was no quiet spell, to him it was just loud. He honed in on the actors, silencing the external noises in his mind even when the headphones that enabled him to hear dialogue were off.

Few people in the crowd could hear a thing the actors were saying. De Niro wasn't hitting all his lines. He wasn't far off but one of the producers, now seated on the sidelines, raised an eyebrow. Did it portend an unprepared De Niro? That could be expensive.

Accardo got up from her chair next to Turteltaub's and walked over to the actor. This was that part about maintaining adherence to the script. She carried her leather script book with her, closed but with marker in place, and chatted briefly. It was the first of a couple of visits over a brief time period. The last time she held the script book a little higher, making it just a little more visible. But she waited until he asked for it, which he did.

And then De Niro was on the money. His character flirted with Steenburgen's, both of them gorgeous. Scene 60 was a single page of script, dialogue between the two actors, but it came to life. The human connection came across with amazing clarity on Hennings' monitors. The quality of it far surpassed any of the technologically advanced computer or flat screens on the market and there were many. The contrast made it easy to envision how it would look on the big screen.

This was a crowd scene, dozens of people on camera, and every element of it controlled. But it all looked natural on the monitors, one extra overplaying the role of a drunk, with passersby in the background while Paddy and Diana chatted.

The process played out, dialogue repeated. Each time the decibel level of the crowd quadrupled the second they cut. But it could have been much worse. People in the crowd cooperated a little bit at least. Some would shush others. Whether the noisy one responded seemed connected to how crazy they looked. But all of it had been crazy, the location, the noise, the street people, the tourists, all the moving parts on the creative side that had to connect.

They got the master and the other coverage they needed for Scene 60. There was another scene of De Niro walking, and then it was done. The crew went into motion to take it down. Lunch was next, then the sidewalk scene in front of Bellagio.

They had survived the baptism by fire without so much as minor smoke inhalation. Departments, by nature insular, had worked together. It boded well for the rest of the week filled with location work around one of the wildest cities in the United States. They had stops all around Vegas, the Neon

216

Museum, the Mirage and even the Stratosphere. The thrill ride, the one where they would dangle Michael Douglas and Mary Steenburgen, or their stunt doubles, 866 feet off the ground, was looming.

So far, so good.

There had been some chaos in the Las Vegas production offices. The shipping issue was one thing, then there was a clash between one of the ADs and the bullpen manager. Initially Badalato had seen it as personality conflicts, which he predicted correctly would resolve itself without his involvement. Indeed, the ADs had moved out of the back bedroom office a week sooner than they might have, drawing that to a close. Then a handful of other complaints came in about the bullpen from different departments.

In the end it was learning that the ADs hadn't had paper, more than once, that got his attention. If Peterson had to send a PA to get office supplies and then expense it she wasn't fully focused on her job. As the 2nd AD, she managed a lot of people and paperwork and the last thing he wanted was for her to be distracted.

Badalato, Kamishin and her Vegas counterpart had enough info by now to take a view from 10,000 feet. What was happening? Personalities were a factor but a key stress point was the amount of work to be done. Attrition hadn't helped. The driver who had helped out in the office was now driving and, aside from one, none of the local PAs hired for the Production department had thrived. If anything, the opposite was true. The failed furniture-builder was the first of several entry-level hires they hadn't brought back. The most serious situation involved a PA who made a mistake about where he dropped off a document and then tried to cover it up, compounding the error. He got to go home early and did not return the next day.

The challenge was in finding competent movie crew in Las Vegas. It might seem that a town that existed on shows would have trained crew in abundance, but the woman brought in to manage the office said that wasn't the case. Movie production was different from a stage show and required different experience.

Peterson, who was now working from the Annex, had worked around it. She brought several crew with her from Atlanta but it wasn't enough. So she advertised on a popular Internet site and screened candidates mightily. That had netted a couple of promising production assistants for her department. She also had a budgeting mechanism to pay them, the union-allowed daily rate.

There was no chaos in the travel office but it was too much work for one person. All of it was documented and time-stamped. The normal workload included the transportation needs of various producers and crew going back and forth to Los Angeles and Atlanta.

Changes to existing itineraries remained steady. But there were plenty of additional work. The week earlier it had been the influx of studio executives for the table read. Now it was getting all the actors and specialty background people in L.A. to Las Vegas for the pool scenes next week.

Badalato, Kamishin and the local production coordinator had all the evidence they needed that the bullpen was understaffed. The budget for *Last Vegas* hadn't included a production secretary in Vegas. That was a more-experienced hire, one that paid better than a PA. They'd also had plenty of time to reconsider a second in the Travel department.

Samuels agreed that the solution for the bullpen was to hire someone else to assist in the travel office and to bring in two additional outside crew from L.A. for the production office. Elizabeth "Libby" Anderson was hired as production secretary. They knew she was good. She had worked on two movies with Badalato and Samuels and was the sister of Jordan Anderson, the PA in Atlanta. She was also available: They called her on Friday and she arrived Sunday.

They also hired Sam Patton as the runner and office PA. Like Anderson, he was a known quantity. That was important for the runner, since they were entrusted with the raw material shot that day -- the "gold." All the scenes shot over the course of a day are on cards managed by the digital loader on set, a member of the Camera department. That material was packaged at the end of the day. Patton's job as a film runner -- a title that hadn't shifted despite the age of digital -- was to get it to the airport. There it was shipped special to EFilm, a unit of Deluxe, in L.A., where the dailies were processed and moved online to editors, who prepared it for review by Turteltaub and producers.

Just having the experienced hires, particularly Anderson, had lightened the mood in the bullpen. She fit right in and now sat at her desk, phone to ear, in search of a missing PA. It was one of the local hires who had worked out. He showed up on time, followed instructions, stayed late and generally took initiative. One day the previous week they had even entrusted him to take the gold to McCarran International Airport. The day's work made it

218

onto the flight to L.A. without incident. Even so, everyone agreed it wasn't ideal. It was another reason to bring someone from L.A. who was known.

Anderson had sent the young man on a series of errands, the most important of which involved getting a key document signed. No one had told him its significance or that he needed to return promptly, and as a rule he generally had. She hung up the phone and started on something else. Within a few minutes one of the ADs came in to the bullpen to drop something off. Anderson asked after the missing PA.

"He's at catering eating lunch."

"Oh, lunch?" said Anderson. "Production doesn't eat. Didn't anyone tell him?"

Anderson's comment prompted a laugh because it had a ring of truth. The bullpen ate last both metaphorically and as a general practice for good reason: It was in a position to avoid additional or hidden costs because it was aware of them. Getting the signature on the document and returning it was key to getting the ball rolling on something else. She radioed someone at catering, who got word to him and he returned in short order.

No one had told the PA to hurry back and he was inexperienced enough not to know. But what if it had happened the evening he carried the rushes to McCarran? It made the case for hiring known crew. There was a lot of pressure to hire locally, particularly in Georgia. While they made effort to hire people in Vegas to work in the bullpen, they had not flowed from the slot machines. This young man was one of the good ones. Anderson knew time was already short. It was also unlikely there would be any more, given they were already starting to think about shutting it all down. She would explain to the young man about lunch rules.

Back on Mailing Avenue in Atlanta, the bullpen was enjoying a low-stress environment. There was plenty to be done but a distinct buffer from anything happening 2,000 miles away. With the skeleton crew there was a minimum of drama. Most would have said they'd rather be working in Las Vegas but this wasn't bad work if you could get it. Besides, soon enough it would all be happening in Atlanta and they'd get their fill.

The action was on the sound stages. The recreation of the Aria penthouse suite, the biggest effort as it contained multiple sets, was well under way. A large building had taken form in the back warehouse. It was still under construction but now walls were in place, windows and doors framed. There were beams overhead to support the second floor, which was in the process of being added.

It seemed massive, given it was inside, and now rose better than two stories high. A 12-step staircase was in place just to access the first floor of the set. The purpose for the elevation, to give the feeling of looking down from a high view, now had physical reality. The floor-to-ceiling windows in what would become the living room set felt high, a long-standing trick in Hollywood.

In one corner a dozen sets of sawhorses were set up with 4x8 boards being turned into faux marble. Behind them, in neat stacks carefully spaced were completed boards. They were just getting started. In yet another area a man worked at a table saw cutting wood into two-foot squares that would be turned into faux tile.

In the next warehouse space finer elements were being constructed. Craftsmen built circular pillars out of wood that would be transformed into marble pillars of the penthouse. Two men worked on what would become the bar in the Deuce Lounge set.

With a $600,000 budget, no significant expense was being spared. Yet at the same time, it was all about money. Just building the sets in Atlanta was about saving money. It was less expensive than shooting in Las Vegas, and an elevated set with a photographic wall of the city skyline was just as effective on screen. Faux marble sheets and tiles, different colors and looks to be used in more than one set, represented significant savings from the real thing. And all of it took artisans.

The other added benefit of shooting on sound stages was the ability to control the environment. There were no slot machines programmed to make irregular sounds that were cutting into a scene. The grass-like covering on top of the warehouse, to quiet the sound of rain should there be some, was now in place as well. And no extras could wander in behind De Niro and creatively light a cigarette.

Patrick Cassidy got into a cab outside Aria shortly after 4 a.m. Tuesday morning. The transportation wouldn't start running for at least a half hour and he needed to get to the Neon Museum. They were shooting a scene with Douglas and Steenburgen, whose characters were on a play date. Normally, set decorating would have been finished the night before but an event at the

Boneyard, as they called the outdoor park filled with old signs, had prevented it.

"There's a surreal quality that can only come with four hours of sleep," Cassidy said as the cab wound its way around the hotel. It went through City Center and then north on Las Vegas Boulevard. Planet Hollywood and the Paris Hotel passed on the right, the Fountains of Bellagio on the left. Then the cab stopped at the intersection of Flamingo Road. The light changed as the cab continued down the Strip past living Vegas history, Caesar's Palace, the Flamingo, the Mirage.

It was an appropriate path given the concept behind the Neon Museum, which was founded in 1996 to save the vintage signs that had once defined the city. Caesar's Palace, now a mega resort, was inaugurated in 1966. The Flamingo went back to 1946, the brainchild of mobster Bugsy Siegel who wanted more than the El Cortez on Fremont Street. The Mirage was a relative newcomer, having first come online in 1989 with its by now well-known volcano. *Last Vegas* would be shooting on the sidewalks in front of the Mirage on Day 4.

The business practice of the early sign companies in Vegas was to lease their creations, which meant that eventually signs were returned. That left a surprising number of them intact, albeit left to decay in the weather in some cases for decades. Many signs sat in the back yards of businesses like the Young Electric Sign Co. or YESCO, as it is known today. Some were literally the size of large dinosaurs. Until the Neon Museum came along, the signs had been slated for the same fate.

Turteltaub credited Bomba with suggesting the location. The signs would provide an excellent backdrop, providing a clear sense of place and at once colorful and historic. The challenge for Cassidy and Bomba in perfecting the set was a museum rule: No one was allowed to touch signs in the cemetery, including movie stars. Given that Turteltaub would have Douglas and Steenburgen stop to say their lines, they needed a little more flexibility. The solution had been to find signs that would blend in. That way the actors had something to lean or stand on, if that's what director wanted, without breaking any rules. So Set Decorating leased or purchased additional signage that the actors could touch if needed.

The signs, collected by the Set Decorating department's Vegas-based crew, had slowly multiplied until they filled the Set Dec storage office in the Annex. Some ended up in the big common room. The signs were varying sizes and had meaning or none, Killer Eats, Fine, Run, Be MMAX, Proof Good, Fine,

Poker and assorted loose letters like, L, T, C, W. Some signs were large enough they stayed outside, while others were delivered directly to the location.

Cassidy had the cab driver circle catering for *Last Vegas*, which was setting up in a large parking lot on the other side of the museum. Then he continued to the Boneyard and other signs of life. The costumes trailer, hair and makeup, and the trailers or Steenburgen and Douglas were set up in a smaller lot. Makeup crew was due at 5 a.m. for Steenburgen, who had a 5:30 a.m. call time to begin preparations. Douglas had a 6:36 a.m. pick up time and make-up at 7 a.m. The ready call was 45 minutes later.

Cassidy paid the driver and got out where a group of eight men awaited him near the entrance of the Boneyard. It was the leadman and the swing gang for Vegas, terms still used for the set decorating crew.

As leadman, Daril Alder's job was to oversee the Set Dec crew, keep track of the items they used, and then remove it all and make sure everything was returned or otherwise disposed. The leadman was still occasionally called the gang boss, given that collectively the group was known as the 'swing gang.' The term had been in use on movie sets since at least the 1920s. In that era, there was a distinction between permanent movie sets and temporary ones. Sets built for the short term were known as "swing" sets, hence the swing gang.

The duties remain largely the same today in that they put the set together in advance of shooting and remove it all when it's done. In between they stand by to make changes to the set, whether called for in the scene or something that occurs suddenly to the director. It can be moving furniture or giant letters and words made of metal.

Cassidy noticed several of the crew shivering. It wasn't yet 4:30 a.m. and felt much colder than 50 degrees, thanks to a strong wind that kicked in hard every so often. "You won't be cold long," Cassidy said, heading down one outdoor path to an entrance to the road just outside the Boneyard where the trucks were parked, the swing gang in pursuit.

The signs had looked deceptively light and airy on the floor of the Annex. Now that it came time to carry them it was clear many of them were heavy. Loose letters, the easiest, moved first. Then the bigger pieces started to come in carried by two men. A steel-frame word "Run" took three men. It took four men to unload the "Poker" sign and bring it back. Cassidy directed traffic, this here, that on the other side.

A rep from the museum arrived to talk to Cassidy while the swing gang continued unloading. The conversation finished as the last of the signage arrived. He stood back to take it all in but something was missing. He stood there looking puzzled for a minute.

"Where's the A?"

Now Alder looked perplexed. "The truck's empty," he replied, looking at the group. "Can someone go look for the A?"

Two men left and returned with the letter. It had been left at the entrance about 30 yards away, likely because someone picked it up but it was too heavy or awkward to carry alone for far. Cassidy watched as the A was set with the group. He looked happier but still wasn't satisfied.

"We want to see the face of the A," he said. The swing gang went into motion and shifted it again, but this way it leaned slightly to one side, off-kilter. Something was needed to weigh it down enough to keep it upright. They'd brought sandbags for just such an occasion, which they now brought in. It took seven to hold it in place.

"So that's all the sandbags for now, boys," said Alder.

Bomba and the assistant art director had arrived a few minutes earlier and stood in the background watching the makeshift set take shape. Bomba and Cassidy conferred on the island of signs a few feet off that ground in the middle of the wide path.

"I think the 'Run' is great," said Bomba, as he sipped his coffee. Cassidy agreed.

There were a lot of things like 'Run' that Bomba and Cassidy, as his set decorator, had woven into sets that weren't requested or even necessarily noticed. The plot centered on Douglas' character getting married late in life, and this scene had him out with someone other than his fiancé, so Billy Gherson was in effect starting to consider whether he should run from the wedding. Other things were less subtle, like the palm trees. Some of the letters in the new display had working lights, so they could be turned on, adding brightness that didn't exist in the signs that made up the rest of the Neon Boneyard. All of it was designed to give the director options. If he didn't like something, they would turn it off or take it out or bring it in, whatever was needed.

"Let's move the Poker sign," Cassidy said to the set decorators, who were hovering nearby. "It should be the same orientation of these other signs."

"The camera will be coming from this direction," Bomba agreed, pointing to what was behind them. The men moved as a team to shift it, some moving the "EATS DINER" sign while four of them shifted the Poker sign.

"Thank you," said Cassidy, the heft of the sign evident.

They were all sweating when Cassidy remembered the last thing. There was an urban ruggedness, despite its location, and a barren feel to the place. To address that Bomba had added some foliage. Three large palm trees, planned for the background, were at the entrance.

"Where are the trees?"

"I was just wondering that," Bomba said. The set dec guys faked groans as they left to bring the palms closer. A couple of tweaks later and they were done.

"Wow, " said Bomba, pointing at something. "That's good." They all looked at a nearby sign that read "Good." Everyone laughed.

"We could just do this all day," he said.

They were all in a good mood by then, the most intense work finished in the short term. They had created a whole new museum display, one that could be touched.

Turteltaub and Rake arrived about 5:45 a.m., ahead of call time. It was still dark but instead of being obscured by it, as had been the case of individual crew trickling in, the director was a beacon. Crew seemed to naturally move toward him from different directions as he passed giant sign dinosaurs to the set. A PA had been walking in the giant pathway in front of Turteltaub and did an about-face, recognizing him. He kept moving, staying just enough ahead to be out of the way. Others kept some distance, just enough to remain in his orbit.

Turteltaub wasn't 30 steps down the path before he stopped.

"You guys can't start following me until 6 a.m.," he said.

The crew withered back and he took the remaining steps to the newly created neon sign exhibit on his own. There he went into his own world, or the world of Billy Gherson and Diana Boyle on their afternoon outing. Turteltaub stood in one place facing one direction, silent, for several minutes. Then he walked to the other side and did the same thing looking in the other direction. A few more minutes passed. Then he stopped somewhere between those two places and looked again.

Some sort of resolution on his face, he walked toward the cinematographer and the rest of the Camera department, which were setting up. The grips had installed a ladder and Hennings was eight feet in the air. He held a long lens to his eye and looked over the boneyard like a captain in a crow's nest with a monocle. As Turteltaub approached he climbed down and handed him the lens without a word. The director climbed up the ladder and surveyed the set the same way.

It was 6 a.m. by then. As light started to edge in the sky the magnet clicked back on. All the crew had arrived. The Sound department was set up and video playback was there. A few people were shivering. It was cold and evidence of the sun did little to stop it. The wind remained the culprit, picking up every so often to remind them of it.

People ask why crew stands around on a movie set. It's because their jobs don't all happen at the same time. There are some departments that work heavily on the front end, like Art, Costumes and Locations. Most of the crew in those departments don't have to be on set although they are represented. Other departments are active only when they are shooting, as with Camera, Sound, Video playback. Then there are departments that provide the infrastructure, Construction, Production and Accounting.

Setting up the first shot was laborious and the setup and shot were not the same thing. In the prep stage, a shot list was prepared and it was what Turteltaub envisioned on the other side of the lens. Today a shot was what the director, and more accurately Hennings, was seeing through the lens and ultimately capturing.

The set-up was bigger. It was everything they did to get the shot. And every time they changed it, whether it involved repositioning the cameras, changing the lighting or moving the actors -- or any combination thereof -- it was a new set up. But it was only one set-up when it came to the cameras, since they had two cameras and were shooting at the same time.

The actors rehearsed the scene, then left for hair, makeup, and costumes. Stand-ins for the actors came in and took the places to be occupied by the actors. There were stand-ins for each actor, whether part of the entourage, as Freeman and De Niro had, or assigned to the actors by the production.

The justification for stand-ins was the same argument in favor of entourages but broad enough to include most actors working at a professional level on camera. Tiring out actors for any reason was counterproductive. The goal was to get the best performance possible and even having them sit still while prepping a shot took away from that. Especially when stand-ins, as a rule, weren't very expensive hires.

All of the technical side accomplished, they called in First Team, which brought Steenburgen and Douglas back to set from the star trailers nearby.

Good acting is knowing the character well enough to convince others they are that person, and hopefully bringing meaning to a story. Sometimes it's also about acting as if it's a sunny day when it's cold. This was one of those scenes.

Costume departments keep dive jackets and other large warm clothing big enough to fit over wardrobe for just such occasions. It helps keep the actors warm right up to the point they take their place in front of the camera. The on-set costumer or the actor's assistant, or both in this case, were standing by if anything else was needed.

The wind had continued. Samuels, who had arrived perhaps half an hour earlier, stood quietly in the background. As the gusts picked up, the executive producer grew worried. If it was this strong on the ground, what would it be like on top of the Stratosphere, where they were shooting in the afternoon? He called Badalato to have someone check the weather. The last thing he wanted was to put a crane and 100 people at cloud level with a fat wind. It felt extreme enough that he should be prepared to stop the shot -- an expensive proposition.

The scene called for Billy and Diana to ride the X-Scream off the top of the Stratosphere. Douglas and Steenburgen didn't have to be sitting in the ride itself in order for that to happen on screen. Nothing in the actors contracts required they do it. There were green screens and stunt doubles to help. Green screen technology enabled the integration of two video streams, which meant they could get a shot of the actors saying their lines in a moving X-Scream car without them being in it. It wouldn't look as good, and it would cost more, but it was accepted and budgeted. Film editors, who routinely work miracles, would merge the images of the actors with stunt doubles and with crowd shots and the one from the helicopter planned for Saturday, most viewers would never be the wiser.

The actors wanted to do the scene themselves but asked to have a look at the X-Scream before cameras were aimed at them. Production set up a private visit to the Stratosphere over the weekend. The word Monday morning was the actors still planned to ride the X-Scream. Douglas had joked he didn't want to tell his 12-year-old son Dylan he hadn't done it.

But no one was taking it for granted. In the event the actors changed their minds at the last minute they would have stunt doubles on site. They would be wearing identical costumes, something long-planned by the Costume department. The plan was to put Douglas and Steenburgen -- or the stunt doubles -- in the front row, camera mounted in front of them, and send it over the side of the building.

Samuels' concern about the wind remained, although less than in the morning. Weather reports and other research had shown some improvement but it was still 25 miles an hour at times. It was the bullpen's advance communication with managers of the Stratosphere, then his interaction with them when he arrived, that made him okay with the scene being shot. Dealing with wind was part of managing the ride and there were strict rules in place as to when the ride had to be shut down. The limit was 40 mph, someone said, and they watched it closely.

Four Fellas set up a short-term base camp across the street from the Stratosphere. The biggest task was getting all the equipment up to the 108th floor. For Kerry Rawlins, it was one of the more complex set-ups he would oversee the entire shoot. But that wasn't why he didn't like it. Rawlins didn't like heights. He'd done that rigging before, even a few stories in the air, but this was different.

As key grip, Rawlins was responsible for the placement of any ancillary equipment used for benefit of the camera. That was anything that diffused light or facilitated moving it, whether dolly, boom or crane. That equipment would have individual technicians, but it all fell under his purview.

This scene would involve three cameras, which was one more than they would typically use, but that was just the start. Scene 84 required a number of specialty items, including a crane, a special effects camera mount for the X Stream Car, Libra head, Fisher 10 dolly, Fisher 23 arm. The Libra head was a digitally stabilized camera mount. The Fisher dolly and arm enabled a sound recording of the ride, not just the actors but also of the noise and reverberation of it moving over the side of the building.

Rawlins was out of sorts as they rolled equipment from the trucks to the elevators, then up an interminable 108 floors, only to then roll it back off. Still, that was fine until they came to four steps, which couldn't be rolled over. All of it came off the rollers to be carried over, then back on the carts to the final parking space.

The department had four grips working on average and added two for the day. That didn't include Rawlins and grip best boy Mackie Roberts or the dolly grips, since they worked with the Camera department. One of the additional hires had expertise on camera platforms. He focused on attaching one to the front of the ride. An unmanned camera would be mounted to that.

It was harder than it sounded. The platform, and then the camera mount, had to be positioned in a way to get a full frame shot while the ride was in operation. But the ride car wasn't designed to accommodate anything on the front. Whatever they put on it had to be stable not just at 30 miles an hour over 68 feet of track, it had to withstand the jerking motion when it stopped. That would happen numerous times in the process of checking it and shooting.

Rawlins offered commentary throughout the set up that revealed his thoughts about being on the top floor of the Stratosphere. He was a natural comedian and it entertained the others. "We are 108 stories up in the air and on rollers!" "Thousands of people ride this safely every year!" "This is how we make our money!"

There were railings and areas where the public walked, which spoke to general safety, but it was also true the movie crew was going out farther and in areas the public didn't go. All of them wore safety harnesses, which was protocol, and it wasn't as though they were that close to the edge. But it was unnerving, even for people who didn't mind heights.

With the platform built they attached the mount. The ride's full-time engineer, who had never been far away, took intense interest when they were finished. Cameras had been mounted on the ride before but it still made him nervous. He ran the empty ride to test the platform and mount. That worked without issue so the next test had the camera attached. There were more tests. Satisfied, the engineer signed off and the normal process of prepping the shot began.

Stunt doubles were prepared and on set. They were on stand-by, and relatively inexpensive compared to the risk of missing a shot if either of the actors balked. It didn't matter that neither of them bore a striking resemblance to Douglas or Steenburgen. The Costume department had them in matching attire and makeup had worked on skin tone.

The decision to tour the X Stream over the weekend -- an actor scout, in effect -- hadn't been the only homework for Douglas and Steenburgen. There had been subtle changes to the script that had affected their characters, including fresh dialogue. The current version of the script, the result of changes made after the read-through, had been delivered to the actors nine days earlier.

Scene 85 had been cut entirely and changes made to four others. Scene 85 had Diana Boyle and Billy Gherson on a walk after their play date on the Stratosphere ride. Queasy from it, Gherson vomits into a trashcan. In its place, they widened Scenes 84 and 86. Scene 86 added dialogue between the two actors that explained the triangular relationship between Billy, Paddy and Sophie, Paddy's deceased wife, when they were young. Scene 84 was the Stratosphere ride itself, which improved on dialogue once they are on the ride and added a joke.

Douglas and Steenburgen worked to have their lines right. Both of them did that as a matter of routine, but it was even more important with a scene like this, given the intention for there to be one take of them going over the side of the Stratosphere on camera.

Steenburgen's character had suggested the ride and would be calm. Douglas' character was uncomfortable but acting cool to impress her. His real thoughts would come out after the ride went into motion and lurched over the side. He assumes it's over. Relieved, he pretends he loved it, whereupon Diana Boyle informs him the car will plunge over the edge three more times. Then it jerks forward.

The current version of the scene, which reflected changes from the weekend after the table-read, had been steered by the screenwriter. Dan Fogelman was busy with another project so he could only spend a couple of days in Las Vegas. Suggesting repairs at the meeting had been "daunting," but he did it anyway. Turteltaub took him seriously because he wrote the screenplay but it was also easy, because Fogelman chose his battles. He had accepted numerous changes gracefully so if he had some issues, so be it.

Last Vegas had changed in a number of small ways since prep began, but it had changed significantly from his first draft. Through the first month of prep everyone worked on a draft with a June date. Another working draft came out the first week of September, but it was still a draft. It wasn't until October, the day before principal photography, that they "locked" the script, which made all changes official. The first two sets of changes happened the same day in rapid succession, white version and then blue. This version was pink. More revisions would come with time, all of it a standard part of the process.

The ADs, walkie buds in place, had locked up the Stratosphere early on. There was limited access granted to the public already, which made that easier. Background actors were checked in. This time there were 22 extras for the scene, six riders, 12 observation deck employees and four ride operators.

The ride operators were the real thing, which made sense since they were trained to run it. There wasn't much room up there and there wasn't a lot of time, given the lease governing the production's use of the facility.

Everything in place, Douglas and Steenburgen got into the car, fresh lines memorized. Gherson hollered as it went over the edge. Diana Boyle laughed with delight. Both actors looked a little wobbly and windblown as they came back inside. They went to video village and asked for a replay, something neither had done on the show to date. The stunt doubles, who were near the monitors, stepped back to make room for the actors. When the replay had run, the set erupted in laughter and applause.

The actors were laughing. It was over and they got up to leave when someone hollered a question. It didn't sound like Turteltaub.

"Ready for another take?"

"Hell no!" said Douglas, which brought more laughter and applause as the actors left.

When things were quieter Turteltaub admitted it had been "scary" up there, particularly with the wind. He had pressed the actors to do the scene. "They are two people who hated this height. They didn't want to go on." He understood that, given he didn't want to ride the X-Scream. He said it made him nauseous just looking at it.

"There were 28-mile-per hour winds and I told them it was 16. It shuts down at 40!" He gave Douglas and Steenburgen a lot of credit for their commitment to getting their roles right. "They hated it and they hate me!" he joked.

An aerial shot would finish the raw material for the scene. They had scheduled a helicopter for establishing shots of Vegas that would also include footage of the Stratosphere from the sky. The stunt doubles would be back, dressed as the actors, with cooperation from the ride operators and limited crew to usher them to front row of the car. Hennings would get a shot from the helicopter and it would be edited in as part of the scene.

CHAPTER TWELVE
Shoot Week 2
Oct. 29-Nov. 2
Day 6, 7, 8, 9, 10

A N OUTSIDER MIGHT ASSUME the second week of photography would be easier. After the challenges of location work all over Las Vegas, the production would now be in the relative safety of Aria. There were scenes at gaming tables and slot machines, in the nightclubs and by the pool. One scene had De Niro, Freeman and Kline strutting down an Aria hallway in brand-new suits. Then there were the scenes that made up the large pool party, complete with Playboy centerfolds and a famous L.A. celebrity DJ, who had been confirmed.

Surely staying in one place like Aria would lighten the load? "Right," said Kristina Peterson. "What could go wrong?" There would be just as many twists and turns at the casino resort, just different ones, the 2nd AD said with normal assuredness.

The scenes planned for the remaining six shooting days -- all that was left before the production would return to Atlanta -- included the actors individually and in groups. It also involved getting something bigger. They needed to capture the general feel of an upscale casino, the specific feel of Aria, and the vibe of Vegas as a party destination.

The first shots Monday were scheduled for outside the Deuce Lounge, one of several smaller bars and restaurants inside Aria. The scenes centered on Freeman's character and included De Niro and Kline. But in the process of getting the actors and the plot on camera, they would get the atmosphere of the place. One of the shots was specifically notated to look out into the casino. The scenes that took place inside Deuce Lounge would later be shot on the sound stages in Atlanta, where they were just beginning work on the lounge set. The shots at Aria could then be used to expand the sense of place, all of it sown together later in post-production in Los Angeles.

By 5:30 a.m. Monday crew began appearing with equipment. It was a dense-feeling area of the casino, one filled tightly with slot machines and other games of chance. They established a perimeter but at that hour it was pretty quiet.

The complex machinery took up a lot of space. Normally, the show had two cameras, A and B. But the addition of C camera for the day, particularly the Steadicam, made the area seem even smaller.

There were carts for each camera and each cameraman. The carts were the easiest way to move equipment as well as the cameramen's kits. The shelves on each of their carts were filled with various accessories. Once all the equipment was there, the cameras were assembled and plugged in. They connected to the cinematographer's custom-designed cart. The Hennings-mobile, his self-designed DP cart, normally had two monitors along with other equipment, one each for A and B camera. Now it had a third for C camera.

Each camera had its own dedicated equipment and crew of three people, plus the dolly grips. With threee cameras, then, there were eleven camera crew, since the third camera didn't have a dolly. And that didn't count the digital loader or the cinematographer. Every contingency for planning and prepping the carts had to be accounted for at this stage.

Generally A camera is the lead camera, and the one the cinematographer works with most closely, and that was true on *Last Vegas*. Jody Miller was the person who controlled the camera, both composition and framing. His position was known, logically, as camera operator. He was also a skilled Steadicam operator, which they would use in this scene.

Chad Rivetti was first 1st AC (assistant cameraman), a position also known as the "focus puller." It was his job to keep the images sharp, pulling or changing the focus, based on how the camera moved. To a layperson the work was probably most noticeable when an image in the background was more in focus than the one in the foreground. "Rack" focus or focusing was changing the focus of the lens during the course of the shot. As 1st AC of A Camera, Rivetti also had broad responsibilities for managing both the equipment and the department, including hires. It made it easy to understand why Rivetti and the second camera assistant paid so much attention to the equipment during prep at Panavision.

Even people with very little knowledge of movie production could pull the 2nd AC out of a lineup because of the iconic tool he used. Chris Flurry managed the slate, or the clapperboard, as it is also known. In the simplest terms, it is the device with the arm that slapped down to mark when a scene began. The term "slate" came from when its surface material was slate like a chalkboard so scenes and takes could be written and erased. Some were even painted in stripes because with black and white it stood out more for editors. The other name for the equipment came from the "clap" sound the arm made when it hit the frame, the arm a "clapstick."

Nowadays it was a digital slate that synced with the Sound department and provided metadata used in editing. Every day Flurry coordinated with the script supervisor to get the scene and take number, and with the sound department to sync their systems. There were other responsibilities, including putting marks where the actors would stand. Each actor was assigned a color and it was up to Flurry to mark it. De Niro was red, Douglas blue, Freeman green and Kline yellow. Steenburgen, like most female leads, was pink. To that end, Flurry took his large roll of different colored tape off his cart and marked where De Niro, Freeman and Kline, would start.

Putting the marks down for the actors sounded simple enough but it could be problematic. Each actor was assigned a color for the run of a show. Flurry assigned the colors if he hadn't been told anything in advance. With *Last Vegas*, he was told De Niro was red, so on the first day of shooting he put down red. Freeman's first scene was later, and his stand-in saw Flurry put down green. "Morgan is always red," he told Flurry.

There wasn't much the 2nd AC could do about that. He figured it would be best to address it directly. So, when Freeman came out a few minutes later, he asked if he was okay with green. The actor looked back at him blankly, just long enough to worry Flurry. Then Freeman burst out laughing and said green was fine. They had joked about it a couple of times since.

Kelly Borisy was the dolly grip for A camera. He controlled the motion of the dolly that carried A Camera and often both Rivetti and Miller. A big man, Borisy was strong enough to do that, and he had a lot of experience. Like everything else, there was more to being a dolly grip than gracefully pulling or pushing five hundred pounds of man and machine at a smooth, even pace while a camera rolled.

Getting the equipment to and from set and putting it together was its own challenge. Setting up the tracks the dolly ran on -- called "pipes" -- required different techniques based on the surface of where they were shooting. Sometimes they needed shims or padding. It had to be right in order for Borisy to control its motion. Fremont Street had presented a challenge because it wasn't a flat surface, at least not where Hennings and Turteltaub wanted the camera.

233

The same team structure was true on each of the other cameras, although in this case there was no need for C camera to have a dolly grip. *Last Vegas* also had a digital loader, whose job was to manage the raw material they collected on memory cards, back them up, track them, and make sure they were packaged for delivery at the end of the day. He worked with all three cameras. On smaller movies, the second AC would have the responsibility. The digital job is parallel to that of a film loader, who loads camera magazines, tracks them, and gets them back for development. However the gold is spun, whether film or digital, it's still gold.

Theo Bott, the rigging gaffer, was rolling out a two-inch-wide colored cable from where they would plug in nearby to the casino power source. It was a family of snakes, red, white, blue, green and black. It wound around nearly 200 feet. He stayed off the main paths of the carpeted floor, hugging the back of rows of slot machines and short wall breaks on the casino floor that separated gaming areas. He tried to dodge "crossovers" where foot traffic would have to pass over. When it was unavoidable, "yellow jackets," raised rubber safety bridges, were placed overtop to alert passersby.

Hennings had an alarmed look on his face as he walked briskly through the area with Rawlins and the gaffer. The place seemed darker to the DP than it had during the camera test. He was right about that, although it didn't seem logical. It was earlier in the day but not significantly. And it wasn't like there were windows shuttered now where daylight had slipped in before. There were no windows.

It seemed like recessed lights had been turned on that perhaps weren't on before. They gave a wide spotlight effect, one after the next. Hennings jabbed his finger toward one of them, took a few steps and did the same thing toward another, and then another. Rawlins, who probably had it the first time, nodded agreeably. Soon the best boy was on top of a 12-foot ladder unscrewing bulbs. Others brought in lights and screens and filters to replace the light, which was softer and would show up evenly in the picture.

The scene had De Niro and Kline hurrying between rows of slot machines away from the Deuce Lounge, rushing to stop Freeman's Archie from gambling away his retirement. Turteltaub and Hennings wanted to use the Steadicam for one of the shots. It would add a sense of urgency.

The Steadicam was introduced in the mid-1970s. By effectively isolating the movement of the camera operator, it was able to stabilize the camera enough to get meaningful images. Prior to that, the options were the tripod and the dolly. The technology has continued to improve over the years but it still takes a lot of skill. It isn't unusual to bring in a camera operator just to run a Steadicam. Some 99 percent of all its users have taken formal workshops, according to Tiffen, which owns the brand.

In Miller, the camera operator, they had someone who could do it all, including the Steadicam, which was part of his kit. Balancing, moving and adjusting a camera while following action of any kind was challenging enough but the equipment also weighed somewhere in the neighborhood of 70 pounds. Fortunately, he was in the physical shape of someone who could wear a 70-pound weight on his back and run with it.

Miller had the looks of someone who might have landed in front of a lens instead of behind it, but then the camera crew was a handsome lot. Part of that was they dressed well, at least compared to other departments. It wasn't a requirement. Movie sets, and locations, current location excepted, could be grimy. The goal was to dress comfortably enough to do the job.

Camera, perhaps more than any department, showed its legacy. Its members had worn ties for decades. Those were long gone, but the language between Turteltaub and Miller was out of another era. Miller called Turteltaub "sir." It wasn't stilted, but genuine and natural. "It's a matter of respect, for the director, but also the set," said Miller.

The Camera department, as a whole, was perceived as carrying a high sense of self esteem. Several people across departments offered the same general observation from earlier: "Camera thinks it's the only department you need to make a movie." No one in the Camera department had argued when asked. If anything, there was a case to be made: "Can you make a movie without a director? Yes. Can you make one without a production designer or costume designer? Yes. Can you make one without a producer? Yes. Can you make a movie without a camera? No." They figured that was a fact and that was hard to argue. The ADs were the next department most likely to be perceived as bossy. But then, the ADs ran the set. They were bossy.

Miller put on the supportive vest used for the Steadicam. It looked paramilitary with a chest plate, black and vaguely reminiscent of a bulletproof vest. It had padded straps and knobs and spars and clips on it. The device worked because of a stabilizing element that hung below it, which meant the camera was less on his shoulder than it was in front of him, occasionally balancing on his leg. The camera fit on that.

To get the shot, Miller stood in front of De Niro and Kline. As the actors hurried to the gaming table to save Freeman's character. Miller jogged backwards in front of them, getting it on camera. It was a narrow area. 1st AC

Chad Rivetti was behind him, handling cords and taking the Steadicam from him to place on the cart when there was a break or the shot completed.

The next shot had Freeman in it as well. They were shooting a scene amidst slot machines, centered on Archie. In the scene, he takes a call from his son, Ezra, with his friends nearby. They took the master shot and Freeman, looking a little fatigued, sat down off to the side between two rows of slot machines. It was subtle, but anyone who had been watching him closely -- particularly his entourage -- saw it. The sense with Freeman was that he would work through any illness.

Freeman's people may have been on the payroll but the care and concern was real. He was going to take a minute. Someone handed him his wrist brace, which he put on. The actor had injured his arm in an airplane accident years earlier and occasionally wore the brace off camera. By then the on-set medic was crouched next to him asking questions.

Karen Strutynski ran the normal checks, temperature and pulse and whatever else, and reviewed the actor's medications. A trained Emergency Medical Technician-Intermediate (EMTI,) she worked occasionally on movies and other productions but her regular job involved assisting a plastic surgeon in the operating room.

It turned out Freeman was running a low-grade fever and likely dehydrated. She did a medication check to ensure there were no conflicts and then recommended an over-the-counter medication in her kit. She also gave him a beverage to help hydrate him.

He was back to work within a few minutes. Rake told him he could take more time, but the actor insisted he was fine. As far as what showed in the monitors, he was. Nothing Archie did on camera would reveal to someone watching the movie that Freeman wasn't feeling well.

"If you listen closely, Morgan has a horrible cold. He sounds a little gravelly," Turteltaub said. "Most actors, if you're really sick, you're allowed to stay home. Not him." They could replace dialogue later if it was needed but he didn't think it would be.

Montage is a filmmaking technique where shorter shots are taken and sewn together in editing with the purpose of condensing time or transmitting an idea. Viewers get a lot of information more quickly than they would in the general flow of the movie.

Dating back to the early days of film, montage was groundbreaking at its birth and slightly different than today. Montage meant sewing individual shots together to create specific meaning that was as important, or even more important, than the story itself. It didn't have to stand alone with separate or special meaning. It's a broadly used technique that adds support to the story.

Whether the images are shown more quickly on screen does not guarantee they are simpler to shoot, any more than a scene with a short description ensures it won't take long. The two montage scenes planned for the day were good examples. A scene that had three of the main actors strutting down a hallway in new threads had taken months to pull together. The other, the scene that had De Niro handing out flyers to Cirque du Soleil acrobats performing in Zarkana at Aria, wasn't as time consuming but required considerable director finesse. Each scene had a simple description, required no dialogue, and probably wouldn't be on screen more than a few seconds.

The initial script for *Last Vegas* had three sections that used montage as part of storytelling: showing the main characters from boys to senior citizens, a flamboyant pool party, and the characters passing out flyers for another party, one they would throw in their suite. The last one, the party the characters throw, is a core part of the plot. They had already taken montage shots of Kevin Kline and Jerry Ferrara handing out flyers.

A review of the scripts showed how the montage scene had been perfected. Initially the screenplay had party prep shots playing out over 13 separate scenes. The yellow draft of the script had come out a week earlier. It had incorporated all the previous tweaks and then relisted those shots, once individual scenes, within a single scene. Scene 62 had the characters making plans to have a party and then added in an alphabet of shots to show it. Scene 62F was where De Niro would hand out flyers to members of the Cirque du Soleil troupe and 62P had the actors walking the hall in their new threads.

"Guys walk like bad asses," originally imagined De Niro, Freeman and Kline walking down the Vegas strip in "amazing new suits." The final version tied it better into the narrative. Now the actors would be walking down a big Aria hallway, having just left the high-end tailor who made their threads, which itself was a new scene.

The core of the scene remained the amazing new suits. Costume Designer Dayna Pink's effort was on full display for the first time. This was the first scene that would have the actors in the suits they would wear in all the penthouse party scenes to be shot in Atlanta. The decision to go with a designer-tailor she knew and trusted had been expensive and had taken a toll on the department's budget. But it had been the only call.

There was another element to the costumes that provided contrast. In the scene, the characters' one-time nemesis and now sidekick, Todd, eagerly followed behind them as an assistant. He would wear casual clothes.

Members of the Costume department who didn't have to be on set showed up for this one. While they exuded confidence in public a two-second glance revealed nervousness. Less time in prep meant fewer meetings, fewer chances to check a fit, fewer opportunities to find a subtle mistake or even a big one.

The costumes were almost guaranteed to be gorgeous. They had been cut to fit each man individually and then tailored further as needed. All of them looked good. But if it had just been about making attractive, high quality suits, they'd be in a different part of the fashion world. This was bigger. It was whether the clothes spoke to each character on their own as well as in relation to the other characters.

The only reaction that mattered in the moment was Turteltaub's. Cameras were in place, the stand-ins lined up, adjustments made. De Niro, Freeman and Kline, along with Ferrara, assembled around a corner, out of sight of cameras. Turteltaub went and talked to them about the scene.

He returned briskly to his director's chair at the monitors. "They're dressed so well! You feel like they've come a long way, just the way she costumed them." That was the point, ultimately. The characters showed a change, one that could come across subtly in 10 seconds on screen. Turteltaub had been in on decisions about costumes, but like everything else, the proof was in the monitors.

They went through the normal commands. ACTION! Archie, Sam and Paddy rounded the corner together walking purposefully toward the cameras, the actors balanced in the frame. The colors of their costumes blended into the scene, none standing out more than the others. The characters looked happy, entertained, as they strutted down the hallway in well-tailored style. The change it reflected was subtle. It made sense.

Todd ran after them, slipping and sliding as he tried to carry their garment bags and keep up with them, his casual clothes another subtle contrast. Ferrara, as Todd, made the scene.

All of it looked remarkably easy when it had been anything but.

The Cirque du Soleil shot was simpler in terms of preparation. The meeting with Turteltaub, Rake and members of the cast and management two weeks earlier had been fast. Turteltaub had looked at the glossy program and picked characters. There had been a language barrier with individual performers, given the show is based in Montreal and draws heavily from the region. A Cirque manager who spoke English had been there to talk with the director. The ADs followed up to confirm scheduling. The same characters would be wanted again for later scenes to be shot in Atlanta. Cirque du Soleil did its own makeup and showed up as agreed.

This time cameras were set up near the escalators, the Zarkana sign above that. Extras were lined up, the acrobats nearby and ready to be spaced among them. Once it was all in place, De Niro ne Paddy would hand flyers out to them, all as the escalator moved. Timing was important with moving stairs.

But where the shot had been one of the least time consuming in terms of crew prep time, it demanded that much more of the director. Turteltaub didn't speak French and they didn't speak English. It was the same language barrier as before only this time he would bypass verbal communication. He would act it out.

The Cirque performers, in character with elaborate costume and makeup, stood by the escalators. Whatever Turteltaub said made them laugh even if they didn't understand it. They didn't need words. The director went into motion near the escalator, and then on it, showing them what he wanted. He danced a little, spun a half circle, bent left and pretended to take a flyer, the point of the scene. Then he bent right, again with a flyer, and took a step back and forward again all with fluidity. He might have been in the scene himself.

All of it delighted the Cirque du Soleil acrobats, who had laughed and nodded throughout the display. Somehow he also got across a message that they didn't need to imitate him, they could do their own thing in character. The point was more that they be animated as they took flyers from De Niro. Finished with direction he looked at them. Did they get all that? "Oui, oui!"

De Niro, who was nearby, understood as well. Katrina Rice, the assistant prop master, handed him flyers and returned to her cart. They did the scene several times. Paddy, a rare detectable smile on his face, handed out party invitations as the escalator moved. And just as fast, the montage shot was done.

Turteltaub loved shooting in Vegas because he liked being in Vegas. "Most people I know who hate it haven't been here," he said, more than once. As the days had accumulated there were signs of stress on some crew but from him it had vanished. He had never once looked tired. One of the cameramen called him "the hardest-working person here." He could still sting someone with a comment but it wasn't often. Most of the crew liked him.

The director had continued to play Pai Gow poker, which added a single joker. He was good at it, the word was, because he knew when to quit. He saw it a little differently. "I had a good run. I wouldn't say I was a good player."

Now it turned out Turteltaub had a mission that extended beyond winning more than he lost. He had been scoping out card dealers for a role in the movie. He laughed at the thought it sounded creepy, like he had an ulterior motive. "I'm a Hollywood director. Want to be in my movie?"

But Turteltaub was serious about putting one of the dealers in the movie. He didn't want an actor who looked like a casino card dealer. He wanted a blackjack dealer who could act like one on camera. Several turned down the offer but he finally picked one who accepted. She was the best of all, he said.

The storyline had Archie winning a lot of money, which is how the characters get invited to the penthouse suite and have enough money for suits and a party. How much money had been a topic the creative producers debated with Turteltaub. The producers thought a lot of money could be a million dollars but the director talked them down. The final version had the character playing a high-stakes poker game with proceeds from his $15,000 retirement account. He would bet it all and come out more than $100,000 ahead.

When Archie first sits down to play he knocks over a drink. This introduces the character Todd. He is angered by it, setting up a conflict with the main characters that they ultimately resolve. The shot required the normal master and coverage of the actors from different angles. Take after take, the card dealer looked comfortable enough on camera to have been an actress.

The scene kept the Set Decorating and Props departments busy. Every time Freeman knocked the drink over, the set decorating crew would replace the cover on the blackjack table. Then Rice would replace the beer, so Archie could knock it over again. The ADs had set it up in the usual way, getting it locked up. PAs were carefully placed around the area. One had been assigned to a yellow jacket, one of the black and yellow cable protectors. It amounted to a speed bump for foot traffic, covering electrical cables the size of fat snakes that crossed the hallway. It was clearly marked but the PA was there to remind everyone anyway. For 90 minutes as they shot the scene, he stood there pointing to the yellow jacket whenever someone approached, alternating his greeting.

"Careful, watch your step."

"Watch your step, please."

"Careful, please."

He stepped away to use the bathroom and within a minute a casino patron had slipped and fallen, right on the spot where he had stood. She shouted loudly as she was going down and then began a howling that could be heard above the din of the casino. Strutynski, the medic, was there within seconds.

Samuels also was there within a few seconds. Within a minute an Aria official arrived on the scene, standing off to the side to watch the medic and the woman, who had continued to wail. Within five minutes Kamishin and the local production supervisor were on the casino floor, down from the fourth floor offices, talking to Samuels. A couple of other people joined them.

"There's one every show," someone said.

Samuels smiled but didn't say a word.

Strutynski huddled over the woman to find out how she was injured. The pain was coming from her shoulder. The medic gingerly checked out the red area. Where did it hurt? Was it a shooting pain or just the one area? Did she want to go to the hospital? The woman, who by then had stopped howling, said yes.

Strutynski had noticed a whiff of alcohol, which wasn't unusual for a casino patron, and they were near a club. Had she been drinking? She asked other questions to understand what happened, not just of the woman who had fallen but also of her daughter, who was with her. The daughter said she wasn't sure exactly what happened but wanted to know. Not to worry, the medic said, nodding over to the closest surveillance camera, they would figure it out. By then the ambulance was there to take the woman away. The medic offered up her card and said she could give them a copy of the report about the incident if they wanted.

By then they had finished shooting the scene. Crew was taking equipment down, Aria people counting chips. Something was wrong. They were down one $5,000 poker chip. It had to be someone working in the area, a casino worker or a day player. Whoever it was didn't understand casinos. Speculation was that they figured no one would notice just one chip. What they didn't know was that it wasn't just any poker chip. It was a tournament chip, which is differently marked and can't easily be cashed in. They apparently also overlooked the half-dozen security cameras trained on the area.

De Niro was late. It wasn't the first time and if anything, it looked like it might be a pattern. The good news for Rake and Turteltaub was that it was never more than 30 minutes, and consistency was easy to manage. The bad news was they hadn't firmed up the theory in time for the day.

Scenes to be shot in the same location were scheduled together as a general rule. It could be timed to get scenes that would portray dawn and sunset in a two-hour period. It could be to get all the cab shots at the airport, even though the scenes involved the characters coming and going days apart. It's helpful if the scenes happen on the same script day, which means the actors don't need to change costumes, but not necessary. So it was that the first half of the day was planned for inside Aria's massive lobby and the second half, in front of the resort.

The general crew call time was 6 a.m., which meant Peterson was due before 5 a.m. and the other ADs not far behind. Aria's lobby was huge but it also opened up to the casino floor. That made locking it up every bit as challenging as what they had done in and out of Binions. Aria wasn't shutting down registration at the front desk. It was quiet now but within hours there would be perhaps 1,000 people within 100 yards. They also had plenty of extras to corral, and a lot more actors working than on the first day. On top of that, Dan Akroyd and Bradley Cooper were planning separate visits to the set.

ADs fanned out to establish a perimeter. There were tricks to locking up a location. They wanted clear paths for foot-traffic, at least two in this case, given the size of the lobby and the cavernous casino. Ideally those paths would feel natural, so passersby would gravitate comfortably in that direction with minimal instruction. They had use of the velvet ropes, on loan from Aria, and those worked well for the type of clientele at Aria.

Finding a place to park the actors was a different challenge. The resort had provided space at Bar Masa and Deuce Lounge. The first they would use for extras holding, and the second would be for cast. But the Deuce was too far away. The Production department had picked up screened partitions the day before and the ADs scouted for a good place in or near the lobby to set it up.

By 6:15 a.m. the area was dominated by crew. They were planning three cameras for the day. Cranes would lift C camera up to get shots of the lobby as well as the main actors. It was heavy machinery. Nico Bally, owner/operator of Cranium Cranes, assured Samuels and Badalato they would protect the marble flooring.

Cranes were how directors got above scenes, providing expansive or loft shots. But they had been in short supply in Vegas. The culprit again was *Hangover III*. With its large budget and special effects, it had scarfed up a lot of specialty entertainment contractors.

Hangover III, was spending a lot of money in Vegas. The city was braced for three weeks of delays along the Strip. Stunt men would parachute onto the strip at night in a highly choreographed scene, with cranes and whatever else they needed to have multiple cameras in place to catch the action. Another scene had Bradley Cooper's character rappel down the side of Caesars Palace. It would take a day to set up rigging and safety precautions for the parachute scene, which took place over several blocks. That gave Cranium Cranes a couple of days to fit in *Last Vegas*, which is all they needed.

As Bally and another man put the crane up in the lobby, the Locations department was doing its thing. Signs went up at key points to legally warn potential interlopers: "Four Fellas Productions LLC will be filming at Aria today. By entering this area you hereby irrevocably consent to and authorize Four Fellas Productions LLC, its successors and assignees to photograph you and/or make sound recordings of you and to use same worldwide for any purpose whatsoever in perpetuity; All such photographs and sound recordings to be the sole property of Four Fellas Productions LLC."

In the meantime, the ADs found a stellar place for their temporary "green room," a term used for the place where actors or other guests wait before they go on camera. They strategically placed the fabric screens near several large pillars at one end of the long opening to the casino, an area with plants and greenery. From a distance, the room dividers virtually disappeared into the environment. It didn't suggest a separate space much less one that was fairly roomy with snacks, a cooler filled with Evian water and other beverages, and directors chairs.

The Props department was responsible for the chairs, from ordering the personalized backing for individuals who would sit in them, to pushing the rolling rack of director's chairs. It was heavy, perhaps hundreds of pounds. Each chair had an exchangeable canvas sleeve. One side featured the embroidered logo of *Last Vegas*, the same one created in Atlanta that now graced all paperwork. The other side had the name of the person to whom it belonged, in this case Robert De Niro, Michael Douglas, Morgan Freeman, Kevin Kline, Mary Steenburgen.

Director's chairs, which fold in the middle like scissors to become flat, had been on movie sets since the silent era of film but they'd been in existence much longer. Their direct lineage was the camp chair used in the Civil War. The early movie titans had liked the chairs for the same reasons Abraham Lincoln had: They weighed less than folding wooden chairs, were more comfortable on the posterior than wood, and could easily be packed up and moved.

It was the Gold Medal furniture company that began making the chairs for a mass audience in 1892. The product was launched at the 1893 World's Fair that also gave the world Cracker Jacks, Cream of Wheat and Juicy Fruit. Gold Medal is still in operation today, although with plenty of competition, from Home Depot to specialty suppliers who cater to production companies.

Kline's chair sleeve originally came with his name misspelled "Klein," something that delighted the actor immensely. It irritated Rice to no end. The assistant prop master worked hard to get things right and she felt it made her look like an idiot. She double-checked the order form to verify she hadn't submitted it wrong. She hadn't and noted as much when she called for a replacement. A new sleeve was overnighted and the offending chairback removed. When Kline saw the new one he seemed disappointed, so Rice gave him the original with his name spelled wrong.

The two scenes to be shot in the morning were 38 and 39. They also had to get footage of the lobby. The crane shot would enable a wide view that would get at its sheer size. Scene 38 had the actors initially being turned away from Aria when they didn't have a reservation. The plan was to finish there, break for lunch, and move outside for scenes in front of Aria in the afternoon.

Scene 39 was one page and one-eighth in length, while 39 was two pages and three-eighths. That was the standard way scenes were calculated by Rake and other 1st ADs. It was a reasonable way to estimate the time it would take to shoot a scene, although not foolproof. It was also a way to measure work on the movie in the course of principal photography. The Daily Wrap Report, reviewed by the studio and producers and bean counters, noted the number of pages shot and whether the day's work had been completed.

The bigger challenge for Turteltaub and Rake was Scene 39, and not just because it was longer. It was also the number of actors with dialogue. Several things happened in the scene. It started as a trip to a spinning wheel for prizes by two of the characters but would expand when the other characters joined them. They needed coverage of each actor speaking. That meant that eventually the lens would have to be aimed at each of them, while the others were in the background. Given the conversation happened in the same place, it was the cameras that had to move.

Coverage was one of the decidedly unglamorous aspects of shooting movies. It was the actors saying the same lines again and again as they reshot the scene from different angles. The more the better, since it gave the editors options in post-production, but it was time-consuming.

The "shot" was what you could see in the lens and on the monitors. A "set up" was any time the camera or cameras moved. It could mean moving the cameras to an entirely new location, as they would after lunch, or just turning the cameras in the other direction to get coverage of one or another of the actors. Artistically the set up was much more than that. It was where the actor stood and the lighting and why you needed a cinematographer. It was how you got the shot.

The first shot of the day had been at 8:10 a.m. It was still relatively quiet in the lobby at that point, but the place seemed to grow louder by the minute. A line began to form at registration, which had a counter long enough to line the far wall. The ADs had locked up the area, and Aria patrons followed natural paths to either side of the casino floor.

They shot the master and then began on coverage. Rake and the ADs had the same initial success of subduing the crowd as they had at Binions. Commands like "Quiet Please!" "Rolling!" went a long way, but they also had to contend with the dull roar growing on the casino side. There were also acoustics in play. Voices ricocheted off the marble floor as the crowd grew.

After they finished the one scene, the actors went to the fabric cocoon set up by the crew in the middle of lobby. They sat on their high chairs, chatting amiably. It was a congenial lot. None of them had worked together before, a surprise given how long each had been in the business. De Niro joined them for a few minutes but left to make a call, leaving his chair empty.

At one point, Douglas, Freeman and Kline started singing "Sweet Adeline" while they waited. It wasn't just a little humming, either. They got into it, harmonizing like a seasoned barbershop quartet that didn't need a fourth. Everyone within listening distance brightened at the unexpected performance. "Man, these guys are really good," said Bally, noting that the understatement of the day.

De Niro settled into a casino chair in a sitting area perhaps 50 feet from the partitioned cocoon. He sat there by himself, slot machines and other electronic gaming machines on either side that left him out of sight. The actor contentedly read the New York Times, string cheese on the table next to him, occasionally taking a call.

With cameras and cranes and monitors in full sight in the lobby it was clear they were shooting something serious. Word of who was in the cast spread. Every so often an Aria guest, tipped off De Niro was there, took the 25 steps from the pedestrian flow onto the casino floor for a look. One man, wearing an expensive, tailored suit, laughed when he was asked if he was trying to get a glimpse of the movie stars. He admitted it. He said he didn't have a lot of time and wouldn't go too far out of his way, but if it was easy? He'd like to be able to say he'd seen De Niro.

All of the primary actors had huge fan bases but there was a familiarity with De Niro. Some of it was the roles he had played, lines of his that had come into the lexicon. He was Travis Bickle, "You talking to me?" in *Taxi Driver*, Jake LaMotta "I ain't going down for nobody" in *Raging Bull*. He was an actor who defined Hollywood but declined to live in LA.

All of the actors had played memorable roles. Douglas played Gordon Gekko in *Wall Street*. The line, "Greed is good!" had been quoted back to the actor he couldn't always mask his irritability. He'd also anchored enormously popular movies like *Fatal Attraction*. But in some ways his biggest role had been as a producer. He won his first Oscar for *One Flew Over the Cuckoo's Nest* (1975), one of its two producers.

Morgan Freeman, with his booming voice, was sometimes called the world's narrator, thanks to roles in *Shawshank Redemption* and *Million Dollar Baby*. He had even played God in *Bruce Almighty* and *Evan Almighty*. Kline and Steenburgen also had impressive credits. Kline had been on the national radar since 1989 when he won the Best Supporting Actor award for *A Fish Called Wanda*. On top of his Tony Awards, he'd also won a Screen Actors Guild honor for *As You Like It* (2006). Steenburgen won an Oscar for Best Supporting Actress, along with a Golden Globe, for her work in *Melvin and Howard* (1981). She had been a regular fixture in Hollywood since, recently as part of the ensemble cast of *The Help* (2011).

Somehow De Niro's public persona was different. "People tend not to scream, 'Hey Kevin Kline!' But a lot of people love when De Niro is on the street," Turteltaub had commented. "You get a lot of ' Bob-bee!!" It was less so with the production working inside, but still true. Even a job that involved watching the actor work repeatedly prompted the question, 'Did you meet De Niro?'

There was a toll to fame for all of them. At one point De Niro joked with Douglas, pointing at him, "That is Michael Douglas! Right there, Michael *fucking* Douglas!" Douglas laughed. All of the actors, for that matter, got the joke. Each had experienced fans that said whatever came to mind, apparently convinced the actors were fair game.

Some crew had collected to the side as they finished the setup, including two members of De Niro's entourage. Why wasn't he with the other actors in the hidden area? Was it attitude? That wasn't it, they said. De Niro just wasn't one to chat, at least not most of the time. Bob was a regular guy, albeit a wealthy and famous one. They worked for him, and they kept appropriate distance, but both said he was generally easygoing. It echoed the earlier comment that De Niro had learned to take care of himself, which was to do what he wanted. He might run a few minutes late but he wouldn't push it too far, either.

Rake called for the ADs to bring in the actors. The plan had been to finish both scenes and then break for lunch by noon. Then they would resume work at the next location, in front of the entrance to Aria. But it was getting later in the morning and the scene required several setups. It started with De Niro and Steenburgen's characters in front of the spinning wheel that stopped at specific prizes. It shifted to a group conversation when their friends approached. All of the actors had lines and would need coverage. As they worked it became clear to Rake and Turteltaub that time was not in agreement with them staying on schedule, although it would be close.

This had not escaped the attention of the crew, either. Union rules mandate that crew gets a meal break every six hours or they get a bump, or increase in pay, every six minutes until they do. Every member of the crew at work on set was entitled to it. The options were limited. If they broke for lunch and returned to work in the lobby, they jeopardized the afternoon schedule, given all the equipment had to be moved. If they didn't it could be expensive. Buzz seemed to grow by the minute.

It wasn't the potential for a little more money, although no one minded that. It was fanning crew resentment, at least with a notable group at the center of the action. This irritability stemmed from the non-deductible breakfast, better known as NDB. It took a minute to understand but it was worth it because it helped illustrate the role of the unions in shaping structure.

Crew needed to report to set "having had," which meant if they wanted breakfast they had to get it before their call times. Most of them had pre-calls, which meant they were due ahead of the 6 a.m. call time. That early hour was normal, and always challenging, but here there were limited options as to where they could get food. The production provided meals to crew via the casino cafeteria, known as the EDR, which was open 24 hours a day.

The EDR served thousands of meals a day, easily absorbing the *Last Vegas* crew alongside blackjack dealers, housecleaning and buff Cirque performers in street clothes. What it lacked in gourmet fare it made up for in variety, although the variety itself didn't change much day to day. It was the only option at no cost for crew. The issue was its location. At a normal pace it was a nearly 15-minute walk from the hotel rooms to the cafeteria. In other words, it couldn't be done comfortably during a 30-minute break, and EDR rules expressly forbade the removal of food.

What NDB meant was that breakfast would not be deducted from paychecks. Instead crew was allowed 30 minutes off the clock, but that wasn't enough time. Some on-set crew had taken the break after 6 a.m. but most skipped it. Leaving set before you were ready, or when director was there, was against the grain, even if someone could cover for the department.

A group of crew blamed Badalato. The movie paid scale and some had been pinched on their kits. Department budgets were limited and they had to do more for less. All of it was building up. Some wanted to claim an MVP, which stood for a meal penalty violation. That would require the production company pay a violation.

Badalato, for his part, knew he was in the bullseye. He noted that he hadn't invented 'pre-calls must NDB,' which appeared on the call sheet every day. Nor had he dusted it off just for this occasion or convinced Samuels, against his will, to use it. It was standard and appeared on almost every feature and television call sheet in use, because it was by union agreement. It was a point of contention across the industry. To his mind, it was logical because without it productions would be getting meal penalties every day. But it was a fact of life in the business and they were only shooting there a few days.

It was with this backdrop the moments ticked by and crew awareness grew that they would, indeed, go over the six-hour window without breaking for a meal. The actors hadn't left between scenes, and they had gone through the material quickly with a quality Turteltaub accepted and liked. There just wasn't enough time.

Rake had been standing next to Turteltaub when the clock struck the appointed six-hour mark. He turned toward the crew and shouted "Grace!" A scattered sound between a murmur and a grumble passed through the ranks.

Grace was a union-approved measure where a production could ask the crew to keep working for up to 30 minutes for the efficiency of the production. While there were restrictions, it was designed for situations like this. The meal penalty would only go into effect if they didn't break in that time. They would get a full 30-minute lunch, but the clock didn't start ticking until the last member of the crew was in line.

Everyone went back to work. The next set up had been readied and all the actors returned to the colored tape on the ground that marked their spots. Now it was De Niro's turn. He would play with lines -- some thought he might be forgetting them -- but he had done all of that during other takes. Now he was on the money, saying his lines as they were written. They went through a couple of takes, all of them okay. Then he nailed it.

You could see the difference. It was a glimpse on Paddy's face that revealed what he thought of Diana leaving with Billy just an iota more subtle than the other takes. Anyone watching him, whether live or in the monitors, saw the difference, Turteltaub chief among them. "Cut. Print it!" said the director.

In the old days of film, "print it" was a literal command. It meant to mark the best take amid thousands of feet of film, making it easy to find. Turteltaub's meaning was the same, even though they were shooting in digital. This was the take he liked, and the script supervisor made note of it. Rake had repeated "Cut" louder, as soon as Turteltaub had, and it had echoed through the other ADs.

Rake and Turteltaub huddled at the monitors, Accardo standing by. The director wanted to see the last take again, just to be sure. The script supervisor spoke to the video assist, who was at his monitors 50 feet away. Director's village was miked so he could hear everything that happened and within seconds it played back on their monitors.

The camera honed in on De Niro, who was looking after Steenburgen. "Look at his face," said Turteltaub. "Look at how much he does by not doing much at all!" The director was satisfied. They were finished with Scene 39. The 1st AD took a few steps toward the crew. "Lunch time!"

Grace would be noted on the wrap sheet.

The last two days of the week were set aside for the pool scenes. They planned to shoot the huge, babe-filled party on Thursday, something they knew was "ambitious," given weather and all the moving parts that had to come together. The main scenes, centered by De Niro, Douglas, Freeman and Kline as contest judges and a well-known DJ celebrity as officiator, included nine other cast, perhaps a half-dozen women from Playboy Entertainment, 30 Aria employees as themselves, and 210 partygoers. That translated to 300 background actors. The quieter pool scenes, set for Friday, had half that many, and none had to get special attention on camera.

Rake had scheduled it that way on purpose. Sin City wasn't the tropics. There was no guarantee of a perfect day in late October in Las Vegas much less two days. Scheduling the pool party on Thursday gave him a one-day backup plan. If Thursday turned to winter they could conceivably switch shooting schedules with Friday. It was less than ideal, given the number of people involved, but with the main actors on for both days it could at least be done.

The scene for the script had been refined. Gone was any reference to a wet T-shirt contest, just as the 2nd AD had predicted months earlier. In its place was a bikini contest. The closest they'd get to a nipple shot was the comment by Morgan Freeman's character that one of the women must be really cold, which wouldn't hurt them in a quest for a PG13 rating. Even then, there was no guarantee that would end up in its final form.

The bullpen kept an eye on the weather. Predictions early in the week were good for Thursday, with a dip in temperature expected Friday. That was good news for everyone except perhaps Douglas, given one of Friday's scene included De Niro pushing him into the pool, assuming Douglas did the scene himself.

By now things had calmed down in the production office, and even lightened. Part of it was the vibe of Aria itself. The resort had anticipated a festive Halloween and Wednesday night had delivered one. That was true despite the fact the pace of work remained the same in the bullpen while they also began to dismantle the business. The last shooting day would be Monday and the bulk of the crew would return to Atlanta the following day. The production would resume shooting Wednesday.

The travel office, now with two people, made plans to get the crew to Atlanta along with the travel arrangements of various actors, crew, producers and studio executives coming in and out of Vegas for the week. The travel office also handled arrangements for child actors who were coming into town to work, along with guardians. One young man brought his sister as well as his mother.

The pool party required another layer of people be brought in. A well-known DJ-entertainer, along with an entourage of six, would act as on-camera emcee in the scene. The "hot girls" casting call had resulted in plenty of eye candy for the pool scenes. For the core group of women to center the scene, however, they went west. Seven women from Playboy Entertainment were booked, their accommodations handled by the travel office.

Everything about the pool party scenes had been time-intensive. Just getting the set built had been an elaborate process, the biggest challenge in Las Vegas for the Art department. As part of the agreement with the movie production, Aria had temporarily deeded over one of its pools. It didn't come with enough room to throw the kind of party called for in the script so during prep the Art department designed a stage to be built over part of the pool, complete with catwalks. A Las Vegas based stage-building company was hired to construct it and with work under way, Bomba and Cassidy had returned to Atlanta to work on the penthouse and other sets in process. Soon everything would be centered in Atlanta.

Bomba had left the assistant art director in charge in Las Vegas. In his mid-20s, he was competent and comfortable in the role. He had done drawings of the set in prep and went back and forth from where they were shooting to where the set was being built. He was also at work on other sets happening on location, particularly one planned Monday at McCarran airport.

It was up to the locally based Locations department lead by Kim Houser-Amaral to liaison between the hotel and construction company. The Locations department was an area of movie production outsiders thought self-explanatory. But it wasn't just looking at properties and ultimately negotiating a lease. It was seeing it all the way through the process. Sound stages were closed to the public while location work happened in the real world and any myriad issues could and would arise. All departments faced challenges, but most were internal. The Locations department was consistently dealing with outsiders who were not committed to the project.

For Houser-Amaral, the week was filled with "nerve wracking" logistical challenges. She had worked on a commercial at Aria before, but that was in-house. This was different. "I had to meet with three guys in suits and I've never worked with a stiffer group of people." She understood why: Their concern, and rightly so, was their guests. At the same time, the movie production hadn't just showed up unannounced.

An agreement like the one between the studio and Aria, which meant MGM, happened high up in the respective organizations. The people who had to see the agreement through were executives on the ground. They had existing responsibilities, some of which they believed conflicted with added projects. In other words, they hadn't agreed to it.

"It was like they weren't completely willing," said Houser-Amaral. "It was, 'You can't do this or that, you can't park here, you can't have cables.'" There was only one way in and one way out for contractors working on the pool party set. Everything needed for construction, all materials and equipment, had to be moved on foot for one-tenth of a mile to the area of the pool where it was to be built. The company hired to bring in the specialized lights and sound system, set decorating in one sense of the word, had the same challenge.

They used an elevator on the west side of the property. "One elevator," she emphasized. "One loading zone." The loading zone could barely fit two of the trusses. "There were 15," she said. They had to run power from three floors, some 1,200 feet of cable. A company that specialized in movie camera cranes returned to the set with two to get elevated shots.

Houser-Amaral's nerves calmed with each hurdle they swung around. They were done ahead of time, the result a completely transformed pool area, unrecognizable to guests who had been to the hotel in the past. Even Aria management did a double take at the big professional stage that emerged, with extensive lights and speakers, and cranes set up on the sides, ready for cameras.

Thursday emerged cold and dark at 5 a.m. when the first crew arrived at the pool. By 6 a.m., the general call time, it had warmed to 51 degrees. A lot of the departments had day players on to help manage the pool party scenes. Four cameras were planned, two of them on cranes. That took specialized crane crew, as well as additional camera crew. There were extras casting people and more people working with the ADs to help wrangle the 300 background actors, 240 of whom were ND or non-descript.

The Aria pool was surrounded by dozens of cabanas. These weren't just for lounge chairs but on the larger side, like small rooms. Each had curtains at the entrance for privacy. The actors were assigned space in the single-digit cabanas, departments spread out from there. Some needed to be closer while others needed more space, like costumes, which had an area for them to work as well as dressing areas.

The Sound department was in one of the closer cabanas. The department was relatively small given how important it was. In addition to the sound mixer there were two other positions, the boom operator and sound utility. The person who did sound utility was once known as the cable man, but the name went away with cable and the requirement it be a man.

Today was one of the more complicated for capturing sound and included the additional of a fourth person, a music playback operator. The party scenes called for it. The scene had a sound system set up in front, but it would be quiet. Instead music playback was controlled from the cabana using Kelson's equipment. The playback operator would listen for Rake's cues. The primary purpose for it was to get everyone in the scene moving to the same beat. Then they would cut the music and shoot the scene, the memory of the beat in the minds of the dancing background actors.

The scenes included a lot of dialogue, which meant a lot of individual mics would be in use. De Niro, Douglas, Freeman and Kline were judges in a bathing suit contest who would sit in chairs on a stage while the DJ was in motion, and a lot of motion at that, in effect making a clipped-on mic more vulnerable. That was a non-issue since the role called for him to use a microphone. But all of it was going through Kelson's board.

Costumes had a cabana for its office and another for dressing areas. The call sheet anticipated nine women in bikinis, seven of whom would be from Playboy Enterprise. Four of those were deemed "heroes"because they would be the leads in the group destined for special camera attention. Moviegoers would know they were sexy and beautiful, but not that they were "playmates," each a centerfold within the past year.

The department scheduled additional costumers for the day to help dress the women. Another actress, an older woman who was out of shape, would also be in the scene, providing a contrast and comedic element. The costumers had another job. One of the scenes had the pool-party hotties flash the actors, their backs to the camera. The department prepared for "modesty," the term used to provide cover for nude or risqué scenes. It could be anything from bathrobes to penis socks. In this case it was bathrobes, towels and pasties, flesh-covered cloth designed to cover private parts.

There were other background actors with specific costumes, 10 "stagehand types," 10 pool cocktail servers, five bartenders, 10 pool attendants and five security personnel for the scene. Aria provided the costumes for any of the people who portrayed Aria employees, some of whom really were employees. Even with them being pre-fit, all of the costumes had to reviewed. Additional costumers were hired for the day to assist with the other background actors.

The mini-cast of characters coming from L.A. ensured the Vegas pool party scene had a wild element. At the center of the scene was Redfoo as DJ. An entertainment renaissance man, he was a musician, singer producer and businessman, best known as part of the musical duo LMFAO, which had just taken a hiatus. As the youngest son of Barry Gordy Jr., founder of Motown Records, he knew his way around music and entertainment.

He knew he wanted to be in the movie. It had been his people who reached out in prep to ask if he would be good for a scene in the movie. It sounded perfect to Turteltaub: "If you need someone to be the life of your party, that's what Redfoo does for a living." The goal was for it to be funny, and to add demographic appeal, but it also had to have Vegas indulgence with a high-end flare. Redfoo was expected to bring a lot of funny, but polished.

Redfoo and the bulk of the Party Rock entourage arrived on schedule, excited. As they got closer to shooting it became clear someone was missing from the entourage. The ADs, and all crew, had continued to use walkies religiously. It was a highly effective way to communicate. On the slowest days it kept everyone coordinated. In times of challenge, it brought help, often before a situation became a problem.

A call went out over the walkie. Had anyone on set seen the man who was to announce Redfoo? It was Peterson's voice. Various PAs responded they had not seen him on set. Someone noted the last time anyone had seen him was the night before when he was actively celebrating Halloween.

Peterson wasn't amused. As 2nd AD she needed to find him, fast, or they had to make a change. But where? She enlisted Blackhawk, a friend of the band and part of the entourage. Blackhawk, so nicknamed for his haircut, agreed to help. Given the potential for it to be something serious, Peterson also reached out to hotel security, who agreed to meet them at the entrance of the entourage suite.

Once they were carded inside it didn't take long to find the young man. He was passed out cold on the floor inside, still wearing his red ranger suit, one of the Mighty Morphin Power Ranger characters. The task of awakening him fell to Blackhawk, who tried valiantly. Eventually he got him to his feet, whereupon the super hero staggered to the bed and passed out again.

Peterson radioed a short version of the news as they made their way back down from the Aria suites to the pool area. Crew jokes abounded. Did anyone know if he had his morpher on? It was a reference to the Mighty Morphin tool that enabled their transformation into super heroes. The morpher had given way to demon alcohol! Rake heard it all play out and was aware of what happened but not concerned. The announcer was part of Redfoo's gig, not technically a cast member. Redfoo could manage it. The scene included the intro but it wasn't key to the story. Besides, he and Turteltaub had enough on their plate.

A short time later Redfoo announced that Blackhawk had landed the role of announcer. The Mighty Morphin man showed up a while later, back in human clothes, but Redfoo had made up his mind. Allowing him to do it after that escapade would "send the wrong message."

Blackhawk looked at ease in the role. He didn't miss a beat and neither did Redfoo. It felt like a party, a Redfoo party, and he got the crowd revved up. The music operator in the cabana was cued by Rake. The 1st AD would alert him whenever it was time to start or stop music. It wasn't what moviegoers would ultimately hear, but it got them dancing at the same time and heightened the mood.

By the first shot it was sunny and mid-60s, creeping toward a high in the low 70s. The actors got in their places at four chairs on the stage, and the contest began. Each of the actors had ratings card props they held up for contestants, drinks and other party props. Redfoo, in his element, looked to Turteltaub when he would add something, and get a nod. There were various ad libs, like Sam lifting his hat up with the straw of his drink. Turteltaub was "using the best of them," as Redfoo put it.

He had a costume that enabled him to rip it off and strip down to a G String, where he would then jump up on the lap of one of the contest judges. He did a dance that had him put his crotch right in front of De Niro's face. "How do you like this package?"

255

It wasn't scripted and the move had surprised nearly everyone. All eyes had been on De Niro. It was ridiculous, particularly the way Redfoo did it. De Niro had genuinely laughed, although he looked a little less amused with each take.

It wasn't a surprise to Turteltaub. When he met with Redfoo to discuss the role, he asked him to describe his show. Redfoo said it was a party and to pull it off he would bring his whole gang, along with party props like beach balls. He said the act included some risqué parts. One part had him rip off his pants, part of a specialized costume, to reveal a tight bathing suit. Then he would gyrate in someone's face, sending partygoers into a frenzy.

"Oh my God, please wiggle in Robert De Niro's face," Turteltaub told him. "That's an Academy Award winner right there!" Producers signed off on it. Most importantly, De Niro didn't balk, and he might have. Instead, the actor went with it, ad libbing a response that made it even funnier. As Paddy grimaced and looked away from Redfoo's package in his face, the character held up a large zero. No one told De Niro to do it, and the "0" brought a natural roar.

It wasn't just that Turteltaub thought it would be funny. It spoke to his theory that iconic actors like these weren't just playing roles when it came to the movie-going public. They were too famous, too much part of the social fabric. "Knowing the wiener wiggle was in the face of Robert De Niro would make that joke funnier," he reasoned. "Not just that it was Paddy but that it was De Niro."

He saw it the same way as the woman playing the comedic non-beauty role alongside the Playboy women. A heavy-set woman would tease Billy on the stage. It was funny because the character was there to marry a much younger woman but also because it was Douglas. The same thing applied to Freeman although in this case the appeal would be the contrast. The actor was so well known for dramatic roles and gravitas that getting him to act goofy in a comedy had special draw, Turteltaub said.

They ran through the whole scene twice and got coverage of all the actors. It was shot in a remarkably short period of time, given the number of people and effort that had gone into it. The weather had more than cooperated for late October. It had been a sunny, bright day that grew warmer with each hour.

Now one of the biggest changes to the script, something put in place in prep by Turteltaub, started to take shape.

The child actors playing the youthful Paddy, Billy, Archie and Sam, were each flown in on Thursday from L.A. or Burbank with the exception of Young Archie, who came from Westchester, N.Y. Costume fittings and meetings with hair and makeup were scheduled for Friday. On Saturday, a rare workday in the movie business, the morning had been set aside for the shooting of still photos of the child actors portraying the main characters as youngsters. Then they would all fly home Sunday, and return to Atlanta when it was time to shoot the scenes.

Fogelman's screenplay imagined a series of still photos of the characters throughout their lives that showed the passage of time in relation to the other characters. That required the actors to contribute images of themselves. Turteltaub came up with the idea of using images of young actors, who would look a lot like De Niro, Douglas, Freeman and Kline. To do it, they would incorporate an old-style photo booth, the type that spit out four images on a black-bordered strip.

It seemed a minor modification at first, one that could convey the passage of time but be simpler than coming up with photos of the actors at the same ages over the course of their lives. There was a lot more to it than that.

The director saw the photos as a creative element that would serve multiple functions, "a little motif" he could use throughout the movie. It would tie the characters to each other and remind people of how long they had all been friends, and create a strand that also could be put to use as a prop or in set decorating.

The photo booths would also contribute to moviegoers buying into the story. The photo-strip product of the machines, and the machines themselves, were ubiquitous at one time. The photo booth prototype machine introduced in New York in 1925 cost a quarter for eight images. It was a novelty. A couple or a group of siblings or friends could jam inside and get pictures. Generally there was goofing around, laughing and pushing or making faces as the machine's flash bulb captured it. The novelty became a fixture over decades, the machine itself often a memory-maker by itself, immortalizing a trip to the boardwalk, bowling alley, town store or pool hall.

There were still plenty of photo booths in operation around the country, even if the price nowadays was $2 or more. The hope was that familiarity would span all four quadrants of moviegoers, male, female, under 25 and over 25 but they knew they at least had the first two.

There were utilitarian reasons for holding the photo booth shoot in Vegas, even though the scene would be shot in Atlanta. It made sense for scheduling reasons. All but one of the young actors was based in L.A., so they were close to Vegas. Various departments that needed to work with them were set up there, none more than costumes. All of the young actors, save Johnny the Greaser, would be pre-fit in their costumes while they were in Las Vegas.

The driving force with regards to timing, however, was the need for the black-and-white photo-strip images of the child actors, which were to be used in set decorating. The 1955 scene had the young actors getting their pictures taken in the booth and playing around in the corner store.

The photo booth was shipped to the Annex and installed by the Set Decorating department. It was an anchor for the most complicated set they had to build, one that replicated Brooklyn in 1955. They were still working on securing the location for it in Atlanta, after a location glitch. The photo booth itself was a separate challenge.

The first part was relatively easy. They found a company that sold working vintage-style machines as well as shells, complete with sharp red velvet curtains and all the externals. Cassidy's main focus was on it being authentic to the time period. He didn't need it to work. So the Set Decorating department had purchased the shell. One immediate challenge was that samples of nameless, laughing people featured in images in the strip were incorporated on its exterior wall. Since there was no telling who those people were, tracking them down to get signed releases was out of the question. So the images were replaced with black-and-white strip photos of various crew and friends or family members, wearing 50s-appropriate attire, accompanied with signed releases. There was a good chance the marketing on the side of the machine wouldn't even end up on camera, but they couldn't take the chance.

The immediate mission was getting all the still photos they needed. It wasn't just mugshots. Turteltaub needed to show personality and the relationship between the characters. They had to be dressed as if it were the 1950s in the costumes they would wear in a scene scheduled for weeks later. Hair and makeup also played a big role because they were locking in their looks for the scene itself. Sophie would wear a high ponytail typical of the time period.

In real life, it took only a few minutes to get into a photo booth, close the curtain and mug to the automatic camera as it flashed four times. This was more time consuming but at the same time it felt easy. Turteltaub directed it as seriously as he would most scenes, acutely aware that it didn't have sound. That meant he could talk them through. It was simple enough, if you had the vision.

In some ways it felt more like they were shooting a scene than still photos because of the way Turteltaub directed Young Paddy (R.J. Fattori), Young Billy (Noah Harden), Young Archie (Aaron Bantum), Young Sam (Phillip Wampler) and Young Sophie (Olivia Stuck). He offered simple guidance to capture the drama between the characters: "You sit down here, you sit here. You give her a kiss, you don't give her a kiss." Young Sophie was advised to react to the kiss the way she wanted, which netted the director the natural response he wanted. This was all moviegoers would see of Sophie, since there was no old Sophie in the cast. They got her with Young Paddy, and in a shot with her and Young Billy, reflecting the triangular connection. They got shots of all of the actors as individuals, including Young Archie and Sam.

Turteltaub was comfortable with the kids, which made them comfortable. Each small instruction went to individual characters and to relationships that were playing out between the adult characters. That connection, and the drama, needed to be evident in the 1950s photo booth still shots. But he wanted the scene to be light. He asked for rabbit ears, which the kids didn't know. He showed them the old-school way to goof around on camera that involved holding up two fingers behind the head of the next person for the photo. They laughed and played in character, easily, as the images were captured. All of the boys shared one striking characteristic beyond being competent for the roles. Each bore a physical resemblance to the adult actors. In some cases it was striking. Makeup painted a birthmark on Young Paddy to match De Niro's "beauty mark," as Turteltaub called it. Kline's younger counterpart wore glasses like the ones the older character wore.

Turteltaub's aim was to capitalize on public personas of the actors. The four men were iconic. For one thing, winning an Academy Award was huge and all five members of the main cast had earned at least one. De Niro and Douglas each had two. But they'd all done something far more difficult: Each actor had stayed relevant in Hollywood for decades. That meant while most

259

moviegoers would see Paddy, Billy, Archie and Sam, they would not fully detach from awareness of the actors themselves.

"As a director, you're always aware of your cast, who the actors are in terms of their persona," Turteltaub said. "I've never experienced a movie -- not just that I've done but that I've seen -- where your knowledge of who the actor is, plays a bigger role in how their character comes off on screen."

CHAPTER THIRTEEN
Shoot Week 3
Nov. 5-9
Day 11, 12, 13

MOST DEPARTMENTS WORKED over the weekend. With Monday being the last shooting day in Las Vegas and the company move on Tuesday looming ahead there was no way Badalato and Samuels could avoid overtime.

During prep, the trip west had been meticulously orchestrated, itemized, compared and contrasted. But now, with principal photography underway, the luxury of extreme detail didn't exist for the return trip. Early plans had the last day of shooting in Vegas on Friday, which would have given the Production department the weekend to problem-solve.

Instead, the company now would shoot scenes at McCarran airport on Monday, travel to Atlanta on Tuesday and check in at Mailing Avenue on Wednesday. Then any needed equipment would be transported to the suburbs, where shooting would resume with a 6 a.m. call Thursday. It was doable, short of unforeseen circumstance. But they were still nervous. Extra effort went into imagining any potential issue to circumvent it before it happened.

Kamishin and Badalato were seated in chairs in his office sipping coffee a little after 8 a.m. They looked bleary, surrounded by his half-packed, black and orange rubber crates. It wasn't that early but it felt like it given they had only been gone 10 hours. Gradually the caffeine kicked in and they started on their inevitable list, albeit a different one than they had used in prep.

Before their list had been forward-looking. Now it could have had columns for past, present and future. The first item was whether they had shut down confusion about the logistics of the move. To do that, they reissued the earlier memo about it with the Prelim on Friday. The "prelim," short for preliminary call sheet, advanced the work planned for the next shooting day. Notices of importance were occasionally attached.

The memo about the move had been issued a week earlier. Crew would wrap at base camp near the airport, once they were done shooting. There had been some second-guessing by crew after the first memo. Why wouldn't they just wrap at the airport if they were already there? Why go to base camp? The question moved through the on set vacuum about whether they should change it. Crew thought it was more logical to wrap at the airport. Days later some wondered if there had, in fact, been a change.

A close reading of the memo provided would have explained it: Not all of it was moving by air. Just as they had in getting there, they would be using all major methods of delivery. It would be a 3D puzzle with moving pieces on a schedule. For the trucks going cross-country, there were two timetables: things that had to be there in time for shooting Thursday morning and things that could arrive Friday. A dedicated truck for other departments would be available for loading at 4 p.m. on Tuesday, as would a forklift and pallet jack. Since it wasn't due in Atlanta until Friday morning it could not contain anything needed for shooting on Thursday.

The camera, sound and video equipment, including the kits of the respective crew, would be expedited. It would be picked up directly Monday night at base camp. Panavision was protective of its equipment. The cameramen knew how to wrap the equipment securely but Panavision dictated how its equipment would be moved. Some equipment was going back to L.A. but most was headed to Atlanta. The rental was effectively being transferred from a California company to a Georgia company, which had benefits to the bottom line. The incentive agreement required the movie company do business within companies in the state. With offices in Georgia, Panavision qualified. That left sound and video playback, which would move on pallets via Federal Express.

Anyone wanting to ship via FedEx had until noon Monday to provide production with the quantity, size and weight of items being shipped. The Production department would be at base camp at the end of the shooting day with pre-printed waybills and shipping labels. The labels were only to be addressed to Panavision Atlanta or Mailing Avenue and would include information about the individual crew attached to the items being shipped. A cargo truck would be there to pick up all items. Crew was to load them on the truck. Both a forklift and pallet jack would be available. A separate truck going to Atlanta would arrive at 4 p.m. on Tuesday in the Annex parking lot. That truck would arrive at Mailing Avenue on Friday morning.

The props truck was easier. It required a driver but otherwise operated independently, since it was owned by Benjamin-Creel. A Teamster would take the truck to Mailing Avenue. As before, once it was fully loaded with

262

things the department needed, most visibly luggage for the airport scenes, it was available for anything the production needed to move. Space leftover was available to crew for personal items, like bicycles belonging to the cinematographer and some of the camera crew, who were avid riders. Nearly every weekend in Vegas the high-mileage rides had helped burn off stress.

There had been no questions about the move since the detailed memo had been reissued the night earlier. Kamishin and Badalato reviewed the immediate needs of the shooting day Monday. Badalato asked about the plan to collect and inventory the leased walkies. Losing just one was pricey. She confirmed they would be collected at wrap on the last day in Las Vegas. Both the prelim and call sheet had reminded crew.

The next item on their list was new. One of the cranes used to shoot the pool party scenes had been damaged. The owner wanted to file a claim. They weren't sure what had happened but initial inquiries pointed to operator error. Badalato and Kamishin decided more homework was needed but it would have to wait until after the move. Then they turned efforts to packing their offices. Badalato was halfway done, as evidenced by the crates. Kamishin said she was not far behind. Both would fly Tuesday, him leaving early in the morning, her in the afternoon. The production team hired to manage the Las Vegas location would remain to shut it all down.

The assistant production manager had taken over the office in the master bedroom suite when the ADs moved. The large bathtub over-flowed with paper. There were reams of it, some of which contained sensitive information such as budgets and timesheets for the actors. A single page with the word "shred" written with an oversized Sharpie floated on top. Mailing Avenue had hired a shredding service but it wasn't clear who would have the duties here.

Someone said guessing how many thousands of sheets of paper were contained in the bathtub would make a fine contest.

"Yeah, but who would count it?" the APOC said. "Not me."

The bullpen had been steadily shipping boxes and suitcases. The room, emptied with the last pickup Friday night, already had a half dozen more. The number grew every few minutes as crew dropped off suitcases or their kits or whatever else they needed to move. They also prepared things for local return, like rolling chairs packed up and put back in the boxes they came in. The lobby of the Annex a block away had its own impressive collection of boxes and crates as well.

But nothing compared to what was happening in the Costume department. Jobst and the key costumer were compartmentalizing. They isolated costumes in the order in which they would be needed. First up were the scenes Monday at McCarran. Those involved all four of the main actors and two script days since the characters were both arriving and departing and would be in different costumes.

Then there were costumes needed for the scenes scheduled for Thursday in Atlanta. They were shooting at Billy's beach house in Malibu, including scenes with Billy and his young fiancé and an engagement party. They prepared the costumes for Douglas and Bre Blair, who was playing the fiancé, as well as for three other actors who spoke in the scene, and various extras. The extras, logically, had to wear attire that looked like Malibu, which was different from the Vegas tone. Jobst also isolated clothes for the fast truck that would work on Friday, specifically those for Archie, since Freeman was on the schedule. When that was done, she and the costumer focused on the larger move, a process that took what was left of the weekend.

They had set up the large offices in the span of a day, aided by its organization. Everything was marked and organized for movement. The move back needed to be every bit as well organized. Either process would have been marveled at by anyone who had ever had to move an office or retail store to the other side of town.

It took the better part of Sunday for the Art and Set Decorating departments to prep McCarran for the seven scenes planned the next day. Sean Ryan Jennings, assistant art director, stood outside Aria at 7:30 a.m. waiting for the valet to bring his rental car. He had overseen the sets in Las Vegas while Bomba and Cassidy focused on the more than two-dozen other sets needed in Atlanta. Given the breadth of the work that went into the pool set, Jennings thought the airport sets were going to be easy in comparison. He called the leadman, who was at the airport already, to check in.

Daril Alder had started work before 7 a.m. along with the rest of the Set Decorating department. The cube truck, which contained the things they needed to create the sets, had reached a barrier. A height limitation sign on Wayne Newton Boulevard, created as a security measure, prevented the truck from entering the airport. That meant the signage and paint and various other things were prevented from getting to Terminal 1.

Shooting scenes at a major airport isn't a regular occurrence. A movie with a negative storyline, say one about a plane crash, was an almost-guaranteed "no," regardless of whether the production company wanted to use the airport's name. But there was more to it than that. Most airports used the space they had. It wasn't easy or convenient to accommodate a movie production. A benign storyline did nothing for the airport's core business either. Even a hefty location fee generally wasn't worth the potential disruption.

However, *Last Vegas* was a story about tourists coming to Vegas so the script was fine. It was upbeat, even, something the city's economic development team might like. Also working in Four Fellas' favor was that McCarran actually had the space. The airport had just opened a brand new terminal, which meant it had an under-used terminal at the precise moment the Locations department inquired. Terminal 1 wouldn't be that way for long, but in that window, with a fee to make it worthwhile, it would work.

Now it was up to the movie company to spruce up the area. The Locations department leased the baggage claim half of Terminal 1 for a single day, which included time to prep it the day before. They leased a nearby airport parking lot for base camp for two days.

Jennings drove down Wayne Newton Boulevard until he saw a member of the swing gang, who had been posted there to flag him over to the parking lot, where he joined the others. Alder had opened the back of the cube truck.

"We need 13' 3," he said, after Jennings had parked. There was another access point into McCarran but it was Sunday morning and too early to secure management approval. It would be easier to transfer the truck's load onto the stake bed truck and take it to the terminal that way. Jennings agreed.

It was easily moved. It wasn't that much, various tools, stanchions and plastic chain to form waiting lines for airline patron extras, paint and signage. The biggest item would be a 16-foot-wide billboard. It was the slot machines that required the heavy lifting, and those were being delivered separately.

Before long the airport's PR manager arrived at the terminal. Jennings, who had been one of several people taping and repainting numbers on the sidewalk for consumer lines, jumped up to greet her. A smart woman with impressively big hair, she took in the work being done in front of the terminal with a smile. The numbers had been dulled by thousands of footprints. She said the new paint gave it a much fresher look.

They talked about the slot machines that were en route to the airport. While McCarran had plenty of them, they belonged to someone. It wasn't just the machines themselves or even the licensed branding on some of them, but the artwork itself. Some artist had designed the flourishes on the belly plate and top plate. That meant the copyright holders had to give permission for the art to go on camera. The easier path was to hire someone who could provide generic machines.

The owner of the slot machine company, clad in a bright shirt with big, red flames, found Jennings. The public relations woman, who had receded to the side of the room but never left, saw him. She was friendly and helpful and called the electrician, who soon arrived to reveal the exact spot of the power junctions, which were hidden below industrial carpet squares. The gaming machines were brought in and a technician began working on them in rotation. He opened each one and cleaned, checking that all lights, bells and whistles worked and replacing or fixing whatever didn't work.

The contract with the slot machine company guaranteed copyright-free machines, but he had gone a step further. Several machines had been designed with special themes that honored the actors without crossing any lines. One read "Seven Deadly Sins" after *Seven*, the thriller of Morgan Freeman's. Another had a *Wall Street* theme, a nod to Michael Douglas' work.

In the matter of a couple of hours Terminal 1 looked refreshed. A new, double row of slot machines were lit up. New signs hung. Fresh paint dried. The swing gang was at work in the corner on the billboard, the last thing they had to get done before they were finished.

Turteltaub had an idea for a gag shot that would show a billboard that featured "Australia's Thunder from Down Under," a male review. The image featured five beefy, shirtless guys who performed a *Magic Mike*-style act in Vegas. The plan was to hang it over the escalator and have the four retirement age heroes come down the escalator below. The entertainment company behind the revue had been happy to provide it.

The sign was prefabricated to slip over an existing digital sign in the airport. It took five workers to finesse the 16-foot ad into its metallic rectangular case. Finished, they carried it across the room to the digital sign, which read "McCarran International Airport Welcomes Automotive After-market Industry Week." They leaned it against the wall while they assessed the sign.

McCarran's public relations executive joined them. She had been out of sight, mostly, and out of mind, but she had been watching from the sidelines.

266

The smile she'd worn early in the day was gone. She got to the point. Did they think they were going to put that huge sign, "Thunder from Down Under" atop of the digital sign? Jennings said yes, he did.

"I don't think so," she said. She looked at Jennings long enough for him to blink. "No," she added for clarity. Jennings asked what her concerns were. She answered succinctly: It was its potential to damage the existing sign. He explained the billboard advertisement was engineered for this purpose and that it looked heavier than it was but she was having none of it.

"I'm just not comfortable with that," she said firmly. The cooperative woman had vanished. This one wasn't going to budge. She softened for a moment, giving a false sense of hope. The airport engineering department would be in early tomorrow, she said. They could review it. As long as they signed off, she was okay. "Tomorrow," she repeated. Then her smile returned. "Are we good?" "Okay," said Jennings. They talked timing. Then she walked back to where she had been standing.

The swing gang carried the sign back to the corner of the room where they'd built it. Someone grumbled along the way about her being over-zealous but Jennings said he understood. It was no big deal. The engineers could sign off and they'd have it up first thing in the morning, well before they needed to shoot.

They leaned the billboard against the corner wall next to a still-folded sandwich board that could also wait until the next day: "Four Fellas Productions LLC will be filming at McCarran Airport today. By entering this area you hereby irrevocably consent to and authorize Four Fellas Productions LLC, it's successors and assigns, to photograph you and/or make sound recordings of you and to use same worldwide for any purpose whatsoever in perpetuity; All such photographs and sound recordings to be the sole property of Four Fellas Productions LLC."

The swing gang was gone a minute later.

Monday began with a 5:30 a.m. call, 30 minutes ahead of the 6 a.m. call time typical in the first two weeks of shooting. That made it that much earlier for crew with pre-calls. On top of the scenes they were shooting, and the move, Daylight Savings Time would go into effect. Adrenaline helped, as did knowledge there would be a break of sorts when they wrapped for the day.

Anyone working with background actors was particularly taxed. In this case they had 253 people due between 4:30 and 5 a.m. Much effort had gone into the mix of background actors to appear in the airport scenes. It might have been a lot of travelers for the scenes they were shooting except they were different script days: One scene had the four heroes arriving, and the other leaving. They didn't want the same extras in both scenes for continuity reasons. Minimally any background actors that did get used would need to change clothes.

The specialty background extras included pilots and flight crew, skycaps and baggage handlers, maintenance crew and limo drivers in dark suits, as well as Southwest ticket agents, part of the placement deal with the airline. It was serious specialty "BG" from there, the abbreviation for background. There was a basketball team and a group of Army soldiers. When Peterson planned it she knew what she wanted: three men and one woman in BDU, or battle dress uniform. All of it was designed for authenticity.

The whole group would be sprinkled in with 180 "ND atmosphere with luggage." ND meant nondescript, or everyday travelers. Altogether, it was enough to make it look like that wing of McCarran was working like a normal day. Some would be outside. Fifteen background actors were instructed to bring cars, which paid extra, to fill in the front of the airport. The production provided picture cars: the #1 Taxi, which the actors would get in once they arrived, and 12 ND cabs, 2 ND shuttle vans, an airport security car, and one Aria limo, for the scene when the actors had finished the adventure and were coming to the airport to fly home.

The vehicles the heroes would take to and from the airport might seem subtle yet it contributed to the story. Upon arriving in Las Vegas, they took a cab from the airport. But when their weekend came to an end, they returned in a limo. The weekend had changed them and that was another way to show it. Turteltaub saw part of the appeal of *Last Vegas* as a buddy movie. He would get a longer shot of Douglas at the airport in the scene where the group departed. Billy Gherson would look after his friends with great affection. They were the greatest thing that ever happened to him.

Turteltaub wouldn't be driving any of these vehicles. The director had put himself behind the wheel for the scene with De Niro when they were shooting the characters' exit scenes at Aria. It was a nod to the 1976 classic *Taxi Driver*. Director Martin Scorsese had ridden as a passenger in the back of Travis Bickle's cab. "I thought, 'If I'm getting in a taxi with Robert De Niro, I'm driving it.' So I did. That's one of the perks to being me."

268

Now Turteltaub's mind was on the scenes to be shot at McCarran airport. There were three exteriors, two interiors and two establishing shots. B camera got the establishing shots, which were of a plane coming "from the west" and another of a plane landing. It didn't need actors or dialogue or sound of video playback and hence fewer members of the crew. The point of an establishing shot was to relay a piece of information in a few seconds, whether it be the location of a city or in this case, an airport. But the shots weren't limited to just establishing place. They could also show an object or a figure, an empty bar, a character with a prop, anything that helped establish context to advance the story.

When they wrapped for the day crew headed to base camp, which had a very different feel given it was also a staging area for the move. There was food but a lot of crew was there just long enough to get on a shuttle back to Aria. The Transportation department ran shuttles to Aria and back to the airport. Others had more work to do to secure equipment for the move.

One of the ADs checked in walkies. The announcement on the call sheet had not escaped the attention of the crew, thanks in part to its larger font and the word "WALKIES" highlighted in yellow. Other paperwork at the check-in table showed it was a group effort. The APOC in Atlanta had ordered them from an L.A.-based company for delivery in Las Vegas. The inventory under way made sure they had all of them back in good working order. Then the equipment would be re-issued in Atlanta in two days.

The technology of portable radio signaling is generally credited to Donald Hings in 1937, a Canadian. A lot of similar things were in development at the time. Motorola had introduced a police radio receiver a year earlier, and in 1937 its line of phonographs and home radios. It was the Galvin Manufacturing Corp. that developed the two-way radios used in World War II. It was effectiveness of the devices on the battlefield, and awareness on the homefront of the lives saved, that made the two-way radios iconic. Use of walkies on movie sets began in the 1950s. Barbara Stanwyck suggested them when they were filming the lifeboat scenes in the first *Titanic* (1953). That followed difficulties in communicating between lifeboats, which held actresses Stanwyck, Thelma Ritter and dozens of extras.

These days it is fairly standard that the Production department order walkies and the ADs manage them, but that wasn't always the case. At one time the Sound department was in charge of them, said Kelson. He had finished securing the sound equipment for the move back to Atlanta, as had the Video assist operator. The Camera department wasn't far behind.

Kelson began in the business in the early 1980s. "It was one thing when we were just handing out a few walkies," he said. As the utility of the two-way radios on set was recognized more were ordered. It became too much for the Sound department, which was relatively small compared to the number of people in the AD department. "These days there can be a hundred walkies or more, he said," as he headed back to the hotel.

Aria had been nice. Even the rooms on the low floors that overlooked a roof had extensive climate controls, interactive televisions that enabled wake up calls and curtains that opened with a button. But it was still a hotel. After nearly a month, all of them were ready to go. They looked forward to the rest, even if one of the days was spent with travel and the other checking in their respective kits and equipment.

The move back had started more than a week before from the vantage point of the bullpen but this was when the big exodus began. Starting well before daylight Tuesday the Transportation department was ferrying people from Aria to the airport, a process that continued all day. There were 10 people from the production on the 7:10 a.m. flight, 13 on the 8:30, 11 on the 10:55 a.m. flight and so forth throughout the day.

First class housed above-the-line people, producers and actors and Turteltaub. By union and guild contract it included 1st AD Rake, 2nd AD Peterson and 2nd 2nd AD Awa, Hennings and A Camera Operator Jody Miller, Badalato and Kamishin, as well as some others. There also were individuals who negotiated in first class travel when they worked out their deal, as was the case with the key hair and makeup artists.

Who ended up in the wider seats with free beverages in flight was a relatively small part of what collective bargaining provided. While unions and guilds had seen a decline elsewhere in the country, the entertainment industry had experienced growth. Every member of the crew on *Last Vegas* who was asked, a process that had continued, said unions were a necessary part of the industry. The cost of membership varied by local and none were cheap. It was worth the money out of their pockets.

They also believed unions had been good for the industry, an opinion shared more broadly outside the microcosm of *Last Vegas* in Hollywood in general. Most people aware of the role of organized labor knew how it had shaped Hollywood over time, as well as present-day operations. And most believed unions were due a large portion of the industry's success. Protecting workers by establishing pay minimums and standard operating procedures had resulted in relatively high standards.

The one general vulnerability was the isolated nature of movie production. There was no on-site oversight of the people in charge. Most of the producers and higher-ups were professional and it worked, even if they didn't make any friends. But things could go south quickly if an actor, producer or director was crazy or abusive or intoxicated, given the power they wielded. There was a long-established hierarchy and most crew wouldn't call them out. The union and guilds were there and crew could report problems, even if they didn't as a rule.

The crew based in Atlanta returning from Las Vegas, including the gaffer, best boy, props departments, and 2nd AD, would get to sleep in their own beds for the rest of the show. The crew who were based elsewhere would move into hotels or short-term housing. Some were going back to the same housing secured in prep.

After Vegas, Kamishin welcomed the familiarity of Virginia Highlands, even if she wouldn't be spending a lot of time perusing the popular neighborhood in Northeast Atlanta. Badalato, a self-described 'homebody' despite his work, returned to the house he had leased. It was five minutes from Mailing Avenue. He found comfort in proximity to the production office. That way if something happened he could be there fast, although if it did, he was probably already there.

Both arrived on Mailing Avenue a few minutes apart on Wednesday morning. All indications were that the move was going smoothly. The Production department offices had been on the receiving end of dozens of boxes and bags in the past week.

The bullpen was decorated with "welcome back" signs, its crew genuinely glad to see those who were returning. Badalato and Kamishin had been in regular contact with Stephens, Jordan Anderson, the APOC and others in the bullpen, but it still felt like a reunion. Other departments may have grumbled about Badalato but his people didn't.

The place felt abundantly more comfortable than its temporary counterpart at Aria. It also had a more lived-in feel to it than when they had left. The smell of fresh paint and new carpet was gone. Badalato and Kamishin made the rounds a short time later, touring the large Mailing Avenue facility, greeting crew who had remained and checking progress.

Eventually everyone settled in to the bullpen. Throughout the morning the pace and size of deliveries quadrupled. Kamishin was detail-oriented and rather than just letting it flow in, she periodically checked where things were. That's how she discovered some of the show's freight had been stopped in Memphis. It took a while to piece together that it was important freight needed on set early the next morning: pallets from the Sound and Video playback departments. She tried to convince the company to move it along, explaining the urgency. The employee of the shipping company was firm. They would not be moving the pallets another foot. No reason was provided but the best guess was that it had been damaged and moving it further would make it worse.

Kamishin admitted she was worried. Something had happened for them to stop the shipment on its way to Atlanta. It was possible there had been some kind of damage to the equipment but the main thing was getting it back to Atlanta. No sound and video playback equipment meant they couldn't shoot in the morning. A lost day would be incredibly expensive on multiple levels.

They talked about different ways to solve the problem. The best one was to have the Teamsters pick up the stranded equipment and drive it the rest of the way to Atlanta. How fast could that happen? It could go right to location but the owners of the equipment would likely want to be there to check it in. A private truck and driver were hired to pick it up in Memphis.

Various departments were on the other side of town readying the location for shooting the next day. They were shooting Michael Douglas' character. Billy Gherson's "home" had been prepped in advance. Now it was making sure all the pieces fit together. The Transportation and Locations departments did their respective jobs. The nearby lot was leased for crew parking, catering and craft services, extras holding and costumes. The Set Decorating department was there making final adjustments. Cassidy, the set decorator, had imagined the finishing touches as if he knew Gherson personally. The home had a high-end look but it lacked feeling, like the character before the trip to Vegas.

There was also mental prep. Turteltaub and Rake came through. The director stood back and looked at the set long enough that he might have been developing film. He moved around, occasionally blocking, but mostly thinking. The director's process in preparing to shoot a scene was becoming clear. No one bothered him, if they'd been inclined to in the first place.

Hennings also came to review the location. He'd gone over it in advance, considering light, but he had the additional challenge of shooting for greenscreen effects to consider. Other camera crew coordinated with Panavision Atlanta to get the equipment checked in to the new city, and then to location.

The set was 10 miles away if you could catapult from Mailing Avenue. Otherwise it was 12 miles through the middle of traffic-choked Atlanta, depending on the time of day. Crew arriving for the early call time would easily avoid traffic. After that all bets were off.

Turteltaub, Rake and the rest of the crew were on Beech Haven Road before the 6:18 a.m. sunrise. The house was landlocked, this being Atlanta, but it would do as the beachfront home of main character, Billy Gherson. Later they would shoot the Pacific Ocean from the deck of Turteltaub's real Malibu home. Thanks to green screen technology, which would merge the two, moviegoers would be none the wiser.

They hadn't cushioned the 6 a.m. call time to soften the landing of the cross-country move. There were two scenes planned, both of them centering on Michael Douglas. The first one had Gherson on his balcony talking on the phone before they left for a funeral. He nodded appreciatively at his girlfriend, Lisa. Gherson would also practice a speech he planned to give at a funeral. It involved a key plot point, because he lamented about aging to those in attendance, then issued an impromptu marriage proposal to Lisa, who sat in the audience. That sets the stage for their trip to Las Vegas to get hitched.

The other scene, the resulting engagement party, took more coordination. There were 36 extras needed as partygoers but there was an important caveat. This group needed to be comprised of two age groups. They were either younger, like 30-something Lisa, or older, like 60-something Gherson. It was another one of the subtle contributions to a scene that helped bring home the age difference. A moviegoer probably wouldn't notice it consciously, but they'd get the point at a deeper level. Less subtle was the part of the scene where Lisa's father, a peer of Gherson's, lets him know he's not thrilled about the marriage.

While the magic of the special effects that put them all in Malibu would happen in post production, they had to get it right on the front end. They brought in a video effects specialist for the day, but most of it fell to Hennings and the camera crew. It amounted to double the work in some sense.

They had to light the actors in the two scenes, and there were different requirements for the engagement party as there was for the scene with

Douglas and Blair. The green screen required a whole other layer. The cinematographer had to make sure the backdrop, better known as a green screen, was properly lit. That was harder than it sounded.

People outside the industry think green screen is relatively new technology, the same thing that enables a television weather person to point to a map when they're really pointing to a blue or green screen while viewers at home see a map.

But Hollywood has been using the technique in various forms since the early days of film. They shot scenes of 1903's *Great Train Robbery* with blacked-out windows and a moving garbage matte to bring them to life. A patent was issued for a traveling-matte technique in 1911 and there have been steady modifications and advances ever since, particularly in the last decades.

The process is "chroma keying," which is a term that is used today as well as in history books, along with "color keying." That term gets to a core description of the process, if primitive. By identifying or keying into a specific color or area of brightness they are able to remove it and replace the green screen with something else. In this case they would replace it with the Pacific Ocean, but it could also have been dinosaurs or aliens.

The screen can be any color. Green can be more effective than most colors because it offers greater contrast but blue has been more commonly used with extreme visual effects. The main requirement is that the screen differ enough from clothing or human skin color to contrast with the backdrop.

The joke that if something happened "they could fix it in post" had gone public. It wasn't as recognizable as "it's a wrap." It also wasn't necessarily true. Yes, they could and did work miracles in editing. But it left a false impression that sloppy work could be done on the front end without consequence. Nobody was blowing off work, least of all Hennings. He was way too serious for that.

There was an art to shooting green screen, even if it seemed technical. It wasn't simply that the actors couldn't be too close to it or too far away. Hennings needed to get a soft but even light across the screen while avoiding reflection or any variant degree of light. Even a small shadow that wasn't visible to a casual observer could show up later. The trick was in lighting the screen separately, but it still took time.

That wasn't the only requirement. The camera operators and focus pullers also had to up their games. They were trained to keep the camera steady but here it became even more important, since a slight movement on their part could make the person on camera appear to move. Focus was another issue. It was always essential that a shot be in focus, something accomplished through adjusting the lens. Now there were limitations, because too much movement on the zoom could change how the actor looked in relation to the backdrop.

It wasn't Newton's Laws of Motion but it took skill and experience to do it right. Then they would fix it in post.

Friday they were on location in Lawrenceville, Ga., to shoot at Bethesda Park and Aquatic Center. In the scene, Kevin Kline's character Sam and his wife, Miriam, played by Joann Gleason, would attend an indoor water aerobics class in their retirement community in Boca Raton, Fl. There was also a pickup shot that had eluded them in Las Vegas of Kline and another actor making party flyers at a business center. That was 1/8 of a page and no dialogue compared to the 1 5/8 script pages of the main scene. There were a lot of moving parts to manage to the scene but it felt like a calm day. The 9 a.m. call time was a first, almost luxurious given the norm. Union rules require they push start times if the previous day runs late, but that hadn't happened here. Crew, most of whom were showing signs of wear even with the extra sleep, welcomed it.

There was a lot of specialty equipment involved with shooting at the aquatic center. The challenges were both environmental and technical. Cameras are not comfortable in high humidity. Indoor pools, even with dehumidifier systems, averaged 60 percent relative humidity. The equipment could manage the moisture in the air given time to acclimate, which is why he was starting early. The 2nd assistant on A camera draped a cloth loosely in front of the camera nearby.

The lenses were fundamentally the same as for a still camera. If you took your camera out of an air-conditioned place and into thick August air, it would fog up. It would adapt with time but Flurry was also mindful of the potential for condensation, since it could hurt the machinery. There were built-in indicators that would signal an error if they detected a problem. Flurry wasn't concerned but he was paying close attention just the same.

One piece of equipment was designed for water. Turteltaub and Hennings planned to get a shot of the aerobics class working out from below the surface. It had the potential to be really funny, the director thought, but minimally it would add to the scene. While the camera wasn't waterproof, there was housing that was and it would enable the underwater shot.

There also was another piece of specialty equipment. Crane crew readied a 30-foot technocrane with Z Head, which would enable the camera to get both loft and various angles on the pool. Even with large windows behind it the crane seemed huge in the enclosed area. It was shaped like a stout "T" with a long top and one end leaning up. A crane operator was on crew for the day to manage the equipment as instructed by Hennings.

Lighting was a different beast all together. In addition to the usual process, two grips worked on a balloon light, although it didn't appear to be cooperating. Lighting was contained with a fabric-looking ball, which diffused the light over 360 degrees, or at least close to it. It was a softer tone more in line with an indoor pool.

The Sound department had done its usual set up. The boom operator and audio utility had arrived a little ahead of the 9 a.m. call. They got the cart set up and otherwise prepared. But after a while there was still no sign of the production sound mixer, who was the head of the department. They called him but there was no answer.

By 9:30 most of the crew knew that Kelson wasn't there. That information had passed through at the speed of sound. Generally if someone was late it was a matter of minutes and no one noticed or cared. Departments looked after each other, even if it meant covering for someone they didn't like since it reflected on them as a group. But it was rare that anyone missed call time altogether, especially someone whose absence could conceivably delay shooting.

There wasn't room for everyone to set up within the pool area where they were shooting. So departments parked themselves along the glass wall on the side of the big pool adjacent to the set and next to an even bigger pool. They were all in a row, different departments one after the next with lights and containers and the director's village and video village. There was another entrance to the smaller pool but it couldn't be accessed as directly. So crew would walk past the row of departments in the big room, around the pool and be visible from a distance by anyone who looked.

The boom operator, who looked miffed as the 10 o'clock hour approached, was relieved to see his boss arrive a short time later. Kelson slinked from the entrance into the main area, through the first half of the 90-degree angle to the second part where everyone was set up. When he got to the sound cart he slipped into his chair quietly. The boom operator leaned forward to tell him something. "Shhhh," the sound mixer answered, putting his finger to his lips. Then he turned to the soundboard, slipped his earphones on, and began sliding levers and turning knobs.

But Kelson's absence hadn't escaped anyone's attention, least of all Turteltaub's. The director had been going back and forth from set to the outdoors, where various other departments had hunkered down. He was on his way back in from one of those trips when he saw Kelson at the sound cart. A few steps later Turteltaub turned back, coming to a stop near him. The sound mixer had his head down as though he were deeply engrossed in the mixing board, a pose he sustained for about two seconds. Then he looked up at the director, smiled and removed his earphones.

"Are these early calls getting to you, David?" Turteltaub might have said it into a microphone the way it played off crew in the vicinity. They were well aware that Kelson was late and had gone silent as the director approached. They looked busy, eyes averted, but they were hanging on every word. Laughter rang out loudly as the director moved on. Kelson quickly had his headphones back on, his attention returned to the board.

It was pure Turteltaub. It was clever but at the same time he nailed him: You're late for a 9 a.m. call? Missing call was serious business, enough to get someone fired, particularly if it happened more than once. Letting any department head go now would pose its own problems but the sound mixer had, in effect, been put on notice.

Kelson knew he was getting off lightly. "I'm lucky he was good humored about it," he said. "Jon might not have been so understanding." He wasn't worried about any additional fallout because it wouldn't happen again. Being late was a fluke because he lived on the other side of the city from Lawrenceville. Ironically, the later call time had contributed because it put him in traffic, he said. On top of everything else, his cell phone was off.

The crew knew Turteltaub's style by now. He always had a sharp wit but on occasion it seemed barbed without clear cause. Earlier in the day he'd gotten after the prop master. The scene included a background actor moving slowly down a ramp into the pool with help of a walker. The props truck had a walker, but no tennis ball to put on the feet of the walker, as was common practice to prevent slipping. The prop master left to get some but returned with only one can of balls.

With other crew nearby the director let him know he thought that was stupid. "Don't you know how many balls come in a canister?" It was a reference to the standard three-ball-per-can occupancy.

Dwight Benjamin-Creel said he didn't play tennis.

"You're a prop master," said Turteltaub.

Benjamin-Creel had something to say but thought better of it. He left to get another canister of tennis balls, but he was pissed. It wasn't the first time he felt zinged. The director's humor was always at other people's expense, he said, adding he was tired of being the brunt of it. Turteltaub was constantly dreaming up things he wanted for a scene the day they were shooting! The Props department could generally accommodate him, but he should give him a break.

Benjamin-Creel soon returned with a canister of tennis balls. The only ones that had been available were a different color, which meant one ball on the legs of the walker wouldn't match the others. Rice worried a little but Turteltaub laughed when he saw it. He liked that better, actually. It was funnier.

It was a small interaction but enough crew heard it to prompt a conversation. They were glad it wasn't them. No one wanted to get caught missing something. This was one of those days. It was hot in there and the humidity had everyone sweating. The smell of chlorine seemed to grow stronger by the minute.

Somebody commented they were steering clear of the director for the day, lest he be in a bad mood. This made Kelly Borisy, the dolly grip, crack up. Turteltaub was a dream compared to some directors, he said. What bad mood? "He's consistently upbeat. He keeps everybody upbeat, even if maybe he's not feeling that way."

Most directors were strong personalities. That was something the whole crew agreed upon. That's what it took to do the job. What made Turteltaub different was his level of awareness of the entire set. It wasn't just that he was aware a key member of the crew had missed call. Any AD would have alerted a director to that if it went on too long.

Turteltaub knew names and he knew jobs. While he dealt primarily with department heads he talked to everyone. He could be prickly but much more often he was funny. "Everything I know about being a director I learned from watching Captain Kirk on Star Trek," he said, a reference to the lead character of a television series that had remained popular over decades and lived on in new movies.

"He knew how to do everything on the ship, even though everyone else was better at it," he said. "Captain Kirk would help Scotty out with the dilithium crystals, he knew the ins and outs of all of it. But nothing took precedence over the Enterprise itself," he continued. "Kirk was married to that ship and when he had to choose between it and a hot girl, he always chose the ship."

Inside the pool area they were getting ready for rehearsal. Rake was talking to Beach Bunny Betty as Benjamin-Creel went by on the walker, testing it. "When do you want me in the water?" she asked. "You may not need to get in," Rake said. "We may want you in an advisory role where we would have you by the monitors to let us know if anything is amiss." He would let her know.

Seeing that Turteltaub was ready, Rake radioed the ADs in the back to bring in the background actors. There were 52 planned for the scene, most of them retirement-age. Twenty would be in the water aerobics class that the two main actors were taking. Then there were 13 more miscellaneous background, five maintenance staff, two lifeguards and three swimmers doing laps. They would be stretching or walking or mingling around.

The extras assigned to the pool were an eager lot. The Costume department, operating out of their trailer and large tent set up in the parking lot, had worked with them. Background actors had been asked to bring robes and flip-flops and other pool attire to the set, and the Costume department augmented from there.

It was in contrast to Turteltaub, in jeans and a button-down white shirt. "This is going to be great," he said, as he shook hands with them. They agreed and nodded excitedly. Rake told them they could start getting in the water. They dutifully complied. They spaced themselves out in the pool, while one of the ADs was on the sidelines making adjustments.

Turteltaub got out in front of the pool like he was walking out onto a stage. He began talking to them, walking back and forth. He was utterly comfortable. He explained how he wanted the scene to play out. One man had his arms across his chest, and the director had him wave them. Now all of them were to bounce up and down in the water. Warm up! Some of them started dancing. He nodded in approval. It was a spry group, the type of retirement-age people who go to aerobics instead of watching television at home. "Let me remind you," the director's voice boomed, "this is a scene about a geriatric aerobics class! Remember, you're retired!" The faux admonishment was a compliment. They were too young to be playing elderly people!

Beach Bunny Betty, the aerobics advisor, had been off to the side advising Polly Craig, the Georgia actress who was to play the aerobics instructor. Then she walked over to Turteltaub with some advice about the logistics of water aerobics. He listened and nodded politely. Then he went over to talk to Rake. A few minutes later, he came and got Beach Bunny Betty. The 1st AD had good news for her. She would be on camera, an elderly swimmer using the walker with tennis balls. Her job was to move creakily down the water ramp and into the pool when the time came. She smiled broadly.

Turteltaub had returned to Craig. She said she didn't have any experience as an aerobics instructor, but she'd been a member of the Screen Actors Guild for nearly 30 years. It was confusing to have instruction from both Beach Bunny Betty and the director, she said. Who should she listen to? "Me, of course!" he said. "I am the director!" He said it in comedic fashion, which made her laugh, and then jumped into motion.

He took a couple of steps back so Craig could see him better. He held out his leg and did a short kick, flopping his calf. Then he took two steps to the left. The dance continued a few seconds, Turteltaub with his hands on hips, swaying, kicking his legs.

She fell in next to him, so they were side by side, and took two steps to the left, matching his movement.

"Bump it, Grind it!" Turteltaub said, two steps to the right.

The line from the script was "Now Grind It! Grind!" But this sounded funnier. Craig repeated it louder, a little more space between words. "Bump. It. Grind. It!" It was funnier still, coming from a little old lady. She was in a flow, two steps to the left, two steps to the right. It was one leg out, one leg back or some variation but she kept up. Turteltaub came to a stop and told her it was perfect. Then he gave his final instructions: "Be funny!" She beamed and nodded enthusiastically.

Crew was in place in the background and the camera went through its tests. The crane was in motion. The operator listened for instruction, swinging the long neck out over the pool. The balloon light wasn't holding up as well. It was supposed to hover overhead but something had malfunctioned. Best efforts to get it up had failed. Hennings said he could make do. There were other lights in place but the images were showing up on the monitors crisp and clear.

In the background, the ADs had brought Kevin Kline in from an inside room. As he got into the pool, Katrina Rice set down weights for use in the aerobics class. Joanna Gleason, the actor playing Miriam, his on-screen wife, arrived and got in the pool. Kline greeted the actress by reaching his arms out to dance. They waltzed. Turteltaub was at the edge of the pool by then. They were his last stop. Then he was back outside the glass wall between pools and at the monitors.

CHAPTER FOURTEEN
Shoot Week 4
Nov. 12 16, 2012
Day 14, 15, 16, 17, 18

E ARLY MONDAY MORNING Turteltaub stood with his arms crossed in front of his chest on the residential street in the Atlanta suburb of Dunwoody. It was a little after 7 a.m. and the temperature had dipped near freezing overnight. He looked up and down the street, then turned back to look at the house where they were shooting Morgan Freeman's character over the next two days. Archie had suffered a stroke and lived with his son and his family while he recovered.

There were six scenes to be shot at the split-level house on Summerford Road. It was the first time the movie-going audience would see Archie on screen and the last. He would be spirited away by Sam, Kevin Kline's character, and dance with a baby.

The house's look was important. But it also met the specific requirement of a ground-level window in the right place. A gag shot would have Archie seemingly leap from his bedroom window to escape his overprotective son when he was really just stepping out. The Location department reviewed 53 homes before isolating a dozen to show the director. Turteltaub hadn't been sold on the house but he was pleased with the interior sets. He was less sure about the scene in the front of the house, where Sam picks up Archie for the Vegas weekend.

The director stood there for several minutes. He looked in each direction, and again at the house. This was a nice neighborhood but something was missing. Neighborhoods like this came with kids, and there were no kids. How could he make it better? He mulled a street hockey game. That would liven it up. Given they had two days there was time to rustle up some school-age kids to play in the street.

The production had leased the house for two weeks. The family was provided with corporate housing and paid enough to make it worthwhile. The production paid to store their belongings safely and installed the furniture and artwork designed for the sets. They also would put it back in place before the family's return.

Set Decorating had provided this furniture. Archie's room had framed photos of his life, adding subtle credibility to the scene. These were the images recreated from the photos Freeman supplied in prep. The one with hin uniform was displayed prominently. Then there was the small, framed black-and-white photo of boys, a memento of his friends. It was one of the strip images taken at the photo booth shoot in Las Vegas, the device Turteltaub came up with to tie the boyhood characters together. Other images from the strip would appear in set decorating elsewhere in the movie.

Dunwoody, an upscale suburb of Atlanta, wasn't designed to be a place that could easily host crew parking and tents for catering. In this case, it didn't lend itself to signs either. The map for the crew had warned everyone to pay attention: "City rules will not allow us to put out directional signs, so know where you are going before you leave."

Base camp was at the nearby Cavalry Assembly of God on Chamblee-Dunwoody Road, with additional parking next door. Shuttle vans went back and forth to set. The Locations department had also struck deals with various neighbors near the house where they were shooting. Craft services were set up on a nearby driveway.

Freeman had arrived and was at base camp in his trailer with hair and makeup. Peterson and Awa were inside the house. Awa, the 2nd 2nd AD, managed the babies who played Archie's granddaughter. Twins have been used in scenes with babies and young children for decades as an effective way to work within labor rules, and state and federal laws. Archie would spend time with his granddaughter in scenes before and after the trip. One scene preceded the trip to Vegas. The other took place months after Archie returns. That meant the baby had to appear older.

The Costume department had matching clothes for each set of twins. They also had pre-fit Michael Ealy, the actor playing Archie's son, and the actress playing his wife. They fit Freeman's stand in as well. His job didn't normally put him on camera. As a stand in, he filled in for camera tests when they set up a scene. This was the exception because it would be his legs and feet coming out of the window rather than Freeman's. He looked enough like the actor that it was possible he could end up on camera and no one would be the wiser.

Peterson was going through paperwork inside the house when she learned about Turteltaub's idea of a street hockey game. She looked at the list of scheduled background actors for the scene, and noted, in Peterson fashion, that none were children. This was a quiet neighborhood. A male jogger and a jogging mom pushing strollers were planned. Another neighbor would be there with a dog. But no kids, aside from the babies, and they couldn't play hockey. If that was something the director wanted to pull off, she needed to make some changes.

Some semblance of normalcy, or at least what passed for it, set in on Mailing Avenue. Even Kamishin and Badalato, who had less sleep than anyone in the past week, looked rested. Having most of the crew on location in Atlanta amounted to a built-in transition for the bullpen crew. There was time to adapt, instead of going from relative quiet to full on-site production with crew, cast, extras, catering, overflow parking and portable toilets. It was an emotional luxury.

Planned, sit-down meetings, once held in Badalato's office, had ended in prep. Instead there were more frequent informal discussions about the day and week ahead. Generally that involved Kamishin standing in the bullpen between the desks of Stephens and the APOC, the rest of the bullpen listening. Topics rolled through quickly and easily.

There had been an issue involving someone in De Niro's entourage, one of the office PAs offered. The rate he had been paid was different from the one he thought was due. The APOC said it appeared to be a question of whether the minimum number of hours had been worked. "I already talked to Billy about it," Kamishin replied. "I'm just going to email it to Jeremiah." The person who had the pay issue was below the line. But since he worked for someone above the line, Samuels could deal with it.

Other questions left over from Friday had to do with boundaries or potential overstepping. The one most talked about was the young woman hired as a PA who became concierge. After the larger crew had left for Las Vegas she moved into an unused office without asking anyone if it was okay. They laughed about it at first. "We have a Celebrity PA!" "A Celebrity concierge!"

But instead of her attitude receding with time it seemed to expand. She asked bullpen crew to "take a message" and said other things perceived as condescending. It was humorous to some degree since almost everyone in the bullpen had more experience and was higher on the food chain. But there was no sign of the attitude abating, either. After the larger crew went to Las Vegas, she came into the Atlanta bullpen and announced she was taking a desk and switching it with a banquet table. Someone was with her to help carry it, and they lifted the desk and took it out as the others looked on, amused. They didn't mind except that she hadn't asked anyone if it was okay.

It was the job of the bullpen to help the departments. The Production department was the hub of the wheel, to recall Badalato's description. But there were a lot of times people wanted something they didn't need or hadn't negotiated. The challenge was giving crew what they could while holding the line. Some chotchke or another had been dropped off. Someone came in, picked it up off the table, and left. Kamishin looked irritated for a second, a facial expression that prompted laughs.

But she wasn't kidding. "It's the entitlement that gets to me," said Kamishin. This was her pet peeve, and she had mentioned it before. It was one thing to ask for a T-shirt or Tervis Tumbler, like the ones that had been dropped off by the Atlanta Film Commission, but another to assume it was theirs for the taking. "Just ask," she said. "It's not that hard."

Jobst had come into the far side of the bullpen at some point in the conversation. The costume supervisor stood patiently near the desk of Jordan Anderson, two neatly wrapped bundles in her arm. The phone rang in the background. That was a constant during the day, but much less in the early morning, given it was three hours earlier on the West Coast.

"Mary Steenburgen's agent is on the phone," the PA offered. "Does she get an assistant in Atlanta?" "Absolutely," Kamishin said, heading out of the bullpen. "I'll take it in my office." The topic shifted to whether and who they had hired to be Steenburgen's assistant.

Jobst handed the bundles to Anderson, who was still tuned in to the larger bullpen conversation, which had turned to perks and other things needed to prepare for the major actors. The costume supervisor paid it no mind. "This needs to be on the first shuttle to set," she said. Anderson looked at her, nodded politely, and reached for the bundles before returning her gaze to the conversation. But Jobst held firm to the costumes, which meant Anderson was unable to grasp them well enough to put them on her desk. She looked back inquisitively.

"This needs to be on the next shuttle to set," Jobst repeated, this time more deliberately and with the slightest of tones. "It's for Morgan. It works today." That cracked Anderson up. Jobst laughed as she released her grip.

285

"Got it," Anderson grinned.

"It's two things," Jobst continued. "The second one is for the interior scene with Debbie and the baby. He wears something else when he gets picked up by Sam out front." Debbie, who had a single line in the movie, played the wife of Archie's son. The other costumes were already on site.

There was no doubt the costume packages would have been on the shuttle to set. Anderson was sharp and Jobst knew it. But Jobst wasn't leaving anything to chance. Freeman would wear the clothes on camera within hours and it was entirely too easy for the package to get lost.

That done, Jobst returned to the costume wing. Dayna Pink had received a call from Rake that they were adding 25 background actors to the 1955 scene, which meant they needed to dress them in period attire. The location had changed from a corner to one in the middle of the street block. Just as Set Decorating had to manage that change, so did Costumes. Instead of needing five extras milling around in the store, they would need people outside on the street, as well.

It was an expensive proposition. As a new production town, it wasn't as if Atlanta had a costume company with a back room dedicated to quality mid-century clothing. Yet they needed to dress background actors like they were shooting a crowd scene in "I Love Lucy."

It wasn't just the clothes either. The scene had not needed pre-fits before, but with that many additional people there was no other way around it. There was no way to do all of that on the existing budget. So Pink asked Samuels for more money. It didn't go well.

The next shuttle left with Freeman's clothes and a number of items. There was a big envelope for Bomba from the art director. There was a more detailed memo about costumes needed for the 1955 scene. Also in the mix were images of the Las Vegas skyline for Hennings' review and ultimately Turteltaub's. The images would be turned into the giant faux skyline, the backdrop of the city that would hang behind the windows of penthouse sets. There was also something for Samuels to sign. The shuttle, along with two people going to set, passed another one returning to Mailing Avenue.

Benjamin-Creel had awoken suddenly that morning, sitting bolt upright in his bed. He'd missed something. Or was he dreaming? His mind raced to sort it out. License plates! They were shooting a scene with cars and they needed special plates. License plates used on screen aren't just floating around. Filmmakers must use numbers that have been retired. He had faux tags in the prop truck but it wasn't just any state he needed. This scene took place in New Jersey.

Benjamin-Creel jumped up and as he got ready for work he called Rice. He was certain the tags were on his to-do list, not hers. But she could verify that the props truck lacked tags from the Garden State. His fear confirmed, his next call was to another prop master working in Atlanta. Within an hour Benjamin-Creel had rustled up a couple of plates, which he then used to create others, 18 in all. They shouldn't need that many but with Turteltaub you never knew. Then he headed to set.

When Benjamin-Creel pulled up with the license plates, Rice filled him in on the new idea: Turteltaub wanted a street hockey game. He asked if she was kidding but she assured him she wasn't. The prop master shrugged and said he would go get equipment for the game. He asked if she needed anything else. "Not until he thinks of something else," she said.

Rice had Archie's pillbox, his gold watch, a burp cloth and a realistic looking baby doll. She also had a record player with 45s for a scene where Archie danced with his grandchild. All that was left was to mix up a batch of baby spit-up, but she needed to consult with Awa. Did the babies have allergies? Rice didn't want to put any ingredients in that could set off an allergic reaction. Awa went to check with the parents.

The swing set scene was ready to go in the backyard. Monitors showed a swing set and the back of a nice home on a beautiful fall day. In reality, the temperatures of the early morning hadn't improved much. Crew huddled near two oversized outdoor heaters. Set up 20 feet apart, they were noisy and would have to be cut off when they started shooting.

It was chilly enough that when Freeman emerged he headed right to the heater closest to the swing. Crew saw him coming and started to shift to the second heater farther away. But he told them to stay. "It's too damn cold for me to have a heater to myself," he said.

The first half of the scene would show Archie's side of a phone conversation with Billy after they returned from the trip when he was sitting by himself with the baby. Moviegoers would see a change since his trip. Archie had healed even more from the stroke and was alone with his granddaughter, something his overprotective son had limited beforehand.

Turteltaub didn't leave the actor standing by the heater for long. Rake had already radioed for one of the babies and they were in position. They cut off the heaters and Rake called camera commands. Freeman showed no evidence of his lingering cold or the outside temperature, which had crew shivering within a minute of losing the heat. Archie played with the baby while starting his half of the phone conversation with Michael Douglas's character.

"Oh shit, Billy. Prostate?" said Freeman, rocking the baby.

"Cut," said Turteltaub, who circled around taking it all in. He walked closer to the actor.

"This time a little more concern on 'prostate,'" he said.

Freeman nodded. Turteltaub turned back to the monitors to do it again, this time with a little more intensity. Moviegoers would hear the other end of the conversation, which would be Billy responding that his prostate had nothing to do with it.

There was no street hockey game when it came time to shoot the getaway scene, where Sam whisks Archie away for the weekend when his son isn't looking. Turteltaub had let it go when he realized it was too difficult to pull off effectively. Benjamin-Creel, who had purchased street hockey equipment by the time word came back that it was no longer on the drawing board, returned it.

Meanwhile, Kevin Kline and Morgan Freeman livened up the scene. Instead of the two characters just taking off, Kline went into a Keystone Cops routine, and Freeman picked up on it. It's always a good sign when the crew laughs.

Lee Siler was in his windowless office on Mailing Avenue placing an order for a clear windshield. As transportation coordinator on *Last Vegas* he oversaw all aspects of the Transportation department as well as picture cars. The short description of the job was moving cast, crew and equipment but there was a lot underneath that. It was hiring and managing drivers, getting the vehicles to be used, scheduling shuttles or otherwise getting cast and crew where they needed to be. The main actors had private drivers, but it was a large cast. Then there was organizing vehicles to be used on location, like costume and makeup trailers, star trailers and honey wagons, which are mobile bathrooms, or sometimes trailers in general.

Managing picture cars wasn't something he regularly did in managing the department. Siler had crew he hired to wrangle vehicles. But a picture car wrangler wasn't in the budget of *Last Vegas*, so Siler was managing it in Atlanta, as his counterpart had in Las Vegas.

"Wrangle" was another term that dated back to the early days of the movie industry. It had started as a term for someone who handled horses and other animals in early Westerns. Gradually it came to be used as a term for anyone corralling anything on a movie, including cars.

Part of wrangling picture cars was planning for special needs. A scene scheduled in a couple of weeks with all five of the main actors involved a minivan in the midst of a traffic jam. Since most windshields on cars today are tinted or coated, Siler was in the process of ordering a clear one that a camera could see through. It was a specialty item from a company in Los Angeles, which would ship it to Atlanta. Then he would hire someone local to install it. And that was just one of the cars he needed for the scene.

Siler was based in Charleston, S.C., but knew his way around Atlanta and was a logical choice for the *Last Vegas* job. He had worked with Samuels and Badalato on *Dear John* and *The Conspirator*. The first was shot in both North and South Carolina, the second in Savannah, Ga.

The first movie he worked on, *Brainstorm* (1983), was filmed in various locations in North Carolina. It starred Christopher Walken and Natalie Wood, and it turned out to be her last movie. He was 17 at the time and the money was good. The next movie, the one that hooked him, was *Firestarter* (1984.) Written by Stephen King and produced by Frank Capra Jr., it launched a young actress named Drew Barrymore. He drove her trailer. "She was seven or eight at the time," he said. "She was a brat. I used to hold her down and thump her on the head."

Firestarter is the movie that brought Dino De Laurentiis to North Carolina but the studio he founded is why he's remembered there. He remained involved with the studio until 1990, which became EUE/ Screen Gems in 1996. It wasn't the first one in the state but it did put it on the map as a production center.

Some believe the 1983 negotiations for his business are the first time government incentives of any magnitude were offered to lure a movie company. Officials in South Carolina swooped in near the end of the year and tried to steal him away from their northern neighbor. They offered to issue $1 million in industrial revenue bonds and sell him County Hall, a former rice plantation used as an auditorium in Charleston. De Laurentiis declined, as history shows. But he was open about the savings of making a movie somewhere other than California. He estimated making a movie in North Carolina amounted to a savings of between one-third and one-half.

New interest in the state meant steady work for a young Siler, even as it came with a significant pay drop. That's when he learned the difference between a union and non-union salary. Decades later, a big part of his job was knowing union rules and managing Teamsters. Siler said he wasn't sure how much he liked the job. He probably wouldn't recommend the job he had now to a college-educated young person.

"It doesn't lend itself to stability," he explained. He cited the nomadic lifestyle as the reason he got married later in life. It was a similar sentiment expressed by several middle-aged crew, including Rake. Traveling had been fun as a younger person, but it got harder with a spouse and kids at home. "If I were a producer I'd probably like it," he added.

He headed out to the front of Mailing Avenue to check something on one of the shuttles. He found Benjamin-Creel standing in front of Mailing Avenue with coffee and a cigar. The prop master was taking a break. He filled Siler in on a crazy day. Then they shifted to work ahead.

"What do you know about the cabs?" Benjamin-Creel asked.

"I'm going to get them to set and that's all I can do," said Siler. There were five taxis in the scene. He also needed a shuttle bus and a billboard truck. That required creating a large mobile advertisement. Billboard trucks were plentiful in Las Vegas but not in Atlanta. Siler planned to use a stakebed truck and the Art department would create the artwork advertisement. They would also use extras cars, perhaps six or seven.

There was a special look to Vegas taxis, Benjamin-Creel said. Siler nodded. The tops had a distinctive triangle shape, so they need those in particular. The advertisements had to be related to Vegas. If they were real, as in product placement, they would come cleared. Otherwise, they had to be fake ads that looked real, which took the work of the graphics person.

"I've told them for several weeks that we needed to get skins and tops for the cabs," Siler responded. "I still don't know what they're doing."

Benjamin-Creel noted the Las Vegas traffic jam scene was two weeks away. He could handle the cab tops. He would reach out to someone in Vegas and have the tops shipped in. The Art department could pick it up from there.

Just inside the door the Art department was dealing with entirely new work. A big shift had occurred at the location where they planned the 1955 scene. Someone had messed up on the locations side and booked something on a street where traffic couldn't be stopped. The discovery was made after construction crew built a wall inside the one location and painted part of it.

The good news was that traffic on a nearby cross street could be stopped. Better still, there was storefront space for lease but it was in the middle of row of shops. For the outdoor shot, the corner was big enough to get a wide angle. With this, the Set Dec department had to decorate the facades of the neighbors to be 1950s era to get a similar exterior shot.

All departments steadily bobbed and weaved with minor shifts. But big changes took more effort. The Art department, via the Construction department and Henery, had crew at work and a bigger budget to absorb the 1955 sidewalk. But the Costume department needed more money to keep up. Though Samuels had initially balked at increasing the costume budget to cover the added costs of the 1955 scene, he had come around.

That's when the real work began for the Costume department. They turned to Western Costume Co., the storied operation in Los Angeles celebrating its centennial year, for the vintage clothes. The company featured 120,000 square feet of space, offices and three main warehouses. Costumes hung on eight miles of pipe, as well as on walls, accessories on walls or in dressers or drawers or cabinets. They had somewhere between 3.5 million and 5 million items, no one could say for sure how many and no one was going to count. There were entire walls of hats, pairs of shoes and boots. Every size was represented as well as every era in history. There were enough military uniforms to dress an army, or even a couple of them. The Civil War had both Union and Confederate wear, with intense detail that focused on accuracy down to the number of buttons worn. Western Costumes also featured a host of skilled employees, from seamstresses and ager-dyers to milliners. It even had a library.

Pink gave Jobst photos of things she liked and descriptions of the looks she wanted. The clothes had to be seasonal and there were colors to be considered. The clothes had to reflect fashion appropriate for a Brooklyn street of that time period. Jobst worked with extras casting on the size breakdown, the male/female breakdown, and ages of the people they needed to dress.

Jobst reached out to Bobi Garland, director of research at Western Costume, who both women had worked with over the years. Garland was a huge help. She worked with them via photos and telephone to approve all the looks before they were shipped to Atlanta. The four shipping crates arrived within the week. One still had its $758 shipping bill attached.

The delivery arrived while Jobst was organizing the department's move to location for the large nightclub scenes, which they were shooting over the next two days. While the department always had a presence on set -- the designer was usually there, as well as the key costumer -- the supervisor often stayed back on Mailing Avenue to prepare for the scenes ahead. Bigger efforts, like the ones in the nightclub, required that the department set up on location.

The Transportation department delivered to Mailing Avenue both a cube truck and an 18-wheel trailer designed for costumes. The cube truck contained racks and clothes, supplies for the office and assorted boxes. The trailer had the actors' closets and specialty items. The trailer looked brand new, with racks and shelves designed for clothes, a dressing room and a small office with desks on one end. It also had a washer and dryer and various outlets for ironing or a sewing machine or anything else.

Jobst made effort to think each bit of costume work through. The morning of the nightclub scenes would be incredibly busy with managing the scenes they were shooting. De Niro, Douglas, Freeman and Kline were working that day, as were most of the second tier of actors and hundreds of extras. But by the afternoon, most of them would be covered or at least in a holding pattern. She scheduled pre-fits for the 1955 background actors in the afternoon.

Badalato went to the sound stages to meet with Henery. The back warehouses were alive with the activity of a construction site. But it felt much different than a building going up in a city. It was a different flow, finish work happening at the same time new walls were being built. There was also a slight contrast to the olfactory senses. It smelled of sawdust and paint and varnish with an occasional whiff of gas or oil or something industrial, rather than the other way around.

It sounded different, too. There was hammering and intermittent 15-second buzz-grind of saws working, air compressors coming on and off with various tools, the occasional loud mechanized vacuum sucking dirty air outside. The sounds scattered across 10,000 square feet of space and converged in a sensory cloud. But there was no shouting, no dominant overpowering sounds like a battering ram or steel beams or plates hitting the ground or each other.

Construction crew and artisans, almost all of them men, were dispersed around the two warehouse spaces, most in the larger space that housed the giant penthouse set. A woman, the scenic artist, worked in the back corner, surrounded by dozens of pieces of 4x8 plywood separated by inches and drying in racks. She leaned over a piece of plywood, paint brush or other implement in hand, mottling its surface and turning lumber into faux marble for the penthouse set. From a distance the wood looked like crystalline limestone.

The large warehouse space had been almost empty when Badalato left a month earlier. Now the two-floor penthouse rose high in the air, perhaps two-thirds of it constructed. The first floor was seven feet off the floor, two staircases leading up about 70 feet apart. Walls were in place on the first floor, a grand, interior staircase in the middle of the largest set, which led to a second floor. Sets would be built there, but it was largely empty. There was flooring in half of it, and grids set up that would hold lighting, along with other mechanical elements and electrical junction areas.

As in Las Vegas, Turteltaub and Rake had planned location work on the front end. For the next couple of weeks, they would be shooting around Atlanta. That provided a cushion of time, but was it enough? It wasn't as if it all had to be done then. There were 21 days, weekends included, until the production moved to Mailing Avenue full time for the remainder of principal photography. But Badalato would prefer they not work weekends as a rule, given it was much more costly.

Badalato found Henery standing over architectural drawings at the oversized drafting surface. It was more than a drafting table, although he had one of those in the front room of his office as well. This one was 8x8, standing level, with perhaps a dozen drawings on it. It was readily available to anyone who wanted to look.

The construction manager was poring over something on the page and turned his attention to the UPM. It felt amiable but Badalato got to the point quickly. How were things going? Was everything on schedule?

Henery said it was but it was going to be close. "It's always been an ambitious schedule," he said. The UPM nodded. It was a reminder of sorts. That word -- ambitious -- had been used several times with regard to the

293

sound stages, starting when they first talked about details. It went back further than that, really, to when Samuels and Badalato were crafting the budget. How far could they cut costs and still get it done quickly and safely? Almost everything about the production was "ambitious."

Henery said he wasn't going to sugarcoat it. There were challenges. He had hired more workers for the week and would hire still more. Even then overtime was likely. The good news was obvious but that didn't make it any less relevant: They didn't need all the sets at the same time, just the ones they were shooting on. The work could be staggered.

It was the penthouse that demanded the most not just in size, but layers. It had multiple rooms and sets. Badalato assured him he would get whatever he needed and asked to be kept closely apprised of progress. Henery nodded of course.

Badalato reflected on the exchange as he walked back to the bullpen. "That would be an example of 'bad news early,'" he said, recalling his admonishment to Stephens and other crew at the start of prep. He respected Henery for it. He had a very big job and he wasn't panicked. The situation was handled, but he wasn't going to mislead anybody either. Henery had a quiet way about him. He'd got a point across in subtle fashion that said, 'You wanted ambitious, you got ambitious.'

Badalato closed his office door as soon as he got back to his office to call Samuels.

The challenge over shipping mishaps had been draining, particularly on Kamishin. It had also proved the importance of the Production department, even if few people realized it. The Production department was seen as the administrative arm, boring compared to working on set. It was their job to handle the paperwork, keep controls on money and do it seamlessly. But it was far more extensive. The Production department had its hand in everything, large and small.

It wasn't happenstance that Kamishin had caught the shipping problem early. They were following every detail. Without that level of commitment, it was entirely possible hours would have passed before anyone knew there was a problem, much less figured out a solution. They knew the consequences and cost of a missed shooting day, which is what no sound equipment would have meant, and took it personally. A missed shooting day would have been expensive. It was an insurance claim, since delays were indemnified, but given that the schedule was locked in it was hugely problematic.

It was unlikely the creative producers or the studio were aware of the effort. If Samuels had told them anything, it was probably that some equipment had been damaged in the move and had been stopped in process. A claim against the shipping company by members of the crew was expected.

As it was, the damage to the sound and video playback equipment was significant. Fortunately, the equipment needed on set could still be used, although there were dents and other signs of impact. Both the Sound department and the video assist had damaged equipment, although it worst for Sound. The good news is that it hadn't delayed production. Now that a couple of days had passed, the Production department was dealing with insurance claims. There was paperwork and the shipping company had been in touch to say it was sending an investigator.

The pace and tone of life in the bullpen felt more serious with them shooting, a noticeable shift from prep. Foot traffic in and out of the bullpen, even with most of the crew on the location, was heavy enough that people who worked there no longer looked up. The office even felt smaller. More things were happening with less time to handle them, which meant more tension.

In the golden era of Hollywood, the movie lot was often referred to as "the circus" and the term is still used occasionally. The next location, a strip shopping center on Chamblee Tucker Road on the outskirts of the city, showed why. It looked like a traveling show was in town for the next two days and nights.

The production had leased the Velvet Room, a large nightclub that anchored the shopping center, which they were using to recreate Haze, an Aria nightclub. The Location department had also negotiated parking and adjacent space in securing the place for use, and they were using it. The production took up more than half of the shopping center parking lot while other businesses continued to operate. Departments were set up around the shopping center as well as behind it. Care and feeding would take place in an adjacent lot behind the center where they had leased space for two tents for hair and makeup, extras holding, some costumes. Both tents had full power, as did catering, which had space set up to feed people.

The Transportation department began moving in the day before. It always took organization, but this was akin to laying out the lot of a moving show in the old days. There were department trucks and trailers, star trailers, office trailers and a honey wagon. Large tents were set up behind the shopping center on an adjacent site for extras holding, make-up and catering. There was limited area given the number of people involved. All the major actors were working, save Steenburgen, and most of the next tier of actors, along with 375 extras the first day and 235 the next.

It had been up to Bomba and the Art department, specifically Cassidy and Set Dec, to make the Velvet Room the type of club that could command $1,800 for a choice table in Las Vegas. The upgrades they put in place were subtle, velvet ropes for the line of patrons, upgraded couches and table for the scene with the main actors. It also helped that it was dark inside.

Shooting a nightclub scene presented technical challenges. There was added labor for the scenes, audio and video playback. House technicians would work club lighting. A music operator would cue tunes between shots, which kept nightclub background actors dancing to the same rhythm. Special effects people were there to create "atmosphere," a smoky haze to fill the bar.

The costume supervisor arrived at 4:30 a.m., well ahead of her call time, and began organizing two different offices. One would be in a red-walled storefront in the shopping center for the department that would serve as the main office and the other was in the costume trailer. It featured a "Wardrobe" sign. The trailer was reserved for actors only. The entrance of the costume truck read: "EXTRA/BG DO NOT ENTER."

Two costumers soon arrived and before long the cube truck had been emptied of the racks of clothing, boxes of shoes and assorted belts, scarves and skinny ties. The storefront became an office with banquet style tables as workstations, partitions for a changing area. It was a microcosm of Jobst's kit from the main office and contained everything they needed, from shears to sewing machines, safety pins to buttons, and thread.

More than a dozen costume racks were organized in sections. Most of the racks were filled with contemporary party clothes, separated by genre. Noticeable in the racks were more expensive clothing for more glamorous nightlife, some frocks more sparkly and Vegas-like than others. They also held more regular nightclub clothes. Two of the racks contained 1955-era clothes for pre-fits scheduled late in the afternoon.

Pink arrived and she and Jobst went to the costume trailer. The four top actors who were working that day were the obvious priority. By now, four weeks into principal photography, the machinery around them was in place. De Niro, Douglas and Freeman all had dedicated costumers as part of their deals. The production assigned costumers to assist Kline and Steenburgen.

Pink paid attention to all of the actors with focus on the leads. But she was always in close contact with Jobst, who ran the department. Organization was key, but so was maintenance. Any number of circumstances could arise that required attention. Garments could be damaged, actors could gain or lose weight and necessitate alterations, but whatever it was they had to be ready.

At the same time, the main actors were just 10 percent of a nearly 50-person cast. The upcoming scenes included a lot of the rest of them, like Ferrara and Romany Malco, who played the concierge, Lonnie. It also included actors April Billingsley and Michael Beasley. He played a bouncer amid "the biggest and baddest" of security guards. Billingsley's character flirted with Sam in the nightclub as well as in a later scene.

Then there were the specialty background actors, who went through hair and makeup and then costumes on an organized and staggered basis. All of them had been pre-fit but needed to be checked and tweaked by the Costume department. It started with the hot girls and GoGo dancers, and one "scantily clad" girl who needed attention. Most of them needed to be camera ready at 7 a.m. but that would just be the start. There were 10 hot guys, 40 regular guys, 20 hot girls, six GoGo dancers, five bartenders, five barbacks. Then there were the three women dedicated to the bachelorette party, who would interact with Douglas, Freeman and Kline. Those women required a more wholesome look.

The overall look of the larger group of extras was also important. Turteltaub had stressed it more than once: The background actors needed a higher end look to be authentic, given high-dollar tables. The Costume, Hair and Makeup departments did their parts. But as the day progressed it became clear not all of them fit the bill. The challenge of turning Georgia extras into Las Vegas partygoers, identified in prep by the 2nd AD Peterson, was playing out in real time. This group looked like they had come from Georgia, more ballcaps and boots, longer hair and fewer collars. The Costume department helped with that but it was still noticeable. They would make a change going forward if needed, perhaps hiring a different extras casting firm.

Transportation had organized the star trailers in a line perpendicular to the entrance of the Velvet Room. Douglas, Freeman and Kline each had makeup calls at 7:30 a.m. and ready times at 8:30. De Niro, who was in two scenes, had a 10:30 a.m. call.

De Niro's trailer was first, a stainless steel monster that he brought himself, or rather his people did. The other main actors were in traditional, leased star trailers. They were nice, with kitchen and bedroom and satellite hookups for the big flat-screen televisions, and a hair and makeup room with separate entrance on one end. They also could have brought their own trailers if they'd wanted to but this was easier. The production covered the cost and reimbursed De Niro his share as part of the contract.

The names of the characters the actors played, written on blue paint tape, were on the outsides of their assigned trailer. It was standard operating procedure on any movie on location to identify the space by character rather than actor. That way a passerby who saw "Billy" or "Archie" would have no way of knowing it was occupied by Michael Douglas or Morgan Freeman. De Niro's motor coach needed no label.

Then there were split trailers, each with two units, for the next tier of actors. The trailers were comfortable and had private bathrooms, if smaller. Turteltaub and various producers likewise had split trailers, which were set up as offices. There was also a four-pack, a trailer with four smaller spaces for any overflow needs.

Slowly it pulled together, the nightclub lights and sound, the regular movie production lights and sound and the crew in various places. They were again piping in "atmosphere," odorous smoke to make the bar more authentic. The ADs organized the background actors in groups with animal names. The walkies were alive with production assistants guarding over a group of giraffes, or tigers, and so forth. It made it easier to know who had been where in the scene. It also prevented hurt feelings, since it was possible they were divided by groups based on perceived attractiveness.

The scene had Billy, Archie and Sam going out to Haze. It was a popular, trendy club and a rare night out for the retirement aged heroes. But Paddy, still angry at Billy, opted out for the night. When he shows up, unexpectedly, he sees his guys getting mistreated by a drunk and obnoxious young man. Paddy comes to their defense in the scene, just as the young Paddy does in the opening scene when they are kids. He slugs the young guy, played by Ferrara. It wasn't *Godfather* or *Raging Bull* but it was still De Niro taking a swing, which made for an interesting day's work. Ferrara said if he had to get beat up in a scene, De Niro was his first choice.

As a rule, the actors didn't do a lot of rehearsing together. De Niro, in particular, liked to work into his dialogue. The Haze nightclub scene was a little different with the punch. It was choreographed and they walked through it. The scuffle would start when Dean, played by Ferrara, goes after Sam in the bar. Two stunt doubles were there, one each for the characters Dean and Sam. As the punch thrower, Paddy, or De Niro, didn't need a stunt double, although one was available.

There was some wait between the rehearsal and the set up and the actors were standing off to the side talking. No one was sure who started snapping their fingers first, but they burst into a scene from *West Side Story* in perfect time.

"When you're a Jet, You're a Jet all the way From your first cigarette To your last dyin' day."

They were all in it, De Niro and Kline the leads. All four of them, even De Niro, singing away! He wasn't a natural singer but he held his own. Crew, producers, Turteltaub, anyone nearby was slack-jawed as it continued.

"When you're a Jet, If the spit hits the fan, You got brothers around, You're a family man!"

When they finished spontaneous applause broke out. The actors knew the song for different reasons. De Niro's character on *Analyze That* sang *West Side Story* songs. He and Kline also had performed it together, in 2002, as part of a fundraiser. Morgan Freeman was in a stage version of *West Side Story* at the Pacific Arts Theater in Oakland in 1963 when he was 26. Also, Freeman and Rita Moreno, who famously played Anita in the 1961 movie, had worked together on the Electric Company and maintained a friendship. Michael Douglas was also acquainted with Moreno although his executive assistant, Allen Burry said he never performed in the classic.

"Places." Then it was back to business, each of them to their colored tape markers on the floor.

CHAPTER FIFETEEN
Shoot Week 5
Nov. 18-23
Days 19, 20, 21

THERE WAS A GOOD REASON the Art department, and most departments, worked well in advance. Time was a buffer between a snag and a full-fledged problem. The location for the opening scene of the movie was a case in point.

A lot of effort had gone into locating the right place to shoot the 1955 storefront. The scenes, one interior and one exterior, would establish the characters and their relationship for the rest of the movie. Turteltaub's first inclination was to go well out of town but he changed his mind in favor of location at the intersection of Boulevard and Glenwood in Southeast Atlanta.

The Art department was given the go-ahead and the keys and went to work. The assistant art director took measurements of the property and used his design software to layout "Bissel's," the name they'd given the 1955 corner store. The drawing contained more than just base measurements. It reflected a false wall to be built along with the location, where the soda fountain and built-ins would be, and other architectural requirements.

Set Decorating started at the ground level. The place was modern-day so they made changes to reflect the time period they were portraying. Cassidy added flooring squares like the ones used in the 1950s, an old-style ceiling, and a false wall to block a portion of the structure that gave away its real age.

Then the Art department learned there was a problem with the location. While city officials did what they could to accommodate the movie industry, there were some roads it deemed too busy to shut down. Boulevard was not one it would stop in the name of art. Given the scene required moving, vintage vehicles, they needed a street where traffic could be regulated. Without the ability to turn the exterior roadway into an active version of 1955, the building at the intersection was useless to them.

This was one of the more irritating mistakes because of how long it escaped notice. Typically a director wouldn't even be shown a property that couldn't meet the requirements of the scene. It was assumed that permits could be obtained or else they wouldn't have looked at it to begin with. But there was time to fix it and the Locations department redeemed itself quickly.

They came up with an alternative about 100 yards away at 487 Edgewood Ave. It wasn't a corner store, as called for in the script, but in its favor, traffic could be controlled. The Art department began anew with physical prep to the building. The new location needed the same changes as the first building - - different flooring and ceilings circa 1955.

The place also required a false wall, this one to block off the back and side of the store. It needed molding to match older areas and different paint. They selected a light green shade, which was a popular color in that era and light enough for the cinematographer, who could be sensitive.

But there was a bigger, more time-consuming issue because of the change. The first location had the benefit of being a corner store with a wide storefront. They could shoot the entire sidewalk and the exterior scene, which had the young actors running, in front of the store. The new location was in a row of stores. To make it work for the exterior shot, the Art department had to turn all the visible storefronts into something from six-plus decades earlier.

They invented commercial neighbors circa 1955 Brooklyn for the shops on either side of 487 Edgewood. The facades of "Goldblatt's Hardware" and "Finkel's Bicycles" were designed and drawn with distinct personality. The company that offered large lots of vintage materials for lease had other content. But there were plenty of other details.

Other storefronts on either side of Goldblatt's and Finkel's needed modifications. The storefronts across the street were included, since the cameras used to shoot the interior scene would look out to the street. It had a present-day look but they also checked to see what was reflected in the window. It was easy for a camera to inadvertently pick up an unintended image from present day. In some cases it was a matter of covering existing signage but other times it was architectural. Cassidy had awnings, popular in the 1950s, installed in front of several of the stores, including the one across the street. Different types of signs were affixed to the buildings, including heavy use of "shingles," perpendicular signage also used heavily in the period.

Every bit of it had been designed with awareness to a larger canvas. It would look natural but there wasn't anything organic about it. Cassidy used different types and colors with the awnings and the signs to distinguish the shops from each other visually. At the same time, they were staggered in a way to work in a long shot. One sign partially blocking another would stop the eye where these fit without being something anyone would pick up on screen.

All of that had happened before Cassidy pulled up to build out the set Saturday morning. The building was near the Martin Luther King Jr. national historic site, which included the boyhood home of the civil rights leader, his tomb, the Ebenezer Baptist Church and a large visitor's center. Working on a weekend meant no rush hour traffic. The early morning meant abundant parking for crew, at least until visitors started arriving to see the national site nearby or to otherwise shop the neighborhood.

Now sporting a full beard, he wore a warm hat and a buttoned-up coat. Various crew arrived within minutes, including an eager PA, armed with a gallon of Starbucks coffee and a dozen pastries. Within minutes nine crew arrived. They got to work quickly. First on the list was getting the giant soda fountain in place, since it would anchor the back.

The Set Decorating department's Atlanta-based buyer, who had searched for things starting early in prep, had kept her eye out for an old-style soda fountain counter. It was a long shot, but given her knowledge of Georgia's thrift and consignment stores, not impossible. In the end it had been designed by the Art department and built by the Construction department. The counter replicated others of that era and was large, high and wide. It came in heavy pieces and took three men 20 minutes to get it inside.

Bomba arrived a short time later. Cassidy was outside directing traffic and the order of things being unloaded. They moved bigger objects first, then furniture and large set pieces. Signage and other unique items came in next, then boxes of things that would fill the shelves. The volume alone was overwhelming, a thought that brought a shrug from Cassidy. "In some ways this is the easiest part of what we do," he said. "Now we just put all the pieces together."

Bomba and Cassidy, the set dressers and other Art department people spread out around the place. Gradually, over the next few hours, they unpacked 1955. Giant shelving units took up the right side of the set, then a wooden checkout counter was brought in, and other furniture from there, all before they could unload the boxes of vintage material that contained everything from stacks of postcards to boxes of Corn Flakes.

There were still small touches, like a roll of brown wrapping paper affixed to the checkout counter, a standard feature in small stores of the era to package goods for costumers. Bissel's had to be typical of other old style corner stores of the day, particularly in New York, which supplied goods for every family need. That included liquor, a fact they confirmed in prep.

A bottle of whiskey was a central part of the opening scene, and the prop would reappear several times in the movie. Earlier in the week Lipp and other Art department crew had taken two crates of whiskey-type bottles and affixed labels that were created by the graphic designer. They unpacked them and placed them carefully on the shelves behind the counter.

Mid-afternoon Turteltaub and Rake appeared at the door. The director and 1st AD had stayed in Atlanta. With a short holiday work-week it hadn't made sense to fly to L.A. for the weekend. They went golfing on the day off and wanted to check progress. Rake relayed the weather report, which showed no rain in the forecast for Tuesday. The director walked around, taking it all in while the others continued to work as though they didn't know he was there, which they most certainly did. He asked a couple of questions, one about making it more Brooklyn-specific.

A short time later, a local couple stuck their heads in the door only to be turned away by the security guard. The director saw it and intervened, inviting them in for a brief tour. It surprised everyone, including the locals, who looked delighted as they walked around the room. The tour was noteworthy to crew because it showed what Turteltaub thought of the work. He didn't say it out loud but he was obviously pleased with their effort. When the stunned couple left they thanked the director mightily.

"What just happened?" the man said as the couple walked away. "That was like walking into a time machine," she agreed.

Turteltaub and Rake left a short time later. Rake would drop the director at the Ritz Carlton before returning to his short-term rental in Virginia Highlands.

Cassidy and Bomba and the rest of the crew had several more hours of work but gradually it was finished. Exterior decorations would have to wait until they returned early Tuesday morning ahead of shooting. A security guard would be on site full time until then.

Each of the young actors, and their guardians, were flown in Sunday. All traveled first class. Three of them came from Los Angeles. The young man who would play De Niro's character came from Philadelphia; Freeman's counterpart was from White Plains, N.Y. Danny the Greaser, played by Stephen Scarpulla, flew in from New York City. He was older so no guardian was needed.

The actors also stayed at the Ritz Carlton. They were in town three nights, limo service taking them to and from the airport on either end, while transportation delivered them to rehearsal and to set. A studio teacher was on crew for Monday and Tuesday.

The Costume department had fittings for the child actors while they were in Las Vegas but the three greasers and Scarpulla, who played the bully in the 1955 scene, still needed fittings. The Costume department had them on the schedule for Monday.

The workweek began with that uniquely American feeling that Thanksgiving break would end it early. Around the country people often take a few extra days off, creating a slowdown across many business segments. That wasn't true of the movie production. No one asked for a day off. They had a full schedule or close to it.

The shooting schedule for the week -- Day 19, Day 20 and Day 21 -- was no lighter than any other, and the contingent of on-set crew was the same. Awareness that the week would end early was high but the break was coming at a good time. The crew on location looked tired for a Monday, as if two days of rest hadn't been enough.

The stress level was higher on Mailing Avenue. The holiday weekend meant fewer workdays to have everything ready before the full company would converge on site for the rest of principal photography, as Kamishin pointed out. Once they returned from the break, there would be three days before the entire company moved to the soundstages for the remainder of principal photography.

Any suggestion they might not be ready was to be taken seriously. Badalato had taken the heads-up from Henery to Samuels. 'Bad news early,' in their vernacular, meant getting ahead of it. This situation didn't have an answer as easy as yes or no. They called a meeting on the soundstages after wrap.

Turteltaub, Rake and various department heads, as well as Badalato and Samuels, moved briskly through a tour of the soundstages, reviewing progress of various sets. Bomba said his job was to recreate the Aria and that's what he was doing. Henery nodded and chewed gum. Turteltaub took it all in. The director's attitude seemed to be that while there was still a lot to be done it wasn't anything to be alarmed about.

Turteltaub zeroed in on the second floor. There were plans to complete more of it, but he didn't need it. They could finish what they had started on the second floor and eliminate the rest because he had plenty to work with. The meeting hadn't taken long.

Samuels and Badalato were clear they supported any overtime needed. What wasn't said was that they were still within the budget. They had figured the cost of building the giant Aria suite was about $650,000, the lion's share of the $1.42 million planned for construction, and it was all in line.

The soundstages bulged with workers, not that it had been short on them before. Henery looked at his clipboard as he got a count: 55 people were working at the moment, 53 men and two women. The number would remain in that ballpark for the next two weeks.

The construction coordinator was confident. The deadline he cared about was the one on the shooting schedule, and that worked in his favor. The whole company would move to the soundstages on Day 24 to spend two days shooting on the Binion's set. That meant he needed to have the Binion's set finished. The Aria penthouse set wasn't needed until Day 26, a Monday. That provided a cushion to finish the biggest set. He thought he could get it done by the weekend, which would be left for Set Decorating department to do its work. That wasn't ideal but they would do what was needed.

There were other construction limitations Henery had to navigate. The warehouse with the soundstages wasn't soundproof. Sound carried easily from the adjacent warehouse workshop as well as the next one. Once they began shooting on the soundstages noise had to be controlled. That complicated how he would shepherd the work through.

Jobst was dealing with the return of a $2,400 dress. Pink had spent a lot of time on the dresses to be worn by Mary Steenburgen. Not all of them made the cut. This one had been ordered from a German designer although the costume designer had ultimately decided to go with something else. That wasn't unusual but there were deadlines associated with returning them, which is why it was on her radar.

Then she prepared for the fittings scheduled later in the day. In addition to Scarpulla and the other greasers a number of specialty background actors were coming in. Some of them had elaborate costumes planned for the splashy Las Vegas funeral scene being shot the next week.

Each of the three days of work for the week had about two pages of script to cover. Monday involved nightclub scenes with extras shot at a bar in Midtown Atlanta. This was a different nightclub scene, one modeled after the Deuce nightclub at Aria. Tuesday they would move to Edgewood Avenue for the 1955 period scenes. Wednesday would be at Georgia World Congress Center, which would double as the Ft. Myers, Fla., airport.

Monday kicked off with a 7 a.m. call time at Vanquish, a nightclub at 1028 Peachtree Street near the intersection of 11th Street in Midtown Atlanta. This was the Peachtree Street in a city with more than a hundred Peachtree streets. It was also Midtown Atlanta, one of three urban centers that comprised the large city. Even on a holiday week Midtown was a traffic and logistical challenge.

The Locations department had secured a parking lot on Juniper Street behind Vanquish to park vehicles for working trucks. Base camp for other trucks and crew parking was on Spring Street, a location they would use again. Transportation ran a van back and forth between the two addresses well in advance of the 7 a.m. call time. Departments and catering were spread out in the parking lot and adjacent retail space.

Vanquish felt a little like Vegas, certainly more than most Atlanta nightclubs. It was ideal for the scenes that took place in Aria's Deuce Lounge. It had a décor that came with a lot of gold and red velvet. There were huge murals throughout the place, most of them featuring either women or tigers or both, with scrollwork over the top. The women were posed in sultry fashion and appeared to be naked without a full reveal. One prominent image had the perspective of looking down the top half of a body of a woman from above the head. The main bar also featured a woman, this one in a red dress, who sat in a chair above one tiger, another one off to the side. Slot machines were installed to ensure identification with Las Vegas.

The nightclub had large sitting areas alongside the central floor, and large bars in front and on the side. Bomba didn't want a big floor, as they had for the earlier nightclub scenes. These were more intimate scenes. He had screens built to make the space feel smaller. The design of the screens incorporated the scrollwork contained in the murals. They also spruced up the nightclub in subtle ways, replacing couch covers and adding chairs and lamps.

A plot point in *Last Vegas* was Kline's character's permission-to-cheat, which was granted by his wife. The main scene they were shooting at Vanquish was his pursuit of that goal. Sam's pals tell him his glasses make him look older, so he takes them off, hence mistaking the Madonna impersonator

306

for an attractive woman. The camera would get a blurry shot of her that could be edited in later to reflect what Sam was seeing.

Kline was there ahead of call, as had become normal for the actor. He stood off to the side of the club talking to Katrina Rice. She had the glasses he would wear -- or not wear -- in the scene. There were other props as well, like bar napkins, drinks and trays.

The actor and assistant prop master were friendly, something the ADs had noted and liked. It was their job to shepherd actors to and from their trailers to set or wherever they had them waiting. Kline could and had eluded handlers in an instant. But he liked Rice well enough that she almost always knew where he was, which had led to Rice being hailed on the walkie whenever someone needed Kline. She generally knew where De Niro was, too. The actor's assistant in Atlanta was provided by the production and new to him and he was doing a fine job. But Rice had helped him get up and running by advising on things that De Niro needed and liked.

Kline was the main character in the scene but it was Roger Bart who had the biggest acting burden. His day began with a 4:48 a.m. pickup before several hours of hair and makeup. The iconic rock star actress Madonna had many looks over her career. The one selected for the scene was her role in *Desperately Seeking Susan*. That 1985 film had Madonna playing a spirited New York City partier with a unique style of dress featuring lots of accessories, jewelry and ties and hair bow.

Bart's character wasn't Madonna but a middle-aged straight man who played her in a Vegas show, and that's exactly what he looked like. He was dressed similarly to the character except with more makeup. They also had him wearing nylon stockings, which he tugged and pulled at off camera like a little boy. The Atlanta-based female impersonators hired for the scene were infinitely more comfortable in ladies attire. The group included a passable Cher and an exquisite Marilyn Monroe. They seemed delighted to be there. At one point someone called for a group photo centered by Turteltaub, who happily obliged.

As the morning progressed, the space in Vanquish grew increasingly stuffy and grumbling among crew increased. To make the set more authentic they again created the hazy smoke called "atmosphere." This time there was less ventilation and it quickly thickened the air. With various crew nursing colds there was scattered coughing. Some worried it was the flu first seen in Las Vegas incubating its way back. And "atmosphere" didn't help.

Safety Bulletin #10 was attached to the call sheet, as it had been before. It was required under union rules and it stated requirements in operations. "Fumed and hydrolyzed chlorides were not to be used but cryogenic gases such as carbon dioxide and liquid nitrogen could be used with proper care."

The safety bulletins were one of the changes made in the wake of actor Vic Morrow and two children dying during filming of *Twilight Zone: The Movie* in 1982. The helicopter accident was covered widely, as was the trial and acquittal on involuntary manslaughter charges of director John Landis, the special effects coordinator, the production manager, an associate producer and the helicopter pilot. Live ammunition had been used in the scene, which disabled the aircraft, causing it to crash into the actors. Witnesses said Landis had instructed the pilot to go lower to get a better shot.

Landis, along with the production manager and the coordinator, also faced charges of violating California child labor laws. Neither of the children had ever worked on a movie. Their parents, Asian immigrants unfamiliar with movie industry operations, were on set after 6:30 p.m. without necessary permits or the supervision of a licensed teacher.

Landis admitted he had hired the children illegally. He reportedly offered to plead guilty to that charge if they would drop the manslaughter charges but they declined. He won.

The incident didn't seem to impact his career but that was the 1980s. Insurance, generally considered essential for any major movie production today, wasn't a factor then. Were the same thing to happen today it's unlikely any studio would immediately put Landis in a leadership role again, as happened then. But even if a studio wanted to hire a director whose choices led to a high-profile, avoidable on-set death, an underwriter might not be.

The positive changes to safety protocol that came of it stemmed from a joint union-management safety committee. It had been established before the incident but was broadened to include all unions and guilds. The group turned efforts to creating safety guidelines and standards that became the Safety Bulletins, which are periodically updated. Ironically, the guidelines are also credited with helping to entice insurance companies to do business with movie productions, which they had previously avoided. Detailing the rules, regulations and standards of conduct within the industry had been good for business.

The artificial haze at Vanquish grew more irritating as the day progressed. The coughing and sniffling seemed to increase. Someone surmised if the smoke was harmful then producers wouldn't be there. That prompted a nod to Amy Baer, who had her schoolage son with her. They giggled on a couch beyond where the sound cart and video playback were set up. "Or expose their kid to it," someone else added.

The creative producers, Baer and Mark, had been a steady presence in Atlanta. They were generally there at the same time, but if not it seemed at least one was around on a shooting day. As predicted, the presence of other top-level producers and studio execs had abated after Las Vegas.

After they finished shooting scenes Monday at the Midtown club, the company moved to Edgewood Avenue in Southeast Atlanta to be ready for the new shooting day. Various departments dropped off equipment and finished for the day. Turteltaub and Rake and a few others left to meet the young actors who would play the 1955 versions of the main characters.

The rehearsal was with Young Paddy, Young Billy, Young Archie, Young Sam, Young Sophie and the nemesis character, Danny the Greaser, who would bring conflict to the scene. Sophie is deceased by the time the main story takes place but the triangular dynamic between her, Billy and Paddy carried on, so the relationship needed to be reflected in the opening scene.

That the actors looked like the men playing the adult characters was criteria in their hire. The director would put the names of the famous actors on the faces of the young ones as a clever way of doing the opening credits. But the kids could also act. Turteltaub was sure of that when he hired them but even more confident after their visit to Las Vegas. He had built a rapport with them when they got the still shots at the old-time photo booth and he reconnected easily. The director again put them at ease by joking around.

The next morning the Art department was there early to transform one side of the street into 1955 Brooklyn. It was reminiscent of the images that initially graced the wall of the Boom Boom Room in the summer. A U.S. Mailbox was affixed on the exterior wall between two stores. An old style fire alarm, a four-foot tower, stood just in front of signage of a 2012 architectural firm, blocking it from the view of the camera.

The main set, Bissel's, might have been a real store if the food was edible. It was impressive when they'd finished the primary interior installation. The final version was staggering in detail. There were thousands of time-appropriate items from individual postcards on a rack to big items like the penny scale.

Full-store signage was now in place. Gold leaf lettering, or at least a reasonable facsimile, graced the storefront windows. They looked like they could have been right out of a town scene in "Leave it to Beaver" or "Father Knows Best."

The window displays on either side were filled. One had "Remedies," "Reliable Prescriptions," "Air Conditioning" and "Fountain Drinks." The other had "Sundries," "Drugs," "Ice Cold Drinks," "Novelties" and 'Stamps." Inside the bay window was an organized display hemmed in with three-foot high curtains. Glass shelves were arranged with vintage Ivory, Charmes and Palmolive soap bars. Other advertisements in the window looked more temporary and balanced the look, "Experienced Waitress Needed" for the soda fountain, "Grape Mint Limeade 10 cents" and "Smoke Viceroy." There also were manufacturer-built displays visible from the outside, like "Have a Hank," which featured handkerchiefs.

The other window had a neon sign, each word stacked on top of the other in yellow, blue and orange, "Whiskey Package Liquors." It was brighter than the other signs but behind the glass it blended in. They had verified the use of neon signs in advance. Times Square was covered with neon in the 1950s, so it was safe to assume a successful Brooklyn store would have one.

The soda fountain, now with stools in place, was decorated with signs. "Ice Cream," "Add A Topping," and "Banana Split" dominated one area. The fountain also sold hot dogs, French fries and cheeseburgers. For every "Malts and Milk Shakes," there was something else like, "Drink Coca Cola Pause Refresh."

There were other standout features, like a vintage phone booth with seat and door. It had a Ma Bell sign and phone. A tan, chest-high Character Readings scale machine, the future generations of which still dot truck stops, stood off to the side: "Your doctor says Weigh Yourself Daily."

But the magnum opus of the set was the photo booth that had traveled to Las Vegas and back. It was a Model 11, which technically came online in 1958, the rare item on set that didn't generate from 1955 or earlier. Even that fact which would never been noticed by a moviegoer, had been considered. By the mid-1950s new patents were issued and the machines became more plentiful. The newer machines were styled differently, more art deco with curved sides, but they continued to sell. This one had a standard look assumed from the time period.

The decision to purchase a shell, rather than a working photobooth, was noted by one of the crew who had moved it. The real machines could weigh 800 pounds and this was much lighter. It looked like the real thing: "BLACK and WHITE PHOTOS," "4 Different Poses in Complete Privacy Only 25¢." A closer look at the sample photo strips on the side of the machine revealed the faces of several crew in the Art department.

As good as the big items were, it was the detail that locked it in as a real store. Every shelf was filled, not haphazardly but organized by type and item. The front counter had vintage chewing gum and candy bars. These weren't facsimiles, but the real thing. Chocolate bars still contained some remnant inside that might have been petrified wood for its texture.

The shooting day arrived early and with it the promise of a sunny, crisp fall 1955 day. The Set Dec department was there first to put together anything on the street or that couldn't be done in advance. They unloaded the goods for the exteriors of Goldblatt's Hardware and Finkel's Bicycles, which soon had a dozen vintage and pristine bicycles lined up in front. Goldblatt's took more effort. There were displays for brooms, another with outdoor yard tools. It had rakes, shovels and tools no longer used in contemporary landscaping. The base of it read: "Geyer Farm Tools – Garden Tool," with smaller print showing "Geyer Manufacturing Co., Rock Falls, Ill."

Just inside the window was a vintage cardboard cutout advertisement of Dutch Boy Paint. It was the iconic Dutch Boy himself with wooden shoe, resting his foot atop paint cans at the base of the ad. A giant key hanging outside showed that copies could be cut inside. One window sign proclaimed, "Plumbing Supplies," another "Disston Land Saws." The best one offered "Johns-Mansville Asbestos Shingles."

The Locations department had leased several vacant storefronts, some of which were being used as offices by the various departments. Most of the businesses in the area were offices or companies that didn't require a lot of foot traffic. There was novelty in having a movie shoot nearby, given it didn't happen a lot and was only one day. That was another benefit to shooting in Atlanta. Angelenos had long ago ceased caring about movie trucks.

The Costumes department set up its office and dressing area inside one of the closer storefronts. The department had fittings for 25 background actors in period costumes; 15 of them would be behind the wheels of 1950s autos. Production assistants worked around the neighborhood. Some were with the vehicles, others were at the intersection to stop traffic, and still more handled

311

crowd control. By then word was out that this would be a different day in the neighborhood. Observers began to collect and local television news appeared.

When it was time, the cars and trucks began moving in two different directions down the same street, a PA pacing them. They would each turn at different corners and return to the starting point, all part of a walkie-talkie choreography. The kids did their part. They goofed around in character even between shots.

After that, Wednesday arrived with relative ease, save for a sharp drop in temperature. One of the things that a job on a movie set required was adaptability. Things changed and that was especially true if on location or outdoors. Generally, you had to make it work. It could be weather or a noisy environment or even a stinky one, as had happened when they shot De Niro's character at the condo building downtown.

Thus far they'd been fortunate. The elements had largely aligned with the shooting schedule for *Last Vegas*. There had been high winds and cold weather on the second day of shooting but the sun stayed out and the wind calmed. The day they shot the outdoor pool party in Las Vegas, which had dozens of people in the water, the sun had again come to the rescue. Atlanta had just delivered a bright, sunny fall day for the 1955 scenes. All of those scenes were scheduled for a single day. There weren't "rain dates," although had it poured rain they would have created one or otherwise found a solution.

The temperature hovered around 40 degrees when the crew began assembling in front of the Georgia World Congress Center in Atlanta. It was 6 a.m. and the doors weren't open yet, although it wouldn't be long. Mark McManus, the video assist operator, was at his cart cracking jokes and lamenting the difference between a job on set and one in the Production department or elsewhere on Mailing Avenue. "When it's cold outside, they're inside. When it's raining, they're inside. When it's ugly at night, they're inside."

Set Dec was converting the exterior of the convention center into the Fort Myers airport and with any luck, the sun would come up boldly to honor Florida. But it was chilly in the meantime. The on-set medic, a local man, had a golf cart style vehicle with anything he might need. It included enough power for a small heater, but there was only so much to go around.

Both scenes involved Sam and his wife so both actors could be scheduled for the same day. One had Sam leaving on the trip, and a conversation with his wife in front of the airport. The other was more intimate once he had returned. Set decorating had built a bedroom set for that scene. It popped up in the first warehouse a few days earlier, disappeared and now only to be relocated to one of the numerous meeting rooms within the convention center the previous day.

The bedroom set had popped up inside a convention center meeting room. It looked bizarrely out of place, a bedroom within a giant folding-wall partitioned room in the nearly empty convention center. Once inside, Turteltaub and the creative team walked down the wide, empty corridor and stopped in the room to look at it.

The director spent seven minutes walking it, stopping at different angles to look at it, while the rest stood silently to the side. Something wasn't sitting right with him about the set. The scene was when Sam and his wife reunited after the trip to Vegas and this didn't seem to fit the bill. He wanted the reunion to have something more than this. He figured he would shoot it, but he also filed it away as something he'd improve on later if given a chance.

Meanwhile, Set Dec had worked its magic. Southwest Airlines, which provided the signage and other items, now had an exterior check-in area in front of the Georgia World Congress Center. It looked like an airport, with its automatic doors and traffic lanes in front. The Costume, Hair and Makeup departments, inside where it was warmer, had readied the background actors playing travelers, who were soon in place.

In the scene, Sam and his wife pull up in front of the airport and talk before he gets out. She gives him a condom and express permission to use on the Sin City adventure. Then she drives away. Kline played it up, Sam dancing around when she pulled away amidst the background actors portraying passengers. It looked like Florida on the monitors, but it was a cold day that had done only a little to warm itself as it progressed. None of the chill was reflected in Kline's performance, nor did any background actors give it away.

McManus' cart, like Kelson's and the cinematographer's, contained a lot of equipment, but it wasn't his only cart. It was his company, McVideo Assist, that owned the equipment at director's village, and the other one like it, called "video village" by the crew. He explained his job: "I log everything from rehearsals on, all the takes. I maintain all the files for everything we've shot."

But that left off the interactive aspect of it. When called upon he had to find whatever was wanted within those files and have it up on the monitor on director's village as quickly as possible, which meant seconds. He joked he couldn't leave his cart, even for the bathroom. During set-ups, when non-camera crew might have a moment, the director and script supervisor often were still at work. They would be talking about scenes and need to have a look at something already in the can. That term, meaning something was completed, stemmed from the early days of the film world when a reel was placed within its flat circular tin.

McManus was easygoing and people often stopped by during breaks to chat with him. He was in tan trousers, a black T-shirt and a thick red button-down shirt under his coat, along with tan plaid cap on his head. It protected his glasses but not his ears, which were cold. They also seemed to have a refined ability to separate sound. One of them was always tuned to the speaker on the cart. It was usually at such a low volume it was barely detectible to anyone nearby.

McManus could be talking to someone and suddenly turn away mid-sentence because he heard something in the other ear no one else had. It was usually Alicia Accardo, the script supervisor, checking in from director's village with something like, 'Hey, Mark, can we see Day 11, scene 112, takes 4 and 5?' He'd drop into his chair, hit a few buttons, and it would be up on a monitor in front of him as well as the monitor in front of her and Turteltaub.

McManus had come to the movie business later in life than a lot of the crew. He'd been a buyer in the apparel industry before that when the bottom suddenly fell out. "They figured they'd pay us less and came up with a new commission structure." It wasn't enough to live on. "I was nearly 40 without a job and a family to support," he recalled.

One day in Wilmington, N.C., he ran into a man he knew from college who had a line on work. They were coming back to reshoot *The Crow* (1994) and needed someone to help them. The star of the movie, Brandon Lee, had been killed on set in a firearms accident and filming halted. The new scenes would reshoot from the perspective of the crow.

The Crow was McManus' first credit. The next five years he worked as an apprentice and operator. Then he got his own equipment. His first job with it was *Shake, Rattle, & Roll*, a television movie. His first feature film was *The Patriot* (2000). His arrival in the business had been pragmatic rather than driven by a love of film but it hit him that in addition to making a decent living he was involved in something cool. "It was the biggest production I'd been on," he recalled. The first day of shooting was the scene where the son of the character played by Mel Gibson was killed by a British general. They had two cranes and 100 foot silk. Another scene had the cavalry, 600 horses strong, galloping over a hill. "That was moviemaking!" he recalled. "I thought it was just incredible."

He had worked steadily since, primarily in North Carolina. The tax breaks put in place -- and left in place -- had led to a robust and seemingly permanent production business. It offered 25 percent where Georgia gave 30 percent, but it brought steady work. Eventually, state leadership would take the tax credits out and put a grant system in place. McManus and other crew would relocate to Georgia for work and pay their taxes there.

His equipment was state-of-the-art but like the camera crew and Kelson, he paid close attention to technological changes and improvements. "They expect me to keep up with it," he said. "Day 1 is when you prove yourself. There is no Day 2 if you're not ready." McManus valued his equipment at about $100,000, but planned a major upgrade. When that was done the system would be closer to $160,000. About a quarter of the additional investment would be for storage, since digital data took up a lot of space.

On *Last Vegas* he had about 1 terabyte of capacity, which translated to 1,024 gigabytes. By way of comparison, 4 gigabytes on a laptop was enough for most non-professional gamers. He had more than enough for a two-camera package deal he had with Four Fellas, which also included the occasional addition of a third camera, or whatever extra they needed on the movie. The upgrade, when he got to it, would be two 2 terabytes, capacity for more than four cameras, and another village. He would finance it, as he had before, and pay it off with his kit rental. That's where the money was, certainly more than the pay for being an operator.

As the video assist, he kept a backup of all creative material that had been shot on the show until it ended, and provided it to them on a hard drive. It wasn't the raw material -- that was the gold they shipped out daily -- but it was a reasonable facsimile. It had come in handy more than once. People asked if he ever kept any of the material but he had no interest in that. The longest it ever stayed on was until the next show when he needed the storage space.

The day wrapped a little on the early side. McManus and the others got the respective equipment back to Mailing Avenue. Technically he was part of

315

the Sound department, and he stored his equipment in the same office. That done, he joined the exodus of crew headed out for the long Thanksgiving weekend.

CHAPTER SIXTEEN
Shoot Week 6

Nov. 26 30
Day 22, 23, 24, 25, 26

MAJOR METROPOLITAN ATLANTA is parted by I-85 and I-75, which merge for a time in the unartfully named Downtown Connector. Some 250,000 vehicles pass through each day on 10 lanes of traffic that wind through the core of the city amidst dozens of skyscrapers. Traffic always slows and occasionally stops, particularly during rush hour. The Monday morning after Thanksgiving weekend it was slower than normal.

It was there, on the northbound side of the Connector that *Last Vegas* set up base camp for the next two days. The large lot at Williams and 8th Street would someday be home to a behemoth building but in the meantime it was available for short-term lease. It was the closest they could get the bulk of the company to the urban residential neighborhood at Peachtree Place where they were shooting De Niro's character in his home.

As normal, the Transportation department, courtesy of its Teamster drivers, had moved the various trucks and trailers to the end closest to the highways in advance of the day. The vehicles were parallel to each other in two rows, a billboard to the far right aimed toward the highway. It was the usual semis and mobile offices, various department vehicles for the Props, Costume, Hair and Makeup departments. Crew parking filled in from there, leaving most of the lot still empty. White vans, also driven by Teamsters, shuttled people back and forth.

On the left, to the far end of both rows, was a single motor coach. It looked isolated, even lonely, separated like it was but what it lacked in neighbors it made up for in quality. De Niro's road-going home away from home was a stunning specimen. The stainless steel machine, with its large pop outs and satellite dish, was state-of-the-art, with two bathrooms, including a master bath, a quality kitchen and a large makeup and dressing area. It also was outfitted with electronics, comfortable furnishings and personal items.

This motor coach was actually a downgrade for the actor. At one point he owned one that didn't just pop out, it popped up with a retractable second story. It had a winding staircase and featured an area for as many as 30 people to watch dailies.

Still, this one was nice, very nice. It hadn't garnered any media attention and it didn't stand out as much as the other one had, which was the point. The only identifying marks on the tractor-trailer designed vehicle were on the cab, which linked it to Four Fellas. A brand new Lexus RX, a luxury SUV, was parked in front of it. Its driver sat behind the wheel talking on his phone. On the other side of the row of vehicles two white vans took turns ferrying people to set or back.

Turteltaub, all of the producers and main actors, and many of the crew, had traveled home for Thanksgiving. The largest contingent had commuted to Los Angeles. The word on set was that De Niro had traveled the farthest. He had gone home to New York, attended a fundraiser and then to China for the opening of a Nobu restaurant -- all since he'd last been seen on *Last Vegas*.

There weren't any news accounts confirming it but it was entirely possible. De Niro hadn't been on the set since the large club scenes so he'd had more than just a long weekend to travel. He also often attended openings of his restaurant around the world. Already worldwide, Nobu was also expanding into the hotel business so there might have been some related business that didn't involve an opening.

Nobu was just part of what was on his plate. De Niro also had Tribeca Enterprises. While best known for the Tribeca Film Festival it was actually a diversified global media company. It operated several branded entertainment companies, including Tribeca Cinemas and Tribeca Film, which was a distribution initiative, and partnered in other endeavors. All of that was on top of the actor doing a couple of movies a year.

De Niro's executive assistant called Rake early in the morning. Would they be using Bob today? "We're shooting his character in his apartment," the 1st AD replied. "I think we'll need him." It wasn't clear what had motivated the call. The assistant hadn't asked for anything. It was possible, particularly if the actor had gone to China, that he was just tired and getting a feel for the day. Rake had passed it along and gone to set.

But it wasn't the first time a call like that had come in for the actor. The producers, Turteltaub and Rake had worked hard to accommodate his requests, and for that matter, the requests of any of the actors. De Niro, Douglas and Freeman were all icons in the acting world. All three men were paid the same for their work on *Last Vegas*, and had the same perk packages. It's just the others hadn't asked.

Taken together one could get the impression that De Niro was a primo uomo. He brought his own custom luxury motor coach, flew in his own jet, stayed in a different hotel. He also had an aggressive executive assistant who had done battle with Samuels when the actor approached the end of his $100,000 perk package while the others were within bounds. In that case the issue was whether a personal trainer and associated expenses were appropriately deducted.

But none of it was outrageous by Hollywood standards or evidence the guy was a jerk. He wasn't. It just meant De Niro was more of a management challenge. Neither Freeman nor Douglas, with their own sizeable fortunes and business interests, had machinery in place like his. De Niro needed more accommodation and no one was complaining, which Rake said was key.

The issue was that by now, with the number of shooting days dwindling, shifts were harder to coordinate. The actor's most recent request was time to tape a message in honor of Dustin Hoffman, who was receiving a lifetime achievement award at the Kennedy Center in Washington. Rake scheduled it but in the end De Niro planned to fly to Washington to do it live, which they were also able to make work without disrupting the production. The event would be taped next week for broadcast later in the month.

Amy Baer drafted a letter to De Niro. She read it to Turteltaub as the two of them sat in their high chairs at director's village at the condo. It essentially said that was the last change they could accommodate. Then she paused.

"You should sign it," she said.

"Oh, no. No," Turteltaub said. "I'm the *director*. You're the *producer*. You sign it."

Paddy's apartment was a unit in the Palmer Building at 81 Peachtree Place. Built in 1907, the building received an exterior landmark designation from the City of Atlanta in 1992 but it wasn't a look unique to the southern city. It had a classic look of buildings of the era that could be found in older cities. In this case, given it was supposed to be Brooklyn, they would add an air of authenticity with overflowing trash cans and New York City cabs in front.

The problem for the cinematographer, gaffer and grip, was that older units were hard to light. Hennings knew the interior production lights would not give him what he needed. The apartment was three stories up and better light would require a crane. The condor, better recognized as a "cherry picker" when it came with a bucket, would lift a BFL -- a big fucking light -- from the outside of the building skyward to the exterior of the living room window and blast shaped light into the living room.

Gaffer Stephen Crowley had 10 people working for him on the movie, depending on the day. Today, it was the best boy and five lighting technicians, a rigging gaffer and best boy rigging gaffer, and a genny operator, who was in charge of generators. Crowley was in many places on set in the course of a shooting day but if you needed to find him at any particular point he was probably standing near Hennings.

When he was first offered the job of running the Electric department on *Last Vegas* Crowley wasn't sure he could do it. He would be wrapping *Scary Movie 5* on the start date. It was just a couple of days so they worked with him, allowing Steve Zigler, the rigging gaffer, to start the movie as gaffer. Crowley finished on *Scary Movie 5* and two days later was on a plane to Las Vegas.

Zigler's full-time job on the movie involved pre-rigging the set for the electric department, which he did with the help of a best boy rigging gaffer. They surveyed the condo, and the building, ahead of time and worked out a plan for it based on what Crowley and Hennings told them. Then they put the foundation in place for whatever lighting would be used and made sure it all worked. It varied by location what that entailed. Having the basic plan handled in advance saved time because the focus was on getting individual lights right, which was time consuming.

Crowley had a different story than a lot of the crew, most of who started in the industry in Los Angeles. He was from Georgia and began his education in camera work with a small church operation in south DeKalb County. At first, it involved shooting concerts every few months with a remote truck. Then that gig became quarterly. He maintained his ties to the organization while he went to a trade school in North Carolina to learn television production. The church operation steadily grew, eventually becoming a mega-church. Crowley was the main camera guy. He directed youth shows along with directing its youth services program. It had "MTV rock and roll style" of production that had broad appeal.

From there he took a job at an equipment rental house where he met people doing documentaries. That led him to several social commentary projects, where he did everything from writing narration to working sound, utility and videography. It was also his first taste of the traveling required to work in production and it led to other things. He worked at the "Cosby Show" when it first started shooting at Spelman College in Atlanta. Then that led to a job at Turner Broadcasting, where he stayed for several years before going freelance.

Crowley took time to praise two mentors and the importance of mentorship in the industry. Marivee Cade was the lighting designer for churches and took him along. She also worked in features and helped him to transition to the freelance world of features. He still marvels at how much she taught him. She was incredibly busy yet took time to teach him and he appreciated it. As a best boy he worked for several gaffers, and one in particular, now a camera operator, taught him a lot.

His first love wasn't an electric box. "I was taken by the camera," he said. Having a mentor was important in the industry because filmmaking was a mix of craft with various trades. There were a lot of nuances, especially in the Electric department because it didn't stop at the power source. Working on movie production lighting required skills beyond what a general electrician would do, and the more you could learn from people who had done it, the better.

Crowley stayed close to his Georgia roots, working freelance on movies as an electrician, a best boy and a rigging gaffer as he worked his way up. "They called me the billy goat," he recalled. "I would climb up the grids," referring to structures built to hold lighting. He worked a lot, including on television, but his focus was features. Over the years that *included Fried Green Tomatoes* (1991), *October Sky* (1999), *Gods and Generals* (2003), *We Are Marshall* (2006) and *The Blind Side* (2009). Gradually, he began taking more jobs as a gaffer, as on *Wanderlust* and *Scary Movie 5*, and fewer as a rigging gaffer.

A rigging gaffer had to have exceptional technical understanding but not everyone who could do that job well was destined for the role of gaffer. The skills needed to be a chief lighting technician today, particularly on a bigger movie, involved a lot of management, up, down and sideways. It extended beyond designing a set-lighting plan, wiring and installation or even being a good electrician.

"That person is usually more politically savvy, has good social skills, a good grasp of the big picture," he said. The historic hierarchy within movie productions remained firmly in place, Crowley said. But it was more pronounced on some movies than others. "So many films have a disconnect between what the director does and the crew. There are elite workers and non-elite workers." *Last Vegas* had "no class consciousness," he said. That came from the top. Turteltaub knew everyone had a job and he took time "to respect that job."

Understanding how it all fit together was part of the job, he said, adding he didn't have a problem with people above the line. "Robert De Niro had to work hard to get where he is," he said. "Society sees the recognition, the glamour, but not what he's had to give up to do it, whether relationships have suffered, how it's limited where he can go." All five of the famous actors on *Last Vegas* had made it over the long haul, which was the hardest thing to do. "Longevity is the telltale sign of success in this business," Crowley said.

Crowley even defended Badalato, by now less of a target by some of his brethren in the Camera, Electric and Grip departments. A handful of them still thought the UPM had crossed a line in efforts to save money for the movie. More than Samuels, who was ultimately calling the shots, it was still Badalato who absorbed the heat. Some of it was due to technique but not all. The unit production manager had a job to do, and it was not a popular job, said Crowley. "I know I wouldn't want to do it."

Turteltaub had liked Unit #6 at the condominium for the scenes with De Niro as soon as he had seen it, which hadn't been the norm in the early scouts. All elements needed for the scenes got check marks, from the age of the building to the apartment layout and front hallway entrance where they would shoot a scene. It also had a different quality entirely that immediately pushed it into the yes column.

It already looked like someplace Paddy would live, from furnishings to books to decorations. The director could see the cranky, grieving widower hunkered down in a chair -- that chair -- when his buddies showed up to take him on a trip. They wanted the apartment as it was. That wasn't unheard of but it wasn't typical, either.

It made for different elements in the contract secured by the Locations department. It shortened the amount of time they needed to lease a second unit, since they didn't have as much to store. And it was easier on the Set Dec department in terms of furniture, given the department normally would have been designing that as well. They could work backwards, removing what they didn't like.

But it wasn't simple, either. It still had to be personalized to the character, time and place. The apartment was in Brooklyn. A vintage sports shirt, signed and framed, hung on the wall. As a grieving widower, Paddy would be awash in memories of his wife. Framed photos of her filled the place here, 10 in all, both alone and with De Niro, representing different times in the characters' lives over decades. The picture of the bar they owned together, an image created months earlier, was in the mix. Pictures of his wife were so prevalent that they hired someone to stand in for the still shots, since there was no Adult Sophie cast in the movie.

There wasn't room for all the crew upstairs, and base camp was far away, so small encampments formed around the Palmer Building. It was the opposite of Aria, where Four Fellas had blended into the giant resort-casino. The Palmer Building was attached to another one constructed a few years ago and were considered one, but even the combined structure contained just 23 units. There was no mistaking a movie company had taken it over.

Craft service somehow found a triangular wedge on the neighbor-hood street to set up the food truck. They soon had the coffee station and snack table out. "Crafty" was generally popular with the crew for obvious reasons but it was even more true on this show. The woman who ran it and her assistant were known and well-liked by a number of crew before the show even started. That popularity only grew. They didn't just put out packaged goods. They made hot snacks, generally twice a day, and either had fresh coffee out or would make it, including lattes and other prepared beverages.

Equipment was unloaded in front of the building by the Grip and Electric departments. The grips handled anything that wasn't electric. Set decorating handled anything going to set. Given there wasn't much space for storage upstairs, Kerry Rawlins figured out what had to go up when and organized the Grip department around it. He had 10 people in all, including two dolly grips dedicated to moving their respective cameras.

With the elevators busy moving equipment, the rest of the crew used the back entrance. It was a staircase wide enough that they could pass each other as they hurried back and forth. The Sound and Video assist departments set up a good 20 feet beyond the ground-floor entrance to the stairs behind the building. There was an overhang in front of the separate garage with nice, new fencing to one side. They led cables from Unit 6 out the window to the ground floor and to their respective systems.

The weather forecast called for a temperature between 40 and 60 degrees and a 10 percent chance of rain. It was on the low end of that and chilly but with the overhang, at least the equipment wouldn't get wet if it rained. The area was soon dubbed "Cement Video Village."

Before long a stench arose. It seemed to come on gradually but was soon so pronounced that everyone joked that it never could have seemed subtle. It was dreadful, like a partially emptied garbage truck had been hosed down and the water left to collect in pools. The culprit was just that, seepage from an overflowing dumpster on the other side of the fence partition.

There weren't a lot of options to relocate. The production sound mixer quickly moved his cart to the other end of the concrete hallway, as far as he could get. It wasn't as easy for the video assist operator. He was able to move a few feet but not far enough to evade it, so he devised an alternative plan. He rounded up mats to cover the area closest to him. The coup de grace that made the difference was fans, which were put inside the fence to blow the stench in the opposite direction. It was one reason to be grateful for the cold because it would have been that much harder to contain on a hot day.

The condor in front of the building had been delivered in advance and stood to the left of the building. Lane closure signs were set up, blocking the area in front of it with cones. The Locations department had secured the permit for the lane closure in advance. It wasn't a busy street but it was a routine safety requirement. Gradually, the Electric department attached equipment to the platform, and it was manipulated into place three floors up, a BFL aimed inside the living room window of Unit #6.

The four scenes at the condominium comprised more than six pages of script. Those were divided over two days based on the actors in the scenes, De Niro being the common denominator. Monday's work was easier, except that it straddled the second and eighth script days, meaning two very different places in the life of the story. Day 1 was 1955 Brooklyn. Day 2 was present day. In this scene it was Paddy as he lived his life before the trip to Las Vegas. Day 8, a few months after they returned, was one of the last scenes. It would reflect the shift in Paddy since his return from the Las Vegas trip.

For the first scene, in which Paddy resists the friendship of his neighbor, Dayna Pink had the actor wearing a bathrobe. In the later scene, after his trip to Vegas, a renewed Paddy is fully dressed and hosting guests. Other more subtle things would be changed for the later scene. The apartment would be neater. Lighting would be brighter. The Set Dec department would remove pictures of Sophie, not all but some, to show Paddy's grief had abated.

But a wall was getting in the way of a shot. The scene near the end of the movie had Paddy in the kitchen cooking with his guests but the camera couldn't fit there. The grips could open the wall, there wasn't any doubt about that. Turteltaub wanted to know what it would take to reinforce the walls in order to cut a hole in it safely. Badalato wanted to know how much it would cost. A figure came back: $6,460 to cut and brace and repair the apartment wall. That seemed high to Badalato, but not as high as delaying production. He would get another estimate.

The second day at the condo was De Niro's scenes with Freeman and Kline. Turteltaub spent several minutes walking around the set a few minutes before the call time. He looked intensely at things. He stopped to look at the Brooklyn Dodger jersey framed on the wall and wondered aloud if that was enough to show they were in New York. No one said anything out loud about that but they might have. Cassidy had looked into getting New York Yankees memorabilia, which would have been ideal, but it was a tightly controlled trademark and time-consuming to sort out. This wasn't a movie with a ton of prep time.

Turteltaub had moved on, his mind on Paddy. "Are there any plates of uneaten food?"

This was also met with silence but Rice stood at attention. This was her ballpark and she quickly saw he was serious.

"Paddy would leave food uneaten on plates around his place," said Turteltaub.

"No one told me that," Rice replied.

"That's because I just thought of it," he said, brightly, as he left the dining room.

Two points came across clearly. No one had done anything wrong but he wasn't kidding, either. He wanted uneaten food on a plate or plates.

Rice got it. Paddy was a lonely widower. His friends arrived unexpectedly to find him in his bathrobe. There were wilted flowers on set and other indications that Paddy was depressed and still mourning Sophie, including many framed pictures. Plates with food that hadn't been eaten or hadn't made it to the kitchen to be cleaned would help get the point across.

The question was whether she could make it happen on such short notice. Catering had shut down by then but she picked up the walkie and radioed them. They thought they could help, although they weren't sure. Food had been taken down but they were still cleaning up. There were bound to be breakfast scraps. Next she radioed Miles, the props department assistant, since Benjamin-Creel was at Mailing Avenue and too far away to be of help. Miles headed to a drug store in the neighborhood to pick up other food items. That way Rice would have something if her catering request turned up empty.

Turteltaub went to his roost at director's village while the crew put the finishing touches on the set. Baer sat with him as she filled him in on details of a major marketing coup. The pitch had been in the works, and there was interest, but now it was official. NBC's Today show would be doing a segment about *Last Vegas* and various producers and staff, along with Matt Lauer, were coming to Atlanta the next day to shoot the segment. In exchange, Four Fellas agreed to a private interview with De Niro, Douglas, Freeman and Kline in one sitting, and access to the set while they were working. That would enable the producers to get b roll, as well as footage of Lauer interacting on set and giving directorial commands as part of the bit.

Today consistently had 4.3 million viewers, and while off its peak earlier in the year, it was an exceptional opportunity to promote the movie. It was a legitimate news-feature story. The movie had some of the biggest names in the industry, which in turn would draw viewers to the network. The news hook was that these famous actors, household names, had never worked together. But even with all that being true, it was still a remarkable bit of marketing. Few things build buzz for a movie as well as a segment on the Today show.

Turteltaub knew it was great for the movie but wasn't nearly as enthusiastic as Baer. He had three scenes to shoot the next day, including a Las Vegas showman's funeral scene with most of the cast and 150 background actors.

And now Matt Lauer was going to stop by and "direct."

The defunct Candler Park Funeral Home took on a surreal quality with the presence of the movie company. It was one-story, long and sprawling. If it had been a house, it would have been ranch-style. Four Fellas was spread out over the property, throughout the interior and edging out over its parking lots. Base camp was on the side with the largest parking lot and it flowed onto an adjacent church parking lot leased by the Locations department. Virtually every production truck was on site along with an abundance of star and executive trailers, the biggest visual display yet of the mobile might of Four Fellas.

It seemed fitting, along with the volume of things to be done, that it was the last day on the road for the company. When work resumed tomorrow it would be on the soundstages for the rest of principal photography.

The funeral scenes themselves -- one interior and one exterior -- would have made for a full shooting day but there were also two others, a Las Vegas traffic jam and a dressing room scene. That was four different sets to have readied on site. Also, the scenes occurred over three different script days. That meant the Costume department needed to make changes for any character that appeared in more than one script day.

There were other things on the schedule. Turteltaub had an idea on how to make one of the Binion's scenes better. He planned to add a couple in the audience where Diana Boyle performed. Those actors were going to come to the site to audition. Time was also set aside for a meeting with Turteltaub and Amy Baer to meet with one of the actors. Then there was the biggest anomaly of the day, the impending arrival of Matt Lauer and the NBC crew. Everyone was delighted but at the same time it was a fresh layer of cluster to a fully clustered day.

It would all fit, as long as there were no surprises. They would shoot the traffic jam first, then the two funeral scenes, then the dressing room scene with Maurice, the Madonna impersonator. An NBC producer and crew would arrive early in the day to set it up and get B roll. Lauer would get there in time for the exterior funeral scene. The group interview would be sometime around 4 p.m. That would give the anchor time to fly to Atlanta after the Today show went off-air in New York that morning. It also would give Turteltaub time to finish the three scenes with the main actors and wrap them for the day before shooting the dressing room scene.

The morning started an hour late, "pushed" because production had run long the day before. This was a normal occurrence in the industry although it had been rare on *Last Vegas*. Union rules required production companies to provide at least 12 hours of downtime before they could require people to come back to work. It meant that instead of starting at 7 a.m., the general call time was pushed to 8 a.m.

Picture cars had been collecting since the night before on the other side of the funeral home from where base camp was set up for the day. A section of the parking lot soon turned into a traffic jam. The lanes were defined and vehicles, many of which had specific Las Vegas markings, moved into place. The back lane got the billboard truck, which featured a Vegas girly ad like those that populate Sin City. The hero minivan, sans windshield, would be front and center. There were five taxicabs, a billboard truck, a panel truck and a hero minivan organized by the Transportation department. Extras driving their cars were staggered in the group while others waited behind the wheel nearby, a total of 15 additional vehicles for the scene. It looked like they were in Las Vegas.

Transportation had organized the picture cars, while Peterson had overseen the background actors bringing vehicles. Benjamin-Creel had made good on his promise to get authentic, triangular Vegas taxi-tops. Any local logos on the cabs were obscured or renamed, the fictional Jackpot Cab Co. in front.

As a rule, when the actors finished with hair and makeup they would come by the sound cart to get fitted with microphones. It had happened organically because the cart was convenient but it also meant the Sound department wasn't running after actors. For the scene in the minivan, Kelson installed microphones rather than fitting the actors. It was better to mic them but they had to wear seatbelts and that was problematic. Planting the mics was the best way to guarantee clean sound.

Outside the grips were getting the condor and flyswatter up while the Electric department set up the lights. The condor was a crane and the flyswatter was a giant frame with material stretched across it like a giant trampoline without a base. They would use it to shape light so it looked more like a sunny outdoor day in Nevada than an overcast one outside Atlanta. The Camera department readied its equipment. Hennings went back and forth between the camera and his equipment and monitors. One shot would come down across the traffic jam. Another would be centered in front of the minivan.

Rake was likewise going back and forth between Turteltaub and crew. Second team was nearby and he sent them to the van for final camera adjustments, then he said something to no one in particular, his finger pushing the talk button on his walkie. The crew heard him, loud and clear. The cast should be told they were 15 minutes out.

Michael Douglas arrived on set a short time later, Mary Steenburgen a minute behind him. The two actors stood off to the side and chatted about the Thanksgiving break. Each had spent the time with family. Douglas had golfed and taken his 12-year-old diving.

Jeremiah Samuels had been nearby at video village talking to Scott Thompson, the actor-comedian known as Carrot Top. They walked over to join the actors. Douglas, consistent old-school gentleman, introduced Thompson to Steenburgen, although they had met the day before.

Samuels brought up the Today segment, clearly pleased about it. "Who's doing it?" Douglas asked.

"Matt Lauer," Samuels replied.

"Bringing out the big guns," the actor commented.

Samuels smiled and nodded at the movie star. "Of course."

Another conversation, this one between crew, was going on just below the surface. The walkies were a tool that facilitated movement and enabled early problem solving. No one above the line needed or wanted one so it was terrain. It provided endless entertainment for the casual listener. The ADs were getting the other actors to set.

"Kevin's walking." A production assistant alerted the group while another voice, which sounded like the 2nd Second, looked for another one.

"Who has eyes on Mary?"

"Mary's on set. We need Bob." That voice clearly belonged to Rake.

"Morgan's walking," said another voice.

In Vegas they had generally referred to the actors by their character names but with fewer crowds they had slipped into calling by their names or a mixture of both.

"Paddy's walking."

De Niro arrived a couple of minutes later. The actors were chatting in a group and he silently joined them. Rake was standing next to Turteltaub by then. He walked over to the group and told them they were ready. The Props department was nearby with the luggage that both Kline and Freeman would carry in their laps inside the minivan and the actors piled in. De Niro was on the left, Steenburgen in the middle, Douglas on the right. Behind them in the back seat was Kline on the left, Freeman on the right, the luggage giving a jammed-in look for the comedic scene.

Scene 35 had been revised several times, the final version distributed to the actors the day before. This was contained in the buff revision, the seventh alteration to the script. These weren't wholesale changes, but shifts to specific scenes as they approached camera time. This one drilled down on the traffic, all of the actors with one line except Douglas, who had two.

The original script had the characters arguing with a taxi driver over the tip. The shooting draft used when they began principal photography had Diana Boyle asking if it was weird that she was in the vehicle with the group. They were a group of old friends and she was a lounge singer they had met a few minutes earlier so it would address the obvious. But it hadn't been needed. Another version had dialogue between Diana and Paddy, which had already been pushed to the next scene, which was after the group exits the minivan. Scene 36, which took place in front of the Mirage as the actors walked, had already been shot in Las Vegas.

The final version tweaked the dialogue to reflect a little more of the characters' personalities. Sam and Archie would be in the back seat visible on either side of Diana, who was the center of the scene. Paddy and Billy would be on either side of her, just as they had as youngsters. All of them were attentive of her.

The call for "Action" opened with Douglas' character's line. "What is with this traffic?" Paddy, who had the next line, would ignore and focus on Diana. "Are you comfortable? I could ask Gherson to sit in the back," was how it read in the script.

But De Niro put his character's spin on it. "Is he bothering you?" Paddy asked. "Because he can sit in the back."

It was a nuanced difference but the shift got to the conflict between the characters better. Paddy had a problem with Billy and it wasn't one that would come with a friendly suggestion he sit in back. It was a loaded comment based on their history together, which included an earlier fight over a love interest. De Niro's version was more Paddy. It was also the way the actor said it, and the amused, slightly surprised look on Diana's face. Turteltaub could get another take with the exact line as written in the revised script but it wouldn't make it better.

De Niro rarely said his lines exactly as they were in the script when they first started shooting a scene. It could look like he was unprepared but it wasn't that. He wasn't just working into the lines either, although that was certainly true. No, the most famous actor in the world was waiting. "He really saves it for the closeup," Turteltaub said. "That's when he gives you his best stuff. He doesn't waste it on the wide or anything you aren't going to use."

By now the respective styles of all the actors were clear. Kline always said his lines as they were but he was also naturally inclined to ad lib other versions. Turteltaub joked about it with the actor. "Hey, don't give him a prop!" because the actor would run with it. It was part of his unique style.

Douglas and Freeman played it closer to the vest. They knew their lines and they held to them. The only time Douglas had a line wrong to date, and he had been close, was in Las Vegas. The actor had acknowledged it and had it perfect the next time.

Based on the laughter of the people watching in front of the two sets of monitors, and at video assist, the scene was funny. The actors, as famous as they were, took on their characters well enough that the group watching the monitors forgot who they were. The guys goofing it up were a bunch of friends in a taxi in a traffic jam on a sunny day on The Strip in Las Vegas, even though it was a chilly morning in suburban Atlanta.

"And, Cut. Let's go again," said Rake, repeating Turteltaub. The actors got back in the van. The extras inching the vehicles forward in the traffic jam in the background inched them backward to start again.

When they needed to re-set the cameras, the actors were led to a comfortable waiting area inside the quietest hall of the funeral home. Chairs were arranged in a semi-circle, refreshments nearby in the open nook. It didn't have a door but it was set back far enough that it wasn't visible from either end of the hall. They were safely out of sight unless someone happened to walk all the way down the hall, at which point they would suddenly find themselves in front of all of the actors at once.

Eventually they went back to their trailers for lunch break. The funeral scene was a different script day and they needed to change costumes. In the meantime, the cameras would move to the auditorium.

The interior of the funeral home was as creepy a place as any that came with an embalming room in the basement. It had a lot of corners and halls and offices and foyers. There were perhaps a dozen viewing rooms, some larger than others, most of them windowless. The smell that permeated the place in prep, the one the realtor said was stuffiness due to being closed up, remained. The bizarre feel wasn't by accident. They leased the location to shoot the celestial sendoff of Maurice, a Madonna impersonator who after being befriended by the main characters, dies in their Aria penthouse.

The NBC crew had arrived earlier and been shown to one of the larger, windowless interior offices. It was two hallways into the interior from where the actors were working, although it might have been a city block given how much was happening between the two places.

The NBC producer and crew had several hours to set up before the anchor arrived. The room where they would shoot the interview was nondescript, big and empty. Nothing about it said, "movie set," which is what the producer wanted it to say. He asked to borrow equipment from various departments to dress it up. The publicist helped make that happen with the movie crew, who were happy to accommodate.

It was set decorating for the news business. The front of the set would have the director's chairs with the actors' names on them. In the background, the NBC crew set up lights borrowed from the Electric department, racks from the Costume department, apple boxes and other equipment from the Grip department.

On the other side of the building in the chapel a large segment of the crew was focused on the next scene. The characters portrayed by De Niro, Douglas, Freeman and Kline would attend a large funeral. They would sit in the center of "thirty of the oddest assortment of Las Vegas types you've ever seen," according to the script, a number that was now up to 37. Surrounding them were more generic BG, for a total of 150. Some BG had double duty. They would work in the traffic jam scene, some with their own cars, and then change clothes to be in the funeral scene.

The extras casting company had started early in the day checking in background actors. There were two call times for them. Specialty BG was due at 7:30 and more general BG at 9:30 a.m. Once they were checked in and all paperwork handled, the background actor would be sent to Hair and Makeup and then to the Costume department, and finally return to extras holding. Peterson and the others would organize them for the scenes.

A large viewing room had been converted to a hair and makeup room with numerous stations and bright vanity mirrors and loud chatter at each one. It was like something out of an early John Waters movie, surreal and not quite right. Specialty background actors got the most attention. In addition to the "Las Vegas characters" there were Maurice/Madonna's friends, a group comprised of five female impersonators, Elvis and Michael Jackson impersonators, and Baton Bob, a local celebrity who had built a career twirling the baton on street corners around Atlanta.

The offices of the Costume department were close. It was quieter and felt much more sane. Jobst and whoever was helping her reviewed the costumes of the BG. Some they augmented and some they changed completely. But one by one they reviewed them all. A lot of the specialty background actors had risen to the occasion. One man wore a matador costume, another brought a ventriloquist dummy ala Charlie McCarthy, another a stuffed animal. One had an empty rolling oxygen canister. There were a number of masks, the best ones high-end Mardi-Gras style. There were also a handful of generic background actors who came through, part of a group of 80 planned.

Dayna Pink had been on set of the traffic scene and came inside the department office at the funeral home. She stood in the largest interior hallway talking to the assistant costume designer. A man in a dog collar and gloves wearing a G-string and fishnet stockings with thin outerwear approached them to review his costume. Pink looked bemused and turned to the assistant.

"What do you think?"

"It's a little much," the assistant answered.

Pink nodded. "I agree," she said, looking back at the young man. "It's a little much."

The young man understood that meant "no." He looked disappointed and for just an instant like he might argue. Instead he turned away without a word in the direction of the Costume department office, where in all likelihood he'd already been told no.

On the other side of the chapel, the check in point for background actors was slow. The second call time had passed and Peterson realized something was amiss. She went to talk to the extras casting person. He said a lot of his people weren't showing up. Worse than that, he didn't think they would. How many BG was he short? He estimated it could be 60 percent fewer than he promised.

Peterson got on the walkie but she also went on foot to the other side of the funeral home property to find Rake in person. This would be serious on any day, but it was also happening on the day they had NBC on site, along with additional studio people and producers.

As she made her way back from talking to him, the 2nd AD racked her brain. Where was she going to find 50 people or more? She arrived at the extras table and began lamenting of the challenge. The preacher from the church next door spoke up. The production had leased overflow space from the church. He had also signed up as an extra to play the part of a preacher. It was a lark for him, but how often do they shoot a movie next door to your church?

How soon would she need the 50 people? He thought he could get a good number of parishioners fairly quickly. Why, some of them were literally within walking distance right now! They'd love to be in the movie, he said. Peterson got back on the walkie to relay the news.

Just as the lunch break was starting it looked like the preacher might just deliver a good number of his flock. Several arrived right away and more were on the way. It wasn't clear how many, but he was doing his part as an extras casting agent.

They checked the background actors in quickly, and then hurried through hair and makeup. Things picked up in the auditorium. Kelson had retrieved his mics from the van and moved his sound cart to the auditorium and set up there. The funeral scene required music playback, and the operator was there. The scene had the funeral goers singing Madonna's "I Remember" and he got it cued up. The grips had already covered the windows in the front of the room, but Kerry Rawlins made adjustments. The Camera department set the cameras up on stage facing into the audience and, that accomplished, stood around.

Rake and Awa were in the chapel getting things in place, while Peterson oversaw the organizational effort to manage the BG outside. A small group stood in a line inside the building and near the entrance chapel. The larger group of background actors -- there were enough although not as many as they wanted -- had been collected together in front of the building in two more groups.

The director had been talking to various people as it was all set up, the noise level in the room rising by the minute. He made a casual sweep of the place looking at the BG, and scoping it all out. One of the prettiest women in the group was chatting up one of the cameramen. She was still there a few minutes later when the director circled back. The two were standing closer together, now deeply engrossed in conversation. Turteltaub stopped at the duo. "Is he telling you he's my son?"

When camera was ready, Rake alerted second team, who were already sitting in the pews. The background actors were next, then the specialty actors sprinkled throughout.

Turteltaub hadn't made any noticeable effort to enhance his appearance for the television cameras, and there wasn't anything wrong with what he was wearing. But several others had dressed better than normal. The NBC crew's boom operator hovered nearby, the news camera aimed at Turteltaub. This was all B roll, Lauer still two hours away.

A few minutes later, the director leaped up and over the two steps leading to the stage. "Hello everybody!" The place was filled by then, funeral-going extras chatting away, and they were stunned silent. Turteltaub scanned the audience, a big smile on his face. He was both comfortable and entertained at the same time, which put them at ease.

"I have good news!" he said, his voice booming out as he waved out actor Roger Bart. The man to be eulogized in the scene, rather, the actor who played him, was alive and well. The crowd was in on the joke, and they laughed and clapped. Bart, who was in the dressing room scene they would shoot last, ducked off the stage quickly.

Turteltaub turned more serious. It was a somber occasion; how could it not be with this bunch of characters? There was more laughter. He talked to them like he might talk to a dozen people. There was no dialogue in the scene, he explained, so any comedy would be silent. "Be funny!"

"I'm going to warn you now that we're going to play the same song, over and over," the director said. "Then we're going to play it again! We're going to play it so much you'll be singing it into next week. But sing out proud, sing for Maurice! Are you ready?" The momentum had built as he had said it and now they cheered. "Yes!"

The music playback operator had the song cued up and let it rip. Turteltaub remained on the stage and sang along, swaying with the music, lifting his arms in the process, which the crowd parroted.

"I'll remember the strength that you gave me,
Now that I'm standing on my own
I'll remember the way that you saved me
I'll remember..."

Once the audience had some practice they called in the main actors. The camera would pan across the kooky bunch of people they had collected for the scene, the audience holding hands as they sang. Another shot had the camera pan across Archie holding hands with Sam holding hands with Billy holding hands with Paddy who was holding hands with ... the Michael Jackson impersonator. All of the actors but Freeman wore yarmulkes.

There were seven people in the Set Dec department in Atlanta. Cassidy, the buyer, a set dec assistant who acted as coordinator, a leadman and three set dressers, one of whom worked on set. All of them, aside from the on set dresser, worked on call.

Their work happened before and after the shooting crew, as had been the case with the interior chapel scene. They had set dressing in place ahead in advance of the shooting day. It was relatively easy compared to a lot of the sets they had put together for the movie. They put the table for the casket front and center in the chapel, added the red velour cover, and then added the casket. The rest was easy. Two giant photos of the deceased, both as Maurice and in full makeup as Madonna, sat on easels. Two Madonna wigs were placed on the easel of the photo of Maurice.

The flowers, which needed to be fresh, arrived in the morning ahead of call. There were a lot of arrangements, the largest for the top of the casket. Then they finished little tweaks from there. A sign on an easel in front of the room with removable letters that read, "Memorial for Maurice J. Tischler." A personalized sign-in book for funeral-goers was in front on the table.

Konrad Lewis had been hired as the on set dresser about a week earlier. His job was the same as the other set dressers with an important caveat. He adjusted the furniture and other decorations on shooting days. His job was to accommodate the movement of the camera, grip and lighting setups and whatever else came up in the course of photography.

That morning it had been securing the largest of the flower arrangements to the casket. The arrangement kept slipping but he found a way to keep them from moving. In the next scene, pallbearers would be carrying the casket, and no flowers were needed. It was an eclectic group that included Carrot Top, an Elvis impersonator, a Cirque du Soleil performer and a magician, and several of Maurice's female impersonator friends, all of whom were in high heels. The cameras rolled, getting the solemn looking actors as they carried the casket. Susan, Maurice/Madonna's widow, followed behind.

The second the pallbearers passed the cameras they would unload the casket, which meant the others caught the weight. Lewis was front and center of the mix, balancing the casket safely to its resting position. "Konrad Lewis! Stronger than 10 men!" someone teased him in carnival barker voice. His reputation among the shooting crew was established.

336

Lauer was at work perhaps 100 feet away. His feature segment was well underway by then. The NBC camera crew was shooting the *Last Vegas* camera crew and Rake and Accardo and Turteltaub and whoever else was nearby. The Today anchorman yelled 'Action!' and 'Cut!' when the real director told him.

Turteltaub played along but only so long, since he wasn't getting his work done. As soon as he could reasonably do it, he took his headphones off, set them on the stand in front of him with purpose. He walked toward Lauer and stuck out his hand, thanking him, very much. The timing was perfect and Lauer had what he needed. He was done.

The anchor's real business, the interviews with the actors, was next. The dark interior room was well lighted, the props shining in the background. It was a good, short interview, the personalities of the actors coming through. Michael Douglas took the lead for the group, Freeman and Kline participated comfortably, and De Niro remained quiet. The anchor asked them what it was like to work with each other for the first time. He asked about their respective ages, which thrilled no one.

Eventually De Niro was the only one who hadn't spoken, and he seemed likely to keep it that way. It prompted Lauer's focus. The Today host had to get something from De Niro.

"If one of you were to be considered the guy who is all business..." the anchor asked, looking at the actor. "Is there a taskmaster here?"

"Not me!" said De Niro. The group laughed.

"I wasn't looking at you for a reason. It's just my gaze ended on you," Lauer said.

"Everybody's at ease about their own and everybody else's process and rhythm, so that's great," De Niro said. "Because it's easy, everybody does what they want, everybody adjusts to everybody. We're having a lot of fun."

The news crew packed up their equipment after the interview was over and headed to the airport. Rather than return the equipment they borrowed to stage the set, they left it where it was. This irked one of the departments who had loaned their equipment for set decorating. They had enough to do tearing down the scene to move to Mailing Avenue.

The bullpen in Mailing Avenue had been quieter than normal as it prepared for the onslaught Thursday of the full cast and crew. It was detail work. That many additional people would tax the plumbing system and there were portable toilets to order, privacy lining for the Costume department cages in the first warehouse where catering would be located, and parking to manage. It was a smaller version of what had happened in prep, in that they tried to imagine anything needed and then got it done in advance. It wasn't advanced science but at the same time it wasn't something done by most businesses.

Kamishin wanted to establish the new parking rules right away so they weren't still dealing with it later. The bullpen crew made and posted signs. A memo to crew was attached to the call sheet Wednesday night that spelled out the rules: The lot in front of the building was no longer open to all. Unless specifically approved, all crew should park in the adjacent lot. The good news, although the memo didn't say it, was that the lot was close, up a short hill in full sight of the main entrance of the studio. Badalato had secured it months earlier for this time period.

The Transportation department laid out the lot that was the backyard of the Mailing Avenue soundstages. Power was put in place ahead of time, large generators contained in an external trailer as well as other machinery close to the far end of the building. A hundred fat, snake-size cords and cables, neatly organized and lined up like a small community, lead inside.

The trailers for the main actors, save De Niro's, were lined up at the back of the property, parallel to each other and perpendicular to the warehouse. De Niro's trailer was parked parallel to the building on the other side of the driveway and paved area that ran parallel to the warehouses, as close as it could be to the entrance to the warehouse without blocking traffic. The multi-office trailers and two-unit star trailers were lined up on one side, between the actors' and De Niro's motor coach. That left a blacktop area, and room for more vehicles to be parked as the need arose. There was plenty of room for that and for vehicles to drive in and out with their charges. The Transportation department was also seeing that leased vehicles used on location and no longer needed, like the costume trailer, were returned.

Work on the sets had continued on the soundstages at a frenzied pace. The Binion's set was ready. Like almost all of the sets built on the soundstages, it was designed to look like its counterpart in Las Vegas. The difference with Binion's was the onus placed on matching the theme, color and tone of it, since the scenes would be edited alongside those shot at the casino. The penthouse suite needed to replicate the Aria but it wasn't going to be juxtaposed on screen next to a real suite.

Carpenters had built the Binion's set over a period of days and it had filled in from there. The layout had the lounge area with bar and stage on one side. It had an intimate feel to it, perfect for meeting and conversing with a lounge singer. A large hallway wrapped around half of the lounge, the two areas separated by a five-foot wall with decorative bars on top. The back area would be populated with gaming machines, giving the lounge a more expansive feel while subliminally reminding people they were in Sin City. All of it had to be wired.

The Electric department spent days on "practicals," a term used for lights that appear in shots. Sconces lined the hallway wall and power was installed to light slots or other gaming machines to be brought it for set decorating. The lounge had multiple western-style chandeliers and behind the bar was a glass-topped cabinet with staggered shelves for alcohol. Lighting was installed underneath it, which would force light up through the bottles to brighten the bar and bring out the beveled glass backdrop. Above the bar was a row of light bulbs like those used in a vanity light. Even exit signs were lighted.

Painters applied a first coat of paint or stain on Monday and added a second coat Tuesday. Carpet was installed on Wednesday. Gaming machines were wheeled in and set up along the perimeter shortly thereafter. Dozens of tables and chairs, two different kinds, were spread around the lounge. Stools stood at the bar. The circular stage at one end of the bar had seemed ignored. There were no walls behind it, which exposed the back of the warehouse and giant rolling doors. With the rest of the stage done, the Set Dec department installed long, gold-colored curtains, which also served to block the warehouse from view.

Setting up the bar was easy with the product placement agreement in place and the goods delivered. Boxes of booze had been shipped, courtesy of Bacardi, and were at the ready. Best known for its rum, Bacardi was a booze behemoth with more than 100 brands and labels. Some were well known, like Grey Goose vodka, Dewar's Blended Scotch whisky, Bombay Sapphire gin, Martini vermouth, Eristoff vodka, Cazadores tequila. They mixed in with the non-trademarked bottles unboxed and set up behind the bar. The non-branded bottles were a variety of glass, different widths and designs, and from a distance they would looked like a regular bar set up.

An electric Bud Lite sign would be visible on the wall near the gaming machines, part of an agreement with Anheuser Busch, which also provided buckets and collars for set decorating. The brand had been seen on camera, although that wasn't the same thing as it ending up on screen. It was used both at the bikini party in the form of a banner, as well as in the hands of actor Jerry Ferrara. His character, Todd, enjoyed a Stella Artois.

The last touches were the lightest. Each table had faux candles, which added light, along with small standup ads for casino events. Hundreds of cocktail napkins were in stacks. Waiter trays and note pads were at the ready. As normal, props would handle specific items touched by the actors, set decorating the rest. But by Wednesday night it was ready to go, the lingering smell of new carpet was the only giveaway that it hadn't been there a week earlier.

Dozens of crew were inside at 6:30 a.m. Cinema Catering was an apt name for the company hired to provide meals for cast, crew and extras. It had moved with the shooting crew from location-to-location since the return from Nevada. Now the company had settled in at Mailing Avenue for the duration.

Buffet tables with hot food on one end and cold on the other lined the wall created by the shrouded chainlink fence wall. Another row of tables were next to the closest warehouse wall. That was set up as a beverage area with various offerings. The highlight of catering for this show was quickly identified. A self-serve juicing bar was at the ready. It was an industrial-grade juicer surrounded with fresh fruits and vegetables. It was a fairly extensive offering, with root vegetables, beets and ginger. This was a good sign.

Almost all movie catering is a cut above the food found in cafeterias in most workplaces but there are also levels. It wasn't unreasonable to conclude that the bigger the budget, the better the catering and craft service was but it wasn't always true. Badalato and Samuels had kept their word in terms of going for the higher grade but it wasn't purely altruistic. Badalato's refrain, "You can ask people to do a lot if you feed them well," was proving true.

By 6:45 a.m. anyone on the shooting crew was long gone from catering, off to ready the set. It was about that time that crew on the production side moved in to the area to eat or pick up food to take to their desks. That wasn't coincidence. It was a longstanding courtesy that actors and shooting crew ate first, since they had less flexibility. Someone out-of-the-know might get in

340

line early but they probably hadn't been versed in the unspoken rule or, worse, they had, and didn't care.

The move to the soundstages had changed the makeup of the first of the row of warehouse spaces at Mailing Avenue and it wasn't just catering. Before then it had largely been the domain of the Costume and Art departments, both of which had doors that opened to it. The Art department had used it as the need arose, such as to build the bedroom set later used for the scene shot at the convention center, or to spread out the vintage 1955 material to decide what they would use to decorate the store. The chainlink fence installed in prep for the Costume department now had a privacy cloth. It made it almost impossible to see through. It had the effect of blending it into the background more like a wall than a fence.

The Costume department had also taken charge of the large, unused room with the deck in the back of the building. In a previous incarnation of the building, the room had served as a lunch or break room. It sat empty for the first months of prep but it hadn't escaped Jobst's attention. She made her case quietly. It was a separate and secure place to put the most expensive costumes and accessories -- the main actors' closets -- something that made sense to Badalato. She moved in quickly, almost "stealthily," someone said, taking it over before anyone noticed, but it also made most sense. It was closest to the Costume department offices and they needed secure storage.

The deck, however, remained Badalato's domain. He and Kamishin had resumed taking breaks out there, often staying to work, as soon as they returned from Las Vegas. Plenty of crew, although not all, knew if they weren't in their bullpen offices to look for them there.

No one was happier about the space than Buddy and the other dogs that remained on Mailing Avenue. He had balls and a couple of toys at the ready. The most beloved was a tool used to fling a ball down the green space, sending canines racing after it. Badalato used it, but it also was at the ready for anyone to use, something Buddy encouraged. It got plenty of use, including by people who came out with a question for Badalato or Kamishin and found them on the phone or otherwise occupied. Instead of standing around awkwardly, they could engage in the ball toss.

The first day in the studio was guaranteed to feel long. There was just one scene on the schedule but it was a big one. The scene was 5.25 pages and included all five of the main actors, and a waitress. It was important because it introduced Steenburgen's character. Diana Boyle was an Atlanta lawyer who relocated to Las Vegas to pursue a lifelong dream as a singer. The scene kicked off with her singing on stage.

It was a story that had some resonance for Steenburgen, who had become a singer later in life under an unusual circumstance. About five years earlier she had gone under general anesthesia for minor surgery on her arm. When she awoke, she had a passion for music. It was more than that, even. It was like a radio was on. She had music on the brain. Even a casual comment seemed to be part of a tune. It persisted and at first it frightened her, as if she might be going crazy. Then she embraced it and started writing music. She had stuck with it, getting a home in Nashville with husband Ted Danson. A lounge scene in *Last Vegas* would feature "Cup of Trouble," which Steenburgen had co-written with two others.

The scene opened with Diana Boyle singing, the sound wafting out into the casino where Billy Gherson hears. He is drawn into Binion's to listen. Eventually Sam, Archie and Paddy arrive and Diana joins them for a drink. What made it time consuming was the number of people in the scene with speaking roles, as well as the waitress who comes to get their drink order.

This scene was like the others in that the master shot was done first. They recorded it all the way through with a wide enough angle to include everyone. In the mid part of the last century, the moviegoer might have seen a lot of that. In contemporary filmmaking it was just the start. Once the master was shot, they got coverage of each actor. Most of those required a different set-up. That meant a scene like this was one of the more tedious things to shoot, because it had to be done over and over again.

"For a director, these scenes are not fun," Turteltaub admitted. "Actors are not so thrilled either, although they don't mind as much the parts where the camera is looking at them," he said, laughing. What made it easier was having great actors in the scene, including Steenburgen in the center. He liked the actress and referred to her as the "muse of the movie."

The director was also aware that shooting a scene like that was tedious for crew, particularly the cinematographer and Camera department. It was up to Hennings to match the light and tone of the scene so it could drop in next to what he shot on location at Binion's in Las Vegas without anyone flagging it. Each setup -- every time they did the scene again to get coverage of a different actor -- took effort. Turteltaub's natural inclination with scenes like this was to start with the characters with the most dialogue. In this case he had Hennings weigh in on what order to shoot the actors for greatest efficiency. It went off as easily as any other scene like it.

After they wrapped for the day, they toured the penthouse sets. Hennings wasn't happy with the existing light, particularly in one area. As before, the light, or lack of it, was almost personal. It was core to his nature as a cinematographer and it would not stand. More practicals were needed and it would all have to be tested. That would require working over the weekend, which meant overtime, and Samuels and Badalato happily agreed.

It added impetus to Henery and his crew. They already needed to finish building the penthouse sets in time to leave room for the Set Dec department to do its job. This meant the Camera, Grip and Electric departments also needed time in advance of Monday the following week, when the penthouse scenes were scheduled to start. There were limits to how much construction work could be done when they were shooting, given the edge of the Binion's set was about 60 feet away from where the larger set began. They couldn't hammer or run saws or do anything noisy, which covered a lot of what had to be done. That extended to the adjacent warehouse as well.

The soundstage light and bell system, standard on movie and television sets, had been installed at both entrances. A red warning light, known as a red eye or wig-wag, was on when they were shooting, often accompanied by a PA there to monitor admittance. The bell system provided specific signals so people knew what was happening on set if they weren't close enough to hear Rake and the echo of the ADs. It would cue construction crew in on when they could hammer or use other loud tools. As soon as they called "cut," followed by a triggering of the light and bell system, whirring and hammering started. The construction crew worked while the shooting crew was at lunch. More construction crew came as soon as they had wrapped for the day.

Chloe Lipp, the art department coordinator, had day players at the ready to work. One set up camp at a table in front of a large mirror on the back wall of the dining area where De Niro's character would have a lonely meal. Bomba and Cassidy wanted a higher-end look so the department acquired thousands of pieces of smooth rounded glass as if for a mosaic, each of which had to be glued on. It was a nice design trick. From a distance it looked like a clear Baccarat crystal glass, but they did it for pennies on the dollar.

The large backdrops for the set were also hung. The giant photo images of the Las Vegas skyline, commissioned during prep, now hung like curtains along the back of the penthouse set. One was the daylight skyline and the other night, but they were disappointed with one of them. It was rough enough that they debated whether it could be used. If not it might mean changing a scene from night to day or closing the curtains or something, which was a decision for Turteltaub. There was no replacing it this late in the game.

There was another trick to bringing the backdrop of a skyline to life, regardless of any flaws. Other members of the Art department began to sew tiny sequins on fishing line, which was hung in long strands in front of the backing. On camera they would give the effect of a glistening skyline lights.

The finish work also pulled together. The faux marble was buffed out and touched up, doors were hung, another coat of paint applied in the main bedroom set and any number of other things. One of the biggest tasks involved filling the two small dipping pools in the penthouse living room. The pools went a long way in making the space seem like a high-end penthouse but they were also part of the script. Douglas's character would push De Niro's into one of the pools, payback for him having done the same to him at the Aria pool.

Now one of the pools was leaking.

CHAPTER SEVENTEEN
Shoot Week 7
Dec. 1-7
Day 27, 28, 29, 30, 31

HENERY AND THE CONSTRUCTION DEPARTMENT needed all of Friday to finish the penthouse but they got it done, with the exception of the swimming pools. Those were drained and resealed and left empty to dry over the weekend. That left Saturday for set decorating. Then Hennings and a pared-back version of the Camera, Grip and Electric departments came in Sunday.

The guiding hand of Set Dec, and the extent to which Cassidy utilized product placement, was evident before the swing gang got to work Saturday. Aria had supplied four control touch screens and six wall-light panels, which authenticated the technology-laden villa they were recreating. High-end appliance maker Viking dominated the penthouse kitchen. They used a wine cellar with an estimated value of $7,349, a refrigerator-freezer valued at $3,849, a gas range with a $6,599 price tag. The French Door Bottom-Mount Top Grille Kit had a thrifty $189 value.

They had used three sinks provided by MTI Baths estimated at $949 each, two in the master bath and one in the bar. Kohler provided various fixtures, including three Loure lavatory faucets valued at $693 each, a Sallie toilet at $926, and an antique faucet at $1,023, along with a handful of other less expensive items. Those were the purchase prices estimated for accounting purposes but the paperwork also noted rental figures, which were lower. The cost of leasing all of the Viking kitchen equipment was $5,395, for instance.

The Olhausen pool table, handmade for the production, had been a nice addition. It had been raised to the top floor and now anchored a set. Olhausen offered a range of pool tables and prices. This one was valued at $8,738, the kit that contained cue, rack and balls $560.

The rental price for the package was estimated at a more palatable $2,789. In exchange, the company wanted brand logo exposure of its table, perhaps on cab toppers or in advertising on the Binion's set. While the script hadn't called for the characters to play billiards, it was the stated goal of Bomba and

Cassidy to provide Turteltaub with options. They also created a massage room and finalized a sitting area with a skyline view.

Product placement hadn't helped with furniture needs and it hadn't eliminated Cassidy's budget challenges. He viewed it strategically and opted to spend the money primarily in the big living room set. All of the furniture there -- the couches, oversized multi-person round chairs, the dining table and chairs, the bar and stools -- looked expensive. He rented what he could. When it came to appliances, the movie was a great renter because the equipment wouldn't actually be used. There were no gas lines, and no plumbing to the sinks and toilets.

The downside was in the event of damage, which was a much bigger risk when it came to furniture. Lease agreements required the production company to buy anything harmed at full price. It also took a lot more staff time to manage product placement.

The furniture in the master bedroom suite, where two scenes were planned, also reflected a budget choice. It was attractive, solid furniture and it looked good, just not in the same way the living room did. The difference was only subtle until you looked closer. It prompted an observer to ask Cassidy where he got it. For just a second he looked stricken, as if he had been caught installing a plaid chair next to a striped couch. He admitted, reluctantly, that it had come from Ikea. He preferred that not be publicly known. Cassidy allowed that it wasn't his first choice or even what he thought was best for the set. This place was a five-star penthouse and most five star penthouses were not decorated with Ikea.

With the furniture in place, the Set Dec department turned to detail work, culling through other boxes shipped from Aria. Boxes contained Aria telephones, Aria information books, gray "Taste of ARIA" books that highlighted its restaurants, even Aria notepads. Another contained items for use in the bathroom, set tray and pieces, and tissue holders.

The shipment also included bar trays, ice buckets, martini shakers, ice scoopers and utensil sets. Villa glassware came with red wine glass, white wine glass, martini, highball, rock, shot, snifter, champagne flute and Pilsner/water glass. Cassidy used it all except for the white wine glass, which was broken when it arrived.

The artwork for the walls came out toward the end. Cassidy reached out to his sister, Diane Cassidy, owner of Cassidy Stock Shots, to see what she had. She was reliable, her pricing was competitive, even good, and importantly, if she had what he needed, the images would come quickly --

with clearance. That meant all legal approvals to use it were in place when the seven pieces arrived as promised.

The last task was to try to protect it. One spilled beverage or grease mark could be disastrous this close to shooting. This living room furniture was coordinated, and none of it was commonly available. If something was damaged they couldn't just run out and pick up another.

Peterson included a note on the prelim, which was circulated Friday night, as well as the call sheet for Monday: "The Furnishings on the Aria set are extremely delicate and expensive. PLEASE DO NOT SIT ON THE FURNITURE. No food or drink allowed on set. Thank you for your help." The final step Saturday was to place signage on individual furniture. The signs were the same but bigger: "Do Not Sit On The Furniture" and "No Food or Drink on Set."

There was a relaxed feel on the soundstages on Sunday with the skeleton crew of the Camera, Grip and Electric departments. It was stress free, since they weren't shooting, and it came with overtime. It didn't hurt that their workload was just a little bit lighter for the last weeks of shooting. The farthest they would move equipment from now on was from one connected warehouse to another. Most days it would just be moving it from the cages to the other side of the main warehouse.

Most department equipment could be rolled easily, but lifting it the six-plus feet to the first floor of the penthouse was another thing. The Construction department had leased industrial equipment like a Toyota forklift to lift things up to the first floor of the penthouse. A scissors lift was inside the penthouse to hoist crew or furniture, as it had the day before, to the second floor of the set.

Chris Flurry and Chad Rivetti got to work ahead of Hennings, who was delayed by a fender bender. They got equipment for one camera to the penthouse living room and set it up. The cinematographer's tall, multi-level rolling workstation was parked in the hallway and readied, lights and monitors on.

Hennings had identified the main threat to effectively lighting, at least for the immediate work ahead, in the foyer inside the suite. Double doors opened to the hotel hallway on one side and the foyer eventually stepped down into the large penthouse living room on the other. The foyer was a wide area with relatively short ceiling heights unlike most of the penthouse, which opened up at the top to reveal the warehouse ceiling. The walls had a darker finish while the larger penthouse living room was bright, the opposite wall a long expanse of floor-to-ceiling windows overlooking the faux Las Vegas skyline. There was discussion about whether they needed to add anything to the hotel hallway, which might have been a set in its own right. It was carpeted, its walls finished and adorned with lighted sconces like the ones at Aria. Certainly portions of it would be visible in scenes at the door.

Hennings was harried when he arrived a short time later after a minor fender-bender. He looked at the table and the recessed lighting laid out on it, which they were wiring for installation in the ceiling, then he walked around and looked at other areas of the penthouse. Eventually, the DP grabbed his Smart Water and sat down on one of the couches to wait while they cut holes in the ceiling and installed the lights.

Hennings was based in Los Angeles and worked primarily in television. He did occasional movies, most recently *Horrible Bosses* (2011). He had arrived in terms of cinematography via the world of rock and roll documentaries. He worked on U2: *Rattle and Hum* (1988) and *Madonna: Truth or Dare* (1991). He had earlier mentioned shooting the Madonna movie, part of the Blond Ambition tour, which prompted a follow-up question about the famous scene where her mic goes out. Madonna, who was singing acapella, was angry about it on camera and apparently even angrier off-camera. Hennings was still miffed, all these years later. Camera crew had gone to incredible lengths to get those shots and all she had cared about was the one mistake, he said. And camera had nothing to do with sound.

When they were ready, Hennings went to his cart, newly adorned with a female Styrofoam mannequin head on the top. Intent on the various monitors and dials, he didn't seem to notice it and no one asked. The cart was stacked with a dozen pieces of equipment. The monitor was the dominant presence with the penthouse living room clear and bright. There was just one monitor hooked up, since they were working with one camera, where he typically had two and occasionally three. They had used four for the bikini party.

Hennings pushed a button on one piece of equipment and a ghostly image of waves appeared. The Leader Multi SDI Monitor LV 5330 was reminiscent of a heart monitor with multiple, white heartbeats lined up and shaded in, light to dark. That alone cost about $6,000. Made for camera mounts, the device read technical aspects of what the camera saw, like aperture, brightness, aspect ratios and chroma, a measure of the intensity or purity of color. Like the monitors, the Leader was just seeing A Camera, although it could provide data from any camera working.

He stood there another minute pushing buttons and peering into the monitor and then went out to the camera to talk to Flurry. That began the cycle, Hennings going back and forth, peering into monitors as they tested different things.

Chad Rivetti stood off to the side talking to his father, Tony Rivetti. The older man was on the movie to fill in on B Camera for a couple of weeks before he started another job. He had the same role as his son did on A Camera. Both were 1st A.C.s or "focus pullers," the descriptive name for the job with a primary role of focusing and refocusing the lens.

Tony Rivetti was one of the best known A.C.s in the business. He started as a camera operator in the late '60s and early '70s on animated television shows like "Super Chicken," "Sabrina and the Groovy Goolies," and "Archie's Funhouse," and moved from there to live action camera work. Over the intervening decades he had collected an impressive list of credits, one that continued to grow. He worked on television and a cadre of noted movies, like *The Right Stuff*, *White Men Can't Jump*, *In the Line of Fire*, *Waterworld*, *Contact*, *Black Hawk Down*, *The Bucket List*, *Social Network*, *Secretariat* and *Argo*, which was about 10 percent of his credit list.

Tony Rivetti's reputation not only preceded him it preceded his son. The first thing Turteltaub said when he greeted the younger man in Las Vegas in prep was, 'You're Tony's kid, right?' That was completely normal for Chad Rivetti. He heard it a little bit less as the years passed and he built his own strong list of credits. But he certainly didn't mind it. He was proud of his dad and had learned a lot from him.

"He taught me you can't guess all the time. You have to be out there, actively, looking at what you're going to shoot." One of the tricks was to measure inanimate objects. "The bar is 10 feet away. If the actor is going to walk over to a table, you should walk over to the chair, too, so you have an idea." But you didn't stop there. You cased the whole area. "That way if the actor goes into his own world, and to a different spot entirely, I'll be good."

Chad Rivetti grew up spending summers on location around the world visiting his father. "I loved banging around on camera trucks. If you were working nights, you'd take cases off the shelf, set up furniture pads, make a bed and fall asleep." His goal at 11, 12 or 13, was to make himself useful as an assistant so camera crew would teach him, and they did. He learned how to load film magazines, which held film stock before and after it had been exposed in light-tight chambers. "I'd load a mag and they'd grab it and use it for the shot." It was a process, since film mags weren't uniform. "There was a lot of trial and error back then," he said, laughing.

After he finished high school he started college but that wasn't where he wanted to be. When he dropped out he went to visit his father on the set of *Wyatt Earp*, which was shooting in Santa Fe. Chad Rivetti found some work and hung around a couple of months. Then he heard from his brother, Darin, who had a job as a key set PA, ultimately earning a 2nd 2nd AD credit for *Forrest Gump* (1994). The Camera department was looking for a camera assistant.

Chad Rivetti got the job and headed to Savannah, GA. His first day they were shooting the Vietnam War combat scenes on location in Fripp Island, S.C., about 90 minutes from the small city. It was a realistic set. They had added palmetto trees and other greenery to make it more jungle-like. There were guns and helicopters and pyrotechnics that included loud explosions. He had been on a lot of movie sets and on most of the studio lots in Los Angeles, but this was a bit overwhelming for the young man.

"It was the first time I got thrown into the deep end," he said. "It was the first time on my own, with people I didn't know, and I was walking onto a film set with expectations of doing the job without being the 1st A.C.'s kid." Luckily, he knew enough to do it. There were "a lot of bosses" and he learned a lot. He watched cinematographer Don Burgess, awestruck, and listened closely.

No one knew how successful *Forrest Gump* would become but it had a couple of things going for it. It had a good budget, roughly three times that of *Last Vegas* when adjusted for inflation. And it had director Robert Zemeckis, who at that point was known for *Back to the Future*, which he had also written. *Forrest Gump* went on to gross $677 million, which by the same inflation measure would be over $1 billion.

A couple of years later all three Rivettis were working on the same movie, a rare occasion. It was *Contact* (1997), also helmed by Zemeckis with Burgess as cinematographer. The movie, which starred Jodie Foster and Matthew McConaughey, was about the first radio proof of extraterrestrial life. The screenplay was based on a story by Carl Sagan. The seminal astrophysicist and author also consulted on the movie but was ill and passed away during production.

Coming on the heels of *Forrest Gump*, with six Academy Awards and impressive box office receipts, it upped the ante for *Contact*. Burgess didn't just want a different look for the movie, he wanted different terrain altogether. It is talked about to this day for its camerawork. One scene is said to contain an "impossible shot." It's a memory sequence where the main character, as a child, tries to save her father from a heart attack. She runs up the staircase and down the hall to get to the medicine cabinet. Special effects had placed blue screen in the medicine cabinet, so they could flip the shot after the actress closed it.

It was impressive but not the only remarkable bit of photography that happened on *Contact*. "There were a bunch of shots like that," he recalled. "There was Steadicam and dolly work and three shots they'd put into one," he said. They would get half of a screen shot in one location, Washington DC or Arecibo, Puerto Rico and then the other half in Los Angeles, and make it look like one seamless shot. "It was a giant undertaking for the '90s."

There were two camera trucks on the movie, nine cameras in total, both of them loaded with film stock. "We had three formats, six different cameras working," he recalled. The formats were the types of film they were using, which varied with the cameras. There was standard 35 mm and 60 mm, they would double the 35 mm to come with a 70 mm, and film for the Vista Vision camera, which was a different animal entirely. Vista Vision turned the 35mm negative into a horizontal position within the camera gate. It was similar in some ways to the technology developed by IMAX, although Vista Vision was only in use for a few years.

The other notable blue-screen work on *Contact* he recalled was a shot of Jodie Foster's character talking to her deceased father in another dimension. They used blue screen that was 20 feet from floor to ceiling. The floor was covered in blue screen as well. It was heady stuff for a young man. The job on *Forrest Gump* confirmed he wanted -- and could have -- a career behind the lens. *Contact* opened his eyes to what the camera could do. It made him want to be a director and he still thought about that.

The biggest change in a sea of changes over the years was the shift from film to digital. But there were many others, and constant upgrades. The self-avowed "camera geek" enjoyed keeping up with the changes in technology. He frequently went to the union, which posted information on the website and held seminars and classes about new technology. Panavision and Sony also offered trainings on new products.

Some of it, he admitted, was self-preservation. "If I get a call from a DP I don't know I have to talk in a way that shows I'm competent," he explained. "If he mentions something I don't know, that's going to lose me the gig. I want every advantage over the next guy." What was more important was keeping the jobs he landed. He needed to understand everything about the camera, especially new technology, because it prevented problems from happening on set. It helped ensure he could handle anything out of the ordinary that came up.

Rivetti said there would continue to be big changes going forward. The equipment they were using on *Last Vegas* was state of the art, but it wouldn't be in a couple of years, and never mind 20 years out. There was even talk they could someday automate focus pulling. He couldn't wait to see how that worked.

From the moment Monday began the week seemed divided in two parts. The first four days on the soundstages were scenes of the main characters in the penthouse, which would be relatively quiet. On Friday, the big party scenes began, and with that a dramatic rise in energy that came with a full cast and two hundred additional people on the stages.

The bullpen had laid the framework for the influx of people in waves. The skeleton crew had first braced for the return of the company from Las Vegas, then for when the Atlanta location work was completed and the full crew moved to the soundstages. Now it was girding for the full cast and nearly 1,000 extras by the time the penthouse party scenes were done.

Most departments were working to prepare for the party scenes. When the week ended, there would be two days left of principal photography.

Last Vegas had continued to be a dog show. Most of the crew pets were well known. Two dogs had been added to the movie crew family. Cassidy's dog, Blue, had been there periodically and was again in Set Dec. And Peterson had taken in a rescue pup. It was a young dog with a head so big for its body that it had a hard time lifting it. It was the wacky world of genetics, one parent a pit bull and the other a much smaller canine.

The travel office remained staffed with two people after Vegas. Getting studio execs and producers, Turteltaub and crew back and forth was the main mission, along with detailed accounting and documentation.

A good portion of it was doing the work a second time after the traveler changed plans. In addition to flights they booked limos or other ground transportation, which would also have to be changed. One executive held the record for changes. As with set paperwork, each revision garnered a different color code. That executive regularly had travel docs coded blue or pink and at least once, green, which meant a flight had been changed four times. It was likely people who made changes were oblivious to the paperwork headache and associated costs, and the Travel department wasn't going to tell them.

With the penthouse party scenes, which brought additional cast, Vegas people, and crew, the travel office resumed a schedule like the one it had in Las Vegas. Vegas people included getting the five Cirque du Soleil performers to Atlanta, but it wasn't just them. It was support staff, the artistic director, publicity, makeup and wardrobe. They were staying overnight, so they needed rooms and transportation. Then there was specialized technical crew to get to Atlanta.

All that was on top of the various producers and studio people. Some of it then required two trips because of the weekend break. They would be brought in Thursday to work Friday, then go home for the weekend and return Sunday for work Monday.

All expenses were tracked at the department level, which sent them to the Accounting department. Accounting did a daily "hot costs" report that summarized all of it, which went to Badalato and Samuels. Hot costs were a slice of what a department had spent that day compared to what they had been allotted for it. If the Grip department had seven people working, but had planned nine, they were under, and if it were the other way around, over. The weekly Cost Report tallied a week of daily hot costs together for distribution to the studios, which provided a more meaningful snapshot.

Then Badalato and Samuels had a conference call with executives from both studios.

Movie production accounting did things backward in the sense that they started with a budget and subtracted, where regular businesses added throughout the year and accounted for it in quarterly and annual reports. The hot costs, and the Cost Report, were another way to look at the health of the production as resources were depleted, said Badalato. That's what the studios wanted to see. "If the numbers are good, it's a short call," he said. "If not, it takes longer."

The first warehouse had already undergone a transformation. The Costume cages were on one side and the covering attached to the chainlink fences effectively blocked the interior from view. Catering had filled in the back. Some of its buffet tables were lined up against the fences as though it were a wall. The overall effect from the rest of the first warehouse was that the Costume department had disappeared. Extras casting took over the other side of the room, along with tables and chairs for another 150 people provided by catering. It made the warehouse seem small.

The Costume department area was like a different world. One section had the washing machine and dryer and steamer. Off to the side were several workstations with sewing machines. A costumer sat in front of one of them, her foot on the pedal making a whirring sound. Behind her a clothing rack had a single T-shirt on it. It said, "Paddy's Bar and Grill" and had been aged by the department for De Niro's character. It had been stone washed or stained or whatever they did to add 20 years, although it apparently had not made the Paddy's closet.

There was another area inside where they met with members of the cast. Most of the fittings were long over, but there was coordination, checking the costume or perhaps tweaking or repairing something. The costumes did not stay with the actors. All were returned to the Costume department until the next time they were needed. The actors closets were secured in the largest of the department offices.

There were just a couple of fittings left. Curtis Jackson, the hip hop artist and businessman better known as 50 Cent, was coming in next week. He would be on site for one day to shoot the scene he was in. Then there were two actors who would play a couple enjoying the music at Binion's, a comedic bit added by Turteltaub. Those last two hires pushed the total number of cast to 50, according to the accountant.

As a rule, main actors didn't come to the Costume department. They had private star trailers in the back and individual costumers who brought things back and forth and otherwise coordinated with Jobst. Pink would go to the trailers as needed. Each of them had a room on the end with a separate door that was outfitted with a chair for hair and makeup or costume review.

The costume designer had worked closely with Mary Steenburgen, the sole leading lady, and her character's biggest scenes were coming up. In the mix was a gold sequined Prada dress. All outfits, had been carefully considered long before now. This was the final look of the dress which had been "altered to fit exquisitely," as Jobst put it. Pink planned to personally attend to Steenburgen, who also had an assistant.

The Costume department was preparing for multiple scenes that would include the nearly full cast. But there were plenty of adjustments and new background actors and significant effort in checking plans already in place, like De Niro's closet. At least four of the same costume was needed for a scene like the one where he was pushed into the pool. The suit would most likely be ruined but even if it wasn't they needed a dry one for a second take. The others were kept for reshoots.

The two-dozen specialty background actors planned for the scene would require more time. This bunch wasn't as wild as the people in the Las Vegas-style funeral, and there was overlap. But there were still challenges, like the group of bridesmaids, GoGo dancers and the exotic dancer, who had several lines. The Cirque du Soleil troupe would be in character for their parts, and bringing their own people to do costumes, hair and makeup. Maurice's Friends, the group of female impersonators, also had their own look down, although the department would review them. One consideration was the big dance scene. Archie would be wearing his expensive, tailored red suit. He might dance with one of Maurice's friends, and they wouldn't want the costume that person wore to clash.

Luckily there was still four days to get it all in order. The next few shootings days were with the main cast, which felt like a lot of breathing room, depending on which department you were in.

As busy as everyone else was, the Art department was busier. In some ways it felt like the weeks leading up to the first shooting rather than a movie that was winding down. The Art department starts early in the process, because they are creating the sets. But a couple had been added.

The Art department was actively working on five sets, which they would deliver in the order in which they were needed. First up was the dressing room of a high-end clothier where the characters got their new suits. They also needed a chapel where Billy and Diana go on an errand, and three separate sets for a phone call between Billy, Archie and Sam.

Back in prep, the Locations department had shown Turteltaub a lot of options for chapels. He needed two and while they found one, he never settled on the other. Nothing appealed to him for the scene where Billy and Diana ran an errand, at least none that wouldn't be just as good or better on the stages.

Then there was the set for the airplane scenes where Paddy, Archie and Sam flew to Las Vegas, Paddy complaining all the while about Billy Gherson.

Luckily for the Art department given the rest of its workload, they had opted for the services of David Myers, owner of Jets & Props Aircraft Mockups. Leasing a set from the company was less expensive than it would be for the Art department to build it. Myers was willing to work with them. The hard cost of leasing the large, mockup aircraft was $10,000. They would hire and cover expenses for Myers, who would oversee installation, along with his crew and the cost of transportation. The 50-foot Boeing 737 mockup would arrive in a 53-foot semi next week.

The best part of the arrangement from a set decorator's perspective was that it was the real thing, sans engine and wings and electronics. The set was built from a retired jet acquired from Southwest Airlines. There was no connection to the product placement deal and it wouldn't say "Southwest," although the seats would have the same dark brown and blue coloring.

Jets & Props operated out of a 5,000-square-foot space in an industrial business area of North Hollywood, but it was fast outgrowing the space. It was filled to the edges with set packages and parts, a galley door, lighting, a row of "bottoms." A full seat in the airplane construction business is called a "bottom." The 737 package Four Fellas ordered contained 72 bottoms, a galley, and the exterior of an airplane bathroom.

Building stationary aircraft was a second career for Myers. His first was as a contractor and builder, and after a similar job building a mockup this was a logical transition. He came off more as an engineer than a builder, although he was both. All of the mockups were designed for movie production, which meant they had been widened to scale, but not where it was obvious.

356

There were other commercial and corporate aircraft mockups in the Jets & Props fleet, including a pristine Gulfstream Silver. It was also possible to lease part of a plane, say 10 windows or 20 windows, "or three window seats with Exterior skin" for a photo shoot. Then there was a cockpit, an aft galley with a flight attendant seat, a forward galley and starboard side door, a forward galley with beverage cart in it, a cockpit security door, a door open with jet way.

The question the Art department faced was where, exactly, were they going to put a set the size of the body of a commercial aircraft. As big as Mailing Avenue was, they were running out of places for sets. They could put the airplane fuselage in the mill shop. The Construction department, which was obviously busy, would have to move over.

Bomba also had a plan for the chapel.

The call sheet for the day included a note that a reporter from the Atlanta Journal-Constitution would be there. "EPK ON SET TODAY. Print Journalist on set today for observation only, no interviews (AJC)." EPK stood for Electronic Press Kit, which was recorded cast and crew interviews or other clips that captured the making of the movie to be used for publicity. The AJC reporter wouldn't interview the actors, but she would get to observe the action on set and to talk to Turteltaub. She was there as they prepped the set for Scene 49, summarized on the schedule as "Words can't describe the penthouse."

The scene took place after the four heroes arrive in a high roller suite for the first time. It had been one page in the original script and was now 2 5/8 pages. Scene 49 played off the heroes being out of their element, older men in a world with popular entertainers they knew nothing about, like 50 Cent. None of the characters planned on the fancy penthouse.

Comedy would ensue as the heroes tried to open the curtains themselves before discovering they were electronically controlled. Eventually it would require the assistance of the concierge, who would push the button. Then the curtains that lined multiple windows would magically open to reveal the fabulous Las Vegas skyline.

An issue with the curtains had been identified earlier, but everyone believed it was fixed. So, Turteltaub talked to Hennings about how he wanted to shoot it while the Camera, Grip and Electric departments went into motion to set up the shot.

But the man in charge of special effects was getting more nervous by the minute. The curtains still weren't working. As efforts failed he alerted Rake, who alerted Turteltaub. There would be a delay. Soon everyone, including the visiting reporter, knew about the malfunction. It took about an hour to rig them. They did it the old-fashioned way. Crew spread out along each big window, hidden from view of the cameras. When the time came they were cued, and all the crew opened the curtains in unison.

The big wide expanse of fake Las Vegas spread out in front, the full pools glistening in the foreground. Turteltaub was his most charming self as he chatted with the reporter. He told her some of the things he'd said before and would again. He was so awestruck to work with these world-class actors that half the time he fought the urge to ask for their autographs. Malfunctions were a normal occurrence on a movie set, he told the reporter. "The difference between a $150 million movie and our movie is that we have six sets of people opening curtains," he quipped.

The director had used that same budget parameter before in describing his work. The difference between a $150 million movie and a budget a small fraction of that size was in how many ways you could shoot something. What can we do to make it better? What else can we do to make it better? With a big budget you could think of everything or at least try hard. Smaller budgets meant thinking fast and moving quickly.

That didn't mean he was okay with the pool leaking or being delayed an hour while the curtains were fixed, no matter what he told the reporter. It was a proverbial red line: Do not be the reason a shot is delayed. Shooting time, with the full complement of working crew, was expensive. On the positive side of the ledger, the ground underneath the pool was dry. The repairs were holding, at least for now. It would take 48 hours to be sure before they could test it. The special effects coordinator did not return the following day.

The actors, Turteltaub and Rake, Hennings and crew moved swiftly through 12 scenes in the first days of the week. Most of them were on the short side, establishing shots and visual comedy. Some were 2/8 of a script page, or 4/8 for half of a page. The fractions were never reduced to their lowest common denominator because the measurement was a literal portion of a script page and each page had eight parts.

"Words can't describe" had been the longest, and they'd gotten through that. The actors had ad libbed a couple of takes and it was really funny. The next largest scene was 1 6/8 pages, "Billy apologizes to Paddy; Paddy storms off." It was the peak of the tension between the two main characters.

De Niro's way of working was clear by now. He searched for the right feel and would alter dialogue as they shot the scene. The shots that centered on other actors wouldn't use his dialogue anyway. When it was his turn, and all the cameras centered on him, he generally said the lines as they were but not always. Paddy was angry in the next, and De Niro peppered in cuss words, which weren't in the script. The scene had Paddy stomp out of the penthouse and slam the door, which De Niro had done enthusiastically enough to shake the set. "Don't break the door, Bob!" Turteltaub called after him. The actor did it several times, including ones where he left the cuss words off.

The pools had glistened in the background of the set but they had also held. The call sheet announced the plan: "AFTER WRAP: SAFETY TEST OF "PADDY PUSHED INTO POOL" WITH STUNT COORD AND STUNT DBLE."

Both pools were engineered to withstand the weight and pressure of several people jumping in at once. It was always assured it would be tested but everyone was paying very close attention, given it had leaked. The scene where Douglas pushed De Niro in the pool was now a week away. The actor was expected to do the stunt himself by choice and it would have been hard to find anyone on the crew to bet he wouldn't. The pool test was anticlimactic because it worked. Stunt people jumped in with great force and the pools were solid. Better, there was no shaking or other signs of weakness.

After they wrapped Thursday, Set Dec dressed the penthouse for the party scenes. There were the typical garnishes, balloons and streamers. They added a couple of small, raised dance floors and brought in party equipment. They also set up the party bar, again with the branded products.

Most deals had been finalized by now. Movie Mogul had remained in touch throughout. They had regularly updated an email entitled "integration and placement recap" and sent it to crew in the Art, Set Decoraging, Costumes and Props departments. The CBS Films executive who oversaw product placement was in regular email contact with crew. His title was vice president of national partnerships, integrations and promotions and he was credited with securing the Aria deal. The crew liked him because he was low-key and had a diplomatic approach. His emails asked questions rather than telling them what to do, all while making it clear what he wanted. The immediate focus was on branded products.

Dropped in the middle of one of his emails like an olive in a martini was a question about the scene at the poker table at Aria. "I might have missed it in an earlier round of dailies, but haven't seen a hands-on with an Anheuser Busch beer label visible with one of the leads," he asked. "I remember the Stella Artois bottle in a scene with Archie at the blackjack table, but not sure we see a hands-on and visible label."

The Stella Artois had been on the table with Jerry Ferrara during a scene in the casino. It wasn't clear if the actor was holding it, but in any case, he wasn't one of the leads. "If you're able to get a hands-on with visible label of one of the Anheuser Busch beers," he continued, "it's $10,000." It continued from there, that AB products included Bud Light, Landshark, Shock Top, Stella Artois. Crew clarified that sum was what the company would be paid if the effort succeeded, not individual crew. It was an absurd question, even. "Crew gets nothing," said one.

Landshark, a Margaritaville brand, was a bit of a mystery since it seemed to be part of two companies. Its use was cautioned on the list of items in an earlier email from Movie Mogul. The featured/focused branding of Margaritaville was a "conflict with MGM. NO Margaritaville product (bottles, signage, blenders -- anything with Margaritaville logo) to appear in any scene filmed at Aria (or in a scene pretending to be Aria if shot in ATL)." Apparently it was okay to feature Margaritaville products in a character's home if there wasn't a conflict with another pending liquor deal. It sounded confusing and the email said if there were questions, crew could call. But nobody had time for that given how much work they had just preparing for scenes.

Getting an actor to hold a commercial product on camera wasn't an easy or desirable task. They weren't getting paid to do it. Celebrity product endorsement was a lucrative business, one big celebrities didn't embark on lightly. If a product, say a Budweiser, wasn't in the script and they didn't know about it, nothing required them to take it. It was possible the actor would accept it, thinking it fit for the character, but it was just as likely to irritate them, at least at a certain level. Most crew were not eager to take that on.

The exec had flagged two scenes for follow up. It had to do with how alcohol would be consumed in the scenes. They gave him enough information that he could follow up with someone named Tiffiny at Bacardi. Then he would know whether or not they could show Bacardi products in those scenes. He would report back.

As expected, Mailing Avenue took on a different feel on Friday with the deluge of people. Two women from the new extras casting company were there well ahead of call time. They set up tables inside the first warehouse closest to the inside entrance and the administrative offices, facing inward. That meant they were facing the wider room, the door that opened to the parking lot on the other side. They were organized, clipboards and other paperwork ready to check in 140 people.

The company was only a year or two old but they had quickly established itself in Georgia. Peterson vouched for them and within an hour it was clear she wouldn't lose any of her human capital on it. The owners of the local company had an important point to make about the use of the term "extra." Yes, it appeared on the call sheet and was used to distinguish different types of casting companies. But when talking about people, and certainly when addressing them, the correct term was "background actors," or BG for short.

It was a position shared by the famed Central Casting, founded in 1925 in part to stem the exploitation of people wanting to work in movies. People taken with the promise of Hollywood had moved to Los Angeles in significant numbers in the early 1900s. They would collect in front of the studios in hopes of being discovered or just finding work. They were "extra" actors used to fill scenes.

Background actors did more than just fill scenes. Often they were the scene. Central Casting had made that point in the 1990s in support of background actors, who no longer wanted to be called extras. Central Casting had also resisted the term "atmosphere" for people. That had been easier to disperse with, since it was used for several things. Extras had proved a far more tenacious term.

There were two key differences between Los Angeles and Atlanta when it came to extras casting at this point in time. LA. had enough work that a sizeable pool of people could stay busy as background actors while Atlanta was still developing as a production town. That was changing fast enough that Central Casting would eventually open an office in the southern city.

The other difference, and it was a big one, was in what it paid. SAG-AFTRA represented principal actors and had some coverage for background actors, but only in certain areas. In Los Angeles, as well as Las Vegas, signatories of the union were required to hire 57 background actors at guild rates before they hired non-union members at a lower rate. A union background actor in those markets earned $145 a day, which translated to $37,700 a year, assuming they worked every day of the year, which they didn't.

Georgia was a "right to work" state, which means state residents can't be compelled to join a union. It had a minimum wage of $5.15 an hour. Federal law required $7.25, which lifted the bottom. *Last Vegas* paid more than that but it was still a savings from the background union wage in L.A. and there were no requirements it hire a certain number of union background. The production honored all other terms of the actors' guild contract for extras, such as when there were "bumps," or an increase in pay. Bringing a car for a scene or an unusual costume were some examples.

There was another, more nuanced difference between the two cities. The majority of background actors coming to Mailing Avenue for the *Last Vegas* party scenes weren't looking at it as steady work. Atlanta was still too new of a production town for that. Most of them seemed to be on an adventure. Word spread quickly among them that De Niro, Douglas and Freeman were not on the schedule for Friday but the overall excitement level remained high. Kevin Kline would be there!

The great news for Peterson et al was that the new extras casting company delivered all of the background actors they had promised. Even better, as a group they had a good look to them. Turteltaub was happy but not happy enough. The penthouse living room set was big enough that the existing group wasn't filling it the way he wanted. But that was only the first part of his request for 40 additional background actors. They needed to be upscale, even in formal attire. And he wanted them there when they resumed shooting Monday.

Any request from the director was an immediate priority, regardless of the department, and that had only increased as photography advanced. The problem for the Costume department was that its stock was low. With the budget constraints they had organized and ordered what they needed with a cushion, but not a couch. And they had already stretched the cushion.

Pink and Jobst, either separately or together, had asked Badalato and/or Samuels for more money on a couple of occasions. The biggest prompt had been in prep when the director dramatically increased the overall number of background actors, and they had boosted the department's budget. The location of the actors' second fittings had been another area of discussion. But Costume department costs increased anytime something significant was added.

After Pink got the request for more extras, she went to Samuels to ask for additional money. He hadn't reacted in his normal manner. It wasn't a yell but his voice was raised, enough that crew nearby heard him. Things were wrapping up and the budget was okay but he didn't want to push it. They needed to work with what they had. No one heard Pink's reply but when she walked by a few minutes later, the look on her face was a cross between miffed and worried. Pink told Jobst what had happened and then left to find Peterson. She would confer with the 2nd AD about the additional background actors.

It had already been a long week for the Costumes department. The key costumer, who stayed on set and assisted with costume needs as they came up, had been fighting a cold and if anything it seemed worse. She was solid crew, great at her job on set as well as tuned in to department needs, everything you wanted in your key costumer. More than once she'd seen something in advance and a heads-up had prevented a potential problem. It would be hard on the department if she ended up needing a day off. The weekend was looming and the hope was she would get enough rest to bounce back.

Midday one of the stalls in the bathrooms near the department malfunctioned. The costume offices were closest to the stages, which meant that BG had found them, leading to overuse. It happened when the costumes department was at its busiest. They closed the stall door and alerted the bullpen, which had a plumber there within a couple of hours. But the prognosis wasn't great for plumbing under duress.

After they wrapped for the day, a serious-looking Jobst came to the bullpen in search of Kamishin. She noted that it wasn't the first time they needed a plumber, and that he called the bathrooms in that section the "the weakest link" in the system.

Kamishin knew where this was going. She didn't want another plumbing problem on a shooting day either. The bathrooms closest to the Costume department would be deemed off limits to BG unless they had business there. They could use the main facilities in the administrative side of the building and the portable toilets. Bullpen crew organized signs and had them up by the end of the day, so they would be in place before background returned Monday morning.

CHAPTER EIGHTEEN
Shoot Week 8
Dec. 10-14
Day 32, 33, 34, 35, 36

IT WAS 7:30 A.M. MONDAY MORNING, but anyone coming onto the Mailing Avenue lot from the outside world might have thought it was 11 p.m. on New Year's Eve. A half-dozen people were in formal attire, one in a tux. It was a good sign for the Costume department, which was working with 191 background actors for the day compared to 140 of Friday.

Inside the department cages Jobst was helping to upgrade costumes into a more cosmopolitan look. Any clothes that had been set to the side had been reconsidered or laundered on an expedited basis. Costumers had gone through various bins to see what else might have been stowed that could be used on camera.

When Pink and Peterson talked on Friday about the predicament Costumes faced in not having enough clothes to accommodate the director's new request, they looped in the extras casting company. They happily agreed to help. It was normal to ask background actors to come in wearing certain clothes, and they vowed to stress formalwear. It wasn't clear if the BG added for Monday had been offered a bump -- extra pay -- to dress the part but they had risen to the occasion.

An hour later a glance at the larger group of background actors milling around the first warehouse Monday morning showed more success. Perhaps only 20 percent of the 100 BG milling around were in formal attire, but Turteltaub had been right: The tuxes and gowns, the added silk thread, all of it contributed to a more sophisticated look to the crowd at large.

Mostly it was a party crowd, lots of spangles and shiny things, colorful attire, oranges and reds, faux leopard pants and polka dots. There was a good mix of edgy types so they had the wilder side, gorgeous young women with short-shorts and high heels and lots of cleavage, presumably the GoGo dancers headed for the raised platforms. One man wore a gold cowboy hat with a feathery tail and black leather tights, while another was covered in war paint. Some were more subtle but still eye-catching, like a man who was prancing around in a tiny hat. He pivoted and cavorted and generally seemed to be having fun.

The GoGo dancers were part of the 38 specialty BG planned. Some were coming from Vegas, like the five Cirque du Soleil performers who were in a montage scene shot at the Aria where De Niro handed out flyers for the party. Others helped address the Vegas stereotype: an exotic dancer, bridesmaids, casino dealers, various performing acts. There was a whole group of male and female servers clad in Aria uniforms who would wait on the party guests. Then there were costumed pirates, "Peruvian passers," and five DJ crew.

The Peruvian passers were a tie-in to the scene on the street in front of the Mirage. They passed out cards to meet exotic dancers and were a regular sight on the streets of Sin City. The earlier scene had Sam take one of their cards and give them party flyers. Peterson said the newly hired extras casting company had found them at a Peruvian restaurant on Buford Highway.

The five bridesmaids, a group of young women the heroes protect in the bar scene shot in Tucker, Ga., were returning. One of them had a larger speaking role in a flirtation with Sam. Another woman in the scene was an Art department PA.

Finding the right person for the cameo of a rap star had taken a few turns. Producers worked early to land Kanye West, and it was sure enough that his was name in the script. A scheduling conflict arose and they brought in rapper T.I. for the table read. That hadn't panned out.

Shortly thereafter Turteltaub was lamenting his failed efforts to fill the role. De Niro quietly took it in. When he had something to say, he said it.

"Would you be interested in 50 Cent?"

Turteltaub nearly fell out of his chair.

"Yes," he said. "We would be interested in 50 Cent."

The hip hop artist-businessman wasn't just of interest, it was hard to imagine anyone better for the cameo. De Niro picked up his phone and "hit speed dial," as Turteltaub termed it. A minute later he had Curtis "50 Cent" Jackson on the phone. He was available.

Everything lined up quickly from there. There were three people in Jackson's entourage, a personal assistant, a driver and security, one of them his longtime friend, Barja Walter. Jackson and team initially planned to fly from Vegas to Atlanta for the day and then on to La Guardia. Instead the group arrived from LA. He was just coming in for the day, so he'd use a star trailer but wouldn't need hotel or accommodation.

Everything about Curtis Jackson was easy. He showed up on time. They showed him to his star trailer and asked him what they could bring. He wanted burgers from Five Guys. His entourage was quiet and polite. His visit to the Costume department was smooth. Pink had selected a brown T-shirt with faded lettering, which a costumer had worked on to give it an aged look. She also decided on a skullcap, which would give him a scary look, part of the role. From there he had an appointment with hair, which with the skullcap was brief indeed, and then makeup.

The storyline was that a hip hop artist, someone out of the purview of the out-of-touch, retirement-age heroes, had cancelled the penthouse suite, freeing it up for the oldsters. It was too late for the artist -- 50 Cent playing himself -- to get it back when his plans changed. When he gets to Aria he has to take another suite, only to be disturbed by the loud party. When he knocks on the door to ask if they can keep the music down he is rebuffed. The guys inside, the fearsome foursome, were the real bad-asses, not the rap star.

Curtis Jackson had many fans among extras, cast and crew, but you didn't need to be immersed in hip hop to know 50 Cent had sold millions of records and came with serious street cred. Oprah had interviewed him a few months earlier on OWN. Jackson had grown up in Queens, selling drugs at a young age. He had walked a camera through the neighborhood and told them about the day in 2000 that he was shot nine times.

Jackson had made one record before he was shot, which was sidelined along with him. Another one, once he recovered, got the attention of rap icon Eminen, who signed 50 Cent to Shady Records. The result was "Get Rich or Die Tryin," which came out in early 2003. It sold 870,000 records in the first week.

But he wasn't out of the woods yet. 2003 ended with weapons charges against Jackson after two loaded guns were found in a parked vehicle outside where he was going to perform. His arrest made a lot of headlines while serving as valuable marketing. Fans loved that 50 Cent was the real thing and that was what rap was about. The gun charges ended with two years of probation.

By winter 2012 the audio drum loop of his past had been on fade a long time, as evidenced in the Oprah interview. It didn't hurt that much to be shot, because adrenaline was flowing, he told her. It was later, when he knew he'd survive, that the pain set in. 50 Cent was an icon by now. He had sold somewhere in the neighborhood of 30 million records. He was beloved by millions, many of whom touted his loyalty. He kept in touch with friends from childhood, like Barja Walter.

Fewer people knew Curtis Jackson as an entrepreneur. His investment in Glaceau, the maker of Vitaminwater, was epic. He was approached for an endorsement but instead Jackson and his manager pursued a co-branding deal. The company would launch new flavors linked to 50 Cent. The result was Formula 50. Jackson wanted grape, in particular. Grape was popular and there weren't any good grape beverages out there. The execs at Glaceau initially resisted, they reached the conclusion their new business partner knew the market.

When Coca Cola bought Vitaminwater from Glaceau for $4.1 billion in 2007, Jackson's take was estimated at between $60 million and $100 million. Since then he had moved into several businesses, most recently sports entertainment. He had formed a company to promote boxing. He also co-authored a fitness book, "Formula 50: A 6-Week Workout and Nutrition Plan That Will Change Your Life."

Jackson wasn't new to the camera or how production worked. He came to set prepared and they got through the material quickly. The role had him playing himself but at the same time, he was acting. He was convincingly mean looking, glaring out from the skullcap, and then pleading that he was sick, sweet and vulnerable on camera. Turteltaub knew he had a good thing going. Several endings were improvised, each bringing more laughter from the crowd. When he was satisfied, the director called him forward.

"How about it, everybody? 50 Cent!" It was a loud and genuine cheer.

50 Cent exited the set but hung out on the stages for a few minutes talking to crew. Everyone was used to the big stars in the cast and even the occasional high-profile visitor like Bradley Cooper, Ted Danson and Dan Akroyd. But they were in the normal range of expectations; 50 Cent was different. A couple of crew even got selfies with him, a rare sight on the stages. Most crew were more likely to be seen on a tour of stars' homes in Beverly Hills than to ask for a picture with an actor.

But it hadn't lasted long. He and the other three men were taken back to the Atlanta airport, Curtis Jackson with a first-class ticket and the others in coach, all of them bound for LaGuardia.

Early reports about *Last Vegas* had described it as a *Hangover*-themed movie for the geriatric set. It was about a trip to Sin City, which meant it was possible to go through the script checking off a list of genre expectations: There was heavy drinking, Sam's search for an extramarital encounter, the wild party, and lots of sexy women, a certain number of them lightly clothed.

Now they were adding a couple of risqué bits, a visit from an exotic dancer and establishing shots of ice sculpture of a naked woman that was both prop and set decorating. Crew was asked over the run of production whether they found any of the more salacious bits in the script offensive, although it was most obvious here. Were they bothered? The general response was a shrug and a no. It was part of the job. Jobst noted the genre, wild trips to Vegas, was relatively subdued in *Last Vegas*. When she first read the script, the costume supervisor thought, 'check,' when she got to those parts of the story. As in, this is a trip-to-Vegas story in the age of *Hangover*. 'Of course there were going to be hot babes.' Her mind went to what the department would need to provide for "modesty," which meant pasties or pouches or covers or whatever else actors might need when they shot it.

The scene with the exotic dancer had shifted over the same time period. An early version of the script had Stacey show up at the penthouse with another woman. She would announce that they liked to work together and they would kiss, all to the shock and delight of the heroes. But the hot girl-on-girl kiss was out. Stacey was a solo act, the result of Sam calling the number on the flyers he picked up on the street.

The scene had De Niro, Douglas, Freeman and Kline on the balcony with a drink. The dancer would arrive and be shown to the living room floor beneath them. Her line was, "Which one of you is Sam?" And all of the characters would raise their hands. Turteltaub did several takes. She looked bored in one, another had her putting on an earring as she talked to them. It hadn't taken long to shoot and everyone clapped for her when they finished the scene.

The CBS executive in charge of product placement had followed up with crew. The issue with one scene was whether Sam would pour tequila into the mouths of the bridesmaids. If he did that from a bottle, rather than a shot glass, they needed to use a nondescript bottle. He had stayed in regular email contact with several members of the crew. But this particular email, about the use of branded alcohol, had been routed through a producer. That made it seem more serious.

The email had his light touch, asking rather than telling, but it felt different. "The bachelor party scene is fun and obviously a party," he wrote. "I don't consider it excessive or irresponsible use of alcohol. Confirm if you agree: Anheuser Busch, Bacardi's products and the champagne company won't want to be featured if there is excessive/irresponsible use of alcohol." He included "rules and regulations" surrounding use of the branded products. There was to be no drinking directly from the bottle of liquor although beer was fine. No underage drinking and no lewd or indecent language or images. Products were not to be featured with "depictions of alcohol abuse, drug abuse, drinking and driving, driving under the legal age, alcohol-related violence, alcohol over-consumption or antisocial behavior," he wrote.

He again clarified the perimeters of the bridesmaids doing shots of tequila. He also wanted to understand the ice sculpture of the naked woman, including how many there were, which had been confusing. As set dressing, the sculpture would be in the background of all the penthouse party scenes. As a prop, it would be a liquor luge, which dispensed alcohol from the breasts of the sculpture. Archie and Sam would lean over the statue to imbibe, although it wouldn't be real booze. The comedy was in seeing the geezers look foolish as they acted like 20-somethings but it apparently crossed the line for a big corporation trying to protect its image.

The assistant propmaster wrote him back: "So I'm clear, there's only one sculpture and she does have breasts, so we need an ND bottle for that, and we will get an ND bottle just in case for the shot situation." "Perfect, thanks," he replied. "One sculpture, 2 breasts and no Bacardi bottle directly tied in with the sculpture/booze luge."

Work on the sculpture -- actually, there were three of them, which is what made it confusing -- had begun more than two months earlier. Rice knew about a local businessman who made ice sculptures for events and parties. Better, he had done a risqué ice sculpture for another movie, *American Reunion* (2011). He was one-of-a-kind and busiest during the holiday season. Set decorating put in an order for three of them so they could be replaced as the week progressed and the hot lights took their toll. Now the sculptures were parked outside in a refrigerated truck.

The swing gang prepared the area for the ice sculpture when they first dressed the penthouse for the party scenes. It was up to Konrad Lewis, the on-set dresser, to get it back and forth when they were shooting. The statue moved from the refrigerated truck to the penthouse set on a rolling cart. The good news was that it frosted up on the way because of the change in

370

temperature. A pearly look made for a more attractive statue on camera. It also obscured the mechanics that enabled the liquid beverage to move through the block of ice, along with anything behind it.

The problem was that the more the statute acclimated, the faster the frosted look disappeared. Fans were in place, which helped to slow melting, but they weren't going to do anything to stop the ice from clearing. Rice studied the statue with a bemused look on her face. She had grown up in Alaska but was at a loss for how to make ice frost, particularly a whole block of it. Then she had an idea. She went to her props cart and got an air canister and blasted an area of the statue. It frosted up immediately. Anywhere she blasted, it frosted. Better, it stayed that way, not forever but for long enough. Then the air canister ran out.

Rice hurried to the props truck parked outside. A search netted just one more canister. That wasn't going to see them through. Benjamin-Creel would pick some up but they needed it now. Who had air canisters on set? Camera! Over the course of the show Rice had become friendly with the camera crew and they were happy to oblige. They gave her a whole box of canisters, to be reimbursed later. Soon, the ice statue was frosted.

"Frosty is ready for her close-up," someone said, soliciting groans. It was a paraphrase of the endlessly repeated line from Sunset Strip. "What? Someone had to say it!" The statue, regardless of which of the clones was working, was "Frosty" for the rest of the show.

Rice attended the Savannah College of Art and Design, where resourcefulness was encouraged. But nothing had taught her how to frost an ice statue. "It's the kind of thing you only learn on set," she said. "And then you never forget it."

Wrangling a large number of background actors took patience and finesse, as well as organizational technique. All of it was coordinated through walkies. The ADs divided the extras into groups, which they had also named, like leopards, tigers and bears. When Rake pushed the talk button and said they were ready for BG, Awa, the 2nd 2nd AD, could chime in with more information. For example, 'the leopards should come in through the National Treasure entrance.'

Assigning names to the groups was also a continuity tool in that it was easier to keep track of which group had been on what side of the penthouse living room during a particular scene. They knew who was fresh – not seen on camera thus far – in case Turteltaub unexpectedly called for something different. But it also spared feelings, say in the event they had divided groups by appearance, and one was "hot" and the other not. Calling in the tigers offered a clue but it wasn't like saying, 'Bring in the hotties.'

The focus of the afternoon was the big dance scene centered by Morgan Freeman, who was still struggling with whatever illness had him down in Vegas. It had concerned Rake and Turteltaub enough that earlier in the day they considered shifting the schedule. Rake had sorted out a way to restructure the scenes if the actor needed to rest, and Kline, who was on call, agreed to come in. But Freeman insisted he was okay to work and the day moved forward as planned.

A new special effects person was puffing out "atmosphere," the smoky look that would give the set more of a party and nightclub feel, and now it was thickening. Turteltaub looked at Rake. "Can someone ask Mr. Hennings if that's enough smoke?" Rake walked over to the DP, who could be seen nodding yes. Rake hit the 'talk' button and said they were ready for second team as he walked back.

In this case the only stand-in needed on set was Richard Cohee for Freeman, but just the command for second team set other things in the motion. It was passed on to the actors, which was the same thing as saying they were up next. It would also be a heads-up to bring BG to set. But Freeman walked up within a minute of Cohee, joining Rake and Turteltaub at director's village. He was in costume, the dashing red suit imagined by Pink. He wanted to rehearse the dance. Rake radioed for the choreographer and CiCi Kelley was there in seconds.

When they interviewed candidates for choreographer three months earlier, the primary requirement was to teach the Cat Daddy to the actor and bridesmaids. The APOC purposefully sought out candidates who were African American. The Cat Daddy was a popular urban dance that originated with The Rej3ctz, a hip hop group. Kelley was one of three candidates brought in for interviews.

She fit the bill. Her resume pitched her as a director-choreographer-dancer-actor-model with special skills that included "Hip Hop, ATL Crunk, African, Jazz, Ballet, Modern (Horton, Limon, Graham), Salsa, Partnering, Vogue." It also reflected credits from music and videos and a couple from film and television. She had toured with Toni Braxton and Keith Sweat/Elvis White, a well-known Caribbean artist. She had performance credits for songs with LL Cool J., J Lo, Outkast and Usher, to name a few.

As choreographer on the movie she was also scheduled to work with Roger Bart, whose character would dance himself into a heart attack. With the party dance scenes she worked with the GoGo dancers, and whoever else needed coaching or instruction. But the Cat Daddy had taken the most time. It wasn't difficult but there were a dozen of them and it took practice. The sequence had dancers moving each arm, then moving them in a wheelchair-type motion before dropping to the ground twice, lower the second time. Then it repeated.

At the same time, things shifted for Archie's big dance scene. He was going to do a partner fox trot, instead of the Cat Daddy, for the main scene. Kelley had worked with him on it already and was confident the actor had it down, so it impressed her he wanted a rehearsal. She joined Freeman who was sitting near the dance floor.

There were other actors in the scene including Kline, Ferrara as the goofy sidekick Dean, Romany Malco as Lonnie, Roger Bart as Maurice/Madonna, Kelly O'Neal, the actress playing Maurice's wife. The maid of honor and bridesmaids were in it, as well as Stacey and the Cher impersonator.

Once Freeman was done with the practice dance, Rake gave the go ahead to bring the BG in. Camera was ready and they shot the scene as a rehearsal. Turteltaub turned to the A camera operator. "Jody, I feel like we lost frame in rehearsal, now maybe it's too much." He called a short break, and Jody and Hennings and Rake went to the monitors while Freeman sat down on the couch to rest.

The video assist replayed the scene and Turteltaub and the others looked at the monitors. Freeman was sweating a little but he was dancing, so that was expected. The director looked intently at his face to see if there was any indication on screen he was under the weather. The actor didn't just look okay -- he looked good. Someone wondered about a slight tonal quality to his voice. It was possible someone might notice that, but it was a non-issue because it could be fixed in post.

Kelley, who stayed nearby on the sidelines, knew the actor wasn't feeling well. As soon as the director said 'Cut!' and Freeman sat down, she saw his fatigue. As soon as the director said 'Action,' it was like nothing was wrong.

"He just pushed right through," she said.

Turteltaub came over to talk to Freeman. The director wanted to tweak the routine and reached out his hand to the actor.

"Dance with me," he said.

Freeman took his hand and kissed it.

"I'll never wash this hand again," said Turteltaub.

The director turned a little closer and said something quietly. Freeman nodded and headed back to the green mark while the director returned to the monitors.

The scene amounted to 6/8 of a page. There was dialogue, but it was shooting the dance scene that required careful effort. It was a good group of BG, attentive and responsive. But left on their own for long and they grew bored. Five minutes on their own and a clear pattern emerged. Conversations that began softly by then turned into a murmur. If no one on the crew said anything, the volume rose steadily until it might have been a real party.

Generally Rake would catch them toward the end of the murmur stage. He had a subdued but effective style that brought them under control quickly with a simple "Shhhhh," or "Quiet. Please." Or, if it had gone past the murmur stage, "Quiet. Please!"

Rake wasn't a yeller, something that had been noted by crew from early in principal photography. A lot of 1st ADs yell or even have bullhorns in their kits to be heard, a tool that went back decades. That wasn't unreasonable depending on the scenario. Rake had managed to be heard on this show without any of that, to seemingly good effect. He said his style wasn't always seen as a positive. "A lot of producers think if you aren't yelling, you aren't getting it done."

The same trend happened with the physical space. The background actors knew they were to stay behind a certain point. Over time as a group they would push over it. It happened in inches, as some in the back jockeyed for more favorable position in front, others trying to get a better look. Rake's focus would have been somewhere else, but when he needed to get them to get ready, he would turn and look directly at them. "Quiet. Please." This time he kept looking until they were silent. "Everyone, take three steps back." And the group, easily 50 people on the one side of the stage, stepped back in little shuffle-hops at the same time, one, two, three. It would have made good comedy.

The scene had Archie dancing with a series of women, one cutting in after the next, even dipping one of them. One of them was the Cher impersonator, which added a comedic element. The character was having a wonderful time at the party. One of the dancers stayed too long without letting someone else cut in. "Cut!" Turteltaub cried. This time he came over to talk to the dancers. "This isn't a girl fight over Morgan," he said. "You're happy to let him go." This prompted a laugh from the group, especially the dancer who had held on.

"Oh come on," said Freeman. "A couple of girls can't fight over me?"

It brought a laugh. The actor was a self-described flirt. In Vegas, when he arrived to look at watches and Aviator glasses days before shooting, he asked an attractive, 30-something member of the crew if she liked to fool around with older men, according to the woman. It was an unusual line, so easy to remember. She said the actor later made another comment, but after that, it stopped so she let it drop.

It took a while to shoot the scene to get the different angles of the dance. The people in the center of it needed to focus, but not the BG, who grew restless and eventually loud. That prompted the most serious admonishment from Rake yet. "If you don't have a line, keep your mouth shut. Please."

Freeman had taken it all in. In full earshot of the BG, quieted in that moment, the actor said, "Maybe your line is, 'Shut the fuck up?'" The way he said it was good-natured. He got a smile and a nod out of Rake. It also generated laughter from the BG, even if it was at their expense.

The actor finished the scene on time. Then he went to his trailer to rest.

The next scene that had a lot of buzz on the stages was where Billy pushed Paddy in the pool, in part because they didn't shoot it until the afternoon, so there was plenty of time for the anticipation to build, was how Kelley saw it. The background actors were excited about it -- Douglas pushing De Niro in the pool! -- and even the crew admitted it made for an interesting day.

It wasn't a difficult scene but it had required careful thought and planning. De Niro was going to do it himself, and he would only do it once. Once Paddy went in, a couple of other party-goers would jump in after him. The pool had been tested and they were confident it was safe. They shot the stunt actor first and worked with the crowd. Turteltaub wanted more from them and the BG were coaxed to react more.

The pools set in the floor were potentially hazardous in that they weren't as visible with the many people milling around. Then there was splashed water. PAs were nearby with towels to dry the floor, and still someone slipped. Everything stopped while they made sure she was okay, Turteltaub first by her side.

The scene had Billy and Paddy talking to each other in the dining room. Each was unaware that the other had designs on Diana but as they stood there, both of them eyeing the door, they figured it out. Rake would call out "Ding Dong" to signal the actors to start their competitive walk to see who could get to the door first. A real doorbell would replace Rake in post. In the process, they go past the pool and Billy gives Paddy a shove.

The actors rehearsed the walk and Turteltaub watched intently in the monitor. "Make sure there's room for Michael to get through," he said to Rake. "Other people seem to be moving in from the side." Rake was out, brushing them back. The actors walked through it again. Then they were ready. Paddy hit the water and a couple of young women jumped in after him, like it was part of the party. And in a flash, it was done, De Niro met with multiple towels from different people as he got out of the pool.

Turteltaub had clearly liked what he saw because he laughed out loud. When they replayed it he was even more certain it was what he wanted. He zeroed in on one of the extras in the pool. "Look what she's doing to Bob!" The woman had come up behind the actor in the pool and casually put her arm around him. It looked natural.

"Check the gate!" Turteltaub said.

Rake took a few steps toward the larger crowd. "Thank you. Checking the gate. We're going to break for lunch." It was 3:30 pm.

There were two things Turteltaub regularly said while they were shooting and "check the gate" was one of them. The gate was the part between the film and the lens, and in the old days they would literally look inside to make sure a tiny sliver of film hadn't damaged it. Because if it had, they weren't done. *Last Vegas* wasn't being shot in film and nor was he telling the digital loader to make sure the card was okay.

The other thing the director said several times over the course of a day was "print it." That meant he preferred that take over the others. The term also referred to film, which was expensive to develop so they didn't want to print everything. A director at that time was saying, print this specific take, whereas now Turteltaub was saying to mark it as the best shot.

A couple of other scenes the next day came with a little more stress from the actors than had been typical. It probably wasn't a coincidence that both of them required emotion, one involving heartstrings and the other the death of a character.

The first scene was where Paddy found out more details about Diana and Billy. During rehearsal Flurry went out with his roll of tape to mark where the actors would stand, a normal part of his job. But he apparently got a little too close to De Niro, who told him they didn't need marks for rehearsals, or something to that effect. Flurry had quickly put it down anyway and scooted out of the way. Turteltaub had seen it, but didn't say anything.

The scene followed the one where Paddy gets pushed in the pool. Once he dries off, he goes looking for Billy and Diana. He finds them and overhears a conversation that includes him. It's painful and he makes his presence known. Billy tries to talk to his lifelong friend but Paddy tells him to stop, lifting his hand. De Niro was in a bathrobe, his hair wet, although the scene wasn't shot in the same day.

The actors worked through it. Douglas thought his character would play it a little differently. "There's something false about my continuing on after he says 'Stop,'" Douglas said. "I'd be devastated if I'd misread something and hurt someone." Turteltaub agreed to try it differently. They got the requisite number of takes and wrapped the scene.

Later in the day when De Niro saw Flurry he acknowledged he'd been short with him. It was casual, no big deal, but it impressed the cameraman the actor was big enough to do it. They didn't all do that. "Two highlights of my life in the same day," said Flurry. "One, De Niro yelling at me, and the other, De Niro apologizing to me."

The following day, Flurry went out to mark De Niro's spot during rehearsal but kept a healthy distance. He walked by Turteltaub on his way back to camera. "Look at you," the director said. "You get snarled at by the lion and then you go back with steak in your hand!" Flurry grinned. "Just doing my job," he said.

The heavier scene had Maurice, the Madonna impersonator, dancing himself into a heart attack. In the original script it was the main catalyst for the change the characters underwent, particularly Billy, who performed CPR. It took place during the party. That meant a lot of other cast in the scene, like Sam and Diana, Dean and Lonnie, along with BG.

Sam had been the first to Maurice's side, but it was Billy who came to the rescue. He knew CPR and would try to save him. The shot was set at 7:55 a.m. and first team came in. By 8:11, Turteltaub had gotten two takes of the look on Billy's face when he sees Maurice on the floor.

Bart, as Maurice, had dutifully laid on the floor acting like a man who had suffered a heart attack. It seemed he went into meditation, because his eyes were closed, but his breathing also slowed to the extent his chest barely moved. The next shot was the part of the scene where Billy performed CPR on Maurice. But Turteltaub wasn't happy with what he was getting and Douglas looked irritated.

"Michael, let's see what you can do without hurting him. Does it look fake? Yes." Somebody who knew CPR went over to coach him. A few minutes later, they were ready. "Alright, going again," said Rake. This take kept the cameras on Douglas for what seemed, and must have felt, like a long time, although it was probably less than 60 seconds.

"I can't keep on," Douglas said. "C'mon man!" Everyone laughed but it didn't look like Douglas was kidding. Turteltaub went over to him and they talked quietly.

Douglas was best known as an actor but he had also been a producer since early in his career. His father, Kirk Douglas, had owned the rights to *One Flew Over the Cuckoo's Nest*, based on the book of the same name by Ken Kesey. The older Douglas, now high atop AFI's top 100 legends' list, had been unable to get a studio to bite on the project. The younger Douglas, then in his late 20s, picked it up with his blessings.

Michael Douglas had achieved moderate success as an actor to that point and was at work on the television show "Streets of San Francisco." In the background he worked to bring the project back to life, relying heavily on his father's notes. That led him to Saul Zaentz, who ultimately financed the movie and became its other producer. They hired Milos Forman to direct, whom Kirk Douglas had first identified for the job.

Forman wanted a realism that wasn't commonplace in movies at the time. They had a scouted a number of west coast locations for the movie and liked the Oregon State Hospital, which was in operation. But its superintendent, Dean R. Brooks, wasn't on board. Brooks had read the book and thought it was brilliant but he also knew mental health treatment had evolved. Stereotypes that all mentally ill people sat lifeless and drooling in chairs were prevalent and wrong. Obviously, if they made the movie there, the hospital would be associated with it.

Then Douglas went to Oregon to meet with him personally. The movie was a historical record of how things had been, not how they were currently. The insight the superintendent could provide to the filmmakers would help expose stereotypes and make it more accurate. Brooks could play the superintendent himself, to make sure they got it right. He agreed. They inked a deal that included the movie production's complete access to the hospital.

Forman moved on site and lived there to prep for the photography. Jack Nicholson, the actor playing the lead, came to work two weeks early so he could mingle with the patients. Patients in the hospital, and local people who worked there were hired as cast and background. To prepare for the patient intake scene, Forman gave Brooks a case history. Then he interviewed Nicholson, in character as R.P. McMurphy. They did it on camera. The actor threw in some vulgarity that wasn't in the script, which startled Brooks, and got a rise out of him that worked.

The story was incredibly rich to start with but the details, the locations and realism, the background actors, the performance and direction – the work of the producers in taking it through the process – brought to the big screen a movie that stunned America.

Cuckoo's Nest became the sixth largest grossing film in history to that point, a list that contained movies like *Gone with the Wind* and the *Wizard of Oz*. The movie swept best picture, director, actor, actress and screenplay for the first time in 44 years at the Academy Awards, only the second to do it. Douglas and Zaentz took home the statue for Best Picture. Douglas remained good friends with Brooks until his death in 2013.

It was a huge leap forward for Douglas, who was 32 at the time of the awards. Douglas was quoted saying it was "downhill from there," although he said Forman said it. Regardless, it didn't turn out to be true. Douglas' career had continued on where few even talked about *Cuckoo's Nest*. He earned his second Oscar for *Wall Street*, which he won over Jack Nicholson, who was up for his role in *Ironweed*. There had been numerous highlights over a career that spanned decades.

On *Last Vegas*, Douglas had earlier made a directing suggestion when they shot the scene at the Neon Museum. Turteltaub indulged it, as he did here in talking with the actor. The look on the director's face when he first got up to talk to the actor suggested he wasn't happy, but his words were good, then and later. "Michael Douglas, of all the actors I've ever worked with, is also the best movie producer. He cares about the entire production. Whether you're on time, how quickly you're working, how many hours everyone is working," he said.

The interaction between Douglas and Turteltaub didn't last long. In the interim Kim Jones, the makeup artist, came in and sprayed Bart to keep him fresh. There was general lightness among the actors who waited and various comments flowed, which Bart ignored. "Roger plays a good dead guy. He's been in character the whole time!" Kline looked at him on the floor and said he was "living in the ethereal world," a play on both the peaceful-looking Bart and Madonna's Material Girl.

Turteltaub returned to his chair and looked at the playback, then he walked back rather than sending Rake. "Guys, let's get one more."

Alicia Accardo had been a steady presence throughout principal photography. The script supervisor was one of the few jobs that required the right personality to do it well, according to other crew. That person dealt with the director all day every day, and some were more difficult than others. Turteltaub had a big personality but a quick look at her credits showed he was probably on the lighter end.

There was more to it than the title inferred. The most common online job description said a script supervisor's primary responsibility was continuity -- making sure one scene was consistent with another despite gaps in when the individual scene was shot. Others said the script supervisor was the "writer's representative on set."

Continuity remained as important as ever. Scenes were shot out of order and they had to be seamlessly connected later. But technology had widened the number of people who effectively participated in that responsibility. The cell phone meant the key costumer could more easily record whether a sweater had been buttoned once or twice. Props, likewise, knew where De Niro picked up the hero bottle. The on-set decorator took photos to make sure furniture was positioned in precisely the same way.

But Accardo knew, too. She was ultimately responsible for ensuring that set dressing, as well as the actors' costumes, hair and makeup, matched between scenes and she had the last word. Accardo also acted as liaison to the cast.

However, it wasn't her job to ensure adherence to the script for the script's sake. "The creative producers are more the voice of the writer," she said. "They're the ones to say, 'No, we need that line.'" It was Turteltaub, or whomever the director was, who called the shots. If the line wasn't being said the way he wanted it, which was the way it was in the script, then it was up to her to go talk to the actor. If the director did like the change, she made a note of it.

She was in regular communication with McManus to check things. Video assist was a quantum leap forward because it was easy to go back in time, see exactly what was there, and match it. She knew from her notes that it had been take 4 that he liked best for scene 82, so it was a matter of getting it on the monitor. Not all movies could afford a video assist, and she could do her job either way. But it was easier.

All that overlooked the other key responsibility of the script supervisor, which was to accurately track the creative progress of the movie, something relied upon at the highest levels. Every night Accardo prepared a report that ranged anywhere from 20 to 50 pages. It was the blueprint for editing in post-production but it was also used on a daily basis for reports sent to the business side.

The script supervisor also "gives the slate" to the Camera and Sound departments. That didn't mean the device itself but the scene and take numbers it reflected. Flurry was the keeper of the physical slate, although the equipment was the property of the Sound department. "It's the biggest part of my job, and I have to use someone else's equipment," said Flurry. "Everyone in camera thinks it's a scam that sound came up with it, but it isn't the case."

It made sense because the Sound department had responsibility for recording "sync" dialogue and sound effects during principal photography, and it had the time code generator. Understanding how the equipment evolved helped explain it. The clapperboard was invented in the early days of talkies. Initially it took two people to do the job, one to hold the board with the information and the other to clap the sticks together. It was an Australian who first put the arm on the device, which separated the top strip with a hinge so it could lift up and clap down. Then one person could do the job.

The clap arm no longer served the same function today. Instead they relied upon an SMPTE time code generator that enabled them to sync sound and picture. It sounded like an abbreviation for some kind of technology but it was actually the acronym of the Society of Motion Picture and Television Engineers. That organization established the time code standards for the industry in the late 1960s, and updated them in 2008. SMPTE, founded in 1916, is an international standards organization relied upon around the world.

The device still looked fundamentally the same. The digital slate was an expensive piece of equipment. The one Flurry was using cost close to $1,500, although they were coming down in price. They were also available for rent. It was faced with whiteboard covered with translucent acrylic glass that could be written on. The red *Last Vegas* mark for the movie created in prep was on the left corner, the director and cinematographer's names on the right. It had an A on it, meaning it was linked to A Camera. Across the top were three boxes that contained information that changed: Roll, Scene, Take.

One day it read Roll: 121, Scene 82C, Take 2 p/u. They didn't use rolls, since film was out, so it instead that reflected the card number, the place where the material was located. After the master shot, every time the camera set up changed a letter was added. So the C meant it was the fourth in the series, after 82, 82A, and 82B. The p.u. stood for pick up, which meant they had "picked up" from a certain point of the scene, rather than starting at the beginning. That happened when Turteltaub was satisfied with the first part of the scene and wanted to improve on the second part.

Flurry looked like a man who loved what he did. The hours were long and it could be taxing, and famous people might yell at you, and you couldn't yell back. But the camera was amazing. He was 35 and strong enough to make the camera look light but he also knew every part of the camera and most of its history. He even knew the arcane history of the development of the slate and could talk about how it evolved over decades in a way that made it interesting.

Flurry attended the College of Santa Fe. That's where he met Ward Russell, a working cinematographer who took time out to mentor students. It was a small school but it had a serious film department and Flurry knew he wanted to be a cameraman. He worked on a public service announcement as part of a student project, the first time he got a camera credit. It was 2002 and the PSA was for Mothers Against Drunk Drivers.

He got some very good advice before his first job interview: "Don't tell them you went to college." The skills he needed to be successful in a camera department had to be learned there, and everyone started at the bottom. A college degree was irrelevant and worse, it could piss someone off. So, he kept it to himself. Flurry's first credit was as a grip/gaffer. Then, in 2005 he got two camera loader credits. That job involved loading the film and managing its care and security, the entry-level job in the Camera department. It was the same as the digital loader, a title change that mirrored the technology. One of those credits was for the television series "Wildfire." Russell was in the Camera department.

Flurry spent the next couple of years as a loader and occasionally a 2nd AC, but then the loader credits stopped and he worked steadily as a 2nd AC. He worked on television but also bigger productions, including with Rivetti and Hennings on *Horrible Bosses*. Understanding how cameras worked was fundamental to his job but he also had insight into positions that helped the Camera department that others might not understand. For instance, a lot of people thought that stand-ins didn't do anything. And it was true that they could just stand there while they adjusted lights and camera.

But Flurry said they could make a big difference to the Camera department. "A good stand-in watches their actor, they know where they're going to go in a scene." That was true both in a physical sense, as to how much motion the actor might put into it, but also in a creative sense. "They know the more elegant points of the script," he added. The Camera department still set up the shot, but they got a better feel for it, where the actor might go, what points in the script might bring an unexpected reaction.

Both De Niro and Freeman had used the same stand-ins for a long time. A side benefit was that it created loyalty to the actor. A good stand-in really wanted things to be right. It sometimes was as simple as a heads-up about something going on with the actor or that something might be an issue. That's what happened when Freeman's stand-in told Flurry the actor's mark was the wrong color. "He cared more than Morgan did," Flurry said, but it still gave him the heads-up so he could deal with it.

Flurry's exchange with the actor early on had helped him establish a rapport with the actor that lasted for the rest of the show. Sometimes Freeman would point out the mark on the floor was crooked or in some other way goof on the cameraman. Once Flurry put a zig-zag in Freeman's mark on the floor, which got a big laugh from the actor.

There was a synergy that revolved around the lens, Flurry said. Everyone knew the transition from film brought big changes but there were subtle ones, too. "With film it was a mystery, like the man with the cloak over his head. That was the only person seeing the image." Now there was video assist and monitors. "With digital a lot of that mystique is gone." It hadn't changed the complexity of the camera equipment or the fact it took team effort, he said.

Flurry came to the soundcart twice each day to sync the slate with the Denecke GR2, "the black box" that generated the time code. But it was just one of numerous instruments on Kelson's sound cart. The cart itself was reminiscent of a one-man band centered by a drum and stacked high with 40 other instruments. He was there to capture sound, not make it, but he had at least that many things on mobile cart. It looked slightly haphazard but everything on it had utility. The main shelf held the mixing board and an auxiliary mixing board. There were two shelves set back behind the main shelf and above it, and two full shelves below, all of it loaded with equipment. As a unit it looked expensive and he said collectively it was insured for $225,000.

Kelson wasn't always in sight. Wireless technology enabled a lot more freedom. Cables, even long ones, had limited where the soundcart could go. Working behind the cart could also create an element of privacy or block him from view. It wasn't unusual to find the production sound mixer with headphones on, eyes closed and fingers turning a knob or pushing a lever, a look on his face like he was listening to Miles Davis' "Birth of the Cool." But it wasn't music or even necessarily something pleasing to the average ear. What he heard were the various sounds coming in from set. He would "mix" them and arrive at a balance. He would leave it there if he could, until the next set up or scene change. It was about "fidelity," a word he used a lot.

As with the Camera department there was a highly technical side to being production sound mixer. Kelson provided and operated the microphones and other recording equipment used on the set. In addition to individual dialogue and effects there was ambiance and room tone and other things that helped match the different sound takes. Most of the work on sound came in post production but it was up to him to have all the parts in place.

Kelson grew up in Los Angeles. His pathway to the movie business was through music. He had friends with a rock and roll band who needed a sound mixer and he wanted to hang out, so he learned. He attended Sonoma State, where he earned a degree in physics. One of his classes required students pick a musical track that they thought presented outstanding engineering and explain why. He didn't have to think long: Aja, the Steely Dan record engineered by Roger Nichols.

After college he got a job at the Federated Group, a chain of stereo and TV stores in Southern California. It was during the heyday of electronics retailers like Pacific Stereo and (Nobody Beats) The Wiz. The store he worked at carved out a niche to serve the studios. One quiet Sunday night he was alone in the store when a man came in with his girlfriend. They chatted about music and Kelson was asked what he liked. He again said Steely Dan. He mentioned Nichols and said he was his hero, and told the story of the college assignment. The man turned out to be a close friend of Nichols.

Three weeks later, Kelson was working in back when he was paged to the front counter. "It was Nichols," he said, with a look on his face like the grace of it still surprised him all these years later. Kelson apprenticed for the recording engineer and inventor. It was a remarkable time, and he was still grateful for it. Nichols, who died in 2011, was awarded a Special Merit/Technical Grammy Award in 2012. It was his eighth Grammy.

Kelson loved the work and found himself on the set of Thriller, Michael Jackson's epic music video released in 1983. He couldn't believe he was there watching it all happen. Two years later he was on *Top Gun* (1985). He recalled Badalato from that time, including seeing the future UPM doing donuts in his car in the parking lot of the soundstages.

He had worked since then, both on big features and small, as well as television shows. He had been on "Walking Dead" immediately preceding *Last Vegas*. Sound mixing was the same on movies and television, he said.

Turteltaub wasn't excited about the Vegas funeral scene. He had even begun wondering if the death of Maurice/Madonna was needed as a catalyst. His thought was that there was enough already to tell a story about a trip to Vegas that leaves the characters changed. He'd always thought part of the movie's appeal was as a story about friendship. That's why he got the shot of Billy gazing after his friends for the scene at McCarran airport while they were still shooting in Las Vegas.

As it was, the script had Billy's turning point follow the death of Maurice. Billy had also called off his planned wedding, the reason they'd all come to Vegas to begin with. That would have to carry the bulk of it if they eliminated the death of Maurice and the subsequent funeral. The culminating scene was a conversation between Billy and Paddy, Sam and Archie in the background. A changed Billy would reveal vulnerability for the first time. It put more pressure on Douglas.

The scene was set in the master bedroom set of the Aria, which wasn't big enough for them to put the camera where Hennings and Turteltaub wanted it, so Rawlins and the grips were taking out a wall that had been in place for two months. The camera crew brought in their equipment. B Camera was able to get set up but A Camera had to hang back to wait for the grips to finish.

Rawlins was a burly guy who told his share of jokes. When his pants had ripped on set a few days earlier he announced it to laughter. He and the others were focused on the wall, machinery grinding away. Then it stopped suddenly. "Nails on a movie set, people. Nails! On a movie set." Rawlins' meaning was clear. Screws were used on set because nothing was permanent. Whatever they built had to come back down, often fairly quickly, as was the case today. Screws could be unscrewed, nails, or dozens of them, had to clawed or sawed out, which took longer.

The grinding resumed, the volume again rising and falling and rising and then, suddenly, a deafening "WHOMP!" The wall-ceiling area crashed on top of the king-size bed and damaged a sconce in the process. It was one of those sounds that are loud enough that for just a second, everything else goes silent. The silence extended through the master bedroom suite to Director's Village, which was on the other side of the wall on the next set.

"Oopsie," called Rawlins, which was followed by a burst of laughter across the penthouse. His tone confirmed without saying it that no one was hurt. Rake, who was out of his director's chair the second the sound hit to see for himself, soon returned. Konrad Lewis, the on-set decorator who was always on hand, even if he didn't have to be, left and returned quickly with a vacuum cleaner. Lewis, with his great attitude and willingness to help, and his strength, had remained a favorite on the stages.

Work resumed and with it the murmur of voices. The dolly grip for A camera got to work setting up the tracks, now that there was room. The A camera operator, 1st AC and 2nd AC -- Miller, Rivetti and Flurry -- each worked to get ready. Miller walked the path of the rails. Flurry had his tape out and put down red and blue markers for De Niro and Douglas. Freeman and Kline were in the scene but not on camera for this take.

Rake returned a few minutes later. He stood there for a solid minute, surveying the situation.

"What's taking so long?"

Miller had taken his seat on the dolly to prep the shot and said as much, adding that he needed a few minutes. They had been delayed while the other work happened. Rake nodded and stood there another minute. Then he pushed the talk button on his walkie and spoke quietly.

"Bring in second team. Ten minutes for first team."

Almost exactly as he lifted his finger off, the request quietly issued to the crew, Turteltaub called out from the other side of the wall.

"How's it going in there?" Rake, in motion back to director's village, repeated what he had just said on the walkie, this time a little louder so the director could hear.

"Bringing in second team."

As they tested lights and camera, Rice came onto the set. She had already put a suitcase on the bed. Now she opened it up and put the clothes on the bed. Douglas would be packing in the scene. Then she took out her phone and took pictures of the bed so she'd know, or anyone else who saw them, exactly where they were next shot.

With call for second team, the assistants to the main actors automatically alerted them they were due next. Douglas arrived quickly but the vacuum was running and he turned around. He was back on the sidelines with Freeman and De Niro, both of whom had arrived, two minutes later.

Douglas was clearly agitated about something because his voice carried more than usual. He had a distinctive voice, but that had been true since day one. It was a voice heard by much of the country, given he did the voiceover introducing the NBC Nightly News at the time. Here the actor sounded angry. He was talking about hunting and armor-piercing bullets and assault weapons. "I'm the first guy to say you have a right to own a weapon, but c'mon! This is insane!" Freeman jumped in with similar sentiment. He had his own unique vocal presence, the permanent lead-in for CBS News at that point. De Niro stood there, silently taking it in, but with a look on his face that showed he shared their anger. The talk went on for another minute.

Rake called over to the actors. "There's not going to be a rehearsal," he said. "We're just going to shoot."

"That costs extra," said Freeman, back to his usual self.

"I need a rehearsal," said De Niro.

"Sure," said Rake, completely at ease with the 180-degree turn. "Let me check with the boss."

Douglas went to his mark, De Niro to his. Freeman and Kline sat down in the chairs that would be off camera in the shot. They would speak but not be seen on camera in this take.

They ran through it once. De Niro had it down. Douglas, who still seemed a little flustered, asked for a look at the script. The scene had been reworked from the original, a revised script issued the day before, and the actor wasn't one to adlib. Accardo walked over and gave him the 2nd Blue Revisions, which contained the new scene. He looked at it and nodded, as if saying 'of course,' and handed it back. "Thank you."

Then they were rolling, Billy explaining and apologizing to Paddy. The scene was toned down from the original, but was still packed with emotion. It was about grief over the passing of Sophie, who had been Paddy's wife, but Billy's love. And it was about aging, and time passing by. Billy had been the youngest-acting member of the group, the one with his hair dyed "hazelnut," a laugh line in the movie. The scene called for the actor to look his age and for the first time, Billy seemed his age.

Turteltaub was watching Douglas in the monitors, De Niro's back to the camera. The director came in between takes. "That was good, really good. Let's give it even more emotion this time."

He walked along the path of the camera.

"Jody, what if we hold the line a little more? Does it grow if we do that? It doesn't need to grow so much, it just needs to have motion. I want the motion to help bring out the emotion."

Then he went to talk to Kline. It was a short conversation, the most important part a reference that the scene had "to be enough" if the funeral scene didn't make it. Turteltaub liked the next take. Eventually they reset for coverage of De Niro. He saved his best for that.

Within a few minutes of wrapping the scene the crew got caught up on the same news that had set Douglas, Freeman and De Niro on edge. There had been a massive shooting at an elementary school in Newtown, Conn. Twenty children, ages 6 and 7, had been murdered along with 16 staff. The actors had seen it on satellite television in their trailers. On-set crew had been working and most didn't check their phones until break.

Watching Douglas and Freeman and De Niro in the moments after the news of Sandy Hook revealed something ridiculously obvious. They were just guys at work. Yes, they were famous and they made a lot of money, but just like millions of other Americans that day, they learned something horrible had happened in their country, and it upset them. It was also ridiculously obvious that the actors were just people. That was something the crew knew that perhaps a lot of the world obsessed with celebrity didn't.

One of Lauer's questions to the main actors was whether having achieved so much, they looked at a project like *Last Vegas* and said, "'Let's just get together and do something that is purely for fun?'" Months had gone by in the process of shooting the movie. When principal photography concluded next week, each of them would have worked at least 38 days, 40 for Douglas. During that time, none of them were anywhere near home. In all likelihood there would be reshoots, which the actors were contractually bound to fit in. And then they were obligated to promote the movie.

This was work for everyone, including the actors.

Lewis, the on-set dresser and part of the Set Dec department, had been on the stages, and on location, on almost every scene shot in Atlanta. He watched the actors closely in the process. "These cats aren't playing checkers," he said. "This is chess." That meant that these actors were operating on a higher level, in his view. Their performances were good early in the process. They didn't need the repeated takes he had seen some other actors require. Turteltaub, he said, "kept it real. He tells you straight-up what he's feeling. If you screw up, that's what he conveys."

Lewis had only been in the business a few years but he had worked a lot. Most of the time it was as on-set dresser, including on *Lawless*, *Madea's Witness Protection* and *Trouble with the Curve*. One of the scenes most challenging for him on *Last Vegas* was the scene where Sam finally finds a woman willing to sleep with him. She was partially undressed before he decided against having sex with her. It was a plot point in the movie that the character was looking for a liaison but when he found one he realized he'd want to tell his wife, as he did everything important in his life. And that had been the only rule, that she didn't want to know about it. Lewis had to move the couch out of the way so the camera could pass by, dipping out of sight just in time. It was like an NFL player making a catch on the edge of the playing field and staying in bounds.

It had been a relatively easy show, he said, something echoed by the rest of the crew. The actors were comfortable with each other, with Turteltaub, and for that matter, with the crew and vice versa. Most of the people who worked on set had been in the business long enough to see people above the line, and not just actors, act badly. It wasn't these guys. Actors arguing about how to shoot something better wasn't unusual, nor was it rare that an actor would snap a member of the crew.

Occasionally it seemed like a genuinely good time, as with the scene in the dressing room, which was montage of the characters shopping for their new suits. The Art department had conjured up a stylish dressing room they might have lifted from a fabulous clothing shop on Rodeo Drive in Beverly Hills. The set had multiple doors representing changing rooms, and long mirrors, the walls covered with light blue wallpaper. Hennings took issue with the wallpaper because it had white in it and Bomba said, yes, it did have some white in it.

Turteltaub was scanning for what he wanted. "Is the changing tent still set up? Bring Morgan's red pants to the set please." Then he turned to the actors to set the scene for the montage, starting with Freeman. "You're looking to Romany for advice because he knows. Bob is waiting his turn. Kevin is bored."

De Niro noted there wasn't a clothing rack in the room, which indicated he thought there should be one. "There isn't a clothing rack in this scene," Turteltaub answered. Then he turned to Rake and said, quietly, "Get him a clothing rack." One arrived in short order, which prompted Kline to tell De Niro it was proof of his importance. The comical barbs continued from there. There was no dialogue in the scenes but if the director had changed his mind and decided to add it, he could have culled from the actors as themselves, goofing on each other.

He did his share of it, as well. The scene leant itself to improvisation, a strong suit for Kline. "Don't give him a prop," Turteltaub said. "We'll be here all day." Toward the end, Turteltaub asked Archie to take a nap for one take and soon Freeman was snoring so convincingly he might really have fallen asleep. "Now that's acting!" someone said. It hadn't taken long and it had been fun.

Kline was the actor most likely to talk to crew without having a reason. He was approachable and easygoing. On a couple of occasions he popped into the bullpen, a solid five-minute walk from the soundstages. It was when he needed something, and rather than having an assistant get it, he went himself. One of those times he stopped at the white board on the wall. It was giant and contained work information, like the date and specific bullpen crew work plans.

It also had lighter elements, including Word of the Day. The actor liked that and said he similarly reviewed new words, and pulled out his phone to find them. Encouraged to write them on the board, he did so happily: Jocoserious, horrisonant, sophrosyn, esurient, Lucullan. It was up to the individual to look them up.

Someone asked him about *The Big Chill* (1983), a movie about a group of former college friends who have a weekend reunion following the suicide and funeral of a classmate. Kline starred in it along with a stellar ensemble cast that included Glenn Close, Jeff Goldblum, William Hurt and others. Kevin

Costner had also been cast, as Alex the suicide victim, but those scenes ended up on the cutting room floor.

Director Lawrence Kasdan had famously concluded the scenes with Alex weren't needed since the story was about the people who survived. His vision worked at the box office. The movie, which had an $8 million budget, earned somewhere around $56 million. Kline said Kasdan was an excellent director and noted the two other movies he'd done with him, *I Love You To Death* and *Darling Companion*. Both of those pictures were good, and deserved more attention than they received. *I Love You to Death*, he added, had been a lot of fun to make.

Everyone was in a good mood in the bullpen, which was festooned with holiday directions. That process had been stoked thanks to a contest by Badalato and Kamishin. Each desk in the bullpen had some kind of decoration and virtually all year-end holidays were represented, from Christmas and Chanukah and Kwanzaa to Festivus, the non-commercial holiday started in 1966 but made famous by its depiction on Seinfeld, the hugely successful sitcom.

Later, Peterson's voice came over the walkie. It wasn't the 2nd AD's normal tone. She said specifically it wasn't an emergency, and she didn't sound scared, but she did need help. Despite that assurance, she might as well have yelled 'Fire!' given the urgency with which the AD department arrived on the deck on the back of Mailing Avenue to assist her.

Zoe, the large-headed puppy-dog, had gotten under the fence of the dog run next to it, and she had gone after her. It was enough of a slope, and the dog weighty enough, that Peterson was having difficulty getting them both back up. Two of the stronger PAs were under the chainlink fence in seconds, one lifting it while the other climbed under, as more people joined the group. They easily got to Peterson, who wasn't far.

The walkie call had been heard by anyone in walkie range, including the production office. Samuels, Badalato and Kamishin, and two visitors, were there. Badalato walked down the desk stairs and turned his phone on record to capture the whole thing and coach them along. There were at least a dozen people on the ground trying to help. The mood was light, although the look on Samuels' face said he wasn't sure yet.

One of the PAs picked up Zoe, who was wearing a purple support harness and matching leash. The dog went limp, her legs and paws stretched out in front, as he carried her up the slope. By then it seemed the entire AD department was there, including Awa, and they helped get the dog under the fence or took pictures. Zoe, now safely on the right side of the fence, kept her eyes trained on Peterson, who along with the other PA made their way up the slope. The chainlink was peeled long enough for them to wriggle under it. Peterson said Zoe was probably the only dog in Atlanta that could trip on a piece of mulch, fall under a fence and roll half way down a hill.

An hour later after the excitement had subsided, even as people came and went, a sense of malaise set in. The crew was tired, some of them still sick, but that wasn't it. For most people, it was winding down a little too quickly, to paraphrase a line of Billy Gherson's from a scene shot on Friday. "That's how you can tell if it was a good show," said Stephens, who sat at her desk in the bullpen after one exchange. "Everyone's sorry to see it end."

Wrap gift-giving, a long tradition in the industry, had started. That was organized by the bullpen as well as by departments that did their own thing. Some turned into a marketing opportunity, like McManus who gave out T-shirts that had both the *Last Vegas* mark and McVideo, his company. Myers, of Jets & Props, had also handed out nice T-shirts before he left.

A lot of crew already had new jobs, including the bullpen crew. Mailing Avenue had been released for a season to a television production, "Necessary Roughness." Simpson, Stephens and Anderson all had jobs on the show and, better, promotions to go with it. Simpson would be production coordinator, Stephens APOC and Anderson, production secretary. Felicia Moniz, a production assistant in the bullpen who had lasted for months, also was hired. It was a coup for the show's producers, as well, since they didn't just get experienced crew but a group that already had relationships with the vendors and service providers they would need.

The number of short chats common in prep, where people stopped for a minute in the bullpen and in the hallways, at catering and on the stages, had resumed. Crew compared notes on what shows they would do next or got leads for work and exchanged contact information.

The airplane set took form over the course of the week until it dominated the Mill Shop. The last scenes of the day would be shot there, which would "wrap Bob," since they were De Niro's last scenes.

It looked like a real plane, sans wings, engine and cockpit, because it was. It had flown as part of the Southwest Airlines fleet. Myers bought the remnants when the aircraft was taken from service and dismantled. He engineered the structure around it, one of several airplane sets he offered.

Myers had created a system where all of the parts could fit securely in the 53-foot semi. The first part of the process was unloading the truck, which contained roughly 30,000 pounds of airplane pieces. The biggest pieces were secured on rolling platforms, which came out in 10-foot sections, while others were on pallets and came off with a forklift. Parts were stacked into each other like Russian dolls, protective material packed between them. Inside that was the 10-foot galley and 12 rows of blue and brown leather seats, stacked on each other. Even the overhead bins, attached to what served as fuselage, were loaded in staggered fashion, one on top of another other.

Myers ran around with a tape measure as they rolled out the base of the aircraft and the process began. Two sides of fuselage were brought together and clamped. Then they rolled in two more sides and clamped them until they had 40 feet of fuselage on either side. Once it was lined up they pushed the two sides together and made some adjustments. Next they lined up the bins.

The last stage of installation was set decorating. They rolled out the carpet, then put the seats in place, 72 in all, and screwed them down. The final stage was largely cosmetic, hanging curtains and polishing the galley. The construction crew, the task nearly finished, stood around taking it all in as various people walked through.

"It has real airplane seats, windows, toilets," someone said. Then he paused. "Wait, the toilets aren't real."

"Yeah, don't use them," said Myers. "I had someone do that once."

"Probably a Teamster," one of the construction crew replied.

While they had put the plane together over several days, it could have been done in a matter of hours, particularly with Myers there. Building aircraft that didn't fly was a second career for him. His first had been as a contractor and builder. After one job on another mockup he fell into this easily.

Four Fellas had rented the 737 but he had other commercial aircraft mockups. His 5,000-square-foot warehouse in North Hollywood was filled to the tips of its wings. He also had corporate jet sets, including a Gulfstream Silver cabin. They could be set up several ways, where cameras pointed forward or aft. There were also pieces of sets available.

The mill shop, with its equipment moved back, had seemed roomy enough as the 737 set went in. Now, with it fully installed along with crew it was more than cramped. It seemed like the tightest fit of any set thus far and they hadn't brought in the extras yet. The two scenes on the plane would include 47 passengers and three flight attendants who were patiently waiting in the next warehouse.

The scenes came early in the movie, when three of the characters fly to Vegas together. It established the conflict between Paddy and Billy. Billy had feelings from childhood for Paddy's wife and he'd never really gotten over it. He hadn't attended her funeral, which angered Paddy. There were two scenes on the flight to Las Vegas. One had the Paddy, Archie and Sam in a row of seats. The other had Paddy talking to Archie while he was inside the bathroom. Paddy ranted about Billy in both of the scenes.

The grips installed a giant sky-blue screen outside the windows of the wingless aircraft while Hennings talked to the gaffer. Kelson and McManus squeezed their respective carts alongside the fuselage. Kelson would mike the actors rather than placing mikes inside, since one of the scenes had them moving. Turteltaub, who had been at the main stages, returned.

"Why aren't we rehearsing?"

"We're still dealing with lights."

Turteltaub stepped back to look at the set silently for a few minutes. A short time later the background actors filed in and were directed to places in the various rows. He watched for a minute and said to put Duffy Astriab, the stand-in for Mary Steenburgen, in the seat in front of the row of actors. Steenburgen wasn't on the schedule, which made Astriab available. He looked again and thought she should have a book. Rake hit the talk button on the walkie. "Props. Can somebody get Duffy a book?" Rice had one handy. Second team was next. The warehouse lights were cut, the interior of the jet lighted.

The scenes introduced the specific conflict between Paddy and Billy. Paddy, who had to be manipulated into the trip to begin with and didn't know Billy would be there, complained about him, which provided the background. The funniest scene was Paddy following Archie to the bathroom and then standing outside to make his point, which got a laugh from the crew.

It went quickly, perhaps as fast as any scenes with dialogue had. Turteltaub knew exactly what he wanted. He got the different angles, and they were done. Then the director stood next to De Niro in front of the open fuselage as everyone grew silent. "Everybody, that's it for Bob," the director said. "A round of applause."

He shook the actor's hand as he said it. De Niro smiled and nodded a thank you to Turteltaub and then to the group, who were still clapping. The director went back to business so the others did as well.

De Niro turned to his assistant. "Where's the john?" And with that, De Niro was gone.

CHAPTER NINETEEN
Shoot Week 9
Dec. 17, 18
Day 37, 38

A HANDWRITTEN NOTE ON THE PRELIM Friday had advanced Monday: "Just two more wake-ups!" It was enthusiasm for sleep more than a reminder that just two days of principal photography remained, since everyone knew that. The wrap party on Saturday night had been a big success. It was normal to have it before the last day of principal photography because within 24 hours of when the workday ended Tuesday, half the crew would be gone.

It was a great party, well organized and fun. Most of the crew attended, as did Turteltaub, who stayed a good part of the night. There was dancing and an open bar and the food was good. The concierge, given a budget, had organized it at a local nightclub that featured a hidden room. She figured that was perfect for celebrities. Most of the actors were gone for the weekend, De Niro's work completely finished. The surprise was that Michael Douglas attended. While he didn't stay that long, he didn't hide out in the secret room, which hadn't stayed hidden more than five minutes.

Frosty the ice luge was a decoration. She had lost her luster since the party scene, and no booze flowed. But her presence was unexpected and met with good cheer. It seemed appropriate that she finish her life at the party.

A sense of calm greeted everyone at Mailing Avenue on Monday morning. The absence of background actors made it seem quiet. It felt bigger and airy and almost fresh, although not quite. At the same time it was obvious they weren't done yet. The first warehouse had undergone another change. On one side crew was finishing breakfast where they had all along while the other side opened to an entirely new room.

The solution as to where to build the chapel set given how crowded the warehouses a week earlier, had been to look elsewhere. Bomba landed on the Boom Boom Room, the Art department's conference and display room as the place to build the set. Now the Boom Boom Room was gone and in its place, an entirely different room. Double doors opened from the room into the warehouse, obscured by a large partition. From inside the cameras could point out and the partition looked like a hallway. Meanwhile, they had cut windows into the walls and installed opaque glass, which opened to hallways.

The pressure was off for a lot of the crew but not the Art and Construction departments. Rice addressed it innocently enough as she talked to Lipp inside the Art department office. "I kind of feel like at this point in time they should be dismantling sets, rather than building them." Lipp nodded.

The Art and Construction departments had spent the last weeks working like they had in the lead up to principal photography, delivering six sets and two redresses. As before, they finished sets in the order in which they were scheduled. The chapel set now complete, the swing gang went to the back warehouse to put the finishing touches on the sets needed in the afternoon.

It helped that the shooting crew was in the first warehouse, because the Art department could work unabated. They had been limited during the previous week, just as when they were finishing the penthouse set, and worked off hours. The party scenes were much louder than the one on the Binion's set but it didn't mean they could be using hammers and drills and other tools in the background.

Meanwhile, the Binion's set had to be redressed, which included rebuilding one section. Three quarters of it had been struck when they learned Turteltaub wanted to reshoot a scene there. The entrance was gone, as were the columns on one side, and the circular stage on the other where Steenburgen sang. But the long wall with the bar, the most detailed part of the set, was largely intact. The camera could face that wall. Aside from the edge that needed shoring up the job mostly required cleanup. They would fill in the foreground with barstools and tables and chairs.

Bomba was on the soundstages to check progress and started at the Binion's set. The large glass mirror, with the word "Showplace" etched in it, hadn't been damaged. The large wooden bar that ran much of the length of the wall required minor touch-up. Both had cleaned up nicely. The next step was Set Dec. Photos of earlier scenes, printed out by the video assist, remained on the bar. The photos would be used even more intensely in the next phase. Every bottle on the bar, the faux beer taps, where stools had been, would match the earlier scenes precisely.

Satisfied with the progress, Bomba headed toward the new sets. They were for the scene with the three-way call between Billy, Archie and Sam that sets off the trip to Vegas. He looked tired as he walked the short distance across the stages.

Set Dec had done its part. The set for Billy, the wealthy bachelor with the Malibu beach house, was the largest. One side of the set featured a wall of windows and deck beyond that with an imaginary ocean view. The deck was actually a fourth set for another scene, that one with Billy and Diana. The ocean would come later, courtesy of technology and footage taken from Turteltaub's beach house.

The set was nice but purposely crisp in keeping with the character's personality. Quality art was on the walls, images from his life contained neatly on the dresser. Other images, including the faded black and white photo strip, hung on the wall.

The Art department had recreated Archie's bedroom based on the scenes shot earlier. The character lived in his son's house, and they used photos taken by the on-set decorator, Konrad Lewis, to recreate it. They were from earlier scenes shot at the house in the suburbs. This set rebuilt the far side of the room, with bed and chair and window. It was the same furniture from the earlier scene, the same photos and decorations from the top of Archie's dresser. It was warmer, the dresser top a little more homey and cluttered.

Sam, who was attending a party, would go into a small bathroom of the hosts to take the call. It was also cluttered, the medicine cabinet full. They made prescription bottles that reflected the hosts of the party, since it was their house. Part of the scene had Sam looking at their drugs in the medicine cabinet.

Turteltaub's plans for the scene were ambitious. He wanted to shoot all of the actors simultaneously which wasn't commonly done. Normally they shot one side of a conversation, while a member of the crew said the lines on the other end. They shot the other side of the conversation the same way. The director figured putting the actors on the phone with each other would help make their performances stronger.

It would be hard on the cinematographer to get the three-way call right. It wasn't just having a third camera. That was normal and they had occasionally used C Camera throughout photography. But getting three different places perfect on the monitors, instead of three cameras on one place, require three times as much work to set up. The lighting was different for each of them.

Hennings had likewise come to the stages to look at the sets to prepare for his work. He went inside the small bathroom set, where Sam would take the call. He looked at the walls and turned around, then he looked at the ceiling. He thought it was too dark, and an angry expression came across his face.

It was at that precise moment the production designer walked up from the other side of the soundstages. Seeing Bomba, Hennings stepped forward. "Do you people ever build sets with lighting in mind?" Bomba's eyes flashed a little. The cinematographer wasn't his boss. The production designer answered to the director, or perhaps a UPM or a producer, the same people to whom Hennings answered. It wasn't the first time and he was tired of it.

"Oh, go back to television and Miley Cyrus," replied Bomba, who turned and walked away. Bomba generally did features, while Hennings did television and occasional features. Hennings had been DP on *Hannah Montana: The Movie*, the young Cyrus' best-known work to that point. There were a half-dozen crew within earshot, and some quiet laughter, and the story quickly spread. But no one was surprised. Both men were under a lot of pressure.

The director knew there was tension between the two department heads. He thought they were both doing a great job. The sets that Bomba and his team delivered were amazing, and the dailies, the physical work being delivered by Hennings -- looked at closely not just by Turteltaub and the editors but at the studio level -- was great. Since the director was happy with the work, he felt no need to intervene. They could work it out.

The DP had the Electric department add more practical lighting in the bathroom set.

One of the grips was watching the clip of the Today show on his phone at lunch. The story on *Last Vegas* had aired a few days earlier on the popular NBC morning show. The link to it had made the rounds via text on the day they broadcast. A lot of people had glanced at it quickly. Now there was breathing room and a couple of other people leaned over to see it in entirety.

The segment aired in the 10 a.m. hour, at the exact time the network producer said it would. They ran teases for it. Programming was softer later in the morning, more features and less hard news.

The segment opened with images from the set of *Last Vegas* and a Matt Lauer voiceover: "Four of the biggest names in Hollywood but they've never worked together. Until now. The Oscar winners are teaming up for a comedy called *Last Vegas*. Recently I caught up with them for an exclusive visit to the set."

There was footage of Matt Lauer getting a hug from Douglas and handshakes from Freeman, Kline and De Niro. It showed various crew at work, grips carrying equipment, including the one who was watching it. It showed the B Camera operator and various other people at work. "On the day of our visit, production had moved to Georgia, where the city of Atlanta was playing the role of Las Vegas." The next shot was the middle room where they had set up the director's chairs, each of the actors seated in a row, Freeman, Douglas, De Niro, Kline.

Lauer: Reports on this are that it's like *The Hangover*. But for...

Douglas: Alte kakers.

Lauer: For the audience at home, can you explain what an alte kaker is?

Douglas: It's in your imagination, but probably anybody over 50.

Lauer: So you would all qualify for alte kakers?

Douglas: Last time we looked.

Lauer: Let's talk about that for a second. He looks to Freeman. You are...

Freeman: 75.

Douglas: Jesus. Set the tone... 68.

De Niro: 69.

Lauer: (Looks at Kevin Kline.) Wait, don't say it. I read the note of how old you are and thought it was a typo. I went into the makeup room and said, 'Just for kicks and giggles, how old is Kevin Kline?' There wasn't one guess over 55... You're 65?

Kline: That's my chronological age, yes.

A new series of images began with more Lauer voiceover. "Audiences have given two thumbs-up to this movie genre. The first two *Hangover* films struck box office gold, grossing more than a billion dollars worldwide. The key to the plot of these movies is a little bit of raunch." One clip had been of Bradley Cooper in *Hangover*, then a graphic of a slot machine ka-chinging away a billion dollars, then another clip from the *Hangover* franchise. That one had a guy passed out on the floor, his glasses near his head, and the legs of a barefoot woman holding shoes in her hand walking out.

Then it was back to the actors.

Lauer: How raunchy is this?

Freeman: No raunch.

Douglas: (Looking at Freeman.) It's getting raunchier as we go along. The language has gotten fuller and fuller.

Freeman: That's one way to put it, Michael. Fuller.

The camera cut to A Camera operator Jody Miller and Kelly Borisy, the dolly grip, and then to McManus' McVideo playback machinery, and then to Rake. "Quiet, please. Action!" A shot of director's village was next, Rake on the left, Turteltaub, Amy Bauer and Accardo. Then another behind-the-scenes clip of David Hennings talking to gaffer Steve Crowley and a pan of the various drag queens and interesting extras in the background.

"On the day we were there, the script called for a funeral scene. But being set in Las Vegas this funeral was filled with all kinds of characters, including... Carrot Top. " Actor Scott Thompson picked up an orange cone and talked into the camera, "There's nothing to see here. Please."

And back to the room with the hero actors in their director's chairs.

Lauer: What is happening here? Why this cast of characters? Who died?

Freeman: I win a whole bunch of money so we throw this very lavish party. So we print up flyers and go out on the street and invite all of these characters to come to the party. This one guy, who you met... Freeman nodded to Kevin Kline.

Kline: He plays a Madonna impersonator who I mistakenly mistake for a woman and kind of hit on her, him, it... And um we become good friends.

Freeman: Comes to the party with his wife.

Douglas: Turns out he's married.

Freeman: Dances himself -- to death.

The next scene cuts to the screen image of the guys at the funeral singing the Madonna song, "I Will Remember."

Lauer: He dies dancing? So that's whose funeral it is. So, let's talk about resumes. Six Academy Awards in this group, I think?

Freeman: Where? Really?

Lauer: A couple of Tony Awards.

Kline: Yes.

Freeman: A couple of nominations, he said, raising his hand.

Lauer: Yes. I wasn't slighting you. A couple of Cecil B. DeMille Awards from the Golden Globes. And so, is this fun, at this stage of your career, to be able to say, 'Let's just get together and do something that is purely for fun?'

Douglas: First of all, it was a shock that none of us had worked with each other before. And that first week you kind of think, 'Man I hope this works because all you need is one bad apple in the group.' So I think we were pleasantly surprised.

A camera shot of the pool scene in Las Vegas plays on the screen and then back to a set inside the funeral home with more Lauer voiceover. "The feeling is apparent on the set, even with the film's director, Jon Turteltaub, who literally let me get in on the action."

The camera showed Jon giving a thumbs-up. He had headphones on and was looking at the screen, with Pink, actor Roger Bart and Bauer also in the shot. The next shot, this one outside, again had Turteltaub with headphones but Accardo next to him now and Bauer behind.

He points like a maestro to Lauer, to let him start the scene.

Lauer: ACTION!

And back inside to the four guys on the chairs in the interview. The scene where De Niro ended up on the spot with the taskmaster question had made it in. "Because it's easy, everybody does what they want, everybody adjusts to everybody. We're having a lot of fun."

The last shot was back to Turteltaub on the set, this time pointing to Lauer, who yelled, "CUT!" And then back in the Today show set and the couch, live with Lauer and Savannah Guthrie.

Lauer: I directed. For the record, I directed a scene with Morgan Freeman, Kevin Kline, Robert De Niro and Michael Douglas.

Guthrie: That's good. And for your bossy side, you're really well prepared for that.

Then a surprise clip, back to Lauer, the director, who called, "ACTION!" Turteltaub had his fingers to his mouth as if with a kiss as if saying, well done. Lauer gives a thumbs-up to the camera.

One more time, the Today show cameras were aimed back at the couch.

Lauer: It's a good group of guys and I think it's going to be a very popular movie when it comes out next year.

Al Roker: Yeah!

Guthrie: Pretty cool. Still ahead...

It was a sweet story seen by a couple of million people, who now knew about a movie that was coming out in a year, something that hopefully would jog a memory or two when it came time.

The chapel scenes had been straightforward, as had the other work for Monday. The set was good, the lighting fine. At the end of the shooting day Accardo packed up and went to the hotel. She still needed to prepare the Script Supervisors Production Report, in this case, for Day 37.

Accardo already had a new job lined up. She was headed to *Transformers 4* directed by Michael Bay, whom she had worked with before. There was a big difference in making a movie with a budget of its size and that of *Last Vegas*. *Transformers* would probably have 10 cameras and a lot more equipment, as well as a lot more crew.

"And I may make more money on a show like that," Accardo said. *Last Vegas* paid scale, where shows with bigger budgets paid more, meaning they had first choice of crew, assuming their picks weren't already booked. That's what happened in Las Vegas when the movie wanted to hire experienced crew and found the market light, given so many were at work on *Hangover 3*.

Accardo had been doing the job for 25 years. She studied radio and television in college but wasn't sure what she wanted to do. A friend of her father's was shooting a television pilot in Northern California so she went there. She took to the work and had stayed busy since.

The movie she did before *Last Vegas* was with Bay, the third in the franchise, *Transformers: Dark of the Moon* (2011). That had a budget nearly $200 million. Before that she had worked with director Michael Mann on *Public Enemies* (2009), which had a $100 million budget.

She had an even longer history with Turteltaub. The first movie she worked with him on was 1995's *While You Were Sleeping*, which starred Sandra Bullock. She was hired again on his next project, which was *Phenomenon* (1996) and on the first *National Treasure* (2004). *Last Vegas* was the first time their schedules and projects had lined up since.

The report she prepared for Day 37 was 25 pages, a little shorter than was typical. It showed both the date and the day, a Monday. It showed crew call was 7 a.m., the first shot 8:40 a.m., that the lunch break went from 12:48-1:18 pm, and that the first shot after lunch began at 1:45 p.m. Camera wrapped at 4:05 p.m.

A chart summarized the work that had been done during the day and tallied the completed work into totals for all of principals. They shot five scenes, which were done in 10 setups. All of that translated to 2 3/8 completed pages of the script, and the time of those scenes translated to 02:30.

The daily summary was tallied into completed work totals of all productivity during principal photography. At the end of Day 37 they had shot a total of 107 scenes with 952 setups, covered 106 5/8 pages of the script, all of which translated to 1:55:57 of script.

There were six scenes left, 5 3/8 script pages. The section for camera roll numbers correlated to digital cards, 238-241 for A Camera and 170-171 for B Camera. The sound roll number was 45. She wrote in a note in the remarks section that a scene scheduled for the day had already been completed. The other pages showed what work had been by script page. Each scene was detailed.

She sent the finished report to Kamishin, the APOC and Stephens in the bullpen and five people at efilm, which was processing the raw material, along with others.

Accardo's dream was to tell the story of her grandfather, Tony Accardo. He had been part of the same crime family as Al Capone. As a character he was appealing because he didn't fit a lot of the stereotypes for mobsters, one of which was that Tony Accardo had died of natural causes in 1992. Early versions of the project tentatively called it "Big Tuna," his nickname. When it was officially announced it was "Untitled Tony Accardo, Sam Giancana Biopic." Michael Mann would write, direct and produce, and Accardo would be an executive producer.

Asked if she would serve as script supervisor when it got made, she said, "I'm not sure I could watch anyone else do it."

The script supervisor report was the longest of the reports that came in to the Production department each shooting day but it wasn't the only one the bullpen used to create the Daily Production Report, called the "PR." They incorporated reports from the Camera and Sound departments, as well as paperwork from the ADs, most significantly for payroll. As the 2nd AD, Peterson oversaw it, but Awa also contributed to it. Who worked -- and for how long -- was documented three ways: crew, background actors and cast.

The extras breakdown identified when they arrived and when they were wrapped. It showed whether they were due additional pay, perhaps for bringing a car or an unusual costume. It also had other details like lunch.

The production time report for the actors, known as "Exhibit G" and generally called "the G," was much more detailed. The form had the name of the union on it and was based on the current contract. The main actors on *Last Vegas* were paid flat fees, so hours didn't determine pay as it did a lot of the crew or actors who had been hired at scale. All actors were required to initial it to confirm its accuracy, and it ended up with the Accounting department.

The daily Exhibit G included all actors working for the day, and even the stand-ins. It was thorough, their names and the characters they played, and closely tracked their day. It was when they reported to work, when they reported to set, when they were dismissed from set, and final dismissal, which with portal to portal meant when they arrived at "home." It also contained meal and travel time.

The PR looked like a call sheet because it was structured like one. It came from the same software and used the same data to auto-fill areas that were known. The front side had the *Last Vegas* mark on it but different information boxes, while the back was a duplicate of the backside of the call sheet with crew names, only this used for payroll purposes.

The front was everything but payroll. Most of the information on the top half was gleaned from the script supervisors report, scenes and pages minutes, set-ups. It also included details from camera report, which in this case came from the digital loader. That was different than the camera information collected on Accardo's report. And it contained the information from Exhibit G.

The back looked exactly like the back of the call sheet except with hours. It contained the job/title and crew member's name, then the hour in and the hour out using military time. With the exception of people who were OC (on call), like the Art, Construction and Set Dec departments and the Production department except Badalato, it showed everyone's hours. Turteltaub was the only person above the line whose hours were recorded on the back of the PR.

Day 37 showed the director had come in at 6.8 and left at 16.7, or just shy of 12 hours, the same as Badalato. Rake, Peterson and Awa were in the same range, with Peterson coming in the earliest at 6.2. Accardo had started at the same time as the director but finished at 17.3, which reflected the time it had taken to finalize the report.

For Day 37, the digital capture footage amounted to 115 gigabytes for the day, pushing the new total to 9990 gigabytes and ensuring they would top one terabyte by the time they wrapped.

A handwritten note from the director was on the bottom of the call sheet for Day 38, the last day.

To The Entire Crew:

This has been the smoothest, easiest, most enjoyable production I have ever been a part of... and that is 100% because of all of you.

Thank you for your kindness, your enthusiasm and your great work.

I couldn't be more impressed or happy –

With love,

Jon

Turteltaub had been described as "warm" and "really funny" as well as someone whose humor could be at other people's expense. It was true he could crack a verbal whip that stung the ass of whomever he aimed at from a stage away. By the same token, he moved on quickly. Once he'd made his point, he dropped it, even if he hadn't forgotten. He was also generally in a good mood, animated and positive. He wasn't big on overt praise. It seemed he expected the crew to do a good job and he wasn't surprised when they did.

That made the note even more appreciated.

The last day pulled together like the clock was in charge. The big scene to be managed was the three-way call. Turteltaub went between the sets. "This is going to be a disaster!" he said, only half joking. There was banter from there. "I told ya." "No you didn't." "Yeah, I did."

A lot of effort went into lighting the scenes. Grids had gone up over all the stages, and they held lights as normal, but there were others. Archie's window had a powerful light outside of it reflecting daylight. A large black tarp had been stretched over the Malibu bedroom set.

A slightly different process would be used to shoot it, one camera on each scene, rather than two. They finished getting the first shot ready and called in first team, then the actors. Turteltaub, sitting at Director's Village, was still joking around. "This is the worst idea I have had!"

Kline came up to the sound cart to get his mic, he stopped at Turteltaub's chair and surreptitiously dropped a hat in his lap. "Oh, no you didn't!" Turteltaub laughed as he looked at it. It read "Ritz Carlton Fuckhead," a play on the hotel in Buckhead where much of the cast, and Turteltaub, had stayed. Kline was already gone, to the bathroom set where Sam would take the call.

Soon Turteltaub was talking to the actors. "Action is Michael. Then ring, Kevin, your action is opening the medicine chest. Archie, not till the second phone ring.

The scene didn't look like a disaster on the monitors and it went more quickly than shooting three separate scenes. Once the scene was done, Turteltaub gave the same public nod to the work of Kline and Freeman, one by one. Both got big hugs from the director.

That left the last scene. The grid over Binion's had been struck with the set but it was back up now. The wall that provided the backdrop for the scene was in place, now with the full bar. The stools and tables were in place in front of it, all of it back in its original glory.

Both of the actors were in costume, Steenburgen in the gold gown. She was surrounded by last-look people putting on the finishing touches, and Douglas' people were nearby. When a train sounded in the distance, Steenburgen commented that she didn't mind the sound. Her father had been a train conductor.

They got to work recreating the on-camera kiss. In the meantime, the reason for the reshoot had become clearer. The editors working in the background thought it could be better, and that it needed to be better in the event they eliminated the death of Maurice/Madonna. That was the main catalyst in the script for the change in Billy. The character had come to Vegas to marry a woman half his age. His planned wedding was canceled, and instead he had fallen for a woman much closer to his age. That would make Diana Boyle a more significant catalyst.

"Gorgeous!" said Turteltaub between takes. "Even the guys are diggin' it! Let's get one more."

The director was trying to keep things light but interestingly, a lot of the crew wasn't looking. Aside from camera, who had to look, a lot of them averted their eyes when the actors kissed. It was something else out of the tradition of Hollywood, a politeness.

At some point Douglas seemed irritated by the number of takes. He indicated to Turteltaub that the director had what he needed. Steenburgen, who looked visibly flushed but not unhappy, kept quiet. The actor went to her side and said something privately. Whatever it was, she nodded and laughed.

"Let's get one more," Turteltaub said.

And before long, it was a wrap. Rake announced that Jon would be saying a few words, a call repeated and then echoed again on the walkie. Word of mouth spread from there throughout the offices, most of which cleared out as people hurried to the soundstages. The director's personality was well known. This was likely to be a roast, particularly with the heartfelt note on the record. Being mentioned was a scary prospect, but it was guaranteed to be funny if it wasn't you.

When enough people had arrived Turteltaub said he had a few words, and that he and Rake had worked on it over dinner. Then he jumped right in.

"Thank you to David Hennings, an amazing 4th choice who could walk into St. Peter's Basilica in Vatican City and say, 'Who built this shit?'" Laughter erupted as the cinematographer grinned.

"To David Bomba, who made the penthouse real and Vegas light. I was worried you would be dehydrated from all the criers."

"Kerry, I worked with your dad and the apple doesn't fall from the tree. But what a fucking tree!" It was an apparent reference to the key grip's father, Alan Rawlings, who owned Gentleman Grips, which had leased equipment to the show.

"Crowley, geez were you boring." Boring was good for the chief electrician.

"Dayna... Where's Dayna?" He looked around for the costume designer. "Dayna, the only thing you had in common with these guys was the number of extras you undressed." This was an old joke recycled for the day, but it kept them laughing. Part of it was his timing. Turteltaub might have been a stand-up comedian. Next he turned to the A Camera operator.

"Jody, I don't know how you did it. You had me in one ear and Hennings in the other and had to figure out how we could both be so wrong."

"A question for Chad. When you were in kindergarten, did your dad come to school to play second base?" Rivetti, in his role as 1st AC for A Camera, had been behind the hire of his dad, Tony Rivetti, although it was obviously approved by Hennings.

Badalato had been miffed when he saw the rate Tony was paid on the first day he worked without having been consulted. The older Rivetti had been given the same pay as the 1st AC, the highest in the department because it had management responsibilities. It wasn't a rate that applied to all ACs, and in this case Tony Rivetti was filling in on B Camera. Badalato had called Chad Rivetti into the office to talk about it although he let it stand.

The director said a couple of other things that not everyone heard. It was about grip and rigging and Peterson, the key 2nd AD and Awa, the 2nd 2nd

AD. Whatever he was saying, the people in earshot loved it. Then he got to the actors.

"Mary -- you are everything I could want in an actress whether she played a mother, a daughter, or a wife. You were the muse of this movie."

"Kevin Kline, thank you for being in my movie and whatever movie you were on."

"Michael Douglas, you knew how to do every job on a movie, and still look good on camera."

Turteltaub again turned, making it hard for some people to hear. He liked Freeman, who he initially feared would be too serious for him. The director mentioned some of the Art department crew as well as hair and makeup, then he looked around for Rice.

"Here was this flaky prop girl in an absurd skirt," he said, referring to his first impression when he met her in prep. "And you made the set better for everyone. Never were you not-ready."

Then it was Accardo's turn. "They kept telling me about the limits on where I could hire from, and then I found out I was going to get a fat, bald dolly grip from Chicago. So, I thought maybe I could pick somebody in Chicago, too. Thank you to Alicia, who had to sit next to me and hear all those things Mark McManus was overhearing." This had been his stealthiest joke, folding in the video assist in the meantime.

"To all the grips and electric -- None of you were as good as Konrad." That also had several layers. It was praise because Konrad Lewis, the on-set decorator who had done everything from skim the pools on the penthouse set to moving furniture out of the way of actresses. He wasn't part of the Grip or Electric departments.

Turteltaub, who had asked earlier if Samuels was in the room, was headed for the grand finale.

"Fuck you Jeremiah for having no focus problem," he said, a sideways complement, since it meant the executive producer had his eyes on things. "And fuck you for hiring Billy Badalato," this brought raucous laughter as Badalato beamed.

"Most of all, thank you, Gary Rake, for the inspiration. You were the soul of this movie and I'd have been such an ass without you. You are loved and you are loved by me." He looked at his paper and back at the crowd.

"If I didn't mention you maybe I didn't see you. Or you are David Kelson. Just kidding. Everyone thinks I hate Kelson. I don't hate Kelson. Gary hates Kelson.... Just kidding!"

"But seriously, everyone. Thank you for a great show. See you at lunch."

A minute later everyone was headed from the stages back through the middle warehouse, laughing and talking like a group just let out of a Broadway theater. Catering had a buffet with steak and lobster, better sides and more dessert options. The tables had been arranged to face in one direction. The stills photographer had prepared a slide show that was a highlight of cast and crew over the course of principal photography. Producers sat near production assistants, as it had been all along. Screens had been set up to show photos taken by the still photographer. Some wrap gifts were handed out but most of that happened in private.

Call sheets usually perish with the day like a newspaper used to before the Internet. Several crew had folded one up and put away Day 38, with Turteltaub's note.

Almost everyone -- not all -- said it was a good show. So, what was it like when a difficult show ended? "Quieter," said Stephens.

"It's less personal," agreed Jobst.

"Everyone just goes home."

Sometimes, they didn't even say goodbye, someone else added.

PART THREE: WRAP
4 Weeks

CHAPTER TWENTY
Dec. 19-21, Jan. 4-25

THE NEXT DAY IT WAS LIKE SOMEONE had thrown a switch on Mailing Avenue. Tuesday they had been shooting, then eating the best meal of the run of production. Wednesday, principal photography was a memory, tables stacked to the side awaiting pickup, and the catering company packing up. Now they were "in Wrap," a different stage of production.

Turteltaub was scheduled for a noon flight out of Hartsfield, an exodus that would include two-dozen other people by day's end. Close behind him were the department heads, Gary Rake, Dayna Pink, David Hennings. David Bomba, the production designer, was also finished although he remained in town. Alicia Accardo was likewise headed home, as were all set support people and assistants to people above the line.

As the week wound down more crew would leave, depending on if they had one, two or three days of paid wrap. There was grumbling about that, since they used to have more time to wrap. Then everyone would be gone for the holidays. Because of how the calendar fell, wrap was happening in two parts. Hollywood, whether it manifested in Atlanta or LA, took its holiday season seriously. All crew would finish on Friday, Dec. 21. Some crew would return Thursday, Jan. 3, while others would return Monday, Jan. 7.

If wrap worked as budgeted -- and a lot of organizational effort had been put in place throughout prep and principal photography so it would -- they would shut down the physical side of the $36 million company in a total of 21 business days.

To get there, everything Four Fellas brought into Mailing Avenue had to be dispersed or accounted for one way or the next and the facility returned to its owners. A lot of the set dressing, costumes and props had to be stored in case there were reshoots. All of them had things that needed to be returned. The amount of product placement luggage alone promised to keep the Props department busy.

Detailed organizational records had to be prepared. These were binders although they called them books, the biggest of which would be the wrap book put together by production. But there were similar efforts in various departments, Travel, Costume, Art, Set Dec, Locations and so forth.

There was a subdued feeling in the bullpen on Wednesday. There was a steady stream of boxes dropped in the middle of the room between the desks. Then someone saw a rat, which sent the place into a frenzy. There wasn't time to call the building owners to address the immediate problem. For that, they turned to the accountant. His door was closed but he heard them, and his name, and opened it before they could knock. He was happy to assist, perhaps to shut them up. Soon, the rat was gone and the accountant was back at his desk behind the closed door.

By mid-morning there were so many items packaged for shipment that the floor in the large room was covered and layered, requiring it be shifted so a path could go through. Dozens of suitcases and boxes and trunks and hard rubber bins, even a couple of sets of golf clubs. Los Angeles-area addresses dominated but there were plenty of other places in the mix, like Albuquerque, Chicago, Dallas, Houston, New Orleans, New York and London.

With just three days until the holiday break the priorities were clear. Any accounts or equipment that was accruing costs and no longer needed would be closed first. The focus would be on leases rather than things that had been purchased. Assets would be sold later as part of an organized process. Other things would take more time. Items needed for reshoots would be isolated and put in storage, although where remained to be seen. Loss and damage claims across departments could be processed when they got back, since the cost associated with the claims wasn't going to change.

The back of Mailing Avenue still had the star trailers and they could go immediately. The travel office was dealing with a parking lot full of vehicles used by crew under the corporate rental agreement. Since they had picked the cars up on Mailing Avenue, that's where they returned them. Then shuttles took them from the soundstages to the airport. Now the vehicles had to be processed back out. The rental company had staff for that, but not in large numbers.

Returning the 85,000-square-foot facility to its original condition under the terms of the lease would be a longer process. A lot of the work, striking the sound stages, could be done when crew returned in January. The official walk-through with the building owners would likely be within the first week.

Badalato and Kamishin wanted to do an early walk through to get their minds around anything that might need to be repaired. They stopped in the bullpen on the way amid a minor commotion.

"Was he wearing his Old Velvet?" someone asked, which brought laughter to what otherwise didn't seem a happy occasion. It turned out a PA had just hung up the phone after a conversation with Prickly Guy's assistant. Simpson prompted the PA to repeat it to them.

"He said, 'Can you just think before you talk again?'"

"Wow," said Badalato in a flat tone.

"Nice," someone else said.

The call had to do with a canvas chair back for one of the studio execs. The PA told him the piece, which slipped over the rails of a director's chair and bore the exec's name, had gone back with her. Prickly Guy's assistant didn't believe it and that had been his response.

"Alright," Badalato said cheerfully. "Let's see if we can get another one to send it to the studio." Props handled chair backs and someone said they would talk to Rice.

The duo continued toward the soundstages. Badalato had gotten to know the owners as part of the leasing process. They had just purchased Mailing Avenue and Four Fellas was their first tenant. Since it had never been used as a studio before, Badalato and the owners had worked out a deal where they would split the cost of upgrades, assuming the owners approved of them. And they had liked most of the improvements.

The soundstages were busy with Set Dec dismantling its work in the three sets used in the phone conversation. Plants had been moved away from the deck that was outside the Malibu bedroom set. Someone was unscrewing the boards of the deck.

To the side, where the cages were, the Sound department and Video assist were getting their equipment ready. About 50 feet away near the remnants of the Binion's set were the camera crew. Badalato and Kamishin said hello and kept moving.

Rivetti and Flurry were organizing the Panavision equipment for shipment, but they also had a lot of their own equipment. The equipment going back to Panavision would take eight pallets.

The items attributed to Flurry, who as 2nd AC took care of the equipment, seemed the most of any individual, save perhaps Jobst. It would take three pallets to secure his list of items: Duffel Alexa Cases, Alexa AKS, Oconnor Panna Head, Cartoni DH Lambda Head Monitor 11:1, Casses LG Prime Case, SM Prime Case, PCZ case, ABHC case, VCLX case, Clr Fltr #1, Clr Fltr #2, Clr Fltr #3, Kristin HME Ezups, Lite Panels, Lite Characters, Yager Cart Utility Cart, Digital Cart, Lens Cart, Rubbermaid Orange AKS.

The cameramen stopped to greet Mindy Bee. She was a marketing executive with Panavision Atlanta. She wasn't there for the equipment, since it was going back to Los Angeles. She had come bearing gifts, T-shirts with both the Panavision logo and the *Last Vegas* mark.

A few minutes later she headed to the bullpen. The T-shirts were marketing and Bee a well-known player. She had spent three years at Panavision Orlando before moving to Atlanta in 2011 to help open that office. Before that she worked for 15 years as a camera assistant on various motion pictures and network television shows. Badalato and Kamishin had already returned to the bullpen by the time she got there. They had something for her, too.

The bullpen PAs were getting wrap gifts out. While there wasn't a timed element, they still wanted to get as much out as they could before the holiday. Ironically, wrap gifts and the wrap party were two things that production departments in general disliked organizing, Badalato said. "If you were the decision-maker, it would be fun," he said. But in real life, wrap presents required a lot of approvals, which was time consuming and required a "wrap gift scout."

When it came to who among crew got one, the general guideline was anyone on the show for more than half of it. Experience had shown that T-shirts or clothing wasn't the best thing for the production department to hand out, in his view. Departments loved giving out shirts, but sizes were tough to get right. Backpacks were the solution this time. One size fit all. The decision was hastened by an opportunity to get decent backpacks through product placement. The production paid to have the *Last Vegas* mark stitched on them. There was also a limited edition publicity photo signed by Freeman, Douglas, De Niro and Kline, who were standing in a row with a "Welcome to Fabulous Las Vegas" sign behind them.

Anderson and Moniz were packing up packages of swag for the actors. Their wrap gift, however, was the same cufflinks the character Billy gave his friends at the party. It was insults the character exchanged in childhood and again in the movie. One had the word "asshole" and the other "prick,"

The rest of the effort was toward getting things in a good holding pattern until they returned.

Wrap resumed Jan. 3, as planned, but without Samuels. He had taken a tumble from a horse over the holiday and was in the hospital. It sounded serious enough that everyone was worried, although on the positive side he was on the phone handling work from his hospital bed. The list of items on the calendar for the week read, "We Miss You Jeremiah Wrap Schedule."

Wrap, as a word, was both noun and a verb. In the movie and television industry it always meant something was finished or finishing, although the time element attached to it varied. The word had been in use at least since the 1940s although it had evolved. A glossary in a book about making movies published in 1945 defined "wrap it up" as "that's all for today."

When they "wrapped Bob" after the airplane scenes, it meant De Niro's scenes in the movie were completed. When they said earlier in photography that Bob was wrapped, it meant for the day. The script supervisor's daily summary had a "camera wrap" place to put in the time the department finished. There was a Wrap Report and they had thrown a wrap party.

Wrap as a stage of a production meant finishing in the global sense. All of it had to go somewhere. Everything had to be accounted for, and every dollar that had been spent, itemized. The Accounting department would get an additional week of wrap to finish. Aside from the payroll manager, who was nearly finished, the department remained the same core group.

All of the departments had already started on wrap books, which were binders that would document their part of the show. They had put books together during the show, so they could cull from there. The main wrap book would be created by the bullpen but there was also a travel book, a costumes book, Art department books, a locations book, a DGA book, and so forth, with some of each incorporated into the larger wrap book.

It was a normal part of the process, with the studio executive in charge weighing in on the specifics of what she wanted it to include. It would contain payroll and deal memos and actor contracts, the final crew list with contact information, the list of locations and contact information. It would detail what things were in storage for potential reshoots and exactly where to find them. The books would be delivered in paper and electronic form.

The bullpen crew was back in their seasons. After touching base on the holidays everyone settled in. A little later Moniz summed it up: "I love wrap. Said no one, ever." Even with the Accounting and Production departments at full complement, and the Construction department working away on the other side of the facility, it was eerily empty. Most of the crew was gone, even as certain departments remained busy.

416

Periodically a member of the crew who had worked on the show trickled in to the bullpen. Some had checks to pick up or others reasons to come in. The buyer from Set Dec, as well as the on-set costumer, reported illnesses that took a couple of weeks to fully recover from. It made several people grateful for just getting a little sick. Whatever bug had invaded the ranks had taken a toll but everyone was back to normal.

The Travel department was working on its report. They had purchased 400 plane tickets, just 50 of which had happened before the company moved to Vegas. That number did not include tickets that had been cancelled, only what was ultimately used. The report looked at it several ways, including by individual. In that case it summarized how many times someone had come and gone and at what cost. There was also documentation for the corporate rental vehicles. Someone else was processing De Niro's plane accounting notes, which was about 20 pages.

The Locations department was ahead of everyone else when it came to wrap, because it closed out accounts after they finished with a location. Any insurance claims, and for that matter most department paperwork, was either well along in process or completed. Closing out insurance accounts and claims had been a significant part of the wrap process for everyone.

Both Rice and Benjamin-Creel were in the office, but it was her last day on the show. At the end of the day she came to the bullpen to say goodbye. They thought Miles, the assistant, was going to come in to help Benjamin-Creel, and she made a point of telling them how much he was needed.

Rice had landed a job as prop master on an indie, *Last of Robin Hood*. The movie was about Errol Flynn, the Golden Age actor who had starred in the *Adventures of Robin Hood* (1938) and was known for his other swashbuckling roles. The movie had a limited budget and just three weeks of prep. Rice noted that Kevin Kline was going to star in it. That prompted surprise from someone in the bullpen, which in turn surprised Rice.

"How could you figure Kevin Kline wouldn't want to play Errol Flynn? Kevin was the pirate king!" The script was good and the role was challenging, and he liked that, she said. He cared more about roles than he cared about money, in her opinion.

Rice had developed more of a relationship with the actors than perhaps any other crew, Kline the most. Not in the sense that she would keep up with them but just in general. Her job had her on set most of the time, but she was also attentive and smart and gifted with some personality. One of the producers had said to Rice, within earshot of others, that she helped put the

417

actors at ease. The assistant propmaster thought things through, as with having multiple books at the ready for De Niro to choose for his character, rather than just giving him one.

Slowly Badalato and Kamishin packed up their boxes, the occasional yellow and black bin in the bullpen. Fed Ex and other delivery services continued to pick things up. Stephens tracked all of the shipments, something Simpson watched, and Kamishin from there. It was easy to see, as the costs mounted, why Kamishin had kept the account number quiet.

Stephens had also overseen distribution of scripts. De Niro had received scripts with strengthened pages, but others in crew had things they wanted as well. Accardo only wanted white scripts. Others wanted the script changes collated in, which reflected the colors. Some wanted two copies of the script, one for notes, and one to keep. They had reprinted it, the full run, 11 times, and the copy machine had never blinked.

Badalato asked if she had heard from Samuels yet that day and she nodded yes. "Has he come to grips with the fact that he's not coming back to work?" She shook her head. "No, not yet." Samuels, who was clearly still suffering from the fall, wanted to return to Atlanta regardless of how he felt. They thought the accident was too serious for him to travel so soon. Besides, he didn't need to be there, he was working from home. A PA could pack up his stuff. Neither of them planned to tell him that, at least not yet.

The Art department had a pared back staff and they were busy. Mark Garner and Chloe Lipp were organizing two, fat three-ring binders, and two other crew were at work in the department. One of the books was for wrap and the other for clearance, which would contain all permissions for various artistic elements used in the movie.

Set Dec was also at work and it wasn't pared back. If anything, they seemed as busy as they had during principal photography, although the pressure had lessened. It was Cassidy and the coordinator and the leadman, along with other members of the crew as needed. The leadman oversaw the crew that handled set dressing. During photography it was getting it on and off the stages and keeping it safely stored. Now it was about returning the items or otherwise organizing final disposition, as directed by Cassidy.

The Costume department seemed emptier because Jobst had fewer people helping here but there was plenty of work. Like the other departments, she had kept careful notebooks documenting everything. All of it was tracked, it was a matter of creating the books for distribution. She had several binders already, a continuity book and another that was just expenditures. She had handled the department budget herself. Typically, she had someone in the department to handle budget management. It wasn't something she liked and she didn't mind admitting it. The wrap books would take effort, but it wasn't the biggest part of her job.

She had to get all the costumes where they needed to be, something that involved multiple layers. The first challenge was creating capsules for any potential reshoots, and then getting them packaged and ready to be sent. They weren't all going to the same place. The main deliveries were back to Warner Bros Costume Dept. and Western Costume, which provided the period clothes for the 1955 scenes. Both of them would store items as short-term holds. Typically, those holds were for 16 weeks, although it could be extended. That way they had been returned but were also available for reshoots.

The third place costumes would go was to storage, something still being finalized by the studio. That's where most of the costumes the main actors wore would be kept in the event they were needed for reshoots. To do that, Jobst separated the costumes by principal actor based on cast number. The actors each had closets, so it was a good starting point. It was trickier from there, since what was in them hadn't come from the same places. For instance, Billy had worn a sweater that came from American Costume Co. That had to go back, although they would also isolate it for a period of time in case it was needed.

Henery had said on Tuesday they could have the penthouse down by Thursday or Friday at the latest, and the top floor was gone the first day. He had at least ten construction crew working in the back, and they were making progress on striking all of the sets. He also had numbers for the penthouse set. It had cost $642,000. He thought the change leftover was about $18,000, a topic that had obviously been covered before between he and Badalato.

There was also potential for reselling some of the materials. About $150,000 of the cost of the set was for materials used to build, some $50,000 of it just in joists. Most of them were in very good condition, Henery said. The same could be said of other things. Now the issue was finding out where and how -- and if -- they could offload them quickly. That was one of the side effects of a shorter wrap period, less time to sell assets.

The sale of assets was already well under way. A spreadsheet listed every item for sale. As a general rule, they wanted 50 percent of what they had paid for the item, and 75 percent for electronics. Most of it was a deal for the buyer, but it satisfied the need to move items quickly. Various pickups had continued, from pallets to large numbers of boxes. Benjamin-Creel shipped 24 boxes of product placement goods back to vendors one day, and 11 the next. There were still more suitcases to go from there, part of the Travel Pro deal.

Jobst' plan was to work at the soundstages through the 15th and then go to Los Angeles, where she had started the show, and finish there. There had been a conversation about it. The costume supervisor said it was acceptable to ship them back without anyone going to Los Angeles. It would save additional wrap days, and expenses, although she was certainly willing to go. "No, we want you there," Badalato replied.

That was the smarter spend. The costumes were going to three places so it was easier for things to get lost. Having Jobst there meant she could help check things in. If something were missing, she would know where it was. One lost costume could be expensive so the added wrap day and expenses were worth it.

It was finishing in Atlanta by the 15th that seemed remarkable. By the end of the day, the Costumes department was empty. All of its contents, aside from the furniture that came with the offices, was gone. Seven pallets, Jobst' kit, had gone to Chicago. Others went to Warner Bros., which would have 25 costumes on hold. There were 26 boxes, from oversized tall cardboard wardrobes with hanging racks to E Containers, which could hold up to 600 pounds.

Others costumes had been shipped separately, including one to Michael Douglas. He had a relationship with Canali, which provided the suits the actor wore on camera. It amounted to product placement but it had more than met with Pink's approval, and it helped with their budget. When the Costume department contacted the clothier about returning them, they said it was okay to ship them directly to the actor.

All of it was happening quickly. The walk-through with the building owners happened as estimated, and it went well. There was no need to convert the room used for the chapel scenes back to the Boom Boom Room. It was fine or even better in its new form. The cages that had gone in, chainlink fences installed in concrete for secure department storage, were an industry standard and would remain. The windows installed in Badalato's office, along with the renovation of the Art department, would likewise stay. The owners had upgraded the back parking lot to create space for star trailers and trucks as part of the initial lease. However, there was some damage to the asphalt that the production would pay to fix. There were other things Four

Fellas would remedy, like a small portion of the floor in the back warehouse where carpet had been glued.

Dealing with insurance claims had been a tedious part of the process which a lot of people were involved with, depending on the origin of the claim. Many people with auto and homeowner policies are happy to never make a claim, but the movie business -- and the insurance companies that sell policies -- fully expected them. Given the number of people working around expensive equipment and locations, history had shown that things happened. And it was budgeted as Loss and Damage, or L&D.

Claims begun earlier in production were naturally further along in process. A claim for a crane damaged in its return from location in Vegas back to California was approved and settled by the insurance company. Both Badalato and Kamishin believed it was an error on the part of an employee of the contractor rather than the production company, but the insurance company handled it so they moved on.

Set Dec had its share of damages to contend with. Cassidy had kept the bullpen apprised and popped his head into Badalato's office for an update. "Can I talk to you about the chandelier," he asked. "Sure," said Badalato. "What's the latest?" Kamishin, who was in her office, got up from her desk and stood at the door between the two offices for the conversation.

They knew the giant light in many of the scenes in the penthouse had been damaged. Someone said a camera hit it, although it wasn't clear that was true. It didn't matter, the production had to make good on it regardless. "I'm not sure how you want me to handle it," Cassidy said. "I think you're better off buying it and absorbing the cost. At least there's something tangible." They talked about the terms of the lease. "I can try to make a deal to pay for the damage, they may go for that." That sounded good as a first step, Badalato said.

It was the downside to renting set dressing, something the limited budget required, and they all knew it. The lease contracts contained purchase price in the event things were damaged or destroyed. That tended to be full value, no breaks, as was the case here. If Cassidy had purchased the leather couch or chandelier, instead, he could have gotten it at a discount, and now they'd be trying to sell it, lessening the overall loss. There was always a tradeoff, Badalato said.

Badalato and Kamishin held a meeting to go over the list of people and vendors who should be thanked along with the credits. Above the line credits were tightly controlled, both in terms of the order in which they appeared and the size of the credit. The DOOD, the form that quantified the number of days the actors worked, played a role in how the actors names would appear. At one point something had been amiss with the DOOD, but it had since been updated and they wanted to review it.

They also had prepared a list of companies and people deserving of special thanks. Who had gone the extra mile to help the movie production. A couple of places up for consideration were dropped, one of them after Badalato observed, "No way. They cost us a fortune." Others were added.

Crew credits that appeared at the end of the movie stemmed from the call sheet. It was possible someone started the movie with one job and moved up the ranks, or for whatever reason, earned a better credit. Kamishin's final credit would be as production supervisor, and Simpson's would be production coordinator, a move up from APOC.

Gradually Mailing Avenue had emptied out. The large semis loaded with set dressing, costumes and props were gone. Kamishin worked on a general memo about outstanding issues. The giant wrap books took form in the middle of the bullpen atop a banquet table set up for that purpose. Requests had continued to come in from the studios, now a total of 14 of them needed. No one could remember that many being needed. They got special boxes just to ship them.

Insurance across all areas was a $307,900 budget line. The biggest portion of the expense protected the movie's investors -- primarily CBS -- from anything extreme. It indemnified the production from a game-ending event, like the loss of an actor or a weather strike or a fatal injury that could shut the movie down. As with home and auto policies, insurance made it possible to manage risk. It did that at a corporate level, but a side benefit was that it also protected Badalato and Samuels from going over budget. Insurance was a budget item they could plan around. It stayed the same and limited the potential for one problem to push the project into the red.

Processing L&D was one of the more time consuming elements of wrap. A number of expensive things had been damaged or destroyed in the course of production. Set dressing had a lot but they weren't the only ones. Claims were made against anything greater than the deductible.

They had handled the claim for damage to a leather couch on location. It happened on the Paddy's living room set, inside the condo leased in downtown Atlanta. Rake called a safety meeting and the natural response for anyone standing nearby was to take a seat. One of them was a grip with a screwdriver in his pocket. It made a dreadful sound that everyone heard and he quickly stood back up, eyes wide. Badalato happened to be standing there, so of course they all turned to look at him. He shrugged. It had been easily covered when they shot the scene. The repair had taken longer and was now complete at $2,000.

A condor used to lift equipment had smashed an expensive, large leased light and stand owned by Pascal on one of the nightclub sets. Something else had been damaged, as well. The lease agreement with Pascal, which just covered the weeks in Atlanta, had been about $10,000. At first it looked like the total charge, with damages, would be $19,000. Ultimately the damage landed at $7,700, $5,000 of which was the light and the rest to cover its stand. That brought the bill down to $17,700. It sounded like T.I., the rapper-actor who auditioned for the cameo ultimately played by 50 Cent, also would be paid for it, although it wasn't clear why and no one wanted to say.

Other claims were on their way to resolution. Kelson's sound equipment was a $3,000 claim. The cinematographer's fender bender turned into a $3,500 deductible, which he was going to pay. He had opted for a higher end vehicle, so that was part of it. Walkie L&D was weighing in at $2,945, a combination of eight damaged headsets, a case and the loss or destruction of a couple of the devices.

Cassidy had succeeded in getting 10 percent off of the chandelier, so that was handled. He reported on some final numbers. The two sconces that had been destroyed were $580 total. He also alerted them to the costs to repair the section of floor in the warehouse. The company that put down the carpet on the Binions set had glued it to the cement. It was one of those things that brought laughter and head-shaking across the stages when it was first discovered. The contractor installed it as though it were permanent, suggesting they worked with the movie business before. It cost $900 to restore it.

Insurance had covered some of the costs and the production the rest, but the numbers worked. They were still under budget. Stephens, who had been there from day one, checked file cabinet drawers to make sure everything really was empty as they packed up for the last time.

Badalato's cell phone rang and it was Samuels checking in. "I'll call you as I'm locking up," he said. "Five minutes."

Then it was time to go. The accountants, who would remain another week, came out of the offices. There were hugs and goodbyes. They'd see each other later on another show.

EPILOGUE

L*ast Vegas* opened on 3,065 screens on Nov. 1, 2013. By the time it closed Feb. 20, 2014, it had grossed $134.4 million. Less than half of that sum was earned in the United States, where it was the 55th largest grossing movie out of 720 in 2013. It was released on DVD and Blu-ray on Jan. 28, 2014, and earned about $16 million. Then it was picked up by Showtime for its viewers.

A lot of people assumed it hadn't done well. It wasn't unusual to hear, "It seemed like it was everywhere, and then it was gone." That's because most of the advertising budget was aimed at driving people to theaters for opening weekend. Trailers started running in movie theaters first. Then the airwaves were saturated with ads for the movie leading up to release, almost too much. Then the advertising was gone, just as had been observed. But it didn't mean the movie was gone. It continued in theaters for several more months.

Hollywood's top grossing movies still live and die by opening weekend. How a movie performs in its first days determines how much it will command in other markets, internationally but also in DVD rights, cable or any other aftermarket opportunity. It's also typically a benefit to the studio to get more people in earlier. That's because the revenue split between the distributor and the theater changes as time goes forward, with the greatest percentage for the distributor happening opening weekend.

*Last Vega*s earned an estimated $16.3 million its first week, more than 50 percent of costs, according to publicly available information. It cost $30 million to make and roughly $150 million had been generated. What business wouldn't like those numbers?

Because movies are a revered art form, it's natural for movie buffs and fans to think the primary aim of the studios and producers making them is to earn attention from the Academy of Motion Picture Arts & Sciences. And, that would be nice. The reason movies are made is to make money. It's a business. If you don't make money, you don't get to make another picture, at least not easily. The producers of *Last Vegas* and the studios behind it wanted a financial homerun. They followed a strategy and hired good people to carry it out. It's the director and the crew, from production assistants to department heads, editors and sound supervisors, whose primary aim is the Academy. No matter how tight a budget, they want to tell the best story they can tell. The challenge is in making the art and the business merge. "We don't shoot movies. We shoot budgets," was how Badalato put it. "They turn out great, so it's working."

The budget consisted of three equal parts. The people above the line -- the writers, producers, director and actors -- got one-third; all costs of making the movie, including salary for crew, was one-third; and marketing and distribution the rest. The size of the budget within that framework ensured most of the people above the line would get paid well, while the costs of making the movie would be kept down. It meant limiting crew hires when possible and paying the crew at scale. It also put strong limits on the budgets departments had to spend on the movie. Crew had to do more with less help, time and resources. That's a global trend, not one unique to the movie industry.

People ask whether crew is invited to premiers and the answer is no, not as a rule. Any crew that is invited are likely to be department heads. "A premier is a marketing tool to draw media. The producers come, you bring stars, there's an event afterward," said Rake. "But it isn't a crew event." There were occasionally crew screenings, depending on where the movie was shot. Last Vegas was shot in two locations, and he wasn't aware of one. Most of the crew wasn't looking for one. They planned to buy tickets to see the movie in the theater when it came out.

ACKNOWLEDGMENTS

I could list hundreds of people who deserve personal thanks from me and it would start with the crew list from *Last Vegas*. You were completely worth the effort. Thanks also to the dozens of industry professionals who have answered questions or sat for interviews to provide additional insight.

Next is raw appreciation for my friends. This book took years to write, and I talked about it endlessly. I saw eyes glaze over and I know some of you had to be thinking, "Well, bless her heart. She's *still* writing that book." Thanks for listening or pretending really well.

I've been a journalist long enough to know how important editors are, and that it would be smarter of me to put them in the lede. I also bent the ear of a lot of journalists, both friends and colleagues and some I knew only peripherally. Your support was essential. Given how far out on a limb I was -- alone -- your collective experience and wisdom kept me grounded. That can't be understated.

Two editors read every word. Jim Molis helped, off and on, over the life of the project. Lynn Medford stepped in during the last year and was key to my finishing it. I cannot thank either of you enough. Kay Zuna, who I've known since adolescence, said something that got me to print out the manuscript, which it turned out was 400 pages. Then she proofread it with a great eye. At that point, I could no longer hide. I also want to thank Mollie Gregory, Mary Anne Marshall, Elaine Ash and Deanne Stillman for their contributions. A very grateful nod to the many others who helped with editing and/or insight, beta and proof reads – most of them without pay.

Thank you to the stellar authors and teachers who took the time to give me blurbs for the book: Kenny Chaplin, Mollie Gregory, Carolyn Johnston, Steffan Piper, Allen Salkin, Tracy Thompson and David Wallace.

Heartfelt thanks to this eclectic mix of individuals in my life for insight into the movie industry, as each contributed in hugely significant and different ways: Kenny Chaplin, Gary Romolo Fiorelli and Carlane Passman. Thanks to Kenny for instilling in me the need for better education in the industry. To Fiorelli for that as well as a love of the business -- it was contagious. And to Carlane, for patiently answering questions and otherwise helping me better understand Los Angeles and its century-plus influence on moviemaking.

The danger of listing some people means I inevitably leave out others who are just as deserving, and all because the deadline is here and I must finish. Please forgive me. I'm grateful to all of the librarians and other professional researchers who helped to lock in harder-to-find details. The research library at Western Costume Co., first with Bobi Garland and then Leighton Bowers, was very helpful. Many of the people who work at Margaret Herrick Library, the main repository of materials of the Academy of Motion Picture Arts and Sciences, went beyond the call to find things and follow up. Special thanks to Midge Costin for the explainer, early in process, on Sound. I would be remiss if I didn't also thank the authors, most of them obscure, who have written about movie production over the past century. (See the Introduction and Bibliography for more details.)

A blanket thank you to this group for support, counsel, friendship or insight with regards to this project: David Ault, Mike & Susie Cosner, Michael Crosby, Don Fehr, Lisa Lisa DeMaria, Essy Freed, Jinny Hawkins, Carolyn Johnston, Kim Kregloski, Tracey Owens, Steffan Piper, Karen Ratts and David Sepulveda. A tip of the sou'wester to Capt. Rick Hubbard, who encouraged me from the start. Brandyn Briley added late stage technical editing and much appreciated publishing software support.

To my family: Julia Jordan, Rob Jordan, Grace Maniglia, Jordan Maniglia, Max Maniglia, Stephanie Oberhelman, Virg Russo, Dan Taylor III, Jack and Uschi Taylor, and all Taylors, especially Grace Unruh. I'm grateful to all of you.

Most importantly, thank you to my parents, Mr. and Mrs. Robert Paul Jordan, who met at The Washington Post and valued good journalism throughout their lives. You may have gone to the great beyond but you were with me every day. Thanks for everything.

CREW/JOBS

For fast reference

A

Alicia Accardo, Script Supervisor
Daril Alder, Leadman, Las Vegas
Jordan Anderson, Office Production Assistant
Libby Anderson, Production Secretary, Las Vegas
Duffy Astriab, Stand in
Lillian Awa, 2nd 2nd Assistant Director

B

Billy Badalato, Unit Production Manager (UPM)
Amy Baer, Producer
Nico Bally, Cranium Cranes
Dwight Benjamin-Creel, Prop Master
Theo Bott, Rigging Gaffer
David Bomba, Production Designer
Kelly Borisy, "A" Camera Dolly Grip

C

Wendy Calloway, Travel Coordinator
Patrick Cassidy, Set Decorator
Richard Cohee, Stand in
Stephen Crowley, Gaffer

D

Kate Duke, Key Costumer

F

Mark Fincannon, Casting
John Findley, Location Manager
Eddie Fickett, Assistant Locations Manager, Las Vegas
Chris Flurry, "A" Camera 2nd AC
Dan Fogelman, Script Writer
Matt Fortino, Additional 2nd 2nd Assistant Director, Prod Assistant

428

Patrick Fuhrman, Leadman, Atlanta

G

Mark Garner, Art Director
Robert Gaskill, Driver/Security, Morgan Freeman

H

Jerry Henery, Construction Coordinator David
Hennings, Cinematographer
Kim Houser-Amaral, Locations Manager, Las Vegas

J

Sean Ryan Jennings, Assistant Art Director
Jennifer Jobst, Costume Supervisor

K

Damiana Kamishin, Production Supervisor/ POC
David Kelson, Sound Mixer
Ashley Kravitz, Clearance

L

Andree Lago, Scenic Foreman
Konrad Lewis, On Set Dresser
Chloe Lipp, Art Department Coordinator
Miles Logan, Props Assistant

M

Laurence "Larry" Mark, Producer
Mark McManus, Video Assist Operator
Jody Miller, "A" Camera Operator/ Steadicam
Felicia Moniz, Office Production Assistant

P

Sam Patton, Office Production Assistant, Las Vegas
Celeste Pawol, Driver
Kristina Peterson 2nd Assistant Director
Quentin Pierre, Assistant, Morgan Freeman
Dayna Pink, Costume Designer

R

Gary Rake, 1st Assistant Director
Kerry Rawlins, Key Grip
Katrina Rice, Assistant Prop Master
Chad Rivetti, "A" Camera 1st AC
Tony Rivetti, "B" Camera 1st AC
Mackie Roberts, Best Boy Grip
Monica Ruiz-Ziegler, Costumer

S

Jeremiah Samuels, Executive Producer
Dusty Saunders, Transportation, Las Vegas
Lee Siler, Transportation, Atlanta
Nikki Simpson, Production Coordinator (APOC)
Bristie Stephens, Production Secretary
Karen Strutynski, Set Medic, Las Vegas

T

Kai Thorup, Assistant Location Manager
Jon Turteltaub, Director

W-Z

Asante White, Production Assistant
Lisa Yeiser, Graphic Artist
Steve "Ziggy" Zigler, Rigging Gaffer

GLOSSARY

Art director – The second in the art, they manage it, along with the budget, at the direction of the production designer.

Assistant costume designer – Assist the costume designer in everything from research to collaborating on creative decisions on what the actors will wear. They might also directly with the actors. Not all movie productions have an assistant costume designer. APOC – See production coordinator.

Best boy – The second in the Electrical or Grip departments, a job that often involves overseeing crew as well as their department's inventory or equipment. Also the department's representative to Production when it comes to adding crew or requesting more equipment.

BFL – Any of the heavier, larger lights on set. It stands for "big fucking light" or "big fat light" depending on who is asked.

Blocking – A way of determining how to shoot a scene and where the actors will be on set, generally by imagining a frame.

Boom Operator – Operator of the boom microphone and second in the Sound department.

Bullpen – The center of the production department, generally a large room with several work stations but also the functioning hub of a movie production.

Camera operator – The person who physically operates the camera, maintaining composition and angle as directed. Catering – See craft service. Cinematographer – See director of photography. Clapperboard – See Slate.

Closet – The term used by the Costume department for the clothes of a particular character. As in "Billy's Closet."

Continuity – Maintaining consistency within and between scenes while shooting for editing purposes.

Continuity book – The Costume department creates books to detail each character's outfit in each scene. It includes what costumes are needed for each scene and how many changes in a shooting day. Once established it can include photos and written descriptions, even fabric content and weaves or any number of other things.

Costume designer – The head of the department who designs the look of each actors for their character, and then sees it through principal photography.

Costume supervisor – Manager of the Costume department, the supervisor is the main contact with other departments and oversees crew. They also supervise the acquisitions of costumes and organize wardrobe to fill actors' closets and racks for background actors and conduct fittings.

Coverage – Individual footage shot of each actor saying their lines in the course of a scene.

Craft service – A department of the movie, it provides snacks and beverages to the crew. This is different from the catering company hired to serve hot, sit-down meals.

Creative producer – Responsible for delivering talent to a project, securing financing, assisting in casting and creative hires and handling high level issues as they arise during production. Not a formal title.

Day out of Days – The production document that details the actors' schedules. DGA – Directors Guild of America.

Digital loader – The Camera department crewmember who manages the raw material captured each day and is responsible for the physical safety and security of camera cards.

Director of Photography (DP) – Responsible for all photography, the DP oversees the camera, grip and lighting departments. (Also called cinematographer.)

Director's chairs – Chairs used on set that fold to become flat and are managed by the Props department. They have been on movie sets since the silent era of film.

Director's plans – A document prepared by the art director that summarizes all the sets in detail. It adds description where most other documents offer summary information.

Director's village – The name given for the director's work area on set, which on bigger movies include camera monitors. Part of the video assist playback equipment.

Dolly grip – The technician who operates the camera dolly, which moves the camera operator and camera assist in the course of a shot. They are always with the Camera department but are part of the Grip department.

E Container – Bulk cardboard box, generally 49"x29"x27", used for shipping and storage by Costumes department. One can hold up to 700 pounds of goods. Embedded marketing. See *Product Placement*.

Executive producer – The duties vary with every movie. An executive producer whose job is on set is also considered a physical or line producer. They oversee expenditures and all aspects of production and top line issues with the studio and cast. Exhibit G – The form used to track and record cast hours.

First assistant cameraman (1st AC) – A position also known as the "focus puller." They keep images sharp, pulling or changing the focus, based on how the camera and actor moves. The 1st AC also has broad responsibilities for managing the Camera department.

First assistant director (1st AD) – The lead manager of the DGA director's team on set. In prep they build the shooting schedule and assist the director in planning the movie. When photography begins, the 1st AD manages the set with help from others in their department. Also responsible for safety on set.

Fitting – A costume department meeting with an actor or background actor.

Gaffer – Responsible for lighting the set, they build a plan that ranges from determining power sources and where cables will run to overseeing the cinematographer's instructions on lighting a scene. They also are responsible for safety as regards electrical systems in both assessing and mitigating risks. (Also chief electrician or lighting technician)

Grace – A union-approved measure where a production can ask the crew to keep working for a set amount of time for the efficiency of the production, provided the camera position does not move.

Green screen – A green or other color background that enables a separately filmed shot to be merged in later with the main shot. The process is "chroma keying," or "color keying."

Key grip – The manager in charge of overseeing the installation, removal and maintenance of non-electrical equipment. The key grip is the department head and the best boy is his second.

Having had – The union-approved term for crew to come to work having had fed themselves prior to reporting.

Kit – The equipment, tools and supplies needed and brought to work by individual crew to do their jobs.

Leadman – The member of the set decorating department responsible for getting and removing set dressing and overseeing the set dressers/ swing gang that assist.

Location casting – Coming up with actors in or near where a film will be shot.

Location manager – Finds places for non-studio scenes shot on location. Spends much of their time on the road looking at places, inside and out. May work with a film commission or government officials.

Mark – A mark is where an actor or actor is to stand, generally a colored piece of tape placed by the camera department as directed; Also used to describe the show logo that appears on set paperwork.

Montage – A filmmaking technique where shorter shots are taken and sewn together in editing with the purpose of condensing time or transmitting an idea.

Music supervisor – Coordinates the work of the composer, editor and sound mixers.

Non-deductible breakfast (NDB) – A union term that refers to breakfast and is not deducted from paychecks. Instead crew is allowed 15 minutes off the clock.

On-set dresser – The member or members of the set decorating department who remain on set to assist with moving or replacing set decorating as needed or requested by the 1st AD or director.

Per Diem – Daily living allowance to cover expenses for out-of-state crew based on union requirements or individual crewmembers' negotiations with the show.

Pick-up or P/U – A new take on a scene under way. It picks up farther along in the scene rather than starting at the beginning.

Picture cars – Any vehicle to be seen on screen separate from utility vehicles used by the Transportation department to move and operate the shooting company. Pipes –The tracks the dolly runs on.

Points – Used in the distribution of proceeds from a movie not generally known by the crew or even the cast. Points are divided as a movie is planned. One per-cent is one point.

Production Assistant (PA) – An entry level position on a movie with a world that varies in volume and task depending on department.

Production Coordinator – The top person in the production department, under the unit production manager and producer, to facilitate to coordinate between departments and facilitate the needs of the production. APOC is the assistant production coordinator or next in command.

Product placement – The inclusion of a branded product on the screen. Also called embedded marketing.

Prep – Time spent preparing for principal photography that covers wide terrain, from creating a shooting schedule, scouting and securing locations, designing and building sets, etc.

Prop master – Property master. The person responsible for purchasing or acquiring any props needed for a production.

Production designer – Responsible for the overall "look" of the movie the top designer of the movie and head of the art department head.

Production sound mixer – Responsible for capturing all dialogue and ambient sound on set or location to be used in the movie.

Pull – Costumer jargon for getting clothes off the racks of a larger collection. This may amount to hundreds of items of clothing, most of which may be slated for background.

Rack focus – Changing the focus of the lens during the course of the shot.

Rigging gaffer – A member of the lighting department who works at the direction of the gaffer and DP to install equipment in a shooting location prior to the shooting company's arrival.

Runaway production – Once used to describe a project that originated in the United States but was shot abroad, it now also includes projects lured away from Hollywood to other parts of the country.

Script supervisor – The person in charge of continuity and tracking the creative progress of the movie production each day. They sit next to the director and take detailed notes, act as liaison with the cast as regards the script.

Second assistant cameraman (2nd AC) – Operates the slate. They also are responsible for marking where actors are to stand during filming.

Second Assistant Director (2nd AD) – Focuses on the next day or days as the First Assistant Director (1st AD) focuses on the current shooting day.

Second Second (2nd 2nd AD) – The next level manager in the AD department, after the 2nd AD, who commonly deals with cast at base camp or as needed elsewhere.

Set costumer – The member of the Costume department who takes care of the actors on set. They track continuity and watch while shooting to make costume adjustments as needed.

Set decorator – The head of the set decorating department responsible for delivering set dressing specific to the characters or story for every set in a movie.

Set up – Any time the camera or cameras move. It could mean moving the cameras to an entirely new location or turning the cameras in the other direction to get coverage.

Shot – What you can see in the lens and on the monitors.

Slate – The device used to mark when camera is rolling. It tracks scenes and takes while syncing to Sound for the two to be reconnected later in post-production. (Also known the clapperboard.)

Stand-ins – The cast members who take the places of the actors before they come to set so that lights and cameras can be adjusted without tiring out the actor.

Steadicam – A specific brand of camera that isolates the movement of the camera operator to stabilize the shot that has become a term for all similar equipment.

Stunt Coordinator – The stunt coordinator is in charge of designing and scheduling stunt performances.

Swing gang – One or more members of the set decorating department who install and remove set dressing.

Unit production manager – The lead of the DGA director's team who oversees the 1st AD and the film's department heads. Also responsible for managing the production and regulating costs and the schedule to deliver it on budget.

Wrap – The act of finishing a shot, the day's work, or the entire production; a stage of movie production.

REFERENCES & SOURCES

The vast majority of content in this book comes from reporting done while being embedded on the production, interviews and set documents. The next pages include some additional references and sources.

Crew credits and budget numbers seen throughout the book, unless otherwise stated, have been documented using the International Movie Database (IMDb). This is because IMDb was the source crew most often said they used and relied upon. Rather than putting links to the pages of all the people mentioned in the book, readers should look there for more information. Where IMDb has been used as a source for information other than credits and estimates for budget and box office figures, it is stated here. It also should be noted that the IMDb system is updated and relies heavily upon information it is provided.

Set documents are listed here first because of how heavily the production relied upon them.

PRODUCTION DOCUMENTS

LAST VEGAS scripts & revisions.	Prelim (daily)
LAST VEGAS Prep Schedule	Call Sheet (daily)
LAST VEGAS Budget	Exhibit G
Shooting Schedule	Script Supervisor's Report
Day Out of Days	Camera Report
Tech Scout Itinerary, Atlanta	2nd AC Camera Notes
Tech Scout Itinerary, Las Vegas	Sound Report
Art Department Set Breakdown	Wrap Report
Costume Breakdown	LAST VEGAS Wrap Schedule

PREFACE

"A Tribute to Style", 25th anniversary of Rodeo Drive, special event, 1997.

Mary Lou Loper, "Breaking Bread With Famous Authors," *Los Angeles Times*, September 14, 1997, p. 83.

De Palma (2015). Directed by Noah Bauchman and Jake Paltrow. United Kingdom: Empire Ward Pictures.

Rendition (2007). Directed by Gavin Hood. United States: Anonymous Content.

Ross, Lillian. *Picture.* York: Rinehart & Company, 1952.

Red Badge of Courage (1951). Directed by John Huston. United States: MGM.

Salamon, Julie. *The Devil's Candy: The Anatomy of a Hollywood Fiasco.* Cambridge US: Da Capo, 1991.

Bonfire of the Vanities (1990). Directed by Brian De Palma. United States: Warner Bros.

Bamberger, Michael. *The Man Who Heard Voices: Or, How M. Night Shyamalan Risked His Career on a Fairy Tale.* New York: Gotham Books, 2007.

Lady in the Water (2006). Directed by M. Night Shyamalan. United States: Warner Bros.

Big Momma's House: Like Father, Like Son (2015). Directed by John Whitesell. United States: Regency Enterprises.

INTRODUCTION

Concept to Script

Tatiana Siegel, "CBS Films nabs Fogelman pitch," *Variety*, March 16, 2008.

Fogelman, Dan. *Last Vegas* P&T. Revisions by Kyle Pennekamp & Scott Turpel, June 20, 2012. Working script.

Amy Baer, Producer

Jude Brennan, "Last Vegas Producer Amy Baer is One to Watch," *Forbes.com*, November 27, 2013.

LinkedIn: https://www.linkedin.com/in/amybaergiddenmedia.

Jon Turteltaub, background

Ebert, Roger. Review of *Cool Runnings*. October 1, 1993.

Frank Bruni, "'Cut!' ... 'Cut!' ... 'Cut!': It's Slow Motion Behind the Scenes When a Movie is Filmed," *Detroit Free Press*, March 12, 1995, p. 1G.

Patrick Goldstein, "Keeping Company With Disney: By Hollywood standards, director Jon Turteltaub has remained remarkably loyal to one studio, from '3 Ninjas' to his latest, 'The Kid,'" *Los Angeles Times*, July 5, 2000.

Steve Schmidt, "One for the Ages: In an industry where youth reigns, 65-year-old Saul Turteltaub is suddenly hot," *Los Angeles Times*, June 29, 1997.

Alaine Woo, "Bud Yorkin dies at 89; partner in TV's 'All in the Family,' 'Sanford and Son,'" *Los Angeles Times*, August 15, 2018.

"Jon Turteltaub" IMDb, https://www.imdb.com/name/nm0005509/.

Kevin Thomas, "'Cool': Hot on Trail of Feel-Good Comedy," *Los Angeles Times*, Oct 1, 1993.

Tim Hayne, "10 Biggest Box Office Flops of 2010 (So Far)" *Parade*, July 10, 2010.

Kirk Honeycutt, "The Sorcerer's Apprentice: Film Review" *The Hollywood Reporter*, October 14, 2010.

Jon Turteltaub, discussing *Last Vegas*

Filmmaker Commentary, Jon Turteltaub and Dan Fogelman, Last Vegas (2013). Directed by Jon Turteltaub. CBS Films. Blu Ray DVD, Sony Entertainment, Culver City, CA.

"Director Jon Turteltaub Chats LAST VEGAS with AMC." Interview by John Campea for AMC Theatres, October 28, 2013.

CHAPTER 1

Mailing Avenue Stageworks

Company website, http://www.mailingavenuestageworks.com.

Existing Office Plan, with redline changes, September 20, 2012.

Billy Badalato

"Billy Badalato" IMDb, https://www.imdb.com/name/nm6169478/.

Marketing material, "Motion Picture Aviations Services." Owners Billy Badalato and Al Gerbino.

Top Gun: Bill Badalato, Tony Scott

Vincent J. Schodolski, "LIGHTS! CAMERA! TEN-HUT!" *Chicago Tribune*, April 17, 1994.

Suzanne Stephens, "Creating a Studio on the Beach," *Pensacola News Journal*, June 25, 1977, p. 37.

Andrew Blankstein, John Horn, "'Top Gun' director Tony Scott jumps to his death from L.A. bridge," *Los Angeles Times*, April 19, 2012.

Product Placement

Sam Lubell, "Advertising's Twilight Zone: That Signpost Up Ahead May Be a Virtual Product", *New York Times*, January 2, 2006.

Wings (1927). Directed by William A. Wellman & Harry d'Abbadie d'Arrast (uncredited). United States: Paramount Famous Lasky Corporation.

The Garage (1920). Directed by Roscoe 'Fatty' Arbuckle. United States: Comique Film Company.

"Product placement spending worldwide and in selected countries in 2012, 2014 and 2019 (in million U.S. dollars)," Statista, June 2015, https://www.statista.com/statistics /261454/ global-product-placement-spending.

Steven Zeitchik, "Super sell me: Morgan Spurlock's new film reveals the influential man behind Hollywood's booming product placement game," *Los Angeles Times*, April 21, 2011.

CHAPTER 2

LAST VEGAS Budget, Locked RED Mmb., December 14, 2012.

David Bomba

Awards, IMDb, https://www.imdb.com/name/nm0093549/awards.

Billy Watkins, "Ready, Set, Design: Canton man adds "Walk the Line' to list of credits for art production," *Clarion Ledger*, November 30, 2005.

Tom O'Neil, "Masters of the Craft," *Los Angeles Times*, November 21, 2007.

The Great Debaters (2007). Directed by Denzel Washington. United States: Harpo Films, Marshall Production, and The Weinstein Company. Production Notes, The Weinstein Company.

Robert Beneker, Film Review, "Be it resolved: You'll feel better when you leave the theater," *The Santa Fe New Mexican*, December 28, 2007.

Todd McCarthy, "Tailor-made for maximum inspirational, historical an educational impact," *Variety*, December 18, 2007.

Production design, history

Selznick, David, and Rudy Behlmer. *Memo from David O. Selznick*. New York: Grove Press, 1981.

Taylor, Theodore. *People Who Make Movies*. New York: Doubleday & Co., 1967.

Annette Insdorf, "Just What Production Designers Do," *New York Times*, September 9, 1984.

Film Finance, general

Goodell, Gregory. *Independent Feature Film Production: A Complete Guide from Concept to Distribution*. New York: St. Martin's Press, 1982.

Kathryn Arnold, "The Basics of Film Financing," August, 28, 2010, https://theentertainmentexpert.com/?p=60.

Kelsey McKinney, "Hollywood's devastating gender divide, explained," *Vox*, January 26, 2015, https://www.vox.com/2015/1/26/7874295/gender-hollywood/.

CHAPTER 3

Tax Incentives

Margalit Fox, "Frank Capra Jr., Movie and TV Producer, Dies at 73," *New York Times,* December 22, 2007.

Ben Steelman, "Dino De Laurentiis, producer who brought film to Wilmington, dies-at-age-91" *Wilmington Star News*, November 11, 2010.

"Migrant Film Workers Follow Studios Over Western States," *Lubbock Avalanche-Journal*, October 24, 1954, Section VI, p. 4.

Jeremiah McWilliams, "Atlanta mayor's film office plans meet some resistance," *The Atlanta Journal-Constitution*, November 5, 2011.

Alison Herman, "How Atlanta is Taking Over the Entertainment Industry," *The Ringer*, August 22, 2017.

Movies not made

Mike Fleming, Jr., "Gerard Butler Drama 'Motor City' Stalls Before Reaching Start Line, Crew Sent Home," *Deadline*, September 1, 2012.

Judy Brennan, "Foster Leaves 'Hot Zone,' Cites Script Shortcomings," *Los Angeles Times*, July 14, 1994.

El Cortez, Binions

"Re: Good Morning," email exchange, re El Cortez, August 28, 2012.

Ed Koch, "'Bugsy' Siegel – The mob's man in Vegas," *Las Vegas Sun*, May 15, 2008.

AD Department

Directors Guild of America, November 24, 2012, https://www.dga.org/the-guild/history.aspx.

"SCQL – 2nd Assistant Director," Southern California Qualification List, Directors Guild of America Contract Administration, https://www.dgaca.org/sc-specific-requirements/sc-2nd-ad.

AD Department, history, paperwork

Blakeston, Oswell (editor). *Working for the Films*. London; New York: Focal Press, 1947. "The Assistant Director," Gerald O'Hara.

AD Department, Shooting Schedule

Naumburg, Nancy (editor). *We Make the Movies*. New York: W.W. Norton & Co. Inc., 1937.

Brooks, James L. *Broadcast News*. New York: Vintage Books, 1988. Film script. https://www.dailyscript.com/scripts/broadc_news.html.

CHAPTER 4

Laurence Mark, producer

Janet Eastman, "Cape Cod on Mulholland," *Los Angeles Times*, January 18, 2007.

Bob Strauss, "A producer is the, uh, the guy who, uh...," *The Boston Globe*, December 12, 1993.

Michael Cieply, "And the losers aren't ...," *The Montreal Gazette*, January 5, 2009.

Casting

"Fincannon & Associates: Motion Picture & Television Casting." Fincannon Casting company website, http://www.fincannoncasting.com.

Jeff Hidek, "Fincannons win Emmy for casting 'Homeland,'" *Star News Online*, September 15, 2012.

"Cucalorus + SAG Present: The Inside Scoop on Indie Casting," *Cucalorus*, special event, November 13, 2014. http://www.cucalorus.org/cucalorus-sag-present-the-inside-scoop-on-indie-casting/.

Locations

Rodney Ho, "'October Road' casts Atlanta as New England," *The Atlanta Journal-Constitution*, March 15, 2007.

Costume Design

Chierichetti, David. *Hollywood Costume Design*. New York: Harmony Books, 1976.

Barsacq, Leon. *Caligari's Cabinet and Other Grand Illusions: A History of Film Design*. Boston: Little, Brown and Company, 1976.

Dayna Pink

"Fashion Consultant Dayna Pink points out pros and cons of getting a tattoo," Club Connect, PBS, WSKG, Elmira NY, April 17, 1993.

Adam Tschorn, "She Didn't Need a Time Machine," *Los Angeles Times*, April 4, 2010, p. 80.

Adam Tschorn, "Designer: Clothes Make the Man," *Leader-Telegram*, Eau Claire, Wis. via *Los Angeles Times*, January 15, 2012, p. 80.

Adam Tschorn, "Fashioning a Character," *Los Angeles Times*, July 13, 2011, p. E26.

Lauren Bans, "Style Reconnaissance: Crazy, Stupid, Love," *GQ.com*, July 29, 2011.

Jennifer Jobst

Genevieve Buck, "All dressed up and a place to go," *Chicago Tribune*, December 15, 1994.

Western Costume

"History," Western Costume Company, http://westerncostume.com/about-us/history.

"There's No Business Like Show Business and No Show Business like Costumes," Western Costume Co., undated company history.

Hunger Game Costume Auction, Blacksparrow Auctions, November 16, 2013. https://www.liveauctioneers.com/catalog/46577_hunger-games-costume-auction/.

Warner Bros Costume Department

"Costume Department." Warner Bros. Studio Facilities. Company website. https://studiofacilities.warnerbros.com/costume/.

CHAPTER 5

Tim Kenneally, "Morgan Freeman is alive, no matter what Facebook says," *Reuters*, September 10, 2012.

"Robert De Niro named best living actor," *UPI*, October 28, 2004.

"Judge won't toss suit vs. De Niro," *New York Daily News*, June 19, 2007, p. 50.

"Transamerica to Buy TV, Movie Production Insurer," *Los Angeles Times*, March 13, 1990.

Reg Wydeven, "Bad actors may prompt insurance morality clauses," *The Post-Crescent*, March 11, 2018.

"Assistant Directors Training Program." Directors Guild of America, https://www.dgatrainingprogram.org/.

Cirque du Soleil

"Cirque du Soleil - Reinventing the Circus - celebrates 25 years!" *HubPages*, March 2, 2013.

"Cirque du Soleil History." Help & Contact, Cirque du Soleil website, https://www.cirquedusoleil.com/about-us/history.

Cirque du Soleil Entertainment Group, Zarkana program, Las Vegas NV, 2012.

CHAPTER 6

Mogul Inc.

Movie Mogul website, https://www.moviemogul.tv/.

Daniel Miller and Jerry Hirsch, "Transforming the Tax: GM uses new 'Transformers' film to promote small SUV in China," *Los Angeles Times*, June 14, 2014.

Cleared By Ashley

"Biography." Cleared By Ashley Inc., http://clearedbyashley.com/ pages/bio .html.

LinkedIn: Ashley Kravitz.

Robert De Niro, at home

Jeremiah Budin, "The Roof is On Fire in Robert De Niro's Apartment" Curbed.com, June 9, 2012. Retrieved, March 14, 2015. https://ny. curbed.com/2012/6/9/10363920/the-roof-is-on-fire-in-robert-de-niros-apartment.

Page Six Staff, "Robert De Niro and wife homeless after apt. fire," *New York Post*, June 8, 2012. https://pagesix.com/2012/10/17/de-niro-and-wife-homeless-after-apt-fire/.

Michael Douglas, at home

Catherine Sherman, "Catherine Zeta Jones and Michael Douglas buy New Bedford Colonial," Zillow.com, October 28, 2014. https://www. zillow.com/blog/zeta-jones-douglas-bedford-home-163078/.

Morgan Freeman, at home

Bob Guccione Jr., "Mississippi Calling: Morgan Freeman has spent his life becoming one of Hollywood's A-Listers, but there's no where he'd rather be home in than home in Mississippi," *Garden and Gun*, February/March, 2012.

Kevin Kline, at home

Maria Carter, "All odds were against Phoebe Cates and Kevin Kline making it as a couple," *Country Living*, November 22, 2017.

CBS Films

"About." CBS Films website, https://www.cbsfilms.com/about/.

Props, Dwight Benjamin-Creel

David Goldberg, "Senoia a star with Hollywood producers," *The Atlanta Journal-Constitution*, August 12, 1993.

"Coen Brothers Filmography," IMDb. https://www.imdb.com/ list/ls0690 77341/.

"The Woodchipper in Fargo." Fargo Moorhead, Minn., https://www. fargomoorhead.org/what-to-do/the-woodchipper-in-fargo/.

Props, shopping

Eric Sturgis, "Sex shops thwart licensing: Adult-themed stores scare off development, critics say," *The Atlanta Journal-Constitution*, April 17, 2003.

Studio budget concerns

Billy Badalato, memorandum To All Department Heads and Supervisors, "Department Budget Meetings," September 14, 2012.

CHAPTER 7

The Great Debaters (2007). Directed by Denzel Washington. United States: Harpo Films, Marshall Production, and The Weinstein Company. Production Notes, The Weinstein Company.

Tom O'Neil, "Masters of the Craft," *Los Angeles Times*, November 21, 2007.

Todd McCarthy, "Tailor-made for maximum inspirational, historical and educational impact," *Variety*, December 18, 2007.

Robert Beneker, Film Review: "Be it resolved: You'll feel better when you leave the theater," *The Sante Fe New Mexican*, December 28, 2007.

Dayna Pink. "Does this cappuccino look good? It should. 44.00 to deliver it to my room in NY. #doesthiscoffeecomewithahandbag?" Twitter @moreacidwash, September 21, 2012, 7:37 a.m. https://twitter.com/moreacidwash/status/249155363486707712.

Costume Designers Guild Local 892 Magazine, Volume 12, Issue 3, November 2013.

Robert De Niro

Patricia Bosworth, "The Shadow King," *Vanity Fair*, October 1987.

Morgan Freeman

From Robert Gaskill and Quentin Pierre, memorandum, undated, "Items for Mr. Freeman's Trailer."

"Re: Alias," email, September 25, 2012.

CHAPTER 8

CBS Corp. 10K, 2012 Annual Report, February 2013.

Travel Movement, *Last Vegas*, Four Fellas Productions LLC, Spreadsheet, October 2, 2012.

CHAPTER 9

Cameo role shift, Kanya West to 50 cent

Fogelman, Dan. *Last Vegas* P&T. Revisions by Kyle Pennekamp & Scott Turpel, June 20, 2012. Working script, Scene 49, p. 60: "Cameo role: Kanye West."

LAST VEGAS 9.14.12 Draft CBS script.

LAST VEGAS, Tan Script Revisions 12/12/12, 50 Cent added.

Art department

"LAST VEGAS Set List based on 9/14/12 Script," Version 1, Released October 3, 2012.

Camera companies

"Panavision Atlanta." Panavision website, https://www.panavision.com/worldwide/panavision-atlanta.

Site Visit: Panavision Atlanta, 1250 Menlo Dr NW, Atlanta, GA 30318, August 18, 2013.

Panavision, "Panavision Atlanta Hosts Grand Opening", Press release, April 30, 2011.

Site Visit: Panavision Woodland Hills, 6101 Variel Avenue, Woodland Hills, CA 91367, November 17, 2015.

"Panavision Woodland Hills." Panavision, https://www.panavision.com/worldwide/panavision-woodland-hills.

"The Panavision Story," Panavision, https://www.panavision.com/history.

"History of the Scientific & Technical Awards." Oscars website, https://www.oscars.org/sci-tech/history.

"Academy Awards." Panavision, https://www.panavision.com/awards. Accessed January 3, 2019.

Wallin, Walter. Anamorphosing system. US Patent 2,890,622, filed August 11, 1954, and issued June 16, 1959.

Kim Snyder, Bill Roberts, Haim Saban, Adam Chesnoff, Adam Weene, "Investor Presentation" on Panavision, September, 2018.

Adriaan Bijil. "The Importance of Panavision: The Invention Phase." *The 70mm Newsletter* 67, March 2002.

General notes

MGM Resorts International, 2013 Annual Report, February 2014, 27–28.

Ashley Powers, "Vegas places a huge bet on its newest showcase," *Los Angeles Times*, p. A15.

LinkedIn: Kim Houser-Amaral.

"About Info." Nevada Film Commission, https://nevadafilm.com/about/.

Brittany Frederick, "Aaron Sorkin's next act: To Kill A Mockingbird turns page on his career," *FanSided*, December 2018.

Legislative Analyst's Office, "California's First Film Tax Credit Program," September 2016.

"Re: ice sculpture," email, September 18, 2012.

Product placement, luggage, "Re: LAST VEGAS Integration and Placement Recap 11/20/12"

CHAPTER 10

LAST VEGAS, White Shooting Draft, October 15, 2012.

LinkedIn: Wendie Erickson Mosca.

Morgan Freeman

Richard Cotton, Andrew Stern, and Steve Gorman, "Morgan Freeman injured in car wreck," *Reuters*, August 4, 2008.

Eliza Wilson, "Still living life to the fullest: Morgan Freeman wears compression glove on hand injured in 2008 car crash for dinner with friends," *Daily Mail*, May 22, 2014.

Namrata Dixit, "Morgan Freeman purchases the SJ30 private jet for $7 million," *Luxurylaunches*, December 23, 2009.

Mark Huber, "People: Morgan Freeman," *Q&A, Business Jet Traveler Online*, December 2009.

Script supervisor, history

IATSE Local 871 website, https://www.ialocal871.org/About-Us/History.

"Script Girls Save Studios Many Errors," *The Hartford Courant*, September 10, 1939.

John Chapman, "Add Courageous Women: Artye Beesemeyer" *Daily News*, New York NY, October 15, 1940.

Blakeston, Oswell (editor). *Working for the Films*. London; New York: Focal Press, 1947. "The Continuity Girl," Phyllis Crocker.

Joseph Lewis, "Script Supervisor Plays an Important Role In Movies," *Quad City Times*, Davenport, Iowa, October 25, 1952.

Stratosphere, X-Scream

Stratosphere website, https://www.stratospherehotel.com/ThrillRides/X-Scream.

X-Scream Specifications, Interactive Rides, Inc., Logan UTAH, undated.

CHAPTER 11

Deluxe, "The Ecosystem of Media and Entertainment (What We Do/How We Do It)," Web Archive, January 15, 2019.

CHAPTER 12

Camera, Jody Miller

Tap Dance in One Take by Steadicam Operator, Jody Miller, April 15, 2014, https://www.youtube.com/watch?v=_zMve9T7ml8

"Film Photographer Spotlight: Jody Miller," Istillshootfilm.org website, https://istillshootfilm.org/post/67781875590/film-photographer-spotlight-jody-miller.

Steadicam, history

Cain Rodriquez, "Watch: Follow the Camera in 10-Minute Look at the Art of the Steadicam," Indiewire, August 14, 2014.

"History of Steadicam," Tiffen company, https://tiffen.com/pages/history-of-steadicam.

re dollyless Steadicam, Mario Tosi.

Paul Rosenfield, "Peck in the Role of MacArthur," *Los Angeles Times*, January 2, 1977.

Robert De Niro, time to set

LAST VEGAS Call Sheet, Monday, October 29, 2012

SAG, Actors Production Time Report, Exhibit G, *Last Vegas*, October 29, 2012

CHAPTER 14

Walkies

Motorola website, company history timeline, https://www.motorola.com/us/about/motorola-history.

Thelma Ritter and Joseph Aloysius Moran papers, Correspondence 1952, Margaret Herrick Library, Academy of Motion Picture Arts and Sciences.

Cirque du Soleil

https://www.cirquedusoleil.com/zarkana/faq.

CHAPTER 13

Sean Ryan Jennings

Sean Ryan Jennings website, http://seanryanjennings.com/.

Daril Alder

Greg Hilburn, "'Blaze' workers rebuilding past," Gannett News Service, via *The Times*, Shreveport, LA, April 24, 1989.

McCarran International Airport, Las Vegas, NV, Website accessed June 25, 2018

David Kelson

LinkedIn: David Kelson.

Tax Credits, Dino De Laurentiis

Baxter, Jeanne, "NC Goes Hollywood, State attracts movie moguls, cashes in on box office receipts," *The Daily Tar Heel*, February 10 1987.

Smith, Bruce M., "Official: One Final Detail Remains in Studio Negotiations," Associated Press, *The Times and Democrat*, Orangeburg, SC, December 15, 1983.

Ben Steelman, "Dino De Laurentiis, producer who brought film to Wilmington, dies-at-age-91" *Wilmington Star News*, November 11, 2010.

CHAPTER 15

Picture Cars

Richard Verrier, "Business is Cruising for Picture Car Warehouse," *Los Angeles Times*, May 4, 2011.

Mark McManus, video assist

LinkedIn: Mark McManus.

Rebecca Ascher-Walsh, "'The Crow' cast deals with Brandon's Lee death," *Entertainment Weekly*, May 13, 1994.

Christine M. Holsten, "Lee film resumes May 26," *Tampa Bay Times*, May 12, 1993, p. 22.

Paul Feldman, "John Landis Not Guilty in 3 Twilight Zone Deaths," *Los Angeles Times*, May 29, 1987.

CHAPTER 16

Atlanta Traffic

Georgia Office of Transportation, Office of Planning, Existing Volume Development and Origin-Destination Data: Downtown Connector Study, 2016.

Robert De Niro, Paddy scenes

Cindy Price, "R.V. Shows: Over the Top and on the Road," *New York Times*, September 29, 2006.

Melinda Sheckells, "Stars Gather at Caesars Palace for Grand Opening of Robert De Niro's Nobu Hotel," *Hollywood Reporter*, April 29, 2013.

Josh Rogers, "De Niro and partners buy Tribeca's Screening Room," *The Villager*, December 23, 2003.

Katherine Skiba, "Entertaining and Enduring: Seven artists are saluted for their lifetime contributions to American culture," *Los Angeles Times*, December 3, 2012, p. D3.

Pat Murphy, "Yankees logo at center of lawsuit by New York woman," *Christian Science Monitor*, April 21, 2011.

Funeral home

"Our History." Raleigh Rucker Funeral Home website, https://raleighruckerfuneralhome.weebly.com/our-history.html.

Mary Steenburgen

Nina Myskow, "Sunny, funny Steenburgen," *Saga Magazine*, London, January 2, 2014.

"Mary Steenburgen: Actress, and now Songstress," CBS Sunday Morning, October 20, 2013.

CHAPTER 17

Media

Jennifer Brett, "Hollywood A-listers turn Atlanta into 'Last Vegas,'" *The Atlanta Journal-Constitution,* December 6, 2012, p. D2.

"Last Vegas—On The Today Show!," email, December 13, 2012.

Randee Dawn, "Michael Douglas: All-star 'Last Vegas' movie getting raunchier as we go along,'" Today.com, December 14, 2012.

Product Placement

"Re: ice sculpture," email, September 18, 2012.

"Re: Bacardi Liquor," email, November 7, 2012.

"Re: booze next week," emails, November 30, 2012.

"LAST VEGAS Integration and Placement Recap 11/20/12," email, November 20, 2012.

"Re: Bachelor Party Scenes & Alcohol," email, November 30, 2012.

"Re: Ice Sculpture – do/don't," email, November 30, 2012.

CHAPTER 18

Camera and Sound, Chris Flurry

Maria Hamilton, "Students Learn Filmmaking and Community Aid," *Albuquerque Journal*, May 4, 2002, p. 5.

Camera and Sound, David Kelson

Prof. Mitch, "Shadoe Stevens and the History of Fred Rated," *Retroist*, September 18, 2015.

Ben Sisario, "Roger Nichols, Artist Among Sound Engineers, Dies at 66," *New York Times*, April 17, 2011.

"Anton Bauer Dual Charger D-2722." Imagecraft Productions, http://imagecraftproductions.com/product/anton-bauer-dual-charger-d-2722/.

"A Brief History of SMPTE Time Code." Horita Co. website, "About Us." SMPTE, https://horita.com/brief-history-of-smpte-time-code.

Script Supervisor

"Every Clip of Movie Camera is Caught By Continuity Clerk," *Asbury Park Press*, December 3, 1921.

"Stage Notes: Film Democracy," *The Brooklyn Daily Eagle*, November 14, 1920.

John Chapman, "Hollywood," *Daily News*, October 15, 1940.

"John A. Chapman Papers, M039." University Libraries Finding Aids, University of Denver.

John Horn, Darby Maloney, Cameron Kell, "Tracy Scott and the invisible art of script supervision," *The Frame*, May 4, 2016.

Ray Kelley, "Kathryn Trosper Popper, 'Citizen Kane' assistant and actress, dead at 100," *Wellesnet*, March 8, 2016.

"101 Greatest Screenplays," #4 Citizen Kane, Writers Guild of America West, https://www.wga.org/writers-room/101-best-lists/101-greatest-screenplays/list.

Heylin, Clinton. *Despite the System: Orson Welles Versus the Hollywood Studios.* Chicago: Chicago Review Press, 2005, p. 32.

Conrad, Joseph. *Heart of Darkness.* New York: W. W. Norton & Co. 2016. Originally published 1899, *Blackwood's Magazine.*

Michael Douglas, re One Flew Over the Cuckoo's Nest.

Eliot, Marc. *Michael Douglas, A Biography.* New York: Crown Archetype, 2012.

Bill Hagen, "'One Flew Over the Cuckoo's Nest' Superb Comedy," *Santa Ana Register*, December 22, 1975, p. E7.

Michael Schulman, "Louise Fletcher, Nurse Ratched, and the Making of One Flew Over the Cuckoo's Nest's Unforgettable Villain," *Vanity Fair*, August 2018.

Curtis Jackson

LAST VEGAS, Tan Script Revisions, December 7, 2012.

LAST VEGAS Travel Memo: Curtis Jackson (50 Cent), December 6, 2012.

LAST VEGAS (BLUE REVISED) Travel Memo: Curtis Jackson (50 Cent), December 9, 2012.

Jason Birchmeier, "50 Cent Biography," *All Music*, June 26, 2016.

Jackson, Curtis. "The Woman 50 Cent Loves Most." Interview by Oprah Winfrey, OWN, June 18, 2012.

Larry Celona, "Thugs Shoot Up Fitty Pal's Home," *New York Post*, January 9, 2008

50 Cent, Jeff O'Connel. *Formula 50: A 6-Week Workout and Nutrition Plan That Will Transform Your Life.* New York: Penguin Publishing Group, 2013.

Dan Charnas, "How 50 Cent scored a half-billion," *The Washington Post*, December 19, 2010.

Dance Sequence

CiCi Kelley, Resumenew, 2012.

Jessica A. Koslow, "Know Your L.A. Hip-Hop Dances: The Cat Daddy," *LA Weekly*, November 14, 2011.

CHAPTER 19

Alicia Accardo, "Script Supervisor's Production Report," *Last Vegas*, 37th Day of Photography, December 12, 2012.

SAG-AFTRA, Exhibit G: Performers Production Time Report. Worksheet.

CHAPTER 20

William Safire, "It's a Wrap," *New York Times*, February 27, 2005.

Nick Dager, "Mindy Bee Joins Cineverse Atlanta," *Digital Cinema Report*, December 2, 2014.

BIBLIOGRAPHY

This bibliography includes some books relied upon in text and others that may be helpful in studying the history of movie production.

Bamberger, Michael. *The Man Who Heard Voices: Or, How M. Night Shyamalan Risked His Career on a Fairy Tale*. New York: Gotham Books, 2007.

Barsacq, Leon. *Caligari's Cabinet and Other Grand Illusions: A History of Film Design*. Boston: Little, Brown and Company, 1976.

Bendick Jeanne, Robert Bendick. *Making the Movies*. London: Paul Elek, 1946.

Boughey, Davidson. *The Film Industry*. London; New York: Sir I. Pitman & Sons. Ltd., 1921.

Blakeston, Oswell (editor). *Working for the Films*. London; New York: Focal Press, 1947.

Chierichetti, David. *Hollywood Costume Design*. New York: Harmony Books, 1976.

Dench, Ernest Alfred. *Making the Movies*. New York: MacMillan Co., 1919.

Gershuny, Theodore. *Soon To Be A Major Motion Picture: the anatomy of an all-star, big-budgeted, multimillion-dollar disaster*. New York: Holt, Rinehart and Winston, 1980. About the movie *Rosebud* (1975).

Glimcher, Sumner, Warren Johnson. *Movie Making: A Guide to Film Production*. New York: Columbia University Press, 1975.

Goodell, Gregory. *Independent Feature Film Production: A Complete Guide from Concept to Distribution*. New York: St. Martin's Press, 1982.

Griffith, Richard. *Anatomy of a Motion Picture*. New York: St. Martin's Press, 1959. About the movie *Anatomy of a Murder* (1959).

Hollywood Film Production Manual. Hollywood, Calif.: Cinema International, 1954; rev. 1971, Raoul Pagel, DGA (editor).

Naumburg, Nancy (editor). *We Make the Movies*. New York: W.W. Norton & Co. Inc., 1937.

Ross, Lillian. *Picture*. New York: Rinehart & Company, 1952.

Salamon, Julie. *The Devil's Candy: The Anatomy of a Hollywood Fiasco.* Cambridge US: Da Capo, 1991.

Seldes, Gilbert. Preface by Charlie Chaplin. *The Movies Come From America.* New York: Charles Scribner's Sons, 1937; London: B .T. Batsford Ltd, 1937.

Selznick, David, and Rudy Behlmer. *Memo from David O. Selznick.* New York: Grove Press, 1981. Full title: *Memo from David O. Selznick: The Creation of "Gone with the Wind" and Other Motion Picture Classics, as Revealed in the Producer's Private Letters, Telegrams, Memorandums, and Autobiographical Remarks.*

Schary, Dore, Charles Palmer. *Case History of a Movie.* New York: Random House, 1950. Actress Dore Schary, as told to Charles Palmer.

Taylor, Theodore. *People Who Make Movies.* New York: Doubleday & Co., 1967.

INDEX

222, 225-230, 233, 244, 246, 296-297, 305, 329, 342, 355, 394, 397, 407, 452

Thompson, Scott (Carrot Top) 140, 336, 329, 401, 438

Actors, Child Actors 60, 162-163, 186, 251, 257-258, 304, 308

Actors, Extras 2, 27, 42, 48, 55, 59-60, 71, 72, 79, 82-83, 89-90, 98-99, 109-110, 114, 141, 146, 151, 185-186, 209, 211-212, 214-215, 220, 229, 239, 242, 252, 264-265, 268-269, 272-273, 279, 284, 286, 290-292, 295-297, 306, 328, 331335, 340, 352, 354, 361-363, 365-367, 371, 376, 394, 401, 404, 408

Alder, Daril (Leadman) 222-223, 264-265, 428, 451

Anderson, Jordan (Production Assistant) 46, 93, 96, 130-131, 218, 271, 285-286, 392, 415, 428

Anderson, Libby (Production Secretary; Las Vegas) 218-219

Annex, The 97, 117, 128, 151, 163, 172-174, 187, 189-190, 204, 217, 221-222, 258, 262-263

Art Department 134, 142-149, 15, 161-162, 169-170, 172, 176, 181-182, 185, 213, 223, 225, 251, 264, 266, 274, 286, 290-291, 296, 300-303, 309-311, 315, 317, 341, 343-344, 355-357, 359, 366, 371, 389, 396-398, 405, 409, 413, 415, 420, 429, 431, 432, 435, 437, 447

Astriab, Duffy (Stand in) 394, 428

Awa, Lillian (2nd 2nd Assistant Director) 183, 184, 186, 190, 211, 270, 283, 287, 334, 371, 391, 404-405, 408, 428

B

Badalato, Billy (Unit Production Manager) 1, 3-11, 13-17, 19-20, 23-25, 27-32, 34 - 39, 42, 44-48, 51-55, 59-60, 64, 66-72, 76-77, 79-82, 84, 89, 93-99, 102, 104, 109-110, 113-118, 120, 127-129, 131, 134-135, 143, 146, 152-155, 162-164, 167, 173, 179, 182-183, 186, 189, 192, 199, 213, 217-218, 226, 243, 248, 261, 263, 270-271, 284, 289, 292-294, 304-305, 322, 325, 338, 340-341, 343, 353-354, 362, 385, 391, 405, 408-409, 413-415, 418-423, 425, 428, 440, 446

Baer, Amy (Producer) 22, 86, 88, 126, 155, 156, 181, 203, 309, 319, 326, 327, 428, 438

Bally, Nico 243, 246, 428

Benjamin-Creel, Dwight (Prop Master) 69, 100, 103-106, 176-177, 182, 212-213, 262, 278-279, 286-288, 290, 326, 328, 371, 417, 420, 446

Bomba, David (Production Director) 1, 18, 28-30, 34-38, 56-58, 70, 89, 95, 102, 105, 108, 120, 122, 129, 131-132, 142, 144-147, 161, 165, 168, 169, 176, 181, 213, 221, 223-224, 251, 264, 286, 296, 302-304, 306, 343, 345, 357, 390, 396-397, 399, 408, 412, 428, 440

Borisy, Kelly B. (Dolly Grip: "A" Camera) 233, 278, 401, 428

Bott, Theo (Rigging Gaffer; Las Vegas Unit) 234, 428

461